Regarding *Educación*

Mexican-American Schooling, Immigration, and Bi-National Improvement

Regarding *Educación*

Mexican-American Schooling, Immigration, and Bi-National Improvement

EDITED BY

Bryant Jensen

Adam Sawyer

Foreword by Patricia Gándara & Eugene García

TEACHERS
COLLEGE
PRESS

Teachers College, Columbia University
New York and London

Published by Teachers College Press, 1234 Amsterdam Avenue, New York, NY 10027

Copyright © 2013 by Teachers College, Columbia University

Library of Congress Cataloging-in-Publication Data can be obtained at www. loc.gov

ISBN 978-0-8077-5392-7 (paperback)

Printed on acid-free paper
Manufactured in the United States of America

20 19 18 17 16 15 14 13   8 7 6 5 4 3 2 1

Contents

PART V: BI-NATIONAL POSSIBILITIES

Foreword

This volume is one of a kind. It reflects important shifts in our global experiences related to migration and education, even as it focuses on the students we share between the United States and Mexico. After a hiatus of half a century, a wave of immigration and substantive interaction between the United States and Mexico has once again transformed the United States. With millions of Mexican immigrants entering the United States and many continuing their engagement with Mexico, this segment of our population is changing the dynamics of the educational endeavors of both countries.

The experience of immigration from Mexico is not new to generations of Americans. However, for Latinos, it has been, and continues to be, an ongoing experience with particular attributes that influence present generations of immigrants as well as creating important lingering effects for second and third generations. Educationally, Eddie Ruth Hutton described the essence of such an experience for first-generation Mexican immigrants back in 1942:

> Most of these children come from the poorer homes [and] . . . They are torn between the conflicting social customs instilled in them by their Mexican parents and those imposed upon them by a new society. They are apologetic for the peculiarities of their families, yet fearful of the alien social order in which they find themselves. (p. 45)

This experience has changed very little for today's generation of Mexican and other Hispanic immigrants. Yet our attempts to understand this experience and to build bridges between the educational systems of the two nations have been few and sporadic. Lucas (1997) characterizes the experience of these first-generation immigrants, particularly school-age children, as manifested in confronting a set of critical transitions. Most U.S. students undergo a set of important and critical transitions: from home to school, and from childhood to adolescence. Immigrant children move through these same critical transitions, but this is complicated by the necessity of transitioning to a new culture and language as well. Increasingly, this transition occurs multiple times in many young people's lives as they move back and forth across the border and into and out of different school systems. Mexico now reports that hundreds of thousands of students who have received all or part of their education in the United States are sitting in Mexican classrooms. And Mexican teachers, like their North American counterparts, are often at a loss as to how to educate these "newcomers." Time and again educators on both sides of the border fail to recognize and build on the linguistic, social, and academic assets of students shaped by both U.S. and Mexican value systems. Yet the economies and the social fabric of both nations depend to a great extent on how well we meet this challenge. Given that most migration has historically been northward, the United States has more experience, though not necessarily more skill, in integrating newcomers into its schools. It is nonetheless astounding how little conversation has occurred between the two countries about how to address the challenge.

Mexican immigration today is part of an increasingly transnational phenomenon based on borderless economies, new communication technologies, and new systems of mass transportation. In recent years anthropologists, not always with robust data or analytical rigor, have been arguing that the "new immigrants" are key actors in a new transnational stage. Today, there is much more massive back-and-forth movement—not only of people but also of goods, information, and symbols—than ever before. Compared to many Mexican immigrants today, the European immigrants of the last two centuries simply could not maintain the level and intensity of contact with the "old country" that is now possible. Furthermore, the ongoing nature of Hispanic immigration to the United States constantly "replenishes" social practices, cultural models, and associated competencies that would otherwise tend to ossify. Almost all regions of the United States are generating a powerful infrastructure dominated by a growing Spanish-speaking mass media (radio, TV, and print), new market dynamics, and new cultural identities.

It has become clear that the United States and Mexico share millions of students—young people who have begun their education on one side of the border and then moved to the other side, or whose parents and families are familiar with either Mexican or U.S. schools and then must navigate the educational system in the other nation. Yet relatively little attention is given to the binational issues involved in educating our youth, and little communication exists between education researchers in the United States and those in Mexico, even when in many cases they are working on the same issues. To address this situation, we proposed bringing together some of the most eminent scholars in the United States and in Mexico who are investigating education issues of the students we share. Our objective was to provide a forum in which these researchers could share their work, get to know one another, and create new collaborations to advance both theory and study design through the examination of one another's work. We hoped to establish new connections among the various educational institutions these researchers represent that would continue long after this first conference. Finally, we intended to disseminate the papers from this conference in a publication that would allow wider access to this research and, we hoped, stimulate ongoing collaboration. The present volume, which places a greater emphasis on Mexican-origin children and youth in U.S. schools, meets this last goal.

An organizing committee spent more than a year working to bring about the proposed conference. That committee consisted of Patricia Gándara, Professor at UCLA & Co-Director of Civil Rights Project/ Proyecto Derechos Civiles; Eugene García, Professor and Vice President, Arizona State University; Carlos Ornelas, Professor, Universidad Autónoma Metropolitana (in Mexico City); Agustín Escobar Latapí, Professor, Centro de Investigación y Estudios Superiores en la Antropología Social (in Guadalajara); Adam Sawyer, Assistant Professor, Bard College; Bryant Jensen, Assistant Professor, Brigham Young University; Romualdo López Zarate, President of La Comisión Mexicana de Investigación Educativa; and Ana Soltero López and Mary Martinez Wenzl, graduate students at the University of California, Los Angeles. Dr. Donald Hernandez represented the Foundation for Child Development, which had contributed importantly to this endeavor along with Arizona State University and the Civil Rights Project/Proyecto Derechos Civiles at UCLA. UC Mexus (University of California, Riverside) was also a major sponsor of the conference. This volume represents a first step in what we hope will be an ongoing relationship between the institutions and the researchers on both sides of the border who have both an appreciation for the importance of this work and a dedication to improving educational opportunities of those students that we share in time, space, and culture.

–Patricia Gándara and Eugene García

REFERENCES

Hutton, E. R. (1942). Mexican children find themselves. In National Education Association (Eds.), *Americans all: Studies in intercultural education* (pp. 45–51). Washington, DC: National Education Association.

Lucas, T. (1997). *Into, through, and beyond secondary school: Critical transitions for immigrant youths*. New York: Teachers College Press.

Acknowledgments

When the two of us met in 2007 at a binational symposium in Monterrey, Mexico on bilingualism and educational opportunity, neither figured that 6 years later we would be publishing a co-edited volume on Mexican American schooling. Perhaps Eugene García, who insisted on introducing us while standing in the lunch line between conference sessions, knew otherwise.

Our initial conversations—and many of those that have followed, for that matter—about education research and practice were as urgent and ambitious as they were diffuse. They ranged from anthropological studies of *respeto* to policy papers on Mexican migration management. Perhaps the only common thread between our ideas, and the papers and books we were reading, was the educational well-being of children and youth with some sort of connection to Mexico.

This book, in many ways, is an attempt to weave together, with at least some degree of coherence, quite disparate ideas and literatures—not only for the reader's comprehension, but also for our own. We have discovered many things along the way. Some connections between concepts and assertions came easier than others. Some we continue to work through. Of course, this coalescing has not occurred without the generous, insightful, and at times paradigm-changing feedback from our mentors and colleagues. Risking unintended omission, we want to acknowledge their support.

First and foremost, however, we want to thank the children, parents, teachers, and school leaders who have deeply inspired our interests and commitments. Both of us have lived and worked in Mexico. Adam worked as a teacher trainer for the *Programa Escuelas de Calidad* (PEC) and conducted field research in rural Oaxaca and Jalisco. Bryant conducted observational research in elementary school classrooms in Morelos, Puebla, and Mexico City in conjunction with the data analyses he performed at the *Instituto Nacional para la Evaluación de la Educación* (INEE).

Prior to our respective times in Mexico, Adam was a bilingual elementary teacher in East Palo Alto, CA, and the Pico-Union neighborhood of Los Angeles, and Bryant was a bilingual school psychologist in an inner-city school district in Phoenix. Our tender experiences with Mexican immigrant children and their families during those years spurred an unquenchable interest in both of us to learn more about the communities they came from and the family values they exhibited. In addition to a host of *dichos* (sayings) and *consejos* (general life lessons) and a heartier sense of humor, we wound up learning a great deal about educational inequality in Mexico, and ongoing social dilemmas associated with economic hardship.

As we write this, the faces and names of the children and families we have had the privilege to know and work with over the years flash through our minds and linger in our hearts. We want to capture their incredible solidarity, resilience, and optimism on the one hand, without undermining the desperate school-related challenges they continue to confront on the other.

A huge debt of gratitude goes to Patricia Gándara and Eugene García. Without their wisdom and pointed advice, this project simply would not have been possible. It was because of their leadership that a 2010 binational conference in Mexico City on schooling for Mexican-origin children, titled "Students We Share," was successful. This meeting brought together some 300 U.S. and Mexican researchers, policymakers, journalists, practitioners, and graduate students committed to understanding common educational problems and possibilities for students of Mexican origins in both countries. Patricia and Gene invited presenters, secured facilities, garnered financial support, and helped shape the content and direction of that gathering.

Following the conference, Patricia and Gene immediately encouraged us to develop a book prospectus to send to publishers. They have given freely and graciously of their time and advice to the project since. *Queridos mentores, se lo agradecemos de todo corazón y esperamos que el producto final les agrade.*

Of course, we are extremely grateful to the book contributors as well, many of whom presented their work at the "Students We Share" conference. We are honored to edit their work, and hope they find some new meaning to their scholarship through the *Regarding Educación* lens we present.

We are also grateful to our colleagues who participated in various symposia at annual meetings for the American Educational Research Association (AERA) and the Comparative and International Education Society (CIES), where we have presented portions of this book since 2008. Contributors to these sessions included Regina Cortina, Stella Flores, Patricia Gándara, Eugene García, Frank Gaytán, Ted Hamann, María Alejandra León García, Bradley Levinson, Carmina Makar, José Felipe Martínez, Felipe Martínez Rizo, Carlos Ornelas, Carlos Ovando, María Elena Quiroz Lima, Juan Sánchez García, Ernesto Treviño, Angela Valenzuela, Margarita Zorrilla Fierro, and Víctor Zúñiga.

On a couple of occasions we had the opportunity to present the groundwork of the book, before its release, at invited events. The formal and informal discussions that followed these presentations helped to refine our ideas, and to consider new ways of organizing the volume. We thank Ilana Umansky, Kenji Hakuta, and Guadalupe Valdés of the Language, Equity and Education Policy Working Group at Stanford University, and Wayne Cornelius and René Zenteno at the Center for Comparative Immigration Studies and Center for U.S.-Mexican Studies (USMEX) at the University of California, San Diego, for the opportunity to present and discuss.

At the time of our first meeting in Monterrey, we were graduate students—Bryant at Arizona State University and Adam at the Harvard Graduate School of Education. We were in the midst of our formal academic training. It is difficult for us, therefore, to differentiate those who have contributed specifically to this volume from those who have enriched our thinking concerning Mexican American schooling more generally. So we do our best to recognize and thank you all.

Bryant: I would not know how to begin to thank Eugene García for his professional and personal mentorship through my graduate school years. When I began working for him as a research assistant, I was shocked at how much Gene valued my perspective and treated me as a colleague rather than an advisee. His *confianza* in me and in my work continues to inspire my best efforts. Observing him over the years I have learned that "the work" matters most. All else is peripheral. I learned that *ganas* (sincere effort) matters more than ability, success, recognition, or prestige.

I also want to thank Andrés Barona, Josué González, Wayne Holtzman Jr., L. Scott Miller, Carlos Ovando, and Elsie Szecsy for their encouragement and friendship during my time at Arizona State. Each of them, in their own way, helped me understand the complexities of school success for Mexican American children.

I benefited from the mentorship and support of a host of researchers in Mexico as well. Above all, I want to thank Felipe Martínez Rizo for allowing an overzealous *gabacho* to poke around the ranks of *el Instituto*—for his endless support accessing data, schools, and colleagues. Oh, and thank you for introducing me to Latapí's *Finale Prestissimo*. Thanks also to Edgar Andrade Muñoz, Marisela García Pacheco, Carolina Contreras Bravo, Eduardo Hernández, and Gustavo Rodríguez Jiménez for your analytic support at INEE.

Also, my heartfelt thanks and admiration to Benilde García Cabrero, Carlos Ornelas, and Teresa Yurén for your friendship, and for indulging me in debates related to school reform in Mexico.

And most recently, I appreciate the collegiality and input from Bruce Fuller, Claude Goldenberg, María Guadalupe Pérez Martínez, Leslie Reese, and Robert Rueda, especially in relation to the ideas I present in Chapter 14. I look forward to collaborating to "find synergy."

Saving the best for last, I thank those closest to my heart: *mi familia.* Nothing motivates me like my wife Taryn's unwavering support. She keeps me grounded, reminding me to "close the cupboards," and that "love is really spelled *t-i-m-e.*" Additionally, she never turns down the chance to read my work, offer enthusiastic encouragement, and suggest ways to reduce jargon and increase clarity. Thank you to my young children, Emmy Mae and Peter Frank, for greeting me with smiles, hugs, and kisses after discouraging workdays. And thank you to my parents, in-laws, and siblings for showing your interest and support, each in your own way.

Adam: I would like to start by thanking my long-time mentor (and dissertation adviser) at the Harvard Graduate School of Education, Fernando Reimers. Since the start of my master's degree in 2002, Fernando has taken me under his wing and shaped much of my thinking on issues of education quality and equity in the Americas. He provided me great encouragement during moments of inspiration, as well as *consuelo* and needed refocusing on my more difficult days. *¡Te lo agradezco mucho, profe Fernando!*

I have also benefited since that auspicious year of 2002 from the support and inspirational example of Patricia Gándara. Since introducing myself to her at Harvard after one of her stirring speeches on the myopic ways of California bilingual education policy, Patricia has embraced my aspirations and provided a brilliant example of focus and attention to matters of social justice through education policy. I am also ever grateful for the many times she has provided me advice and bibliographic references, often at the 11th hour of a crucial deadline.

Three years into my doctorate, I had the serendipitous fortune to meet the great migration researcher Wayne Cornelius. After an energetic conversation on the binational aspects of Mexican migration and social integration, "Profe C" spontaneously invited me to be a Visiting Research Fellow at his vaunted Center for Comparative Immigration Studies at UC San Diego. During my time at CCIS, I gathered data that later laid the foundation for my dissertation through field work in Oaxaca with Wayne's Mexican Migration Field Research and Training Project. During this time and beyond, Profe C has done much to shape my thinking on matters of immigration policy and immigrant integration while also being a loyal supporter and friend.

I am grateful to many other mentors and friends who have helped to refine my thinking and methods, and provided valuable support during graduate school and my early post-doctoral years at Harvard, UC San Diego, and Bard College. These individuals include: Terry Tivnan, Vivian Louie, Catherine Snow, Kathleen McCartney, Mary Waters, Julie Reuben, Gary Orfield, Jorge Dominguez, Wendy Luttrel, Richard Murnane, Ellie Drago-Severson, Pedro Noguera, Marcello Suárez-Orozco, Kevin Gee, Carol da Silva, Alan Aguilar, Jesús Álvarez Gutiérrez, Susan Henry, Michael Kieffer, Jeannette Mancilla-Martinez, Irene Gándara, and Erin Goodman at Harvard; David Fitzgerald, Tomás Jiménez, Agustín Escobar Latapí, David Keyes, Christina Velásquez, Grecia Lima, Scott Borger, Leah Muse-Orlinoff, and Jennifer Blakeslee at University of California, San Diego; and Ric Campbell, Carla Finkelstein, and Norton Batkin at Bard College.

For me an even greater fruit (than this book) catalyzed by the Mexico City conference was the magical fortune of meeting my future wife, Mirna Troncoso, at this event. Mirna has been a tireless supporter and friendly critic to Bryant and me as I have taken on both the substantive and more rote aspects of this project. She and our loving son, Hector, have provided ceaseless love and patience despite the many evenings and weekends I had to lock myself away with my laptop. Thanks for being my best friend and most important blessing, Mirna.

I also give thanks to my mother, Carole Norris; stepfather, Alan Kay; stepmother, Susan Sawyer; and my many siblings, who have shaped my values and believed in my efforts. And last, but certainly not least, I give thanks in loving memory of my father, Paul Sawyer, who always nourished my love of teaching and of Mexico, and taught me through example to fight tirelessly, passionately, and intelligently alongside the "least amongst us." Dad, your ever-present spirit and energy permeate the pages of this volume.

Finally, we both wish to thank the institutions that offered financial support at different points during this project. The Students We Share conference was sponsored by the UCLA Civil Rights Project/ Proyecto Derechos Civiles, the ASU Office of Educational Partnerships, UC Mexus, the American Educational Research Association, and the Foundation for Child Development in the United States, as well as the *Comisión Mexicana de Investigación Educativa*, the *Universidad Pedagógica Nacional*, the *Secretaría de Relaciones Exteriores*, and the *Secretaría de Educación Pública* in Mexico. The *Centro de Políticas Comparadas de Educación* at the *Universidad Diego Portales* in Santiago, Chile, and the David O. McKay School of Education at Brigham Young University provided subventions for the book. And additional support from the Master of Arts in Teaching program at Bard College and the Institute of Education Sciences post-doctoral fellowship at the University of Oregon provided the time, space, and support to finish the project.

−BJ and AS, September 2012

CHAPTER 1

Regarding *Educación*:
A Vision for School Improvement

Bryant Jensen and Adam Sawyer

Un niño educado, translated "an educated child," implies cultural meaning and competence that are easily lost in translation. Studies of Mexican and Mexican American populations (e.g., Reese, Balzano, Gallimore, & Goldenberg, 1995; Valdés, 1996) indicate that *educación* concerns, by and large, the venerable agrarian values of respect for authority, group solidarity, family loyalty, good manners, and self-dignity. This contrasts quite profoundly with its English equivalent–and the traditional U.S. values of individual accomplishment and factual knowledge.

Likely, there are many exceptions to these cultural stereotypes (as there are evidences). Nonetheless, in this book we present the case that "regarding *educación*" accurately captures the most promising solution to the portentous educational dilemma in which the largest Hispanic and fastest-growing ethnic minority population–Mexican American children–are found. Cultural and linguistic hybridity are already a matter of fact for millions of first-, second-, and third-generation (plus) Mexican American schoolchildren. A central problem is that this hybridity is not well understood or nurtured as a way to improve educational opportunities. Some Mexican American children, on their own devices, learn to maintain and nourish cultural and linguistic competencies to flourish in U.S. schools. Others struggle to assimilate both Mexican and U.S. ways of being–often leading to a series of social problems, including becoming a school dropout, domestic problems, and even incarceration.

Ironically, the erratic acculturation and pervasive school failure (Gándara & Contreras, 2009) of Mexican American children and youth continue to occur at a time when educational opportunities in Mexico have never been better (which, we argue, has important implications for Mexican American schooling), and when civic societies and technological economies in the industrialized world increasingly demand the same capabilities (i.e., collaboration, communication, persistence; Darling-Hammond, 2010) that tend to be socialized quite well in traditional Mexican families (Bridges et al., 2012).

Our argument is that through a more systematic understanding and incorporation of Mexican American students' interpersonal assets, deeply rooted in their cross-national experiences, schools can play a more positive role in preparing the fastest-growing segment of the student population *and* labor force in the United States, whose educational prospects will literally shape the future direction of our nation. In addition to a newfound regard for Mexican American students' cultural, linguistic, and interpersonal resources, this new orientation requires a greater awareness of the bi-national demographic, political, institutional, sociocultural, and pedagogical realities of Mexican American schooling.

This volume intends to create a forum for new discussions about cross-national schooling opportunity regarding *educación*. "Regard" is about bringing the issue to bear, with all its complex components. We wish not only to highlight the migration flows and historical patterns of unequal educational opportunities for children of Mexican immigrants during the latter half of the 20th century, but also to contrast these circumstances with historic inequalities and burgeoning educational opportunities south of the border. Indeed, the educational problems and possibilities of children of Mexican immigrants have important roots in their native country, whether through personal or intergenerational experience. These origins, important to improvement efforts, tend to be overlooked by U.S. stakeholders (Jensen, 2008b).

"Regard" also means to show respect for, or hold in high esteem. This is the larger objective of the book. School improvement efforts for Mexican American students are enhanced, we argue, by *esteeming* (not only *recognizing*) the cross-national experiences and interpersonal capabilities of Mexican American students. Multiple levels of school-reform initiatives can benefit from consideration of the social and cultural aspects of learning and development associated with *educación*–to better prepare students for 21st-century demands.

These goals are reflected in the chapters of the book's five parts. In the first part, the authors discuss some of the major educational dilemmas Mexican American students face. In Part II the chapter authors analyze schooling contexts in Mexico as a way of considering improvements in U.S. settings. In Part III, researchers provide case studies of student schooling experiences from both Mexico and the United States that illustrate the transnational dimensions of migration and education that link the two nations. And Part IV examines the interpersonal, family, and community assets of Mexican American students in greater detail, grappling with how cultural dynamics are associated with these competencies. Ending with a more future-oriented perspective, Part V explores how binational collaborations in the 21st century might address some of the opportunities and challenges presented in previous chapters.

To provide context for the main body of the book, we continue this introductory chapter with an overview of the historical, structural, and sociocultural explanations for the inordinately large number of Mexican-origin students in the United States. Finally, we provide a brief history of Mexican American schooling, emphasizing the (often faulty) premises upon which past and current approaches have been based. We then outline the essential components of a 21st-century bi-national *educación*—framed within the lens of student and family assets—articulating how the volume chapters interconnect to argue this imperative.

WHY MEXICAN STUDENTS?

We do not exaggerate when we assert that improving schooling for this large and rapidly growing ethnic group should be one of the most important social domestic issues of our generation (National Task Force on Early Education for Hispanics, 2007). The "demographic imperative" (García & Jensen, 2009) combined with the pervasive academic underachievement of Mexican American students are no longer items that can be shelved. We cannot afford for such a large U.S. student population to continue as an educational—and socioeconomic—"underclass" (see Chapter 2). The "same old" policy and practice solutions are likely not enough to turn the tide.

The numbers indeed are compelling. Currently 1 in 10 children in U.S. primary and secondary schools have a Mexican-born parent (Passel, 2011) and about 1 in 7 are Mexican-origin more broadly (meaning they have a Mexican-born grandparent or great-grandparent). A smaller portion themselves were born in Mexico (less than 10% of all Mexican American students). A majority, however, live with Mexican-born family members at home. Taken together, more than 8 million Mexican-origin children and youth have Mexican-born parents (Passel, 2011).

Migratory Explosion

The vast size of this student population stems from arguably the greatest migratory explosion in U.S. history. Between 1965 and the beginning of the Great Recession in 2008 (Passel, Cohn, & Gonzalez-Barrera,

2012), the Mexican-born population of the United States increased from approximately 740,000 to over 12 million, with peak migration flows during this period occurring from the mid-1990s to the mid-2000s (when about 500,000 Mexicans were migrating annually to the United States; Passel, 2011). At this peak, there were nearly 32 million persons of Mexican origins (i.e., those reporting their origin as "Mexican" on the U.S. Census, including U.S.- and Mexican-born persons; Ennis, Ríos-Vargas, & Albert, 2011) in the United States. Of course, a Mexican presence in what now is the American West traces long before the Mexican-American War (1845–1848), which resulted in Mexico handing over present-day Arizona and California and parts of Colorado, Kansas, Nevada, New Mexico, Oklahoma, Texas, Utah, and Wyoming. And while Mexican migration to the United States persisted throughout the first half of the 20th century (much of which was facilitated by the Bracero Program, a bilateral agreement to import temporary contract laborers from Mexico to the United States between 1942 and 1964), the recently completed migratory boom is by far the largest on record (Passel et al., 2012). Presently, there is a leveling off of Mexican immigration to the United States and a modest increase of return migration to Mexico (Passel et al., 2012), factors caused in great part by the U.S. economic downturn and to a lesser extent intensified border enforcement and detention. Whether migration levels will surge once more to earlier levels when the U.S. economy fully recovers is an open question.

Regardless of what the future holds, there are several misconceptions surrounding the causes of post-1965 Mexican migration, most of which are discredited by four broad findings from decades of sociological and anthropological research (e.g., Cohen, 2004; Cornelius, Fitzgerald, Hernández-Díaz, & Borger, 2009; Massey, Durand, & Malone, 2002). First, migration is a direct consequence of economic development in Mexico, not due to a lack thereof (Massey et al., 2002). The poorest of the poor within Mexico by and large are not among those who tend to emigrate. Economic liberalization over the past four decades alongside international economic policies like the North American Free Trade Agreement (NAFTA) opened Mexico's economy to foreign investment and ownership. This led to concentrations of economic opportunities in urban centers alongside a decreased ability to subsist in rural regions. Many rural residents in Mexico were forced either to migrate to large Mexican cities or head to the United States (Cohen, 2004; Cornelius et al., 2009; Massey et al., 2002). New transportation and communication infrastructure, increased living standards in Mexico, an infiltration of U.S. consumer tastes, inadequate banking and credit markets in Mexico, and a thirst for remittance money from *el norte* (Cornelius, 1990;

Massey et al.,2002; Sawyer, 2010b) all contributed to mass Mexico-U.S. migration.

Second, Mexican migration flows are enhanced by economic, social, and cultural integration between our two nations. Each year the United States and Mexico are among each other's top trade partners. Whereas NAFTA displaced many rural Mexican workers and their families, it also contributed to greater hemispheric concentration of banking, finance, commerce, and research, and a large demand for "low-skilled" service workers throughout the United States. American companies heavily recruited Mexican workers because of their willingness to work hard for relatively low wages (Massey et al., 2002; Portés & Rumbaut, 2001). Employment opportunities spurred a proliferation of Spanish media, small Mexican businesses, and Mexican products in many non-traditional migrant communities throughout the United States (particularly in the Southern, Midwestern, and Rocky Mountain states). This was accompanied by a propagation of U.S. commercialism and strong demands for English proficiency throughout Mexico.

Third, Mexican immigrants by and large make the United States their new home, rather than returning to their communities of origin in Mexico. At the same time, migrants retain strong transnational social ties with the families and friends left behind (Cornelius, 1990; Portés, 1996; Sawyer, 2010a; Smith, 2005). Relationships between the diaspora and the homeland take on many forms (addressed by Zuñiga and Hamann, Chapter 8, and Sawyer, Chapter 9, this volume). Strong transnational social networks increase the likelihood that members of the migrant's family will one day migrate themselves (Cornelius et al., 2009; Massey et al., 2002; Smith, 2005).

Last, U.S. immigration policies often have unintended consequences that influence migration flows. For example, the 1965 Immigration and Nationality Act privileged family reunification for naturalization priorities. These reunification provisions opened the door to greater numbers of Mexican migrants than expected (Cornelius, 1990; Massey et al., 2002). The 1965 reform coincided with the abolishment of the Bracero Program, thereby extinguishing a legal channel for temporary Mexican workers even as they were increasing in demand. This unintentionally contributed to an unprecedented flow of undocumented migration (Cornelius, et al., 2009; Massey et al., 2002). Moreover, efforts in recent years to end undocumented migration through greater border enforcement have "caged in" (Cornelius et al., 2009) Mexican nationals wishing to return to their country of origin rather than deterring illegal entries, which only ballooned the overall number of undocumented Mexican migrants to over 8 million persons (Passel, 2011).

Underperformance in School

The large numbers of Mexican-origin students in U.S. schools resulting from unprecedented migration flows are just one reason for this volume. The pervasive underperformance of Mexican American students
from preschool to college is another. Documented now for several decades, in comparison to Whites, Asian Americans, and most other Latino groups, Mexican American students are more likely to repeat grades
in school, and less likely to complete high school, be in higher-track
classes, and attend or graduate from college (Carter, 1970; De la Rosa &
Maw, 1990; Gándara & Contreras, 2009; García, 2001; Harklau, Losey,
& Siegal, 1999; President's Advisory Commission on Educational Excellence for Hispanic Americans, 1996; Ruiz-de-Velasco & Fix, 2000;
Valdés, 2001; Valenzuela, 2005). These patterns are stubbornly persistent and show insufficient decrease with generational acculturation
into the U.S. mainstream. Whereas Telles and Ortiz in Chapter 2 find
notable educational progress (measured by educational attainment) between the first and second immigrant generations, this upward trend
stagnates after the second generation, a development authors interpret
to be a "racialization" of Mexicans into a national underclass. These
trends are consistent with the academic achievement of Mexican-origin
children across immigrant generations, as shown by Galindo in Chapter
4. Moreover, Mexican-origin children of undocumented parents, as discussed by Bean and colleagues in Chapter 3, are at an even greater risk
of educational failure than children of documented parents.

Just as a bi-national lens clarifies the origins of the migratory phenomenon, it also aids in understanding the roots of poor educational
outcomes for Mexican American students. In Chapter 5, Treviño documents the access and quality divides that have historically plagued
rural regions in Mexico, from where the vast majority of Mexican migrants originate. And in Chapter 6 Pérez and colleagues discuss wide
variations in preschool quality across Mexican communities. Though
school enrollment and attainment are improving at unprecedented rates
throughout the Mexican Republic—including its long-neglected rural locales—rural and especially indigenous students continue to drop out of
school much earlier and perform much lower on academic tasks compared to the rest of the country (Reimers, 2002; Sawyer, 2010b). Improving school quality for children in these communities constitutes a
major policy challenge in Mexico. Thus, poor educational performance
for Mexican-origin children in the United States is in some ways a car-
ryover of problems from their country of origin—problems that have

yet to be resolved in Mexico. Unlike immigrants from other countries, who tend to have more formal schooling that those remaining behind, Mexican immigrants have comparable education levels to those who do not migrate (Feliciano, 2008), which has repercussions into second and third generations following immigration.

A BRIEF HISTORY OF MEXICAN AMERICAN SCHOOLING

The Mexican American schooling problem has not appeared suddenly, nor has it been blatantly ignored. The problems are historically rooted, and efforts to make policy and practice improvements have exhibited much better intentions than results. These efforts are important to re-visit in order to build on past successes without repeating past mistakes. Our position is that 21st-century improvements will require much more purposeful practices, programs, and policies that:

- Address the bi-national origins of educational failure, and
- Build on the cultural, linguistic, and interpersonal assets of Mexican-origin students, families, and communities.

19th-Century Schooling

The initial era of Mexican American schooling roughly began with the 1848 signing of the Treaty of Guadalupe Hidalgo, which spread U.S. dominion over what had been half of Mexico's national territory and instantly converted thousands of Mexican citizens to U.S. residents. Schooling for Mexican-origin children in the new American Southwest during the mid- to late 19th century consisted of a hodge-podge of private religious and secular institutions complemented by a much smaller number of public schools. A holdover from the days of Mexican rule, the most dominant player in these early years was the Catholic schools, established by foreign teaching orders like the Sisters of Loretto, the Christian Brothers, the Sisters of Charity, and the Jesuits. Instruction in these schools was conducted overwhelmingly in Spanish, and Hispano-Mexican culture was preserved through curricular content (Blanton, 2004; San Miguel, 1998). Spanish was also the preferred language of a smaller number of secular private schools founded by members of the Mexican American community. However, newly sprung Anglo-American Protestant schools viewed the culture, language, and religious practices of Mexican Americans as inherently inferior. These schools tended to conduct instruction in English and undertook a project of religious conversion and the molding of young Mexican Americans to Anglo-American values (San Miguel, 1998).

As the Anglo-American population grew in the Southwest through increased settlement in the latter decades of the 19th century, Mexican American political power decreased, as did support for the use of Spanish and the teaching of the Mexican American heritage in public schools (Blanton, 2004; San Miguel, 1998). These changes coincided with the nativist movement that enveloped the entire nation during the late 19th century in response to mass immigration from South, Central, and Eastern Europe. In the Southwest, school officials took aim at eliminating non-English languages from school instruction and revamping school curriculum to reflect Anglo-American values (Blanton, 2004; San Miguel, 1998). By 1914, when the beginning of World War I whipped nativism into overdrive, the consolidation of the Americanization project in the public schools of the former territories of Mexico was complete.

Schooling to the Mid-20th Century

The period from the outbreak of hostilities in World War I to the Civil Rights Movement in the mid-1960s represents perhaps the darkest historical period in Mexican American schooling. During these years, Mexican American students were increasingly sequestered into segregated, substandard schools. The overall size of the Mexican American population remained more or less stable during this period, though the size of the overall foreign-born population in the U.S. decreased from over 14 million persons (11.6% of the total population) in 1930 to under 10 million persons (4.7% of the total population) by 1970 (Jensen, 2008a). The economic depression of the 1930s, the huge strain of World War II on the federal government, and strong ensuing nationalism contributed to decreased immigration through the mid-20th century in general, and deplorable school conditions (infrastructure, materials, teacher quality) for Mexican American students specifically. A report from Texas during the 1955–1956 school year indicated that only 25% of Mexican Americans in the state reached 8th grade and less than 10% reached the 12th grade (Blanton, 2004). President Lyndon B. Johnson (1965), who taught at rural Texas schools for Mexican American students in the late 1920s, later reminisced, "I shall never forget the faces of the boys and the girls in the little [school], and I remember even yet the pain of realizing and knowing then that college was closed to practically every one of those children because they were too poor."

It is important to note that the Jim Crow-like schools for Mexican Americans did not persist unchallenged. The 1940s saw waves of protracted resistance from Mexican Americans who engaged in various protests and direct appeals to school boards and elected officials. Energy for this movement in large part came from a restless immigrant second generation–many of whom had fought in World War II–who formed organizations like the League of United Latin American Citizens (LULAC) (Blanton, 2004; Delgado-Bernal, 1998; González, 1998). These efforts eventually led to court cases (e.g., *Mendéz v. Westminster* in 1946), substantive policy changes (Delgado-Bernal, 1998; González, 1998; Wollenberg, 1974), and successful legal challenges to school segregation in Arizona and Texas. Said accomplishments caught the attention of young Thurgood Marshall some eight years before *Brown v. Board of Education*, which now represents the landmark court case to end the era of legally sanctioned Jim Crow schooling for African American, Mexican American, and other racial and ethnic minority students.

Bilingual Education

Political mobilization of the 1940s and 1950s, however, was only a prequel to the dramatic schooling changes wrought by the turbulent 1960s. Emboldened by the Civil Rights Movement and the Vietnam War, Mexican Americans (or "Chicanos") advocated for greater educational equity and bilingual and bicultural schooling (Delgado-Bernal, 1998). Moreover, scholars began to coalesce around the benefits of bilingualism, and the Cuban exile community (following the 1959 revolution) in Southern Florida was demonstrating for strong dual-language school models with broad political support within the state (Jensen, 2008a). These events set the stage for the signing of the Bilingual Education Act on January 2, 1968, under President Lyndon B. Johnson (1963–1968), who retained deep sympathies for underprivileged students from his young-adult years teaching in rural Texas (Blanton, 2004; Dallek, 1991).

Though the Bilingual Education Act provided an endorsement of bilingual instruction in schools, it did not mandate it (Blanton, 2004; Crawford, 1992). And while the legislation itself garnered wide support on both sides of the political aisle, the perceived purposes of bilingual programs varied among legislators. For most, it was perceived as an opportunity for children in low-income families–most importantly the "disadvantaged" Mexican Americans–to acquire English and succeed within mainstream schooling institutions. Spanish and other minority languages were seen largely as deficits to overcome rather than assets to maintain and develop. Chicano activists, on the other hand, saw bilingual education as a vehicle for cultural preservation and distinctiveness (Blanton, 2004; Delgado-Bernal, 1998).

Others saw the new bilingual policy somewhere in between. Harold Howe II, Education Commissioner at the time, said the new laws showed

> promise of redeeming Mexican American children from the near-certainty of education failure in that they emphasize a bicultural, bilingual approach which says, in essence, that Mexican American children must learn the English language and Anglo ways—but that they can do so without having to reject their knowledge of the Spanish language and of Mexican American ways. (Blanton, 2004, p. 140)

During the years immediately following, several enthusiastic school districts began to experiment with bilingual programs, while many resisted bilingual instruction. Despite the new law, most Mexican American children remained in segregated schools without any sort of Spanish instruction (Blanton, 2004; Crawford, 1992; Delgado-Bernal, 1998). The landmark Supreme Court case *Lau v. Nichols* of 1974, however, was a watershed moment for bilingual education. In the case justices ruled in favor of a class of Chinese American students who charged that San Francisco's schools had violated the equal protection clause of the 14th Amendment by failing to provide them a "meaningful education" (Blanton, 2004; Crawford, 1992; Delgado-Bernal, 1998). This ruling set the stage for the subsequent "Lau Remedies," which required all school districts to identify and provide regular language assessments to all language-minority students, requiring bilingual instruction whenever feasible (Crawford, 1992; Delgado-Bernal, 1998).

Even though the Lau Remedies by no means led to universal adaptation of bilingual education, vigorous enforcement by the Office of Civil Rights during the Ford and Carter administrations led to more than 500 school districts coming into compliance with the new law (Crawford, 1994). These programs were further bolstered by local legislation in California (1976) and Texas (1981)—and several other states—to establish native language instruction as a right. Most of the bilingual program models, however, were "transitional," meaning they only temporarily delivered instruction in the native language in order to eventually teach exclusively in English (Blanton, 2004; Carter & Segura, 1979; Delgado-Bernal, 1998; Gándara, 2002).

At a time when the Mexican immigrant population had nearly tripled from the previous decade (Jensen, 2008a), Carter and Segura (1979) bemoaned this ongoing compensatory emphasis of bilingual school programs for Mexican American children. They argued for legislation that sought not only to "modify the children of poverty" but, more importantly, to "willingly undertake programs to modify the school itself." And they predicted that "bilingual education as . . . a compensatory-transitional program . . . will eventually disappear . . . as it becomes increasingly clear to legislators that the goals of improved Chicano academic achievement are not met." They continued by arguing for "bilingual-bicultural education [with] maintenance-enrichment objectives" (p. 384).

Ultimately, the political pendulum in ensuing decades swung decisively counter to the direction urged by Carter and Segura. At the local level, bilingual education was subject to competing and often contradictory legislative efforts, uneven implementation, and in some instances, hostile resistance (Blanton, 2004; Crawford, 1994; Delgado-Bernal, 1998; Gándara, 2002). At the national level, funding of Title VII and adherence to the Lau Remedies varied wildly among presidential administrations. Even in California, which long had some of the most progressive bilingual education laws on the books, only 30% of English Language Learners (ELLs) in 1994 received some type of native language instruction (Crawford, 1994; Gándara, 2002), despite considerable research evidence to support this approach (August & Hakuta, 1997; Cummins, 2000; García, 2005; Snow, 1990). In the meantime, the 1980s and 1990s saw a crisis in public confidence in public education, which became etched in the national consciousness through such scathing publications as the government report *A Nation at Risk* (1983) and Jonathan Kozol's *Savage Inequalities* (1991). The seemingly intractable problem of Mexican American underachievement—which bilingual education had seemingly done little to ameliorate—was symptomatic of this larger failure.

These policy changes took shape while large-scale Mexican migration to the United States continued to grow at unprecedented levels. In 1980 the total Mexican-born population in the United States was just over 2 million persons, compared to over 9 million by the year 2000 (Jensen, 2008a). More than half of Mexican migration during this period was undocumented. California by far received the largest portion of documented and undocumented Mexican immigrants during the 1980s and 1990s, which led to a growing anti-immigrant sentiment in the state. In 1994 this sentiment showed itself with the passing of Proposition 187 (over 60% voter approval), which declared public schooling and all other public services—with the exception of emergency medical services—off-limits to undocumented immigrants. Though the initiative was later ruled unconstitutional and never enforced, it set the stage for other restrictive policies (Gándara, 2002). Four years later, Proposition 227–which essentially ended bilingual education in California except under very narrowly defined circumstances–was passed with 61% voter approval (Gándara, 2002; Gándara & Hopkins, 2010). Not long after its passing, copycat initiatives were passed in Arizona (2000) and Massachusetts (2002), with yet another failing in Colorado (2003).

Standards-Based Reform

The tide continued to turn against bilingual education with the consolidation of the standards-based reform movement within the landmark reauthorization of the Elementary and Secondary Education Act (ESEA) in 2001 known as No Child Left Behind (NCLB). In NCLB, the former Title VII was renamed Title III (effectively terminating the Bilingual Education Act), which changed a bilingual education focus for ELLs and immigrant students to English-only programs (ESEA, 2001). Within Title III, states were required to test all ELLs in the country at least once a year (with some accommodations) in reading and math and were mandated to create an annual state test to assess the English proficiency of all ELLs. Schools in every state were to be held accountable for specified progress on the assessment in order to attain Adequate Yearly Progress (AYP) (ESEA, 2001). While Title III retained some grant monies that states could use for bilingual programs, it did not incentivize them. Reflecting the new emphasis on English acquisition, the U.S. Department of Education's Office of Bilingual Education and Language Minority Affairs was changed to the Office for English Language Acquisition upon the passing of No Child Left Behind (Crawford, 2002).

Failure of Reform Efforts

Fifteen years after the passing of Proposition 227 and now into the second decade of the NCLB era, educational outcomes for Mexican American students from preschool through college have remained virtually unchanged (Gándara & Contreras, 2009). NCLB has not narrowed racial-ethnic academic achievement differences as intended (Fuller, Wright, Gesicki, & Kang, 2007), and new restrictions on bilingualism in U.S. classrooms have led to major decreases in production of multilingual and multicultural instructional materials and a dramatic decrease in teachers choosing certification paths providing training in second language acquisition and cross-cultural teaching (Gándara & Hopkins, 2010). Thus, although extant research demonstrates that one-fifth to one-third of the overall Hispanic-white achievement gap could be eliminated with high-quality Spanish-English instruction (National Task Force on Early Education for Hispanics, 2007), most Mexican American children attend schools prohibiting or simply not offering bilingual education.

In some ways, however, closing the era of heated bilingual education debates is timely because both sides of the debate possessed a similar flaw in their underlying perspective: language (bilingual *or* English-only) instruction was the "magic bullet" (at least implicitly) to solving the educational woes of underperforming language-minority children like Mexican American students. While there is evidence to suggest that well-implemented bilingual approaches can be beneficial for many Mexican American students, the larger dilemma of providing equitable schooling for this population is much more entrenched. In addition to language of instruction, needed reforms must directly address the origins of educational failure in Mexico on the one hand, while valuing and developing the cultural, linguistic, interpersonal, and family assets of Mexican American students on the other.

To date there is not much evidence that our reform perspective is shared among policymakers. The current trend in education policy for Mexican Americans and other ELLs is one of incremental tinkering. For example, the Obama administration has taken steps at the executive level to grant states greater flexibility in meeting the requirements of NCLB, including provisions related to ELLs (Cavanaugh & Klein, 2012). In addition, a task force convened in 2010 recommended minor refinements to NCLB for the educational well-being of ELLs rather than large-scale changes. Recommendations focused mainly on improvements in the identification and re-designation procedures for ELLs, greater awareness among practitioners of the intricacies of second-language acquisition (especially the time dimension), accommodation procedures and use of English language assessments, and investments in teacher training and district and school capacity-building (Working Group on ELL Policy, 2010). While we stand firmly behind these important recommendations, we contend that securing an equitable education for Mexican Americans in the 21st century will require a much more dramatic reorientation. Importantly, we must rethink the sorts of "competencies" schools should target in our technological age (Collins & Halverson, 2009) in order to build on the cultural and developmental assets of Mexican American students (as addressed in Chapter 10 and Chapter 11) in ways that also nurture the knowledge and skills demanded by 21st-century economies and civic society.

21ST-CENTURY DEMANDS

There is no question that for all ethnic and socioeconomic groups in the United States the technological revolution of the past decade and a half has changed and continues to change our economic life, civic life, and the way we relate with family and co-workers alike (Banks, 2008; Collins & Halverson, 2009). These changes have induced rapid transformations in the labor market, so that the top 10 jobs in demand projected for 2010 did not even exist in 2004 (Darling-Hammond, 2010). Many argue that the new technology-laden environment that unavoidably surrounds us require rethinking the skills children and youth will need to be successful in the 21st century (e.g., Trilling & Fadel, 2009).

Some of these skills are much the same. Literacy, numeracy, and information-processing competencies will continue to be in high demand in the 21st century, albeit with greater complexity (Carnegie Council on Advancing Adolescent Literacy, 2010). There is an overwhelming consensus, however, that proficiency in reading, writing, arithmetic, and an array of digital technologies is necessary but not sufficient for success in contemporary life (Darling-Hammond, 2010; Murnane & Levy, 1996; Organisation for Economic Cooperation and Development [OECD], 2005; Trilling & Fadel, 2009; Wagner, 2008). The argument goes that the *individual* thinking skills can no longer overshadow important *interpersonal* competencies (e.g., communication, collaboration, empathy) demanded by employers (for innovation) and civic society (to solve complex social problems). Coincidentally, new frameworks for school improvement that "regard *educación*," as we have described it, are bound not only to benefit Mexican American students, but also to contribute to systemic changes that better prepare all U.S. children for the 21st century.

Importantly, new theory and research in the learning sciences demonstrate deep connections between complex thinking and socioemotional competencies (Denham, 2006; Meltzoff, Kuhl, Movellan, & Sejnowski, 2009), so that emphasis on interpersonal competencies could also have positive effects on individual thinking skills like reading and writing for Mexican-origin students. This sort of perspective requires us to rethink learning in school, as Jensen discusses in Chapter 14. He affirms that Mexican American students would benefit from a "prefrontal cortex"—a metaphor that is more reflective of the most recent science.

Whether neurological metaphors add value for school improvement efforts or not, what is clear is that U.S. society demands a broader array of competencies from schools in the 21st century than from schools in the 20th century. New individual skills include autonomous critical thinking, where we monitor and regulate our own understanding in light of new information and perspectives. This requires considerable cognitive flexibility, where we can revise our own understanding–searching for additional patterns and relationships–in light of ongoing analysis and synthesis of information and feedback from knowledgeable others.

Particularly important for Mexican American children, who tend to be socialized in non-school environments that value interpersonal aptitudes, the higher-order thinking skills of the 21st century cannot really be separated from the social competencies these skills demand. These competencies include functioning within culturally heterogeneous groups, collaboration (requiring cooperation, compromise, and community-building), and effective communication (including close listening, observing, and empathy) (OECD, 2005; Trilling & Fadel, 2009; Wagner, 2008).

A challenge for future research and program designers will be to match ways Mexican American children are socialized outside of school (Bridges et al., 2012; Fuller & García Coll, 2010) with academic tasks at school that integrate as many of these (individual and interpersonal) skills as possible. Once again, such enhancements will require a better understanding of the linguistic and cultural hybridity of so many Mexican American children in ways that optimize student outcomes that matter. Thus, *Regarding Educación* serves as a promising platform to improve educational opportunities in the new millennium.

BI-NATIONAL CONNECTIONS

Coming to terms with *educación*-related assets in part means understanding their origins, which are found in rural Mexican values with which millions in the United States personally identify. On the one hand, rural communities in Mexico (though in a cultural "state of flux," as discussed by Reese in Chapter 10) are characterized by strong social networks and the traditional values of *respeto* (Valdés, 1996), cooperation, familism (see Chapter 11, this volume), and social cohesion (Valenzuela, 1999). On the other hand, most rural Mexican communities confront profound socioeconomic hardship, and the quality of schools in these regions is subpar at best (see Chapters 5 and 6).

Acknowledging important heterogeneity across students, it is noteworthy that most Mexican American children are exposed regularly to the "cultural models" (D'Andrade & Strauss, 1992) of rural Mexico. While more than 9 in 10 Mexican American school-age children are themselves born in the United States, roughly two-thirds have a

Mexican-born parent. Thus, for a majority, the values, beliefs, and expectations inherent in Mexican cultural models are reiterated through interactions and daily activities in households and neighborhoods (see Chapter 12). By understanding the roots of these cultural models, we can better understand how to engage Mexican-origin students in academic activities in ways that are more interesting and have greater personal application. This includes understanding how Mexican schools tend to operate, particularly in communities most affected by Mexico-U.S. migration.

As explained in Chapter 7 by Regina Cortina and colleagues and in Chapter 5 by Ernesto Treviño, Mexican primary and secondary schools remain quite centralized at the federal level. The curriculum is nationalized (even for private schools, which account for 10–15% of overall PreK–12 enrollment), and teacher hiring and in-service training are negotiated between the Federal Education Ministry (*Secretaría de Educación Pública*) and the national teacher labor union (*Sindicato Nacional de Trabajadores de la Educación*). Long-standing political wrangling, typical of public institutions in Latin America, colors these negotiations. This is evidenced by frequent teacher protests in the streets of Oaxaca, Chiapas, and other states.

The greatest institutional achievement of Mexican schools over the past couple of decades has been the expansion of school enrollments, as mentioned by María Guadalupe Pérez Martínez and colleagues in Chapter 6. School attendance and access to quality programs (with adequate resources) continue to vary quite widely across Mexican states, and especially between urban and rural communities, where students in urban settings fare much better than those in rural settings. Compared to industrialized nations, students in Mexican schools, on the whole, demonstrate below-average performance on standardized tests in math, reading, and science literacy (on average Mexican students perform about one standard deviation lower than the OECD countries [OECD, 2011]). Compared with Latin American countries, however, Mexican students perform fairly well (Laboratorio Latinoamericano de Evalución de la Calidad de la Educación [LLECE], 2010), and gradual, steady improvements—in terms of attainment *and* achievement—are being made every year.

But aggregate and institutional analyses only tell part of the story. Studies underscoring interpersonal dynamics within Mexican schools and classrooms communicate intriguing structures emblematic of *educación* values, on the one hand, yet widely disparate practices, on the other. Descriptive research highlights the importance of intimate parent involvement in the administrative life of the school, socialization with the same student cohort year after year, and a fundamental commitment to group solidarity across classrooms (Jensen, 2005; Latapí, 2009; Levinson, 2001; Yurén & Araújo, 2003). Given the prevalence of rural Mexican cultural models in Mexican American households, the U.S. practitioner benefits from understanding school and classroom dynamics in Mexico. Current evidence describes the public school classroom in Mexico where group work dominates, where teachers follow a national curriculum, and where respect for authority and good manners is the norm. It should also be understood that the public school day in Mexico lasts 5 hours or less, and that teacher and student absenteeism are ongoing problems. Because of this and other distractions actual instructional time can vary greatly within the same school, posited to account, at least partially, for large within-school learning differences (Abadzi, 2007; EQUIP2, 2010).

Of course, these preliminary observations hardly serve as an introduction to the rural Mexican life or the schooling experiences of children and their teachers in these communities. The general idea, however, is that with some binational understanding, practitioners and policymakers alike are better suited to develop and implement viable programs and strategies that are responsive to the previous (personal and/or intergenerational) educational experiences of its intended beneficiaries. But articulating what U.S. stakeholders, including practitioners and policymakers, should know about schooling south of the border is not enough. We need to know how to develop this understanding for specific purposes. These purposes should speak to improvement needs at multiple levels of the U.S. system, including local, state, and federal levels. Moreover, school improvements through binational understanding, which at present enjoy little evidentiary support, should also target enhanced educational opportunities across countries, particularly for children moving both ways across the border.

As mentioned by Mary Martinez-Wenzl in Chapter 13, there is some precedent to develop binational understanding for mutual improvements. The teacher exchange, textbook, and adult education programs by Mexico's *Instituto para Mexicanos en el Exterior* (IME), for example, intend to enhance educational opportunities for Mexican-origin students and their families in U.S. settings. As Martinez makes clear, however, these intentions are dwarfed by the marginal profile, small budgets, and scant evidence of these initiatives.

On the other side of the equation, binational efforts have not really addressed educational improvements in Mexico. Some migration scholars have articulated educational improvements within the larger framework of binational migration management (e.g., Escobar Latapí, 2008;

Escobar Latapí & Martin, 2006), but this approach has not yet led to education improvements through specific policy or practice initiatives. Certainly the notion makes sense: social and economic networks created through Mexico-U.S. migration flows should lead to educational advancements. But much more work is needed to craft this agenda for actual implementation. In the spirit of moving toward this still-elusive goal, we suggest:

- Fitting education collaboration within a broader agenda to manage migration
- Expanding the profile and impact of binational education programs for mutual benefits
- Increasing binational understanding among school practitioners

THE REGARDING *EDUCACIÓN* VISION

The purpose of this volume, thus, is to articulate the tenets for a new framework of Mexican American schooling for the 21st century. This framework directly addresses the historical and pervasive underperformance of children and youth of Mexican heritage—applying lessons learned from past successes and failures—not by narrowing definitions of success, but by expanding them. Chapters in this book, drawing on multiple disciplinary perspectives and data sources, make it clear that while Mexican American students tend to struggle with academic content through traditional curricular and instructional approaches in schools, the values and practices rooted in rural communities in Mexico are associated with positive social, emotional, and community development. As educators, policymakers, and researchers, we must identify substantiated ways of drawing on these assets to improve learning opportunities, school motivation, graduation rates, and participation in higher education. This conceptual shift, one that systematically incorporates the contributions of family histories and interpersonal competencies into school curriculum and instruction, benefits not only children of Mexican origin, but also, we argue, the U.S. student population at large.

On the one hand, our recommendations are consistent with other reform proposals that advocate for

- More collaborative, problem-based learning opportunities (Bruer, 1997)

- Culture-minded teaching and school organization (Tharp, Estrada, Dalton, & Yamauchi, 2000; Tharp & Gallimore, 1988)
- Strong models for professional development (Darling-Hammond, 2010)
- Purposeful infusion of digital technologies (Collins & Halverson, 2009)

On the other hand, we argue that Mexican American students require additional considerations to make these large-scale changes even more consequential. These considerations regard *how* the above changes are carried out to address the specific needs and strengths of Mexican American children. They regard *educación* by developing and applying knowledge of Mexican schooling, including forms of parental inclusion, classroom instruction, and types of competence. By doing so we can identify problem-solving activities for classrooms that are grounded in students' lives, family values, and daily experiences. And parents of Mexican American students can be better integrated into the life of the school to help teachers and school staff better appreciate traditional Mexican values, as well as the conditions associated with migration experiences. The bi-national assets approach articulated in this book can lead to a redesign of our educational system so that the largest and fastest-growing ethnic minority group in the United States can meet the civic and labor demands of the 21st century.

REFERENCES

Abadzi, H. (2007). *Absenteeism and beyond: Instructional time loss and consequences.* Washington, DC: World Bank.

August, D., & Hakuta, K. (Eds.). (1997). *Improving schooling for language-minority children: A research agenda.* Washington, DC: National Academy Press.

Banks, J. (2008). Diversity, group identity, and citizenship education in a global age. *Educational Researcher, 37*(3), 129–139

Blanton, C. K. (2004). *The strange career of bilingual education in Texas, 1836–1981.* College Station, TX: Texas A&M University Press.

Bridges, M., Cohen, S. R., McGuire, L. W., Yamada, H., Fuller, B., Mireles, L., & Scott, L. (2012). *Bien educado:* Measuring the social behavior of Mexican American children. *Early Childhood Research Quarterly, 27*(3), 555–567.

Bruer, J. T. (1997). *Schools for thought: A science of learning in the classroom.* Cambridge, MA: The MIT Press.

Carnegie Council on Advancing Adolescent Literacy. (2010). *Time to act: An agenda for advancing adolescent literacy for college and career success.* New York: Carnegie Corporation of New York.

Carter, T. P. (1970). *Mexican Americans in school: A history of educational neglect.* New York: College Entrance Examination Board.

Carter, T. P., & Segura, R. D. (1979). *Mexican-Americans in school: A decade of change.* Princeton, NJ: College Entrance Examination Board.

Cavanaugh, S., & Klein, A. (2012). Broad changes ahead as NCLB waivers roll out. *Education Week,* February 10, 2012. Retrieved online at http://www.edweek.org/ew/articles/2012/02/09/21waivers.h31.html

Cohen, J. (2004). *The culture of migration in southern Mexico.* Austin: University of Texas Press.

Collins, A., & Halverson, R. (2009). *Rethinking education in the age of technology: The digital revolution and schooling in American.* New York: Teachers College Press.

Cornelius, W. (1990). *Labor migration to the United States: Development outcomes and alternatives in Mexican sending communities.* Working Paper No. 38. Washington, DC: U.S. Commission for the Study of International Migration and Cooperative Economic Development.

Cornelius, W., Fitzgerald, D., Hernández-Díaz, J., & Borger, S. (Eds.) (2009). *Migration from the Mexican Mixteca: A transnational community in Oaxaca and California.* San Diego, CA: Center for Comparative Immigration Studies, University of California, San Diego.

Crawford, J. (1992). *Hold your tongue: Bilingualism and the politics of English-only.* Boston, MA: Addison-Wesley.

Crawford, J. (1994, November). Summing up the Lau decision: Justice is never simple. Paper presented at a National Commemorative Symposium: Revisiting the Lau Decision—20 Years After. San Francisco, CA.

Crawford, J. (2002). Obituary: The Bilingual Education Act, 1968–2002. *Rethinking Schools.* Retrieved online at http://www.rethinkingschools.org/special_reports/bilingual/Bil164.shtml

Cummins, J. (2000). *Language, power, and pedagogy: Bilingual children in the crossfire.* Clevedon, UK: Multilingual Matters.

D'Andrade, R., & Strauss, C. (Eds.) (1992). *Human motives and cultural models.* New York: Cambridge University Press.

Dallek, R. (1991). *Lone star rising: Lyndon Johnson and his times, 1908-1960.* New York: Oxford University Press.

Darling-Hammond, L. (2010). *The flat world and education: How America's commitment to equity will determine our future.* New York: Teachers College Press.

De La Rosa, D., & Maw, C. E. (1990). *Hispanic education: A statistical portrait, 1990.* Washington, DC: National Council of La Raza.

Delgado-Bernal, D. (1998). Chicano/a education from the Civil Rights era to the present. In J.F. Moreno (Ed.), *The elusive quest for equality: 150 Years of Chicano/a education* (pp. 77–108). Cambridge, MA: Harvard Educational Review.

Denham, S. (2006). Social-emotional competence as support for school readiness: What is it and how do we assess it? *Early Education and Development, 17*(1), 57–89.

Elementary and Secondary Education Act (ESEA). (2001). *No Child Left Behind Act of 2001.* Washington, DC: United States Department of Education.

Ennis, S. R., Ríos-Vargas, M., & Albert, N. G. (2011). *The Hispanic population: Census briefs.* Washington, DC: U.S. Census Bureau. Retrieved from http://www.census.gov/prod/cen2010/briefs/c2010br-04.pdf

EQUIP2. (2010). *Using opportunity to learn and early grade reading fluency to measure school effectiveness in Ethiopia, Guatemala, Honduras, and Nepal.* Washington, DC: USAID.

Escobar Latapí, A. (2008). Mexican policy and Mexico-U.S. migration. In A. Escobar Latapí & S. F. Martin (Eds.), *Mexico-U.S. migration management: A binational approach* (pp. 179–216). Lanham, MD: Lexington Books.

Escobar Latapí, A., & Martin, S. (2006). *Mexico-U.S. migration management: A binational approach.* Washington, DC: Institute for the Study of International Migration.

Feliciano, C. (2008). *Unequal origins: Immigrant selection and the education of the second generation.* El Paso, TX: LFB Scholarly Publishing LLC.

Fuller, B., & García Coll, C. (2010). Learning from Latinos: Contexts, families, and child development in motion. *Developmental Psychology, 46*(3), 559–565.

Gándara, P. (2002). Learning English in California: Guideposts for the nation. In M. Suárez-Orozco and M. Páez (Eds.), *Latinos: Rethinking America.* Cambridge, MA: David Rockefeller Center for Latin American Studies, Harvard University.

Gándara, P., & Contreras, F. (2009). *The Latino education crisis: The consequences of failed social policies.* Cambridge, MA: Harvard University Press.

Gándara, P., & Hopkins, M. (2010). *Forbidden language: English learners and restrictive language policies.* New York: Teachers College Press.

García, E. (2001). *Hispanic education in the United States: Raices y alas.* New York: Rowman and Littlefield.

García, E. (2005). *Teaching and learning in two languages: Bilingualism and schooling in the United States.* New York: Teachers College Press.

García, E., & Jensen, B. (2009). The demographic imperative. *Educational Leadership, 66*(7), 8–13.

González, G. (1998). Segregation and the education of Mexican children, 1900–1940. In J. F. Moreno (Ed.), *The elusive quest for equality: 150 years of Chicano/a education* (pp. 53–76). Cambridge, MA: Harvard Educational Review.

Harklau, L., Losey, K. M., & Siegal, M. (Eds.). (1999). *Generation 1.5 meets college composition: Issues in the teaching of writing to U.S. educated learners of ESL.* Mahwah, NJ: Lawrence Erlbaum Associates.

Jensen, B. (2005). Culture and practice of Mexican primary schooling: Implications for improving policy and practice in the U.S. *Current Issues in Education* [Online], *8*(25). Available: http://cie.asu.edu/volume8/number24/index.html

Jensen, B. (2008a). Immigration and language policy. In J. González (Ed.), *Encyclopedia of Bilingual Education* (pp. 372–377). Thousand Oaks, CA: Sage Publications.

Jensen, B. (2008b). *Understanding differences in binational reading development: Comparing Mexican and U.S. Hispanic students.* Paper presented at the annual meeting for the American Educational Research Association.

Kozol, J. (1991). *Savage inequalities: Children in America's schools.* New York: Crown Publishers.

Laboratorio Latinoamericano de Evaluación de la Calidad de la Educación (LLECE). (2010). *Factores asociados al logro cognitivo de los estudiantes de American Latina y el Caribe.* Santiago, Chile.

Latapí, P. (2009). Maestros y pedagogía. In P. Latapí, *Finale prestissimo: Pensamientos, vivencias y testimonies.* México: Fondo de Cultura Económica.

Levinson, B. (2001). *We are all equal: Student culture and identity at a Mexican secondary school, 1988-1998.* Durham, NC: Duke University Press.

Massey, D., Durand, J., & Malone, N. (2002). *Beyond smoke and mirrors: Mexican migration in an era of economic integration.* New York: Russell Sage Foundation.

Meltzoff, A. N., Kuhl, P. K., Movellan, J., & Sejnowski, T. J. (2009). Foundations for a new science of learning. *Science, 325,* 284–288.

Murnane, R., & Levy, F. (1996). *Teaching the new basic skills: Principles for educating children to thrive in a changing economy.* New York: The Free Press.

National Commission on Excellence in Education. (1983). *A nation at risk: The imperative for educational reform.* Washington, DC: United States Department of Education.

National Task Force on Early Childhood Education for Hispanics. (2007). *Para nuestros niños: Expanding and improving early education for Hispanics—Main report.* Washington, DC: Foundation for Child Development.

Organisation for Economic Cooperation and Development. (2005). *The definition and selection of key competencies.* Paris, France: Author.

Organisation for Economic Cooperation and Development. (2011). *Education at a glance: OECD indicators.* Paris, France: Author.

Passel, J. (2011). Demography of immigrant youth: Past, present, and future. *Immigrant Children, 21*(1), 19–42.

Passel, J., Cohn, D., & Gonzalez-Barrera, A. (2012). *Net migration from Mexico falls to zero–and perhaps less.* Washington, DC: Pew Hispanic Center.

Portes, A. (1996). Global villagers: The rise of transnational communities. *The American Prospect, 25,* 74–77.

Portes, A., & Rumbaut, R. G. (2001). *Legacies: The story of the immigrant second generation.* Berkeley, CA: University of California Press.

President's Advisory Commission on Educational Excellence for Hispanic Americans. (1996). *Our nation on the fault line: Hispanic American education.* Washington, DC: U.S. Department of Education.

Reese, L., Balzano, S., Gallimore, R., & Goldenberg, C. (1995). The concept of *educación*: Latino family values and American schooling. *International Journal of Educational Research, 23*(1), 57–81.

Reimers, F. (2002). *Unequal schools, unequal chances.* Cambridge, MA: Harvard University, David Rockefeller Center for Latin American Studies.

Ruiz-de-Velasco, J., & Fix, M. (2000). *Overlooked and underserved: Immigrant students in U.S. secondary schools.* Washington, DC: Urban Institute.

San Miguel Jr., G. (1998). The schooling of Mexicanos in the southwest, 1848-1891. In J. F. Moreno (Ed.), *The elusive quest for equality: 150 years of Chicano/a education* (pp. 31–51). Cambridge, MA: Harvard Educational Review.

Sawyer, A. (2010a). *In Mexico, mother's education and remittances matter in school outcomes.* Washington, DC: Migration Information Source, Migration Policy Institute.

Sawyer, A. (2010b). *Money is not enough: Remittances and other determinants of youth educational attainment in a Southern-Mexican migrant-sending community.* Cambridge, MA: Harvard Graduate School of Education Doctoral Dissertation.

Smith, R. C. (2006). *Mexican New York: The transnational lives of new immigrants.* Berkeley, CA: University of California Press.

Snow, C.E. (1990). Rationales for native language instruction in the education of language minority children: Evidence from research. In A. Padilla, H. Fairchild, & C. Valadez (Eds.), *Bilingual education: Issues and strategies* (pp. 60–74). Newbury Park, CA: Sage.

Tharp, R., Estrada, P., Dalton, S., & Yamauchi, L. A. (2000). *Teaching transformed: Achieving excellence, fairness, inclusion, and harmony.* Boulder, CO: Westview Press.

Tharp, R., & Gallimore, R. (1988). *Rousing minds to life: Teaching, learning, and schooling in social context.* New York: Cambridge University Press.

Trilling, B., & Fadel, C. (2009). *21st century skills: Learning for life in our times.* San Francisco, CA: Jossey-Bass.

Valdés, G. (1996). *Con respeto: Bridging the distances between culturally diverse families and schools: An ethnographic portrait.* New York: Teachers College Press.

Valdés, G. (2001). *Learning and not learning English: Latino students in American schools.* New York: Teachers College Press.

Valenzuela, A. (1999). *Subtractive schooling: U.S.-Mexican youth and the politics of caring.* Albany, NY: SUNY Press.

Valenzuela, A. (Ed.) (2005). *Leaving children behind: How "Texas style" accountability fails Latino youth.* Albany, NY: SUNY Press

Wollenberg, C. (1974). *Westminster v. Mendez:* Race, nationality, and segregation in California schools. *California Historical Quarterly, 53,* 317–332.

Working Group on ELL Policy. (2010). *Improving education for English Language Learners: Recommendations for the Reauthorization of the Elementary and Secondary Education Act.* Washington, DC: United States Department of Education Working Paper.

Yurén, T., & Araújo, S. (2003). Estilos docentes, poderes y resistencia ante una reforma curricular: El caso de formación cívica y ética en la escuela secundaria. *Revista Mexicana de Investigación Educativa, 8*(19), 631–652.

Part I

CHALLENGES AND DILEMMAS

Part I addresses the entrenched educational challenges Mexican American students face, as well as some of their causes. These challenges are rooted in historical dilemmas (e.g., poverty, racial/ethnic isolation, unauthorized immigration) the U.S. school system confronts at large. In Chapter 2, Edward Telles and Vilma Ortíz, sociologists who study assimilation patterns of Mexican American populations, discuss the (limited) progress in Mexican American educational attainment across five generations. In Chapter 3, Frank Bean, Susan Brown, Mark Leach, James Bachmeier, and Rosuara Tafoya-Estrada assess the long-term scholastic impact of parental unauthorized status on Mexican American children. They document alarming educational attainment divides for the children and grandchildren of unauthorized immigrants. And in Chapter 4 Claudia Galindo summarizes her work on national-level math achievement trajectories of Mexican American children from Kindergarten through fifth grade.

CHAPTER 2

Intergenerational Assimilation Patterns of Mexican American Students

Edward Telles and Vilma Ortíz

In 1993, when UCLA's historic Powell Library was being retrofitted to meet stricter earthquake codes, workers found numerous dusty boxes hidden behind a bookshelf in an unused basement room. The boxes contained the original survey questionnaires collected in 1965 and 1966 used to inform Leo Grebler, Joan Moore, and Ralph Guzman's *The Mexican American People: The Nation's Second Largest Minority*, published in 1970. This path-breaking study accompanied the national discovery of Mexican Americans, which Grebler et al. claim began in 1960 with the presidential campaign of John F. Kennedy. Based on random samples of Mexican Americans in Los Angeles and San Antonio, they concluded that although some sectors of the Mexican American population had entered the middle class and begun to participate in American society, there was little overall assimilation, even for those who had lived in the United States for several generations.

Library staff soon brought these questionnaires and other project materials to our attention. Sensing a unique opportunity, we seized on the idea of revisiting the original respondents. We sensed that Grebler et al.'s (1970) survey could once again be important if we could examine the lives of the original respondents some three decades later and thus create a longitudinal study. In addition, we thought to make this genuinely intergenerational by interviewing the children of the original respondents, who would now be well into adulthood. This kind of follow-up study would require substantial detective work to find the survivors and a sample of their children, both of whom we knew would be scattered not only throughout California and Texas but also beyond. Several years later, with generous funding from the National Institutes of Health and several foundations as well as the assistance of many energetic graduate students, we were able to locate and interview 684 of the nearly 1,200 respondents who were younger than 50 in the original survey (nearly 60%) and 758 of their children. The result was our book, *Generations of Exclusion: Mexican Americans, Assimilation, and Race* (Telles & Ortiz, 2008). The title largely reflects the centrality of education to the intergenerational incorporation of Mexican Americans in North American society and particularly their poor educational outcomes.

We believe that this truly longitudinal and intergenerational design would be especially well-suited to address current debates about the integration of immigrants and their descendants in American society. Our research design allows us to address conceptual issues that arise in studies on ethnic integration and methodological issues that arise in intergenerational and longitudinal research. These include the problems of interviewing respondents who might be so highly assimilated that they no longer identify with the group, tracking intergenerational change with cross-sectional data, and selectivity due to respondent loss over time. Our survey examines a randomly selected sample of persons who identified themselves as Mexican Americans in 1965 and returns to them and their children some 35 years later, regardless of how they identified in 2000. In other words, our research design allows sampling without an ethnic bias. It also permits investigating actual intergenerational change from adult parents to their adult children a generation later, overcoming the problem of comparing generations with cross-sectional data. Finally, to overcome the loss of respondents over time, we are able to adjust our follow-up data to reflect the entire original random sample, using information from the 1965 survey questionnaires.

DEBATES ABOUT MEXICAN-IMMIGRANT INTEGRATION

Since we began this survey more than 10 years ago, an academic debate has emerged about the future the children of today's many immigrants face. The case of Mexicans has taken a prominent place in the debate because today's immigrants, unlike their predecessors a century ago, hail predominantly from Latin American and Asia. The intergenerational integration of these immigrants has come to again occupy a central place in American sociology. Theoretical debates about the importance or nature of assimilation have reemerged, but with a decidedly more empirical bent. In particular, two book-length studies have become prominent. As the largest immigrant group since World War II, Mexicans have become a litmus test for the assimilation prospects of the new immigrants. With the experience of new mass immigration already 20 some years behind us, immigration scholars have mostly speculated about the sociological outcomes expected for the new second generation. However, because the oldest of these children are only now entering adulthood and gaining a foothold in the labor market, it is still a bit early to analyze outcomes such as occupation, intermarriage, and adult identity, though at least one study has begun to provide some early evidence on the possibilities. Examining the adolescent children of immigrants in San Diego County in *Legacies: The Story of the Immigration Second Generation*, Alejandro Portes and Ruben Rumbaut (2001) come to the pessimistic conclusion that the children of Mexican immigrants will experience downward assimilation. They maintain that Mexican Americans have little hope of entering the middle class, and a large number resolutely identify as Mexican. Instead of becoming like the assimilating Italian Americans, Portes and Rumbaut predict that they will become more like the stigmatized African Americans.

By contrast, Richard Alba and Victor Nee (2003) have tried to resurrect the assimilation model, albeit a more nuanced version. They are guarded in their interpretations of the Mexican American experience, primarily because of evidence of poor progress by the third generation, but think that Mexican Americans and the descendants of today's Latin American and Asian immigrants will eventually assimilate, much like earlier European immigrants, and that the social boundaries between groups will, for the most part, disappear. Although they recognize race as a formidable impediment to successful integration in American society, they believe it is surmountable.

We believe the experiences of the Mexican American population are likely to be mixed rather than unambiguously assimilated or racialized. Some may do well and more or less blend into mainstream society. Others will not. We know little about the variation in outcomes and even less about what factors best determine outcomes. We see a complex sociological puzzle that needs to be sorted out through careful empirical analysis, which we decided to undertake.

Our goal was to investigate the intergenerational integration of the Mexican-origin population into American society during the second half of the 20th century. We asked whether the cultural, economic, and political characteristics of Mexican Americans change in any patterned way the longer families have been in the United States. We take the generational approach that has become the sociological standard for understanding immigrant integration. Our primary stratifying variables are therefore generations. We divide *generation* into historical or family generations and generations since immigration, which have been largely confounded in the academic literature. We thus take a very long view of immigrant integration, investigating the effects of four generations or more of residence in the United States. Ultimately, then, this is a story that is more than a century long, in which the fourth generation is unlikely to have ever known their immigrant great-grandparents, who were often Mexican nationals.

ISSUE OF EDUCATIONAL ASSIMILATION

In this chapter, we focus on education, which occupies a central place in our book because it underlies almost all other variables of immigrant incorporation and because the outcomes are notably alarming. Today, according to most public opinion polls, education ranks as the most important issue facing Latinos. Despite 60 years of political and legal battles to improve the education of Mexican Americans, they continue to have the lowest average education levels and the highest high school dropout rates among major ethnic and racial groups in the United States. These inequalities generate other social and economic inequalities between them and European Americans throughout their adult lives. However, leading analysts, apparently believing in the universality of assimilation, argue that this is the result of a large first- and second-generation population still adjusting to American society. Although the traditional model generally predicts assimilation within three generations, these and other scholars predict that Mexican Americans will have the same levels of education and socioeconomic status as the dominant non-Hispanic White population by the fourth generation. Borjas (1994), in particular, argues that Mexican Americans are especially slow to assimilate because the immigrant generation has had especially low levels of education and other forms of human capital compared with other immigrant groups. However, most social scientists who have closely examined schooling data for Mexican Americans over generations since the immigration of their ancestors have shown that their educational attainment improves from immigrant parents to their children but stalls between the second and third generations. This occurs even though the second-generation parents of the third generation have significantly more education and understanding of the educational system to pass on to their children than their own immigrant parents had. This pattern is often theorized as reflecting optimism among immigrants, in which the relatively ambitious immigrant parents, who themselves suffered from low education and skills, strive for the American dream. Thus, they drive themselves and their children to do well in school, whereas second-generation parents perceive greater limits to their own and their children's success. Others contend that the second generation's schooling advantage derives from their resistance to assimilation and their ability to mobilize ethnicity as a positive resource to escape the disadvantages wrought on them by public schools. For example, Vigil (1997) found an ethnic resurgence or Mexicanization process among mostly, but not exclusively, second-generation Mexican American high school students in Los Angeles, which resulted in their greater self-confidence in the classroom. By contrast, the third generation no longer benefits from immigrant optimism and the cultural protections against discrimination offered by the second generation's immigrant family.

Despite the apparently strong quantitative evidence showing a lack of educational assimilation among Mexican Americans so far, at least two studies claim that the pessimistic conclusions of halted progress for Mexican Americans are based on faulty or inadequate data. Schooling among Mexicans, they argue, converges with that of non-Hispanic Whites over the generations, albeit at a slower rate. First, Smith (2003) contends that previous conclusions are deceiving because using generation since immigration with a single cross-sectional data set does not capture actual generational change—that is, from parents to children. Using a historical series of data sets to approximate parent-to-child generations, Smith finds persistent gains into the third generation, though the gap with non-Hispanic Whites does not disappear. Second, Alba and Islam (2009), reflecting Alba and Nee's (2003) optimism, argue that the low educational attainment observed for Mexican Americans may be an artifact of how data are collected. They claim that more successful Mexican Americans might be opting out of the Mexican category—thus identifying in other ethnic categories—by the third generation. As a result, the average educational levels for the group are underestimated. Alba and Islam maintain that individuals whose parents may have intermarried, which is indicative of intergenerational assimilation, may be particularly likely to opt out. Available representative data sets do not distinguish more than three generations since immigration and thus do not permit tests of assimilation for the fourth, and perhaps fifth, generation. In this chapter, we reexamine this debate with the Mexican American Study Project data, which we believe overcome the deficiencies that have hamstrung previous studies. We show actual intergenerational changes rather than the synthetic changes common to cross-sectional data sources. The sample was drawn based on the reported ethnicity of the parents in 1965 and thus precluded opting out by children, since we sampled their children despite their own reported ethnicity. We find that there is almost no opting out of the Mexican or Hispanic category, as Alba and Islam suggest. We also disaggregated the sample into a fourth and an incipient fifth generation. We show that, despite improvements, the hypothesis of educational assimilation for Mexican Americans is still not borne out.

A PORTRAIT OF EDUCATIONAL INEQUALITY

To put Mexican American education in context, we first examine official census data for major racial and ethnic groups, regionally and locally. The Mexican-origin population in 1970 is identified only for the five-state Southwest region (Arizona, California, Colorado, New Mexico, and Texas), where the vast majority (about 90%) of Mexican Americans lived at that time. Despite much settlement by Mexican immigrants elsewhere in the United States in recent years, a substantial majority remain in the Southwest. For comparability with our data, we analyzed census data for Los Angeles and San Antonio at roughly the same ages of respondents in our study. Specifically, Table 2.1 shows education indicators for 1970 and 2000 among U.S.-born Mexican Americans, Whites, African Americans, and Asian Americans for the five southwestern states as well as Los Angeles and San Antonio. We focus on those age 18 to 54 in the 1970 census and 35 to 54 in 2000 because these ages roughly match the ages of our original 1965 adult sample and the 2000 child sample, respectively. We calculate the schooling deficit between the average Mexican Americans in our sample and average non-Hispanic Whites in the census, and we present these later.

Table 2.1 clearly shows that education among Mexican Americans lags behind all other major race-ethnic groups in the Southwest, Los Angeles, and San Antonio. Because the data are just for those born in the United States, we are certain that virtually everyone in the sample was educated in the United States. Educational attainment of Mexican Americans fell behind Whites and Asians by about 2 years and behind African Americans by about 1 year in 1970 and 2000. High school graduation rates and college completion rates also were lowest for Mexican Americans in both periods. This gap remained from 1970 to 2000, despite the fact that schooling improved for all groups. More than 90% of Whites and Asians reported completing high school in 2000, compared to 84% of African Americans and only 74% of Mexican Americans. By 2000, fully 35% of Whites in the Southwest and 54% of Asians

Table 2.1. Years of Education and Graduation Rates by Race, 1970 and 2000[a]

	1970[b]			2000[c]		
	Southwest States[d]	Los Angeles	San Antonio	Southwest States[d]	Los Angeles	San Antonio
Years of education						
Mexican Americans	9.7	10.7	9.0	12.3	12.6	12.5
Non-Hispanic Whites	12.3	12.6	12.3	14.1	14.2	14.2
Blacks	10.9	11.4	11.0	13.2	13.4	13.5
Asians	–	–	–	14.7	14.6	14.7
High school graduate						
Mexican Americans	44%	51%	37%	74%	76%	77%
Non-Hispanic Whites	75%	79%	74%	90%	94%	95%
Blacks	54%	63%	57%	84%	84%	89%
Asians	–	–	–	95%	95%	93%
College graduate[e]						
Mexican Americans	3%	4%	2%	13%	13%	14%
Non-Hispanic Whites	15%	16%	15%	35%	40%	39%
Blacks	5%	5%	4%	17%	19%	21%
Asians	–	–	–	54%	56%	52%

Source: Decennial censuses 1970 and 2000 (Edward Telles' and Vilma Ortíz's tabulations).

a Among U.S. born.

b 1970 figures among ages 18 to 54.

c 2000 figures among ages 35 to 54.

d The five Southwest states are California, Arizona, Colorado, New Mexico, and Texas.

e 1970 college graduation figures among ages 25 to 54.

completed college, compared to about 17% of African Americans and 13% of Mexican Americans. Regarding place differences, schooling outcomes for Mexican Americans tended to be substantially better in Los

Angeles than San Antonio in 1970 but by 2000 were more comparable. The fact that education levels for Mexican Americans were slightly better in the urban areas of Los Angeles and San Antonio than for the region overall is probably why our sample has somewhat higher educational attainment than found in other sources. Our sample was entirely urban in 1965, but only 65% of Mexican Americans overall actually lived in urban areas. Thus our sample somewhat overestimates Mexican American educational attainment; nonetheless, it provides the best available data for showing and understanding longitudinal and intergenerational relationships with education.

EDUCATIONAL CHANGE ACROSS THE GENERATIONS

As we have seen, the Mexican-origin population has the lowest educational achievement rates of all racial-ethnic groups. Because this might be interpreted as an immigration effect where years of schooling in another country are not compatible, we excluded immigrants from the results in Table 2.1. Low educational achievement might be readily justified by an assimilation hypothesis that because many Mexican Americans grew up in immigrant households with poorly educated parents, their own levels of education would logically be lower than those of non-Hispanic Whites or African-Americans, the vast majority of whom are third generation or later. To explore this possibility, we examine schooling attainment across generation since immigration.

Table 2.2 breaks down education into three levels of schooling completed by generation since immigration. We show educational outcomes for original respondents in 1965 and 2000 because some respondents may have completed further education in the intervening years. The first row shows that the years of education for original respondents range from 6.8 years to 9.5 years in 1965 but 35 years later, their education had improved, on average, by about 0.6 years for the immigrants, 0.8 for the second generation, and 0.9 for the third generation. The second row and third row also show sizeable gains in the percentage that finished either high school or college. For the first and second generation, college graduation rates tripled, perhaps reflecting the onset of affirmative action.

Table 2.2 also shows that years of schooling for the children sample had greatly improved from that of the original respondents. Although only 16 to 35% of the original respondents reported completing high school, 73 to 87% of their children did. Among the original respondents, years of education and high school graduation rates show constant improvement from one generation to the next. College completion rates, on the other hand, do not vary much by generation since immigration for original respondents. For their children, all of whom are U.S.-born and educated, there are no clear trends, as shown in Table 2.2. Years of education decreases from 13.1 to 12.4 from the second to the fourth generation since immigration. High school completion is similar among all three generations since immigration, and college completion is noticeably lower for the fourth generation (6%), though it is not appreciably different between the second (13%) and the third (14%) generations. However, as shown in Table 2.1, college completion rates among Whites

Table 2.2. Years of Education and Graduation Rates by Generation Since Immigration, 1965 and 2000

	Original Respondents, 1965[a]		
	Gen. 1	Gen. 2	Gen. 3
Years of education	6.8	9.2	9.5
High school graduation	16%	32%	35%
College graduation[b]	2%	2%	4%
	Original Respondents, 2000		
	Gen. 1	Gen. 2	Gen. 3
Years of education	7.4	10.0	10.4
High school graduation	30%	48%	57%
College graduation[b]	7%	6%	5%
	Children		
	Gen. 2	Gen. 3	Gen. 4+
Years of education	13.1	13.1	12.4
High school graduation	84%	87%	73%
College graduation[b]	13%	14%	6%

Source: Mexican American Study Project.

a 1965 figures among age 18 and older.

b 1965 college graduation figures among age 25 and older.

had increased to 35% in this time period. Sadly and directly in contra-distinction to assimilation theory, the fourth generation differs the most from Whites, with a college completion rate of only 6%.

Figure 2.1 shows generational changes for Mexican-origin persons over the span of the 20th century. In addition to the original respondents and their children, we show educational attainment for the parents of original respondents. The parents were educated mostly in the 1900s to 1930s, the original respondents were schooled from the 1930s to 1950s, and their children were educated from the 1950s to the 1980s. At the same time, we present results for three generations since immigration within each of these cohorts. Taken together, Figure 2.1 shows educational progress among the three cohorts descended from immigrants during three periods in which they entered the United States. For example, the first cohort begins with the immigrant or first generation, which was educated between 1900 and 1930, followed (to the right and down one) by their second-generation children educated between 1930 and 1950, and then their third-generation grandchildren. The second cohort begins with the second generation (or more) since immigration that was schooled at the beginning of the 20th century, followed by their third-generation children and then their fourth-generation grandchildren. This cohort is especially likely to include descendants of the Mexican population who resided in the former Mexican territories ceded to the United States in 1848.

Overall, both cohorts reveal substantial improvements in education over succeeding generations. Immigrant grandparents, schooled in the earliest period, had an average of 4.1 years of schooling. Their U.S.-born children more than doubled these levels to 10.0 years. Finally, their third-generation grandchildren tripled the initial educational levels to 13.1 years. Seen in this way, schooling improved greatly across the generations over the 20th century. The second cohort shows a similar pattern: the second-generation grandparents had 6.1 years of education, followed by 10.4 years among their third-generation children, and 12.4 years among their fourth-generation grandchildren.

However, despite several decades of struggle to improve the poor state of education and a century-long effort to achieve equality for Mexican Americans, the gap between Whites and Mexican Americans persists (the average educational level for non-Hispanic Whites is on the bottom line of Figure 2.1). The dramatic result is that poor education persists for the fourth generation, which may be the first generation not exposed to immigrant relatives, and whose ancestral ties to Mexico are predominantly through their great-grandparents or great-great-grandparents,

Figure 2.1. Years of Education by Generation-Since-Immigration, 1965 and 2000

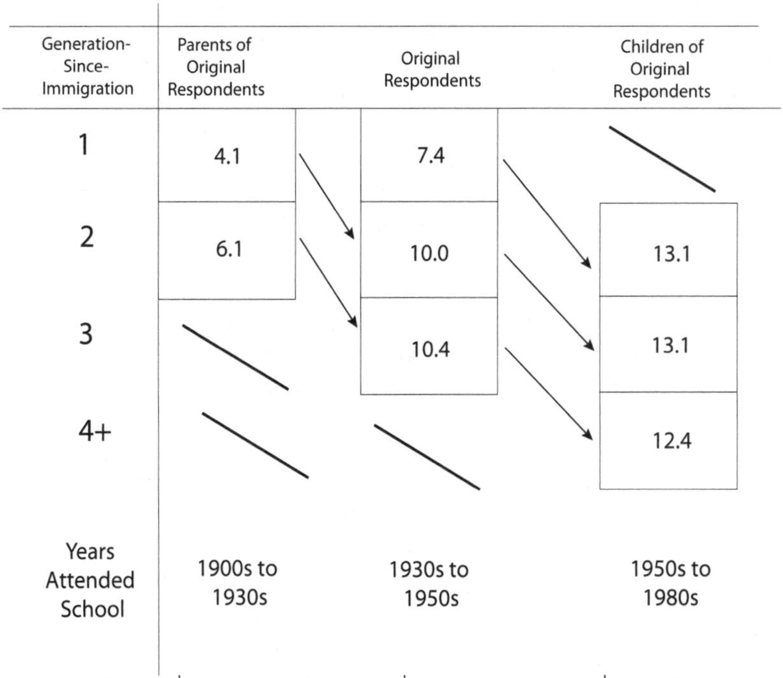

Generation-Since-Immigration	Parents of Original Respondents	Original Respondents	Children of Original Respondents
1	4.1	7.4	
2	6.1	10.0	13.1
3		10.4	13.1
4+			12.4
Years Attended School	1900s to 1930s	1930s to 1950s	1950s to 1980s

Generation Since Immigration	Parents of Original Respondents	Original Respondents	Children of Original Respondents
1	4.1	7.4	–
2	6.1	10.0	13.1
3	–	10.4	13.1
4+	–	–	12.4
Years Attended School	1900s to 1930s	1930s to 1950s	1950s to 1980s
Non-Hispanic Whites	9.5	12.5	14.2

Source: Mexican American Study Project.

whom they are unlikely to have met. Despite the optimistic expectations of economists, such as Smith (2003) and Borjas (1994), and assimilation scholars, such as Alba and Nee (2003), assimilation is very limited, even by the fourth generation. To make matters worse, the expectation that educational attainment improves across generations is turned on its head for the children of the original respondents. Figure 2.1 shows that the fourth generation has fewer years of average schooling than the second or the third generation.

For the original respondents, there is a large gain from the immigrants, most of whom were probably educated in Mexico, to the second generation. The third generation, with 10.4 years of schooling, does slightly better than the second generation. Mexican Americans continue to have lower high school graduation rates than any other major ethnic group in the United States. Figure 2.2 shows that only a minority of original respondents, who were mostly schooled between the 1930s and 1950s, completed high school, whereas around 80% of all children did. Understandably, the graduation rate is especially low for immigrants given that they often completed their educations in Mexico, where high school completion is less common. Only 30% of immigrant original respondents completed high school, whereas 48 and 58% (respectively) of their second- and third-generation counterparts did, suggesting a smooth generational improvement for those schooled from the 1930s to the 1950s. Thus, though improvements from parents to children in graduation from high school, especially for immigrants, are clear, they are less so for the children of the third generation.

Our data also allowed us to investigate the educational achievement of the grandchildren of the original respondents, enabling us to distinguish a fifth generation since immigration. We did not directly interview the children of the child sample, but instead asked the children of the original respondents about their own children's education level. Because many of these children were not yet adults and thus had not completed their education, we limited our investigation to high school graduation rates for those 20 years old and older. Figure 2.2 shows that these grandchildren of the original respondents, who are third- to fifth-generation, seemed to be doing no better than their parents. By this time, the third, fourth, and fifth generations were performing equally, with no significant differences among them. In the third generation, 85% had graduated from high school, versus 84% of the fourth generation and 81% of the fifth generation.

Figure 2.2. High School Graduation by Generation Since Immigration, 1965 and 2000

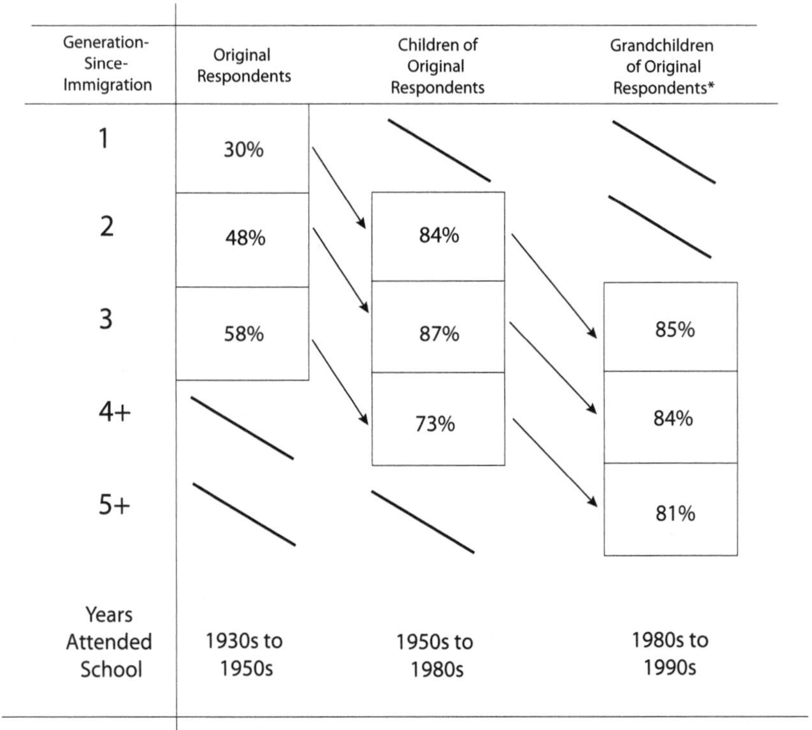

Generation-Since-Immigration	Original Respondents	Children of Original Respondents	Grandchildren of Original Respondents*
1	30%		
2	48%	84%	
3	58%	87%	85%
4+		73%	84%
5+			81%
Years Attended School	1930s to 1950s	1950s to 1980s	1980s to 1990s

Generation Since Immigration	Original Respondents	Children of Original Respondents	Grandchildren of Original Respondents[a]
1	30%	–	–
2	48%	84%	–
3	58%	87%	85%
4+	–	73%	84%
5+	–	–	81%
Years Attended School	1930s to 1950s	1950s to 1980s	1980s to 1990s

Source: Mexican American Study Project.

a As reported by children, among grandchildren age 20 and older.

CONCLUSIONS

Education among Mexican Americans does not improve in subsequent generations–since immigration, as assimilation theory predicts. Gains from immigrant parents to their children aside, Mexican American schooling remained fairly flat in succeeding generations since immigration. Assuming equally resourced children, education actually worsened. That is, when parental education, household income, and other indicators of parental status are held constant, the highest levels of schooling are for those who immigrated as children but were educated in the United States and the lowest for the grandchildren and great-grandchildren of immigrants. In other words, the third and fourth generation did worse than the 1.5 or the second generation. Moreover, our study shows similarly poor educational outcomes for the fifth generation, that is, the adult children of the fourth-generation children. America's public schools have failed Mexican Americans, contrary to what they did for European Americans a century ago. Instead, our research supports the claims of many educators that the failure of public schools derives from a racialized system that stigmatizes Mexican American children in various ways. Racialization through schooling seems to help cement their low status in American society.

Our findings are consistent with the theory of status attainment, in which parents' education and income are the best predictors of their child's education. Mexican American children with more educated parents do better than those whose parents have less education. However, the payoff to any educational advantages their parents may have is lower for Mexican Americans than it is for both Whites and African Americans. Also, various types of social capital improved education.

Our findings are mixed regarding the relationship between segregation and education, once factors such as parental education are held constant. In other words, parental resources mostly shape children's levels of education and the neighborhoods in which they can afford to live. Thus, our evidence suggests that reducing segregation, by itself, may have little effect on the poor educational outcomes of Mexican Americans.

Although status attainment is consistent with assimilation theory, in that children's status depends on parents' status, assimilation theory goes a step further by expecting consecutive and cumulative gains to status over generations since immigration. In other words, with assimilation theory, two conditions must be met: those with higher status inherit higher status from the previous generation, and status is increased with successive generations since immigration. For the Mexican case, the first condition is met but not the second. Status attainment is important, but when it comes to generation since immigration, status gains passed down from parents are stalled or even reversed by the third and subsequent generations. Our evidence thus strongly supports research claiming that racial stereotyping and discrimination have largely contributed to enduring Mexican American disadvantage.

We also find that Catholic schools have a beneficial effect on Mexican Americans. Even when a host of other variables that contribute to education are held equal, including parental resources and aspirations, having attended high school in a Catholic or other private school contributes more than a full year of additional education for Mexican Americans—an amount that would largely overcome their educational deficit relative to other Americans. Certainly, one can identify instances where public schools perform just as well, but these are exceptions. What about Catholic schools could disrupt the racialization process? First, the higher expectations of the Catholic schools themselves provide advantages to students in those schools. This is expressed in the universally high expectations held jointly by teachers and parents that all students can succeed and will go to college. Second, the more personalized and small community identity of these schools may decrease racial and ethnic stereotyping and divisions. This suggests that creating smaller learning communities, a recent intervention in public schools, and working on countering unconscious biases and low expectations on the part of teachers toward Mexican American students could improve public education.

To end this chapter on a more positive note, we consider education outcomes for Mexican Americans over time rather than by generation since immigration. Mexican Americans have seen educational progress over the course of the 20th century. This does not involve progress by generation since immigration but is due to a slow historical trend of improving education. This leads to gradually reducing, rather than eliminating, the educational gap from U.S. Whites. This slowly declining gap over time is partly attributable to state intervention, such as policies that strive toward equity in public spending for schools, and to civil rights gains for minorities, including the end of de jure segregation. These have contributed to educational gains for a considerable number of Mexican Americans. On the other hand, continuously high dropout rates for Mexican-origin children suggest that reversals of this improving long-term trend are also possible.

REFERENCES

Alba, R., & Islam, T. (2009). The case of the disappearing Mexican Americans: An ethnic-identity mystery. *Population Research Policy Review, 28,* 109–121.

Alba, R., & Nee, V. (2003). *Remaking the American mainstream: Assimilation and contemporary immigration.* Cambridge, MA: Harvard University Press.

Borjas, G. J. (1994). Long-run convergence of ethnic skill differentials: The children and grandchildren of the Great Migration. *Industrial and Labor Relations Review, 47,* 553–573.

Grebler, L., Moore, J. W., & Guzman, R. (1970). *The Mexican American people: The nation's second largest minority.* New York: Free Press.

Portes, A., & Rumbaut, R. G. (2001). *Legacies: The story of the immigrant second generation.* Berkeley, CA: University of California Press.

Smith, J. P. (2003). Assimilation across the Latino generations. *The American Economic Review, 93,* 315–319.

Telles, E., & Ortiz, V. (2008). *Generations of exclusion: Mexican Americans, assimilation, and race.* New York: Russell Sage Foundation.

Vigil, J. D. (1997). *Personas mexicanas: Chicano high schoolers in a changing Los Angeles.* Fort Worth, TX: Harcourt Brace College Publishers.

CHAPTER 3

Unauthorized Migration and Its Implications for Mexican American Educational Incorporation

Frank D. Bean, Susan K. Brown, Mark A. Leach,
James D. Bachmeier, and Rosaura Tafoya-Estrada

Ever since the 1880s and the development of rail connections between northern Mexico and the U.S. interior, Mexican migrants have been coming to the United States in notable numbers (Cardoso, 1980; Spener, 2009). Those lacking official permission to enter are often today called "unauthorized" migrants (Bean & Lowell, 2007), although most arriving before World War I (and even long afterward) would scarcely have entertained the idea they were "unauthorized" (Massey, Durand, & Malone, 2002). Indeed, there was no official government agency charged with the responsibility of interdicting illegal border crossers until 1924, when the Border Patrol was established (Zolberg, 2006). But most Mexican migrants, then and now, move because they need jobs and U.S. employers need their labor. Consistent with this, the United States for more than two decades permitted Mexican contract laborers to enter the country legally through the Bracero Program. When that program ended in 1964, the number of unauthorized migrants began to escalate (Calavita, 2010). The difficulties such migrants face have always been considerable (Chávez, 1998; Gonzalez, 2006). And after the penalties for unauthorized entry began to increase in 1996 (National Research Council, 2011), their hardships became even more severe. Yet the country continues to rely as much as ever on unauthorized less skilled Mexican workers (Bean, Brown, & Bachmeier, 2012). This contradiction highlights the growing relevance for public policy of assessments of how unauthorized migration affects the social, economic, and political incorporation of Mexican Americans into the United States.

Numerous research studies have documented that unauthorized Mexican migrants pay an earnings penalty and that earnings rise with legal status (Donato & Massey, 1993; Hall, Greenman, & Farkas, 2010). Such findings have fueled recent theoretical arguments that unauthorized migration status may hinder the social, economic, and political incorporation of immigrants just as much, if not more than, other disadvantages (Bean & Stevens, 2003; Brown & Bean, 2006). Empirical research by Brown (2007) shows that having unauthorized parents reduces the ability of the Mexican American second generation to move to richer, more integrated neighborhoods. And another recent survey-based study provides explicit empirical indication that unauthorized entry handicaps educational advancement, especially among the children of Mexican immigrants (Bean et al., 2011). Because educational attainment "captures the human capital necessary for full social, political and economic participation in society" (Jiménez & Fitzgerald, 2007, p. 344), this chapter focuses on how unauthorized status among Mexican immigrants affects the educational incorporation of their descendants.

We take a five-pronged approach. First, we outline the context of unauthorized migration and its potential effects on the education of Mexican American children. Second, we discuss several critical theoretical and methodological issues involved in assessing the educational incorporation of immigrant groups. Third, we summarize the results of our research on how much difference having an unauthorized parent makes for the educational attainment of the second generation. Fourth, we extend the implications of these findings to the grandchildren of unauthorized immigrants, calculating the extent to which removing the second generation's educational deficits would boost the third generation's attainment. Such a multigenerational approach enables us to draw inferences about what educational incorporation might look like absent the long-term effects of unauthorized status. Fifth, we suggest that among the plausible mechanisms linking unauthorized status to education, the need to work among the immigrants and their children is a major one, and we discuss the implications of this for educational incorporation.

THE UNAUTHORIZED MIGRANT CONTEXT

One of the bedrock issues in policy debates about immigration reform in the United States involves whether to provide legal residency to an estimated 11 million unauthorized immigrants (Passel & Cohn, 2011). Little research has explicitly addressed whether *not* being able to legalize handicaps unauthorized immigrants and their children. Here we focus on Mexican immigrants because they comprise by far the largest U.S. immigrant group in general, and because so many of them come without papers (Bean & Stevens, 2003; Bean et al., 2010). Likewise, Mexican-origin children account for a large majority of children with an unauthorized immigrant parent. According to current estimates, 70% of the 5.5 million children of unauthorized immigrants in the United States have a Mexican-born parent (Passel & Cohn, 2011). These numbers imply that more than half of the 7.3 million children of Mexican immigrants residing in the United States in 2010 had an unauthorized parent (King et al., 2010).

Most children of unauthorized parents, about 80% as of 2009, are born in the United States and are thus U.S. citizens (Passel, 2011). Even though U.S.-born children of immigrants presumably enjoy access to the same education and jobs as any other citizen, their parents' migration-status histories reflect the first membership experiences of these young people with the host society (Hochschild & Mollenkopf, 2009). Unauthorized Mexican migrants endure only the most marginal membership, hardly anything more than mere presence in the country, which makes for a precarious situation likely to exert lasting effects on their second-generation children. To overcome this marginalized state, such immigrants may try many difficult or expensive pathways to obtaining legal permanent residency (LPR), even including marriage to a U.S. citizen. Some of those who obtain LPR status may eventually naturalize and become U.S. citizens. But many are never able to legalize.

Different reasons for migrating can make for varying parental legal status trajectories both within and among couples. Compared with other immigrant groups to the United States, more Mexicans have traditionally circulated back and forth between the two countries (Cornelius, 1992; Massey et al., 2002; Portes & Bach, 1985). Circular migrants often change their temporal intentions over time, gradually becoming permanent migrants (Roberts, 1995), in a process that may occur over many years (Menjívar, 2006; Roberts, Frank, & Lozano-Ascencio, 1999). As migrants move from *sojourner* to *settler* status (Chávez, 1988), their frames of reference shift from the society of origin toward the society of destination. Thus, when poor, unskilled labor migrants (especially males) who initially migrate for temporary employment begin the transition to more permanent work, they often seek ways to legalize. This process may take years to implement, however, because legalization often depends on the migration status of other family members (Dreby, 2010).

By making legal entry for almost all labor migrants dependent on family relationships, U.S. immigration laws encourage the development of complex family-based strategies for achieving legalization (Curiel,

2004; Glick, 2010; Hondagneu-Sotelo, 1994). Whatever the strategies employed by particular families, it is clear that many Mexican immigrants spend long periods as unauthorized migrants and varying amounts of time in transition from one migration status to another. The uncertainty of these transitions appears to reinforce immigrants' need to work, with this tendency occurring disproportionately among those in the most precarious contexts. This dynamic in turn can deter schooling in the second generation and, through legacy effects, later generations as well. The centrality of education to the overall incorporation of immigrants makes clear the importance of examining outcomes across generations, as well as of comparing the outcomes of later-generation groups to those of the non-Hispanic White majority group. To do so, we introduce survey data that include four generations of young adult (ages 20–40) Mexican Americans in Los Angeles. (See Bean et al., 2011 for more details on the survey, called Immigration and Intergenerational Mobility in Metropolitan Los Angeles, or IIMMLA.)

IMPORTANT RESEARCH ISSUES

Studying educational incorporation requires the consideration of several theoretical and methodological issues, each of which can influence research conclusions. Following Jiménez and Fitzgerald (2007), the most relevant of these for present purposes are:

(1) Specifying the appropriate comparative context of
    incorporation,
(2) Resolving the "generation/cohort" problem,
(3) Dealing with measurement error in assigning generational
    status, and
(4) Making sure comparison groups are similar on other variables
    that affect incorporation.

Taking unauthorized status into consideration comes into play in at least the first two of these.

The "Compared to What?" Problem

Concluding that successful incorporation has occurred depends in the first instance on what is being compared. This is foremost a theoretical issue. Perhaps the most basic decision incorporation researchers must make involves deciding whether to compare the experiences of immigrants, including unauthorized migrants, to the situations of people in the country of destination, or to compare them to people in the country of origin. Because the very idea of incorporation (or of assimilation or integration) is framed in terms of country-of-destination dynamics, this usually means that the comparisons of interest are often made between immigrants and others in the destination society. If the United States is the destination country, this means asking in turn any of several questions: To what extent are immigrants like natives in general, like native co-ethnics, like native majority-group members, or like native minority groups? But if the primary research interest focuses on reasons for leaving an origin country (as it might if one were examining how economic development influenced emigration), then the comparison instead might be on how dissimilar emigrants are from those left behind in the origin country, either when emigrants initially leave or after they have been in the destination country for a period of time. For example, research may show that Mexican immigrants are not doing very well in the United States compared with native-born Americans, but nonetheless better than non-migrants in Mexico. Having a job in the United States may be "better" than not having a job at all in Mexico. Becoming less like those who stayed in the origin country has been termed "dissimilation" because of ever-growing dissimilarities over time between emigrants and the natives of the origin country (Jiménez & Fitzgerald, 2007).

Comparisons of certain groups within the United States are also more relevant to assessing some theoretical perspectives than others. For example, a classical assimilation perspective implies that immigrants and native Whites converge with one another (suggesting focusing on comparisons of later-generation immigrant-group members with later-generation native Whites), whereas an "assimilation as intergenerational process" perspective implies that later-generation members of the immigrant group are doing better than the first generation (suggesting comparisons among the first, second, and third generations) (Jiménez & Fitzgerald, 2007). Similarly, a segmented assimilation perspective implies that at least some members of the immigrant group become like disadvantaged native minority groups (which suggests a comparison of third-or-later generation immigrants with third-or-later generation African Americans) (Portes & Rumbaut, 2001). Thus, various comparisons can result in one reaching different conclusions about the degree of incorporation. Here our explicit focus on multi-generational incorporation dynamics makes us most concerned with comparisons that assess the classical and intergenerational assimilation hypotheses (i.e., those that involve comparisons of Mexican-origin generations with one another and those of the Mexican-origin third generation with third-or-later generation Whites).

The Generation/Cohort Problem

Making intergenerational comparisons also requires dealing with generation/cohort problems. From the second to later generations, the educational trajectory among the descendants of Mexican immigrants often yields ambiguous if not contested results. Numerous cross-sectional studies show little differences in educational attainment between second- and third-plus generation Mexican Americans (Farley & Alba, 2002; Grogger & Trejo, 2002; McKeever & Klineberg, 1999; Reed et al., 2005; Zsembik & Llanes, 1996). Other studies find notable and sometimes significantly lower educational attainment for third-plus generation Mexican Americans (or Latinos) compared with second-generation Mexican Americans (Bean et al., 1994; Keller & Tillman, 2007; Wojtkiewicz & Donato, 1995). Moreover, lower third-plus generation attainment also often emerges for groups that are non-Hispanic (Boyd, 2002; Chiswick & DebBurman, 2003; Glick & White, 2004; Kao & Tienda, 1995; Ramakrishnan, 2004), suggesting that this particular kind of ambiguity is not unique to the Mexican case. The fact that this is also true for groups that migrate with higher levels of education than Mexicans implies that the small differences between second- and third-plus-generation Mexican Americans often observed may result from factors other than ethnoracial discrimination against the group.

One of these may be birth cohort heterogeneity within generational groups. Because Mexican immigration has been ongoing for well over a century in the United States, as Jiménez and Fitzgerald (2007, p. 342) note: "Using only a generation as a temporal marker of assimilation is not enough. Each generation of Mexican-origin individuals is made of people from a mix of birth cohorts, and each birth cohort contains individuals from many immigrant generations." One way to deal with this involves controlling for age, or making generational comparisons within narrower age ranges, as we do here.

Evidence of this source of ambiguity also reveals itself in different research designs yielding different results. Studies that compare parental cohorts with child cohorts, or longitudinal ones comparing parents with their children, show more consistent evidence of assimilation than simple generational cross-sectional studies that fail to detect the cohort and time dimensions. Smith (2003, 2006) finds rising levels of education across three generations of men of Mexican origin and a corresponding decrease in the gap between their educational levels and those of non-Hispanic whites; he concludes that Hispanic men have made sizeable strides in closing the socioeconomic gap with Whites. In another example, using longitudinal data measuring individual Mexican American families, Telles & Ortiz (2008; Chapter 2, this volume) find increasing education across the first three generations, although more at the level of high school than college completion. But in the fourth and fifth generations, they find stagnation in educational outcomes.

The "Third-Plus" Generation Problem

In addition, ambiguity in the findings of cross-sectional studies may result from problems in the definition of the third generation. All of the above such studies use measures that aggregate the third with later generations. As a result, the "third-plus" generational measure used actually includes fourth, fifth, sixth, and even later generations. Few studies are able to distinguish a true third generation (consisting of those with at least one Mexican-born grandparent) from later generations (consisting of those whose grandparents were all born in the United States). One study that does make this distinction relied on General Social Survey data from 1972–2002 (Alba et al., 2011). When these surveys were examined cross-sectionally, only modest evidence of intergenerational mobility emerged. But when the education of respondents was directly compared with that of their own parents, the data indicated substantial mobility among both Mexican Americans and Whites, but especially for Mexican Americans, whose parents' education is particularly low. When this study directly examines the educational difference that emerges from using a "third-only" measure as compared to a "third-plus" measure, it finds that the third-only generation is attaining slightly more education, with one exception: third-only generation boys are less likely to finish high school. Using the IIMMLA data, which are more recent, we find a deficit of 0.3 years of school for third-plus generation males compared with third-only males (see Table 3.1). For females, we find results similar in direction, although not as extreme in magnitude. In sum, when researchers have no alternative than to rely on a third-plus measure, as is the case with Current Population Survey (CPS) data, assessments of the third-plus generation education gap between this group and non-Hispanic Whites are biased. Moreover, as a percentage of this between-groups gap, a deficit of 0.3 years constitutes a substantial part of the difference. Similarly, calculations of educational gain from the second to the third-plus generation substantially *understate* percentage advancements in schooling.

What accounts for this distortion? Recent research suggests it results mostly from selective attrition. Errors in defining the Mexican-origin group become more numerous the more generations are included

Table 3.1. Years-of-Schooling Discrepancies Between Third-Only and Third-Plus Measures of Respondents' Generation, Persons of Mexican Origin, Ages 20–40, Los Angeles, 2004

	Generation Measure		
Gender	*Third-plus*	*Third-only*	Difference
Males	13.1	13.4	-0.3
Females	13.4	13.6	-0.2

Source: IIMMLA data (see Bean et al., 2011).

since immigration. Any sampling frame that depends on ethnic self-identification for inclusion in the sample misses those people who no longer identify as either Hispanic or Mexican. This is particularly true for people with only one or two Mexican-born grandparents. For example, 30% of the third-generation children of Mexican-origin women are not identified as Mexican under the Hispanic question in the CPS (Duncan & Trejo, 2011). In a separate study of U.S. censuses from 1980 to 2000, Alba and Islam (2009) also find substantial apparent attrition from the Mexican-origin group. Those who no longer identify as Mexican appear to be highly selected among those whose parents have outmarried. Not only is outmarriage fairly commonplace among Mexican Americans, but it occurs more often among the more highly educated (Bean & Stevens, 2003; Duncan & Trejo, 2011; Mittelbach & Moore, 1968; Rosenfeld, 2002). Selective attrition thus produces substantial downward bias in measures of socioeconomic attainment in samples selected on the basis of ethnic self-identification.

Making the Reference Group Comparable

A final issue to consider involves making the reference group (the one being compared to an immigrant generational group for purposes of gauging the degree of incorporation) comparable to the immigrant group in terms of differences in other factors that could affect the educational levels of the two groups. In national-level studies, this can be achieved through multivariate analyses employing appropriate controls if the study includes measures of all relevant factors that matter. In other instances, this may be more difficult. For example, because of the post-industrial nature of their economic structures, Los Angeles, along with New York and several other major metropolises in the country, both attracts disproportionate numbers of college graduates and experiences out-migration of persons with only high school diplomas or less (the

latter for cost-of-living reasons if nothing else). Moreover, this selective migration occurs to a greater relative degree among non-Hispanic
Whites than in the Mexican-origin population, because the former
group contains a higher proportion of college graduates. Stated differently, the selective in-migration of educated Whites and out-migration
of less-educated Whites means that the Los Angeles gap in educational
attainment between Whites and Mexican Americans will substantially
exceed this same educational gap in the rest of the country. As we note
below, this difference may also capture the influence of other factors,
such as discrimination, that are unmeasured here. We adjust for these
differences below by subtracting from non-Hispanic White levels the
average net differential between educational levels in Los Angeles and
the rest of the country for both men and women, although we interpret
the resulting differences with caution.

Our Research Approach

We focus on examining both intergenerational and classical assimilation dynamics. The former involves making comparisons among Mexican American generational groups, and the latter, comparisons of the
Mexican American third generation with non-Hispanic Whites. Following the discussion presented above about the heterogeneity and likely
distorting effects of attrition in so-called "third-plus" generation data, we
take advantage of the fact that a clear-cut "third-only" generation can
be isolated in the IIMMLA data. Our comparisons thus consist of examining educational attainment levels for young adults (ages 20–40) in Los
Angeles of Mexican immigrants (the first generation) and two groups of
Mexican Americans–the second generation, including some who migrated to the United States as young children, and the third generation.
Our goal is to estimate statistically the lingering depressive effects on the
educational attainment of the third generation of unauthorized status
of grandparents. This enables us to approximate the outcomes relevant
to assessing the intergenerational and classic assimilation hypotheses *if*
unauthorized Mexican immigrants were able to legalize.

UNAUTHORIZED STATUS AND
ITS EFFECTS ON SCHOOLING

More than any other group, Mexicans are diverse both in initial form
of entry and in not having finished the often lengthy process of moving
from unauthorized sojourner to legal settler status (Roberts, Frank, &

Lozano-Ascencio, 1999). The pathways they adopt toward legalization and naturalization are similarly heterogeneous. As a result, their family structures reflect a wide variety of parental combinations of entry and subsequent legalization and naturalization statuses. As noted above, numerous studies have documented the deleterious effects of being unauthorized, especially in the labor market (Gonzales, 2011; Hall et al., 2010; Massey, 1987; Massey et al., 2002). Recent studies have also found negative psychological consequences for the children of unauthorized immigrants, including stress and other anxieties that inhibit learning and cognitive development (Yoshikawa, 2011). Such factors are also likely to limit children's educational attainment.

Educational attainment also seems likely to be reduced by the marginality of unauthorized immigrant parents. Differences in levels of schooling substantially explain differences in employment and earnings between Whites and many ethnoracial groups, with the notable exception of Mexican immigrants and African Americans (Duncan, Hotz, & Trejo, 2006; Smith & Edmonston, 1997). Among Mexican immigrants, this is a function of unauthorized status (Hall et al., 2010), which in turn suggests that the incorporation processes for Mexican immigrants are likely to take considerably longer than those of other immigrant groups because Mexicans must find ways to legalize before they can take full advantage of American opportunities (Bean & Stevens, 2003; Bean et al., 2011; Brown, 2007). Because Mexican immigrants increasingly make up an essential part of the country's supply of less skilled labor (Brown, Bachmeier, & Bean, 2009), the policy challenge for the United States is to find ways to make their incorporation sufficiently successful so that the long-run costs of their remaining unauthorized do not exceed the short-run benefits from the important work they do.

But what are some of these costs? Mexican immigrants show various entry and subsequent migration status trajectories. Among the second-generation Mexican Americans in the IIMMLA sample, for example, many of their parents are likely to have been unauthorized when they came to the country: 34.2% of Mexican mothers and 32.8% of Mexican fathers (see Table 3.2). Nearly three decades after they migrated to the United States, the Mexican parents still have mostly not finished high school (averaging only a little more than 8.5 years of schooling; see Table 3.3). By contrast, their children complete an average of 13 years of schooling. Many of these Mexican Americans did not speak English at home while growing up, although virtually all learned the language, and nearly three-fourths lived with both parents. The predominant migration status factor affecting their educational attainment involves whether the mother had legal status. Second-generation Mexican American

Table 3.2. Percentage of Immigrant Mothers and Fathers with Various Nativity/Migration and Legalization/Citizenship Trajectories, Mexican-Origin Parents

Trajectory	Mothers	Fathers
Unknown	1.0	6.4
Never Migrated to U.S.	8.7	12.7
Authorized to Naturalized	32.1	25.6
Authorized to LPR	13.7	12.6
Unauthorized (or Unknown) to Naturalized	14.8	16.3
Unauthorized (or Unknown) to LPR	15.2	12.2
Unauthorized (or Unknown) to Unauthorized	4.2	4.3
U.S. Born (N = 935)	10.5	9.9

Source: IIMMLA data (See Bean et al., 2011).

Table 3.3. Means and Standard Deviations for Respondent and Parent Characteristics

Attributes	Respondents	
	Mean	*SDs*
Age	27.8	0.19
Years of education completed	13.0	0.08
Male	0.5	0.02
Second generation	0.67	0.02
Spoke Spanish at home while growing up	0.91	0.01
Enrolled in school at interview	0.3	0.02
Lived with both parents while growing up	0.72	0.02

	Mothers		Fathers	
	Mean	*SDs*	*Mean*	*SDs*
Years of education	8.7	0.13	8.6	0.13
Held laborer occupation in home country	0.24	0.01	0.5	0.02
Worked in white-collar occupation in home country	0.21	0.01	0.17	0.01
Migrated from West Central Region of Mexico	0.52	0.02	0.51	0.02
Returned to home country for 6+ months after migration to U.S.	0.15	0.01	0.15	0.01

Source: IIMMLA study (see Bean et al., 2011).

respondents with mothers who became legal get 2.04 years more schooling than those with unauthorized mothers (Bean et al., 2011). With statistical controls (for both respondent and parental characteristics), this gross difference shrinks to 1.51 years, which is still highly statistically significant. The educational advantage resulting from maternal legalization thus does not appear to owe substantially to other kinds of differences between these two kinds of mothers and their children.

However, such a relationship between mother's legalization and children's education could still be spurious (i.e., it could result from factors not observed in this research). An example is parents' level of initiative. Bean et al. (2011) take advantage of the fact that many parents legalized through the 1986 Immigration Reform and Control Act (IRCA) and use this fact to help control for such factors. After employing this approach (termed an *instrumental variable* technique), they find that the education premium for legal status is reduced only slightly, to about one and one-quarter years (1.24) years. In other words, controlling only for factors that are observable in the data diminishes the education premium of mother's legal status by about one-third (from 2.04 to 1.51 years). Taking IRCA legalization into account as a way to adjust further for unobserved factors reduces the premium by about another one-sixth (from 1.51 years to 1.24 years). Thus, a substantial difference of nearly one-and-one-quarter years of schooling still appears related to mothers having achieved legal status.

REMOVING THE EFFECTS OF UNAUTHORIZED STATUS FROM THE GENERATIONAL PATTERN

Now we turn to examination of the schooling pattern across three generations, but focusing on a third-only group rather than a third-plus group. Although the IIMMLA data allow the construction of a fourth-plus generational group, we do not use such a measure because it is subject to the distortions and deficiencies noted above for all "plus" measures that combine multiple generations into one. One of the most notable strengths of the Mexican-origin IIMMLA data is that they permit the isolation of a third-only generation, and this is what we rely on here. When we use this designation, it shows higher levels of schooling completed for third-only generation respondents (see Table 3.4). For example, third-only males exhibit 13.4 years of school, a level up from 12.9 years in the second generation. This in turn is 3.3 years higher than the first generation's level of 9.6 years. We can also compare sons directly with their fathers. As in the case of previous research, the gains when

Table 3.4. Years of Schooling Completed by Generation Among Mexican-Origin Respondents and Their Parents

Generation of Respondent	Males		Females	
	Father's average education	Respondent's average education	Mother's average education	Respondent's average education
0	5.7	N/A	4.7	N/A
1st	7.4	9.6	6.6	8.5
2nd	11.7	12.9	11.2	12.8
3rd-only	12.6	13.4	11.8	13.6
Approximate period of high school attendance	1950–1980	1980–2000	1950–1980	1980–2000
3rd+ non-Hispanic Whites	14.6	14.5	14.0	14.9

Source: IIMMLA data (Bean et al., 2011).

examined this way are even bigger. For example, third-only generation males exceed their father's level of schooling on average by 1.7 years. Females show similar intergenerational mobility patterns.

Despite this evidence of greater educational incorporation based on the third-only generation measure, we must remember that the schooling levels in Table 3.4 still reflect the dampening effects of unauthorized migration status. Next we ask: what would the schooling levels of the second-generation sons look like if all of their mothers had come to the country legally or if they had been legalized instead of staying unauthorized? Since about 20% of the second-generation sons had mothers who remained unauthorized, this means that we would expect about one-fifth of this portion of the Mexican-origin sample might have achieved an additional year and a quarter of schooling on average but for the disadvantage of their mothers' status. Adding this increment to the schooling level of the one-fifth of second-generation sons boosts the overall average schooling level of 13.2 years for this group (see Table 3.5). Turning to the third-only generation, we calculate an adjusted schooling level for this group by assuming it entails the same proportional increment in attainment between the second and third-only generations as was revealed in the unadjusted values in Table 3.4. There, the third-generation attainment for sons was 3.9% higher than that of second-generation males. Increasing the adjusted second-generation level in Table 3.5 by this pro rata amount yields an adjusted attainment of 13.7 years of schooling for third-generation sons. This constitutes the estimated level of attainment we would expect if there were no adverse legacy effect of grandparents' unauthorized status on third-generation attainment. The results of similarly-reasoned calculations for females are also shown in Table 3.5.

However, the schooling levels for third-only males and females still fall below those for third-generation non-Hispanic Whites. For example, the 13.7 years for males lags the level of 14.5 for White males shown in Table 3.4, a difference of 0.8 years. But these levels, even though they have the effects of parental unauthorized status removed, still reflect other differences between Mexican Americans and Whites in Los Angeles, including differential selective in- and out-migration by education. As a rough gauge of these differences, we can compare the difference in average level of schooling for native-born Mexican Americans in Los Angeles to that for Whites in the city, and then in turn compare this difference to the same difference in the rest of the country. Using these data Mexican American males in Los Angeles average 11.9 fewer years of schooling than White males, whereas in the rest of the country, this difference is 1.2 years. In other words, the difference in the degree to which the White schooling level exceeds the Mexican-American level in Los Angeles is 0.7 years *more* than this same difference in the rest of the country. For females, this deficit is 0.9 years. As noted above, this bigger Mexican-origin deficit in L.A. could stem from differential migration into and out of Los Angeles by education on the parts of the two groups, but other factors are likely to be involved as well. If we take this differential excess as a rough proxy for the degree to which all of these other factors make for L.A.-specific educational differences between the two groups (and it is only a crude guide), we could further adjust the differential between the third-only Mexican American schooling level and that for non-Hispanic third-generation Whites by subtracting this difference from the White schooling level.

If we do this for males, we find it accounts for most of the remaining difference between the two groups in attainment levels (as shown in the bottom row of the male column in Table 3.6). In sum, removing the legacy effects of grandparents' unauthorized status, as well as adjusting in a very rough way for other kinds of differences that affect schooling levels for these two groups in Los Angeles, accounts for much of the educational attainment difference between Mexican American and White males by the third generation. More broadly, the extent to

Table 3.5. Respondent's Average Schooling (Years) by Generation, Adjusted for Effects of Unauthorized Parental Status

Generation of Respondent	Males	Females
1st	9.6	8.5
2nd	13.2	13.1
3rd-only	13.7	9

Source: IIMMLA data (Bean et al., 2011).

Table 3.6. Third-Only and Non-Hispanic White Education Gaps With and Without the Removal of Unique City Effects and Unauthorized Legacy Effects

Differences	Males	Females
Gross differences	–1.1	-1.3
Remaining difference		
With city effects removed	-0.3	-0.3
With legacy effects removed	-0.7	-0.9
With both removed	0.1	-0.1

Source: IIMMLA data (Bean et al., 2011).

which these two kinds of adjustments individually and in combination affect the Mexican American third-only generation educational deficit compared to Whites is shown in Table 3.6. For females, much of the gap, as with males, is closed by the third-only generation as well. To be sure, this adjustment for unique L.A.-related influences may not only remove the effects of structural differences, but also the effects of others, one of which could be greater than average discrimination in Los Angeles. That is, the adjustment may take out of the picture some of the influence of discrimination (i.e., discrimination against Mexican immigrants in Los Angeles that could be stronger than elsewhere, thus dampening Mexican-origin attainment in the city compared to that in other parts of the country). Whatever the case, adjustment for city-specific differences undoubtedly captures at least a portion of the influence of other factors that make for particularly large White/Mexican-origin education differences in the city. The results thus suggest that at about 30% of the ethnic differential in years of schooling is explained by the legacy effects of unauthorized migration. Moreover, if one were comparing the L.A. third-only generation educational attainment to average White educational attainment in the rest of the country and removed the legacy effect of unauthorized migration, even more of the education difference would disappear.

WHAT EXPLAINS THE ADVERSE EFFECT?

What accounts for the dampening effect of parental unauthorized status on children's educational attainment? We consider three possible explanations, although there could be more. Sorting empirically through the various mechanisms that dampen the schooling success of the children of unauthorized migrants is an important area for future research. But what do we already know about their experiences? Perhaps first is simply that severe stress probably impairs the ability of unauthorized migrants to motivate and encourage their children to read and do their homework. Because unauthorized parents are forced to lead lives in the "shadows" (Chavez, 1988), shadows that are particularly hard to escape or compensate for when one doesn't speak English, they necessarily keep a low profile. They constantly fear detection and deportation. Most cannot get driver's licenses and thus worry constantly when driving to work or elsewhere that they will become involved in an accident, the aftermath of which will expose them to the police and other official scrutiny. Their continual cautiousness and furtiveness inevitably induce stress and frustration and reduce efficiency. This clearly is likely to take a toll on children's educational success.

At the same time, because most of the unauthorized are impoverished labor migrants, with little education or command of English, they must take poorly paying jobs, often multiple jobs, with nighttime or irregular hours. The lack of education and English ability limits these parents' ability to deal with schooling issues, and the long hours limit their available time. But poverty affects children's education in subtler ways as well. The family's very low income level reinforces a family/household-based "social insurance" orientation to the labor market (Van Hook & Bean, 2009). That is, given their migration and survival exigencies, it is more important to obtain work than it is to spend time finding the best-paying work. In short, it is more important to minimize risk to the family from not having work than it is to pursue individual wage gains, which may be meager in any case. This means that for unauthorized parents, their "reservation wage," or the level of pay at which they are willing to accept a job, is likely to be much lower than for legal Mexican immigrants or native-born Mexican Americans. This may explain the fact that lack of legal status rather than differences in education mostly explains the lower wages and slower wage growth for unauthorized Mexican immigrants compared with legal Mexican immigrants (Hall et al., 2010).

This low reservation wage also makes it important to maximize the number of earners in the family. Thus, children are often encouraged to work as soon as they can, unless they show promise of being exceptionally good students, in which case they are encouraged to concentrate on their studies (Bachmeier & Bean, 2011). This produces a greater tendency toward "role specialization" among the children of Mexican immigrants, especially among boys, for whom the work imperative is greatest. Compared to African Americans and Whites, Mexican-origin immigrant and second-generation youth are more likely to be working when they are *not* enrolled in school, and also they are more likely *not* to be working if they *are* enrolled in school. This tendency can be seen clearly in Table 3.7, which shows the relative tendencies of various generations of 16- and 17-year-old Mexican-origin boys to be working when they are not in school versus when they are in school, compared to this same tendency in comparable groups of later-generation Mexican-origin boys and African Americans and Whites. The differences are large. Boys who migrated to the United States when they were 12 through 17 years old (the 1.25 generation) are more than 10 times more likely to be working when not enrolled versus when enrolled, whereas whites and African Americans show values of slightly less than two times more likely. In short, working and providing income for the family is overwhelmingly important among Mexican immigrants and their children. This imperative seems likely to drive down educational attainment among the children of the immigrants.

Table 3.7. Non-enrollee/enrollee Ratios in the Adjusted Odds of Workforce Participation Among 16- and 17-year old Mexican-origin Boys, by Generation and Ethnoracial Group

Generation	Non-enrolled	Enrolled
Mexican	1.25	10.3
Mexican	1.5	4.4
Mexican	1.75	3.6
Mexican	2.0	2.9
Mexican (3rd-Generation American)	2.2	–
White	1.9	–
Black	1.7	–

Adapted from Bachmeier and Bean (2011).

These subtle effects of long hours, low wages, and an emphasis on staying employed would seem the most likely mechanism through which unauthorized status impinges on educational attainment. These, of course, may overlap with stress. Neither can we fully rule out a third possibility–that ethnoracial discrimination against Mexican immigrants might explain some of the differences. Perhaps discrimination in school against the children of immigrants, many of whom are only learning English, also explains the poor outcomes. The fact that wage differences between unauthorized and legal immigrants are not entirely explained by legal status and education (Hall et al., 2010) appears to lend credence to this idea. But the fact that wage differences between native-born Mexican Americans and Whites are fully explained by education and experience suggests that any effects from discrimination cease after the first generation. This in turn implies that any discrimination effect may derive more from nativity or legal status discrimination than from ethnicity. For example, if employers discriminate against unauthorized workers, then perhaps other people, like teachers, may also discriminate against the children of unauthorized migrants. Yet for discrimination against children based on legal status to explain the results would require that teachers be able to tell which children have unauthorized parents and which do not.

In the final analysis, we cannot say with certainty to what degree each mechanism might account for the patterns of poor educational outcomes. To some degree, the low educational attainment in the second generation on the part of the children of unauthorized parents may result from contributions from all of these–namely parental and second-generation work imperatives, stress, and discrimination (probably in school) against unauthorized migrants' children, many of whom may not speak English very well. Our conjecture is that it is predominantly the work imperatives that Mexican-unauthorized immigrants face, together with the family/household risk minimization strategies these foster, that most hold back educational attainment among their children, especially boys. Parsing out the effects of the various mechanisms more exactly awaits further research.

CONCLUSION

These findings indicate the importance of opportunities for immigrants to legalize for the success of their children. Given that most children of unauthorized immigrants are born in the United States, our analysis suggests that legislation providing the possibility of entry into full societal membership creates benefits not only for the immigrants themselves but also for their children and potentially their children's children. When those unauthorized entrants who have the opportunity to legalize do so, both they and their children are able to overcome many of the disadvantages confronting them. This resourcefulness constitutes strong evidence in support of granting full societal membership. Because parents' socioeconomic status has sizeable effects on children's education (Fischer & Hout, 2006), the positive influence of such membership in the immigrant generation also carries over to later generations, boosting their schooling as well, as our extrapolated results to the third generation show.

Also, while the pattern of findings presented above does not rule out the possibility that discrimination accounts for educational differences between higher-generation Mexican Americans and non-Hispanic Whites, it does imply that a particular kind of discrimination may explain them, namely discrimination against unauthorized immigrants and their children. That is, at the end of the day, even though unauthorized migration exerts a negative legacy effect on education whose magnitude is large enough to explain almost all of the gap in attainment between third-generation Mexican Americans and Whites, this doesn't mean that there is *not* a gap, just that there probably wouldn't be nearly *as big* of a gap if it weren't for unauthorized migration. Indeed, there are a lot of unauthorized migrants in the country now and they have a sizeable number of children, the vast majority of whom are U.S.-born. And their presence in the country, given their importance for the workforce, will probably continue. The twist between our results and those of Telles and Ortiz is that ours suggest that later-generation gaps in educational attainment occur just as much, if not more, as a result of discrimination toward unauthorized migrants (and their children, perhaps, in schools) than as a consequence of discrimination against Mexican Americans per se (including discrimination against the third-and-later generations).

REFERENCES

Alba, R., Abdel-Hady, D., Islam, T., & Marotz, K. (2011). Downward assimilation and Mexican Americans: An examination of intergenerational advance and stagnation in educational attainment. In R. Alba & M. C. Waters (Eds.), *The next generation: Immigrant youth in a comparative perspective* (95–109). New York: New York University Press.

Alba, R., & Islam, T. (2009). The case of the disappearing Mexican Americans: An ethnic-identity mystery. *Population Research Policy Review, 28,* 109–121.

Bachmeier, J., & Bean, F. D. (2011). Ethnoracial patterns of schooling and work among adolescents: Implications for Mexican immigrant incorporation. *Social Science Research, 40,* 1579–1595.

Bean, F. D., Brown, S. K., & Bachmeier, J. D. (2010). Comparative integration contexts and Mexican immigrant-group incorporation in the United States. In A. Chebel d'Appollonia & S. Reich (Eds.), *Managing ethnic diversity after 9/11: Integration, security, and civil liberties in transatlantic perspective* (pp. 253–275). New Brunswick, NJ: Rutgers University Press.

Bean, F. D., Brown, S. K., & Bachmeier, J. D. (2012). Luxury, necessity and anachronistic workers: Does the United States need unskilled immigrant labor? In J. Skrentny & D. Fitzgerald (Eds.), *American Behavioral Scientist* (pp. 1008–1028).

Bean, F. D., Chapa, J., Berg, R. R., & Sowards, K. A. (1994). Educational and sociodemographic incorporation among Hispanic immigrants to the United States. In B. Edmonston & J. S. Passel (Eds.), *Immigration and ethnicity: The integration of America's newest immigrants* (pp. 73–100). Washington, DC: The Urban Institute Press.

Bean, F. D., Leach, M. A., Brown, S. K., Bachmeier, J. D., & Hipp, J. R. (2011). The educational legacy of unauthorized migration: Comparisons across U.S. immigrant groups in how parents' status affects their offspring. *International Migration Review, 45*(2), 352–389.

Bean, F. D., & Lowell, B. L. (2007). Unauthorized migration. In M. C. Waters, R. Ueda, & H. B. Marrow (Eds.), *The new Americans: A guide to immigration since 1965* (pp. 70–82) Cambridge, MA: Harvard University Press.

Bean, F. D., & Stevens, G. (2003). *America's newcomers and the dynamics of diversity.* New York: Russell Sage Foundation.

Boyd, M. (2002). Educational attainments of immigrant offspring: Success or segmented assimilation? *International Migration Review, 36*(4), 1037–1060.

Brown, S. K. (2007). Delayed spatial assimilation: Multi-generational incorporation of the Mexican-origin population in Los Angeles. *City & Community, 6*(3), 193–209.

Brown, S. K., Bachmeier, J., & Bean, F. D. (2009). Trends in U.S. immigration: A shift toward exclusion? In J. Higley & J. Nieuwenhuysen (Eds.), *Nations of immigrants: Australia and the USA compared* (pp. 42–55). Cheltenham, UK, and Northampton, MA: Edward Elgar.

Brown, S. K., & Bean, F. D. (2006). *Assimilation models, old and new: Explaining a long-term process.* Washington, DC: Migration Policy Institute.

Calavita, K. (2010). *Inside the state: The Bracero Program, immigration, and the INS.* New Orleans, LA: Quid Pro Books.

Cardoso, L. A. (1980). *Mexican emigration to the United States, 1897–1931: Socio-economic patterns.* Tucson, AZ: University of Arizona Press.

Chávez, L. (1988). Settlers and sojourners: The case of Mexicans in the United States. *Human Organization, 47*, 95–108.

Chiswick, B. R., & DebBurman, N. (2003). *Educational attainment: Analyses by immigrant generation*. IZA Discussion Paper 731. Bonn, Germany: Institute for the Study of Labor.

Cornelius, W. (1992). From sojourners to settlers: The changing profile of Mexican immigration to the United States. In J. A. Bustamante, C. W. Reynolds, & R. A. H. Ojeda (Eds.), *U.S.-Mexico relations: Labor market interdependence* (155–195). Palo Alto, CA: Stanford University Press.

Curiel, E. M. (2004). The green card as a matrimonial strategy: Self-interest in the choice of marital partners. In E. Fussell (Ed.), *Crossing the border: Research from the Mexican Migration Project* (pp. 86–108). New York: Russell Sage Foundation.

Donato, K. M., & Massey, D. S. (1993). Effects of the Immigration Reform and Control Act on the wages of Mexican migrants. *Social Science Quarterly, 74*(3), 523–541.

Dreby, J. (2010). *Divided by borders: Mexican migrants and their children*. Berkeley, CA: University of California Press.

Duncan, B., Hotz, J., & Trejo, S. (2006). Hispanics in the U.S. labor market. In M. Tienda & F. Mitchell (Eds.), *Hispanics and the future* (pp. 228–290). Washington, DC: The National Academies Press.

Duncan, B. V., & Trejo, S. J. (2011). Intermarriage and the intergenerational transmission of ethnic identity and human capital for Mexican Americans. *Journal of Labor Economics, 29*(2), 195–227.

Farley, R., & Alba, R. (2002). The new second generation in the United States. *International Migration Review, 36*, 669–701.

Fischer, C. S., & Hout, M. (2006). *Century of difference: How America changed in the last one hundred years*. New York: Russell Sage Foundation.

Glick, J. E. (2010). Connecting complex processes: A decade of research on immigrant families. *Journal of Marriage and the Family, 72*, 498–515.

Glick, Jennifer E. and Michael J. White. (2004). Parental aspirations and post-secondary school participation among immigrant and native youth in the United States. *Social Science Research, 33*: 272–299.

Gonzales, R. G. (2011). Learning to be illegal: Undocumented youth and shifting legal contexts in the transition to adulthood. *American Sociological Review, 76*(4), 602–619.

Gonzalez, G. (2006). *Guest workers or colonized labor? Mexican labor migration to the United States*. Boulder, CO: Paradigm Publishers.

Grogger, J., & Trejo, S. J. (2002). *Falling behind or moving up? The intergenerational progress of Mexican Americans*. San Francisco, CA: Public Policy Institute of California.

Hall, M., Greenman, E., & Farkas, G. (2010). Legal status and wage disparities for Mexican immigrants. *Social Forces, 89*(2), 491–514.

Hochschild, J., & Mollenkopf, J. (2009). *Bringing outsiders in: Transatlantic perspectives on immigrant political incorporation.* Ithaca, NY: Cornell University Press.

Hondagneu-Sotelo, P. (1994). *Gendered transitions: Mexican experiences of immigration.* Berkeley: University of California Press.

Jiménez, T. R., & Fitzgerald, D. (2007). Mexican assimilation: A temporal and spatial reorientation. *Du Bois Review, 4*(2), 337–354.

Kao, G., & Tienda, M (1995). Optimism and achievement: The educational performance of immigrant youth. *Social Science Quarterly, 76*, 1–19.

Keller, U., & Tillman, K. H. (2007). Post-secondary educational attainment of immigrant and native youth. *Social Forces, 87*(1), 121–152.

King, M., Ruggles, S. J., Alexander, T., Flood, S., Genadek, K., Schroeder, M. B., Trampe, B., & Vick, R. (2010). *Integrated Public Use Microdata Series, Current Population Survey: Version 3.0.* Minneapolis: University of Minnesota Press.

Massey, D. S. (1987). Do undocumented migrants earn lower wages than legal immigrants? New evidence from Mexico. *International Migration Review, 2*, 236–274.

Massey, D., Durand, J., & Malone, N. (2002). *Beyond smoke and mirrors: Mexican migration in an era of economic integration.* New York: Russell Sage Foundation.

McKeever, M., & Klineberg, S. L. (1999). Generational differences in attitudes and socioeconomic status among Hispanics in Houston. *Sociological Inquiry, 69*(1), 33–50.

Menjívar, C. (2006). Liminal legality: Salvadoran and Guatemalan immigrants' lives in the United States. *American Journal of Sociology, 111*(4), 999–1037.

Mittelbach, F. G., & Moore, J. W. (1968). Ethnic endogamy: The case of Mexican Americans. *American Journal of Sociology, 74*(1), 50–62.

National Research Council. (2011). *Budgeting for immigration enforcement: A path to better performance.* Committee on Estimating Costs of Immigration Enforcement in the Department of Justice. Washington, D.C: The National Academies Press.

Passel, J. (2011). Demography of immigrant youth: Past, present, and future. *Immigrant Children, 21*(1), 19–42.

Passel, J., & Cohn, D. (2011). *Unauthorized immigrant population: National and state trends, 2010.* Washington, DC: Pew Hispanic Center.

Portes, A., & Bach, R. L. (1985). *Latin journey: Cuban and Mexican immigrants in the United States.* Berkeley, CA: University of California Press.

Portes, A., & Rumbaut, R. G. (2001). *Legacies: The story of the immigrant second generation.* Berkeley, CA: University of California Press.

Ramakrishnan, S. K. (2004). Second-generation immigrants? The "2.5 generation" in the United States. *Social Science Quarterly, 85*(2), 380–399.

Reed, D., Hill, L. E., Jepsen, C., & Johnson, H. P. (2005). *Educational progress across immigrant generations in California.* San Francisco, CA: Public Policy Institute of California.

Roberts, B. R. (1995). Socially expected durations and the economic adjustment of immigrants. In A. Portes (Ed.), *The economic sociology of immigration* (pp. 42–86). New York: Russell Sage Foundation.

Roberts, B. R., Frank, R., & Lozano-Ascencio, F. (1999). Transnational Migrant Communities and Mexican Migration to the United States. *Ethnic and Racial Studies, 22*(2), 238–266.

Rosenfeld, M. J. (2002). Measures of assimilation in the marriage market: Mexican Americans, 1970-1990. *Journal of Marriage and the Family, 64*(1), 152–162.

Smith, J. P. (2003). Assimilation across the Latino generations. *The American Economic Review, 93*, 315–319.

Smith, J. P. (2006). Immigrants and their schooling. *Journal of Labor Economics, 24*, 203–233.

Smith, J. P., & Edmonston, B. (1997). *The new Americans: Economic, demographic, and fiscal effects of immigration.* Washington, DC: National Academy Press.

Spener, D. (2009). *Clandestine crossings: Migrants and coyotes on the Texas-Mexico border.* Ithaca, NY: Cornell University Press.

Telles, E., & Ortiz, V. (2008). *Generations of exclusion: Mexican Americans, assimilation, and race.* New York: Russell Sage Foundation.

Van Hook, J., & Bean, F. D. (2009). Explaining Mexican-immigrant welfare behaviors: The importance of employment-related cultural repertoires. *American Sociological Review, 74*(3), 423–444.

Wojtkiewicz, R. A., & Donato, K. M. (1995). Hispanic educational attainment: The effects of family background and nativity. *Social Forces, 74*(2), 559–574.

Yoshikawa, H. (2011). *Immigrants raising citizens: Undocumented parents and their young children.* New York: Russell Sage Foundation.

Zolberg, A. R. (2006). *A nation by design: Immigration policy in the fashioning of America.* New York: Russell Sage Foundation.

Zsembik, B. A., & Llanes, D. (1996). Generational differences in educational attainment among Mexican Americans. *Social Science Quarterly, 77*(2), 363–374.

CHAPTER 4

Math Performance of Young Mexican-Origin Children in the United States: Socioeconomic Status, Immigrant Generation, and English Proficiency

Claudia Galindo

Mexican immigration is significantly impacting the diversity and size of the U.S. population. Between 2000 and 2010, the Mexican-origin population in the United States increased from 20.6 to 31.8 million, representing 63% of the Latino population and 30% of the U.S. foreign-born population (Ennis, Ríos-Vargas, & Albert, 2011; Martin & Midgley, 2006). At the same time, many Mexican-origin students are educationally disadvantaged, as pointed out in Chapters 2 and 3. Over the past 30 years, Mexican-origin students have experienced important educational gains, but continue to lag behind other racial and ethnic groups in attainment and achievement, from early childhood through college (Crosnoe, 2005; Hirschman, 2001; Reardon & Galindo, 2009).

These educational disparities are especially problematic because they are intrinsically related to social and economic inequalities and limit students' upward mobility opportunities. Studies confirm that educational attainment is a strong predictor of employment, participation in high-skill occupations, and earnings (Duncan, Hotz, & Trejo, 2006).

Several theoretical arguments are used to explain Mexican-origin students' poor educational outcomes. Cultural arguments focus on social forces and historical relations between minority and majority groups (Ogbu & Simmons, 1998; Valenzuela, 1999) or on cultural mismatches between schools and homes that affect minority students' educational outcomes (García, 2001; Saracho & Marinez-Hancock, 2007). In contrast, structural theories argue that the position of minority groups within the U.S. social hierarchy is the main determinant of their educational experiences and that schools, as agents for social reproduction and inequalities, reinforce the current power structure and the supremacy of the dominant class (Bourdieu, 1986; Lareau, 2003; Valencia, 2002). These theoretical perspectives bring useful insights for understanding the complexities faced by Mexican-origin students in schools and discuss the impact of macro-level factors, such as structure and culture, which may be related to students' educational outcomes. However, none of the theoretical perspectives alone fully explain Mexican-origin students' educational outcomes, and they may be less helpful for explaining learning patterns among young children given their developmental stage. Furthermore, these theories do not reveal policy-relevant mechanisms that may help reduce Mexican-origin students' educational disadvantages, or how family and student variables interact to inhibit or facilitate educational improvements. Thus, this chapter focuses on the interrelation of students' socioeconomic characteristics, generational status, and oral English proficiency as main explanatory variables of academic achievement of Mexican-origin students in the United States. Given the rapid growth of the Mexican-origin population in the United States, their educational disadvantages, and the increasing importance of educational attainment for upward mobility, it is critical to understand the achievement experiences of these students to make improvements. This chapter provides insights into Mexican-origin students' academic learning experiences in the U.S. by analyzing math achievement from Kindergarten through 5th grade and comparing them to non-Hispanic White (hereafter "White") and non-Hispanic Black (hereafter "Black") students. I pay particular attention to variation in achievement patterns between Mexican-origin subgroups, by generational status (i.e., first-generation children are born in Mexico to Mexican-born parents, second-generation children are U.S.-born to Mexican-born parents, and third-plus generation children are U.S.-born children to U.S.-born parents with Mexican origins), their socioeconomic status, and their oral English proficiency at the start of Kindergarten. I also examine statistical interactions of these factors and their associations with Mexican-origin children's math achievement at the beginning of Kindergarten.

The data I use for this analysis come from the Early Childhood Longitudinal Study-Kindergarten Cohort (ECLS-K; NCES, 2003). This large-scale study focuses on young children's development at the beginning of Kindergarten—a crucial period for children's later well-being

(Entwisle, Alexander, & Olson, 2005; Rouse, Brooks-Gunn, & McLanahan, 2005). Because of the longitudinal nature of the data, I am able to look at achievement trajectories from Kindergarten through 5th grade rather than scores at one point in time, which improves previous research using cross-sectional data. Also, the ECLS-K sample includes a sizeable group of Latino and Mexican-origin children, and extensive information on students' language and socioeconomic characteristics.

Using the ECLS-K data, several studies have shown that Mexican-origin students performed significantly lower in math and reading at the beginning of Kindergarten, in 1st grade, and in 3rd grade than did their White and other Latino peers (Crosnoe, 2006; Glick & Hohmann-Marriott, 2007; Reardon & Galindo, 2009). Although achievement gaps narrowed significantly during the elementary grades, in 5th grade, Mexican-origin students were still scoring significantly lower than White students on math and reading tests (Reardon & Galindo, 2009). In addition, Mexican-origin students demonstrated lower academic performance than Latino students from others countries/regions of origin, including South American and Cuban students.

FACTORS TO CONSIDER

Research on different educational outcomes highlights the educational disadvantages that many Mexican-origin children experience in the United States. These educational disadvantages are observed for Mexican-origin students in terms of attainment and achievement measures, and they are associated with a series of demographic and family factors.

Immigrant Generational Status

The relationship between educational outcomes and immigrant generational status (i.e., the length of time in the United States) is controversial because research has provided little consensus about whether immigrant children actually demonstrate better performance than similar native-born students or whether earlier generations perform better than later generations. Supporting the findings that immigrants have better educational outcomes than native students, the notion of immigrant paradoxes gains strong and consistent support in the literature (Fuller et al., 2009; García Coll & Marks, 2009). While family background and socioeconomic status have typically been considered the most important explanations for poor outcomes, it is surprising that individuals with adverse economic characteristics (as with most Latino immigrants) experience stronger educational outcomes than others in the same socioeconomic strata. Some research with high school students, for example, shows that immigrants (first- and second-generation students) demonstrate higher academic test scores than their third-generation-plus peers (Glick & White, 2003; Kao & Tienda, 1995).

However, other findings point to troubling outcomes among immigrant students, particularly among Mexican-origin children. Duncan et al. (2006), for example, found that Mexican-born students in the United States have fewer years of formal education than U.S.-born Mexican Americans. Also, Reardon and Galindo (2009) found that first- and second-generation Mexican-origin children showed weaker reading and mathematical understanding than did subsequent generations in the elementary grades. Thus, mixed findings regarding the school performance of Mexican children of different immigrant generations are reflected in a variety of approaches represented in the literature on immigrant educational outcomes. In addition, researchers have yet to determine how the differences in achievement outcomes across generations are related to socioeconomic status or English proficiency. More information is needed about specific mechanisms related to Mexican-origin students' educational disadvantages in order to understand how to improve their achievement.

Socioeconomic Status, English Proficiency, and Educational Outcomes

The impact of family socioeconomic characteristics on students' educational outcomes is pervasive in the literature. Research consistently shows that children of formally educated parents tend to obtain higher grades and reach higher levels of education themselves, and are less likely to be retained or drop out of school, compared to children whose parents have less formal schooling (Entwisle & Alexander, 1993; García, 2001; Schmid, 2001). Students from families with more economic, social, and cultural resources tend to obtain more academic knowledge and skills at home. These parents are more likely than others to provide educational materials, assistance, and time for their children's educational needs (Pong, Hao, & Gardner, 2005; Wojtkiewicz & Donato, 1995). All of these benefits and opportunities transmit messages to children about their parents' positive attitudes toward and support for education, which translates into better educational outcomes for students.

In addition, formally educated parents tend to develop more egalitarian relationships with their children's teachers and school administrators. Because schools are more likely to value the cultural patterns, preferences, attitudes, and behaviors of formally educated individuals (Dumais, 2002; Roscigno & Ainsworth-Darnell, 1999), these parents and their children may feel more comfortable at school than children of less formally educated parents because the schools' linguistic structure, authoritative patterns, and curricula correspond more closely to those features at home (Lareau, 2003). Also, parents with higher levels of formal education handle school decisions about their children's placement in special programs, teacher assignments, and retention more proactively than do working-class or poor parents (Lareau, 2003). It is through these interventions that highly educated parents monitor their children's educational experiences and make sure that their children's educational choices and assignments have positive consequences for their future.

Similarly, the impact of students' English proficiency on their school achievement is recognized in the literature. In U.S. schools, many English Language Learners (ELLs) lag behind native English-speaking students in their academic achievement. Compared with English-speaking students, ELLs tend to have lower math and reading test scores, academic grades, and educational and occupational aspirations (Galindo, 2010; Rumberger & Larson, 1998). According to the National Assessment of Educational Progress (NAEP), in 2005, 46% and 73% of 4th-grade ELLs scored "below Basic" in math and reading, compared to 11% and 25% of White students (Fry, 2007). Moreover, in 2002, 8th-grade ELLs students scored 1.2 standard deviations lower than English-proficient students (Callahan, 2005). In addition, in 2000, only 19% of ELL students met state norms for reading in English (Kindler, 2002). Further research shows that among second-generation students, those with higher levels of English proficiency have higher math and reading test scores, and that English Language Learners and Limited English Proficiency (LEP) students have significantly lower scores than native English-speaking students in several content areas and at different grade levels (Gándara et al., 2003). A lack of English proficiency is also associated with a greater likelihood of dropping out of school, particularly for Latino students (Schmid, 2001).

Students without sufficient English proficiency face important challenges in schools. These students not only need to master a new language but must simultaneously acquire the expected academic skills for each grade level (García, 2001). When teachers use English as the only language of instruction, students need at least the minimum of oral English proficiency to understand instruction, conduct meaningful learning interactions, and use inquiry processes that further learning (Gándara, 1999). Additionally, students who are English Language Learners often do not have access to important resources needed to excel in school. They tend to have less qualified teachers (Gándara et al., 2003; Padrón, Waxman, & Rivera, 2002), and be more likely to attend segregated schools with high concentrations of other students who are not proficient in English. Their ELL status also results in higher rates of placement in special education or remedial classes (Callahan, 2005). These conditions interfere with ELL students' learning opportunities and limit their interactions with English-proficient students and other high-achieving peers, which could limit language and academic development further.

Moreover, students who are English Language Learners often experience additional barriers given their levels of poverty and generational status. Capps et al. (2005) indicated that most ELL students have foreign-born parents (83% in elementary and 71% in secondary), two-thirds of ELL children live in low-income families, and 48% have parents without high school diplomas. Mexican-origin students, in particular, are more likely than others to have each of these characteristics that negatively affect success in school. Although these factors may not be disadvantages per se, they could have negative consequences for their academic progress, because they make it considerably more difficult for students and parents to communicate effectively with teachers in order to take advantage of school learning opportunities.

Poverty and English proficiency may be particularly important to understand Mexican-origin students' academic achievement patterns. Many Mexican-origin students have low-skilled labor migrant parents with lower levels of formal education, and they are overrepresented among students with English difficulties in bilingual and Limited English Proficiency programs (Crosnoe, 2006). Among Latino subgroups, Mexican Americans have the highest poverty rates (32%) (Lichter, Qian, & Crowley, 2005). For those older than 16 years, $20,238 is the median annual personal earnings (Pew Research Center, 2009). Although the poverty rates are clearly greater for children under 18 years of age, approximately 32% of Mexican Americans live below the poverty threshold (U.S. Census Bureau, 2003). Also, almost two-thirds of Mexican-origin elementary and secondary students speak a language other than English at home, and about one-fifth have difficulty speaking English (KewalRamani et al., 2007). This double disadvantage has not been deeply analyzed in relation to academic performance. We know little about how socioeconomic status and English proficiency coexist and interact to impact the academic achievement of Mexican-origin students.

ANALYZING THE DATA

As mentioned, the data I analyzed in this chapter come from the ECLS-K study, sponsored by the National Center for Education Statistics (NCES). The ECLS-K provides a nationally representative sample of approximately 21,000 Kindergarteners who were followed through 8th grade. For more details of the ECLS-K study, the user's manual is available online (NCES, 2003). Descriptive results presented here are based on a sample of approximately 14,600 students (the unweighted sample sizes were rounded to the nearest 10 to avoid concerns of participant identification, as specified in the restricted license requirements.) This sample includes Latino students of any race and Black and White students born to a U.S.-born parent. I excluded students who were Asian, other race, or of unknown race from this analysis.

I analyzed students' math learning trajectories and achievement gaps between Kindergarten and 5th grade, using math assessments of students with at least one wave of data and valid test scores re-scaled after the spring of 5th grade. To analyze the effect of socioeconomic status and English proficiency on math test scores at Kindergarten entry, I used a restricted sample with only Mexican-origin students ($n = 1,550$) who had math test scores in the fall of Kindergarten. To measure math achievement, I used the ECLS-K math assessments, which were based on national and state standards to ensure that the skills measured tended to be taught in the associated grades. Trained data collectors individually administered these untimed, adaptive tests. Details of the assessments are provided in ECLS-K psychometric reports (Rock & Pollack, 2002). Language-minority students who were not proficient in oral English took the math test in Spanish; therefore, we had accurate math trends for most Mexican-origin students who were classified as language-minority (or living in non-English-speaking homes). By 3rd grade, all language-minority students were deemed as proficient in oral English. Consequently, all students took the 3rd- and 5th-grade math tests in English.

I characterized the diversity of the Mexican-origin population by disaggregating children by their generational status, socioeconomic status, and oral English proficiency.

- *Generational status.* Mexican-origin children were classified as first-, second-, or third-plus generations. First-generation Mexican students were non-U.S. born to non-U.S.-born parents. Second-generation students (the reference category) were U.S.-born to non-U.S.-born parents. Third-plus-generation students were U.S.-born with U.S.-born parents.

- *Socioeconomic status (SES).* I used the ECLS-K continuous measure of socioeconomic status, which is a composite measure of parent income, parent education, and occupational prestige. I sorted Latino children into the overall SES quintiles to analyze disparities in math achievement.
- *Oral English proficiency.* Mexican-origin students were classified as language-minority if English was not the primary language used at home. For most students, this information was available from their school records or was gathered from teachers' reports. Students were classified as English-proficient the fall of Kindergarten if they scored 37 points or higher on the English Oral Language Development Scale test (OLDS) (scores range from 0 to 60). If the language-minority student scored less than 37 points, s/he was classified as not proficient in oral English.

REPORTING RESULTS

Mexican Students' Socioeconomic and Language Characteristics

As Table 4.1 shows, Mexican-origin students in Kindergarten experienced important socioeconomic and language disadvantages. As expected, the economic characteristics of Mexican-origin students were significantly lower than those of White students. However, while stronger educational disadvantages were observed for Mexican-origin students, larger income gaps were observed for Black students. Among students from different regional/national origins, Mexican-origin students had parents with the lowest levels of education. Around one-third of Mexican-origin parents had not finished high school, and only about 9% had a college degree or higher. Also, Mexican-origin students (somewhat similar to Central-American-origin students) had the lowest mean family income ($30,000) and the most students living in poverty (41.5%). In contrast, Cuban- and South-American-origin students' parents had the highest levels of educational attainment, similar to the parents of White students, and they had the highest family mean incomes.

The majority of Mexican-origin children (58%) were classified by schools as language minorities, as is often the case for Latino students of any country/region of origin, which is not surprising given the large amount of Latino students with foreign-born parents (see Table 4.1). Compared to Mexican-origin students, Central-American-, Cuban-, and

Table 4.1. Latino and Mexican Students' Socioeconomic and Language Characteristics (n = 14,600 students; including n = 4,010 Latinos and n = 1,720 Mexicans)

Race/ National Origin	SES Indicators			Parents' Education		Language Characteristics		Language Spoken at Home			
	Com-posite measure	Mean income ($)	Below poverty level (%)	< than HS (%)	Col-lege + (%)	Lan-guage Minor-ity	Non-proficient in Oral English	English Only Home	Pre-domi-nantly English	Pre-domi-nantly Span-ish	Only Span-ish
White, native	0.183	62,797	9.2	3.6	38.6						
Black, native	-0.428	28,001	43.0	13.3	12.1						
Latino, any race	-0.430	34,057	35.1	26.5	12.7	50.2	29.6	31.8	19.4	19.3	29.5
Mexican	-0.580	30,210	41.5	34.3	8.6	58.7	42.3	23.8	16.2	20.0	40.1
Puerto Rican	-0.282	43,534	27.5	13.9	17.8	32.2	7.0	39.6	27.2	18.3	14.9
Cuban	0.145	56,038	20.8	8.3	41.4	67.9	22.2	18.8	31.8	23.5	25.9
South American	0.020	45,535	19.5	5.8	33.3	68.4	22.7	21.1	15.9	23.3	39.7
Central American	-0.457	33,349	38.8	33.5	18.6	75.8	43.2	17.3	24.4	30.7	27.6

Table 4.1. Latino and Mexican Students' Socioeconomic and Language Characteristics (n = 14,600 students; including n = 4,010 Latinos and n = 1,720 Mexicans) (continued)

Race/ National Origin	SES Indicators			Parents' Education		Language Characteristics		Language Spoken at Home			
	Composite measure	Mean income ($)	Below poverty level (%)	< than HS (%)	College + (%)	Language Minority	Non-proficient in Oral English	English Only Home	Predominantly English	Predominantly Spanish	Only Spanish
Other Latino	-0.139	44,523	16.9	14.2	23.6	24.4	3.2	51.6	24.2	13.0	11.2
Mexican Origin											
1st generation	-0.874	17,476	68.8	47.2	3.0	91.2	78.2	6.8	2.3	15.8	75.2
2nd generation	-0.732	24,940	47.7	42.3	6.4	76.9	56.1	8.3	13.0	25.6	53.1
3rd+ generation	-0.179	44,243	21.1	13.7	14.7	13.7	3.4	57.6	26.8	10.6	4.9

Note: Sample includes Latino students of any race and Black and White students born to a U.S.-born parent. All statistics were weighted by cross-sectional spring of Kindergarten weight c2cw0. Latino students were disaggregated by national/regional origin. From the total sample analyzed in this table, about 4,010 (27%) were Latino, 8,680 (59%) were White, and 1,920 (14%) were Black students. Mexican students were disaggregated by generational status. From the total sample analyzed in this table, about 170 (10%) were first-generation, 990 (58%) second-generation, 520 (30%) third-plus-generation, and 30 (2%) were generation unidentified.

South-American-origin students were more likely to be language minorities (76%, 68%, and 68%, respectively), whereas Puerto Rican students were the least likely (only 32%). Also, Mexican-origin students were the most likely to live in Spanish-dominant homes (40%) and, along with those with Central American origins, to not demonstrate oral English proficiency (about 42%). In contrast, only 15% of Puerto Rican students lived in homes that only spoke Spanish. And only 22% of students from Cuban and South American origins, and 7% of Puerto Ricans, were not deemed orally proficient in English.

Mexican-origin students' immigration status had a significant association with socioeconomic and language characteristics. There were important differences in these attributes by generational status, with fewer socioeconomic and language disadvantages observed for the third-plus generation. Socioeconomic status and English proficiency improved across generations. First- and second-generation Mexican-origin students were three times more likely to have parents with less than high school education as compared to third-plus-generation Mexican American students. Also, particularly low mean family income was observed for first- and second-generation Mexican-origin students ($17,500 and $25,000, respectively), whereas third-plus Mexican American students had the highest family mean incomes ($44,243). On average, third-plus Mexican-origin students had a higher family mean income than did Black students.

Furthermore, the percentage of students classified as language minorities decreased largely by generational status. Almost all first-generation Mexican-origin students were language minorities, compared to less than 14% of third-plus-generation Mexican-origin students. Similarly, a lower proportion of English-proficient students were observed among first-generation Mexican students (about 22%) than among third-plus-generation Mexican students (97%). Thus, the economic and language differences observed between Mexicans and other Latinos and across generations may have important consequences for these students' academic learning.

Achievement Gap Trends from Kindergarten to 5th Grade

Achievement "gaps" I report measure the difference in mean math scores between each group of interest and White students (the reference group), in standard deviation units. An important advantage of using standardized scores is that they allow for interpretation and comparability with other research (Reardon & Galindo, 2009). One standard deviation typically represents the achievement gap between children from low-income and middle-income families, which is a very important difference in magnitude. Figures 4.1 to 4.4 present the main findings of the gap analyses, and the Appendix to this chapter includes detailed tables of the estimated achievement gaps and their standard errors by each wave of data collection. Achievement gaps were estimated for six waves of assessment: fall Kindergarten (FK), spring Kindergarten (SK), fall 1st grade (FF), spring 1st grade (SF), spring 3rd grade (ST), and spring 5th grade (SF). The reference group is represented by the value of "0" on the "Y" axes in figures.

Achievement gaps by immigrant generational status. As Figure 4.1 illustrates, there were significant gaps between White and Mexican-origin students across generations, but smaller gaps were observed for third-plus-generation students. At the beginning of Kindergarten, first- and second-generation Mexican-origin students scored about one standard deviation below White students, whereas third-plus-generation students scored only half a standard deviation below the same reference group. By the spring of 5th grade, although the achievement gap was reduced significantly (by approximately half) for all the groups, differences in math achievement persisted.

Achievement gaps by socioeconomic status (SES). I present two sets of math achievement gaps by SES. The first includes gaps between the average Mexican-origin student in a given socioeconomic quintile and the average White student across SES (see Figure 4.2). The second set reports within-SES gaps, showing the average difference in math performance between Mexican-origin and White students within the same socioeconomic quintile (see Figure 4.3).

Figure 4.2 describes achievement gaps significantly larger for Mexican-origin students in the lowest SES quintiles than for Mexican-origin students in the highest SES quintiles. Mexican-origin students in the highest two quintiles showed relatively similar achievement levels at Kindergarten entry and over time compared to the average White student (across SES). However, most Mexican-origin students were in the lowest socioeconomic quintiles, so the academic advantages observed among the students in the highest socioeconomic quintile were experienced only by a small number of students. Math achievement gaps decreased by half between Kindergarten through 5th grade for students in the lowest SES quintiles.

Within-SES gap analysis in Figure 4.3 shows that math achievement gaps between White and Mexican-origin students are found over and above SES differences. As expected, within-SES gaps are smaller than those observed in Figure 4.2. Mexican-origin students at the start of Kindergarten scored roughly one- to two-thirds of a standard deviation lower in math than White students of the same SES quintile. On average, even within similar levels of SES, Mexican-origin students had lower math performances than did White students. Within-SES gaps decreased steadily from Kindergarten through 5th grade, specifically for Mexican-origin students in the lowest two SES quintiles. But within SES gaps for Mexican American students in the highest three SES quintiles showed smaller reduction or fluctuations over time. By the spring of 5th grade, in the lowest SES quintile, Mexican-origin and White

Figure 4.1. Trends in Estimated Math Achievement Gaps, by Generational Status

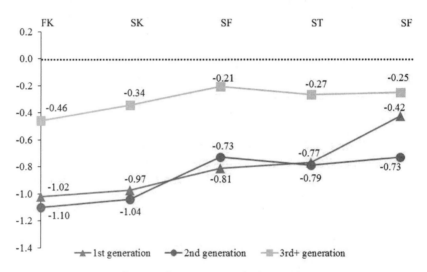

of Cases by Group and Time Point

	FK	SK	SF	ST	SF
1st generation	90	90	100	100	100
2nd generation	750	800	780	780	770
3rd-plus generation	330	360	350	340	330

Note: White students are the reference group, represented by the value of "0" on the "Y" axis. Gaps are measured in pooled standard deviation units. FK=Fall Kindergarten, SK=Spring Kindergarten; SF = Spring 1st grade; ST = Spring 3rd grade; and SF = Spring 5th grade. Unweighted sample sizes were rounded to the nearest 10 because of restricted license requirements.

students' average scores are no different from each other. Yet, although within-SES gaps are smaller by the spring of 5th grade, Mexican-origin students in the highest three SES quintiles still scored significantly lower than White students in the same quintile.

Achievement gaps by English proficiency. Figure 4.4 illustrates that native-English-speaking Mexican-origin students scored higher than language-minority Mexican-origin students. Also, Mexican-origin

Figure 4.2. Trends in Estimated Math Achievement Gaps, by SES

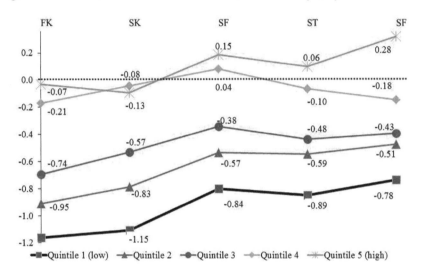

————Quintile 1 (low) ——▲—Quintile 2 ——●—Quintile 3 ——◆—Quintile 4 ——✳—Quintile 5 (high)

of Cases by Group and Time Point

	FK	SK	SF	ST	SF
Quintile 1	590	630	630	610	620
Quintile 2	240	260	260	250	250
Quintile 3	150	160	150	160	150
Quintile 4	130	140	130	130	130
Quintile 5	70	80	80	80	70

Note: White students are the reference group, represented by the value of "0" on the "Y" axis. Gaps are measured in pooled standard deviation units. FK = Fall Kindergarten, SK = Spring Kindergarten; SF = Spring 1st grade; ST = Spring 3rd grade; and SF = Spring 5th grade. Unweighted sample sizes were rounded to the nearest 10 because of restricted license requirements.

students who began Kindergarten proficient in oral English had better math scores than those who were not proficient. Compared to White students, math achievement gaps were significantly larger for non-English-proficient Mexican-origin students, whereas native-English-speaking and language-minority students who were English-proficient showed math achievement gaps significantly smaller at the start of Kindergarten. Math achievement gaps decreased steadily over time for all groups, but they still persisted. Native-English-speaking Mexican-origin students scored about one-third of a standard deviation lower than White students, but those students who were not proficient in English scored four-fifths of a standard deviation lower than the same reference group by the spring of 5th grade.

Interactions among SES, Generational Status, and English Proficiency

Based on their descriptive analysis of Latino subgroups' achievement gaps, Reardon and Galindo (2009) argued that socioeconomic status and language spoken at home may be key variables to explain Latino students' educational disadvantages. To further analyze this claim and to focus on Mexican-origin children, I present four statistical models with math scores in the fall of Kindergarten as the dependent variable (see Table 4.2). The first model only includes generational status as a predictor variable (3rd+ generation is the reference group). This is expanded in Model 2 to include the socioeconomic composite measure. Then I include language-minority status and oral English proficiency score (OLDS) in Model 3. Finally, Model 4 includes two interaction terms: student SES and language-minority status, and student SES and OLDS scores. The interaction-effect model tests whether the association between English proficiency and math achievement varied as a function of students' SES. Table 4.2 reports findings for the models, each of which controlled for assessment dates.

Corroborating my previous findings of math achievement gap analysis, I found important differences in math achievement at the start of Kindergarten across generation groups, with better outcomes observed for the third-plus generation. On average, first- and second-generation Mexican-origin students scored about 3.5 points lower than third-plus-generation Mexican-origin students in the fall of Kindergarten. Also, Model 2 revealed that socioeconomic status had a very strong effect on math achievement, over and above immigrant generation status. A unit increase on the socioeconomic status composite measure was associated with a 2-point increase in math achievement at the start of Kindergarten.

Figure 4.3. Within-Quintile Trends in Estimated Math Achievement Gaps, by SES

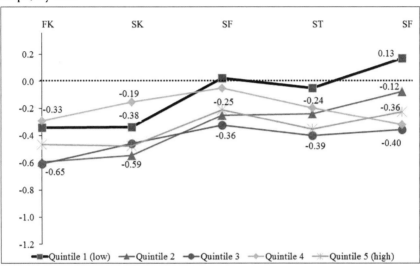

Note: White students are the reference group, represented by the value of "0" on the "Y" axis. Gaps are measured in pooled standard deviation units. FK = Fall Kindergarten, SK = Spring Kindergarten; SF = Spring 1st grade; ST = Spring 3rd grade; and SF = Spring 5th grade. Unweighted sample sizes were rounded to the nearest 10 because of restricted license requirements. The numbers of Mexican-origin students across waves are the same as in Figure 4.2.

In addition, after including the socioeconomic measure, the original difference between third-plus-generation and first- and second-generation Mexican-origin students decreased by 50% and 60%, respectively. These results suggested that a significant part of the association of math achievement with generational status was due to the association of socioeconomic status with students' math achievement.

Next, in Model 3, I added language-minority status and students' OLDS scores (English proficiency measure). As shown, both variables were highly important. On average, Mexican-origin students with higher English ability and socioeconomic status began Kindergarten with better math skills than Mexican-origin students who did not possess these family and personal resources. When both variables—socioeconomic status and language characteristics—were included in the model, initial differences in math scores at Kindergarten entry across generations became meaningless. Both had strong and independent effects on students' academic outcomes. These variables also had interactive effects on achievement. The association between oral English

Figure 4.4. Trends in Estimated Math Achievement Gaps, by Language Status and Oral English Proficiency

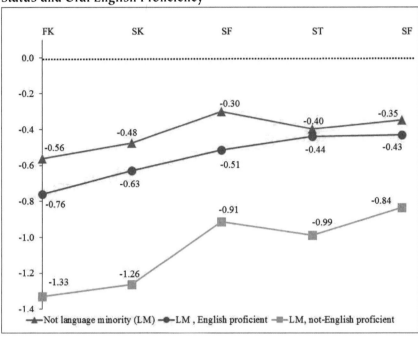

of Cases by Group and Time Point

	FK	SK	SF	ST	SF
Not language minority	470	510	500	500	490
LM, English proficient	210	210	210	200	200
LM, not English proficient	500	550	540	536	540

Note: White students are the reference group, represented by the value of "0" on the "Y" axis. Gaps are measured in pooled standard deviation units. FK = Fall Kindergarten, SK = Spring Kindergarten; SF = Spring 1st grade; ST = Spring 3rd grade; and SF = Spring 5th grade. Unweighted sample sizes were rounded to the nearest 10 because of restricted license requirements.

proficiency and math achievement varied as a function of students' socioeconomic status, which means that the relationship between English proficiency and math achievement got stronger at higher socioeconomic levels (Model 4).

Table 4.2. OLS Regression Estimates of Effects of Socioeconomic Status and Language Characteristics on Math Scores at Kindergarten Entry (n = 1,550)

Variables	Model 1	Model 2	Model 3	Model 4
1st generation	-3.869***	-1.545***	-0.112	.0434
	(0.531)	(0.528)	(0.578)	(0.575)
2nd generation	-3.464***	-1.730***	-0.723+	-.632+
	(0.318)	(0.325)	(.373)	(0.372)
3rd + generation (reference)	-	-	-	-
Socioeconomic status (SES)		2.023***	1.684***	1.309***
		(0. 146)	(0.154)	(0.357)
Language-minority status			-1.668***	-1.731***
			(0.347)	(0.358)
OLDS score (continuous)			0.8176***	1.249***
			(0.187)	(0.203)
SES*Language minority				1.558***
				(0.302)
SES*OLDS				0.409*
				(0.204)
Adjusted R-squared	0.08	0.18	0.20	0.22

Note: Generational status regression coefficients represent gaps in math scores compared to reference group (third+ generation), not absolute scores. Continuous variables, socioeconomic status, and OLDS scores were grand-mean centered. Regression models were adjusted for date of assessment. Standard errors are shown in parentheses. P-values: $+ p \leq .10$, $* p \leq .05$, $** p \leq .01$, $*** p \leq .001$.

SUMMARY OF FINDINGS

This chapter builds on previous knowledge about racial/ethnic educational inequalities by analyzing Mexican-origin students' math performance from Kindergarten to 5th grade, specifically in relation to their socioeconomic status and English proficiency. Below I discuss four main findings from this research.

First, compared to other Latino subgroups, Mexican-origin students experienced important economic and language disadvantages.

On average, Mexican-origin students experienced the worst economic characteristics and showed the highest percentages of non-English proficiency (comparable to Central-American-origin students). These disadvantages were more pronounced for Mexican-origin students with foreign-born parents than for those with U.S.-born parents.

Second, there were important differences in math achievement among Mexican-origin subgroups, based on generational status, socioeconomic status, and language characteristics, which usually are masked in studies that treat Mexican Americans as a homogenous group. Those with Mexican-born parents, those from the lowest socioeconomic groups, and those with limited oral English proficiency showed greater disadvantages in math achievement. In contrast, Mexican-origin students with U.S.-born parents, those from the highest socioeconomic groups, and those who were English-proficient showed smaller differences and more similarity to White students' math achievement over time.

Third, math achievement gaps decreased over time, yet important gaps remained at the end of 5th grade. For instance, first-generation and English-proficient language-minority students with Mexican origins scored half a standard deviation lower than White students in math by spring of 5th grade, whereas the achievement gaps observed at the start of Kindergarten were between four-fifths and one standard deviation. Even still, within-SES gap analysis showed that Mexican American students from middle- and higher-SES families continued to perform substantially lower than their White peers (in the same SES group), suggesting that economic resources do not generate similar educational or academic returns to Mexican American students as they do for White students. It is important to further our understanding of the sources (e.g., teacher, characteristics, school policy, family dynamics) of disadvantages of Mexican-origin students with economic resources, as this group is likely to increase in size over time.

Finally, students' oral English proficiency and family socioeconomic status were very important variables to understanding Mexican-origin students' math achievement, at least at the start of Kindergarten. On average, Mexican-origin students with stronger English proficiency and those from higher-SES homes demonstrated better math performance than Mexican-origin students who did not possess these family and personal resources. The effect of each of these variables was observed even after controlling for the other, confirming the independent importance of the variables on students' achievement. These findings have important practice and policy implications because they can inform interventions to counter Mexican-origin students' educational disadvantages in early school settings.

CONCLUSIONS

Even though policies for reducing poverty might decrease Mexican-origin students' educational disadvantages, macro-level interventions require a long-term strategy and do not necessarily have an immediate impact on students. School-based reforms to improve students' English proficiency in the early grades, on the other hand, may help increase Mexican-origin students' achievement trajectories and diminish the devastating socioeconomic effect on students' learning. These interventions are even more important if we take into account that Mexican immigrant families are overrepresented in low-quality schools, as demonstrated by Crosnoe (2005).

It is important to note that the findings presented here do not have implications or relevance for discussion of language policies or specific language programs (i.e., bilingual education, English-only programs, or ESL). Language programs for non-English speakers have been a main topic of concern among policymakers, researchers, and the general public. Proponents of bilingual education argue that these programs increase the acquisition of relevant abilities for students' future, decrease the learning gap between majority and minority students, and reinforce cultural and linguistic diversity (Cummins, 2000; Krashen, 1999). In contrast, proponents of English-only programs argue that the previous programs have negative impacts on students' lives by restricting learning opportunities, increasing their likelihood of dropping out of school (Murr, 1998), and decreasing their wage potential in the labor market (Porter, 1999).

Regardless of discussions on language policies, implementing concrete measures to increase English proficiency of Mexican-origin students in the early school years may be an important mechanism to reduce their educational disadvantages in math achievement in Kindergarten. Additionally, schools may focus on other mechanisms that could neutralize the association between poverty and Mexican-origin students' educational outcomes. Active parental involvement and family and school partnerships could be one of these mechanisms (Galindo & Sheldon, 2012). Epstein (2001) argues that the home and school are two very important contexts of influence on children's development, and that the degrees to which educators and family members maintain positive relationships with one another help determine children's academic success. When we consider the positive social development of young Latinos nurtured by robust parenting practices within Mexican-origin families (Crosnoe, 2006; Galindo & Fuller, 2010), the potential benefits of parental involvement initiatives are even greater. Thus, Mexican-origin children could benefit from their families' support if schools were able to provide guidance to parents about specific mechanisms that could help improve learning opportunities.

As the number of Mexican-origin individuals in the United States continues to increase, their well-being and social mobility opportunities are central issues of concern. Without any doubt, Mexico is one of the most important sending countries of immigrants (Martin & Midgley, 2006), with a self-reinforcing process of immigration that most likely will continue, given the consolidated economic and historical relationship between the United States and Mexico (Massey, 1999). From a policy perspective, it is essential that research continue to identify key mechanisms that may contribute to the improvement of educational outcomes of the Mexican population in the United States. At the same time, it is important to better understand school quality and the main educational challenges in Mexico, especially in sending communities, to suggest policy interventions to improve the educational experience on the other side of the border. By improving the educational experiences of Mexican-origin children in both countries, we will likely see spillover benefits on both sides of the border.

REFERENCES

Bourdieu, P. (1986). Forms of capital. In J. G. Richardson (Ed.), *Handbook of theory and research for the sociology of education* (pp. 241–258). New York: Greenwood Publishing Group.

Callahan, R. (2005). Tracking and high school English learners: Limiting opportunities to learn. *American Educational Research Journal, 42*(2), 305–328.

Capps, R., Fix, M., Murray, J., Ost, J., Passel, J. S., & Herwantoro, S. (2005). *The new demography of American's schools: Immigration and the No Child Left Behind Act.* Washington, DC: The Urban Institute.

Crosnoe, R. (2005). Double disadvantage or signs of resilience? The elementary school contexts of children from Mexican immigrant families. *American Educational Research Journal, 42*, 269–303.

Crosnoe, R. (2006). *Mexican roots, American schools: Helping Mexican immigrant children succeed.* Palo Alto, CA: Stanford University Press.

Cummins, J. (2000). *Language, power, and pedagogy. Bilingual children in the crossfire.* Clevedon, England: Multilingual Matters.

Dumais, S. (2002). The two meanings of social capital: The role of habitus. *Sociology of Education, 75*, 44–68.

Duncan, B., Hotz, J., & Trejo, S. (2006). Hispanics in the U.S. labor market. In M. Tienda & F. Mitchell (Eds.), *Hispanics and the future* (pp. 228–290). Washington, DC: The National Academies Press.

Ennis, S. R., Ríos-Vargas, M., & Albert, N. G. (2011). *The Hispanic population: Census briefs.* Washington, DC: U.S. Census Bureau. Retrieved from http://www.census.gov/prod/cen2010/briefs/c2010br-04.pdf

Entwisle, D. R., & Alexander, K. L. (1993). Entry into school: The beginning school transition and educational stratification in the United States. *Annual Review of Sociology, 19*, 401–423.

Entwisle, D. R., Alexander, K.L., & Olson, L.S. (2005). First grade and educational attainment by age 22: A new story. *American Journal of Sociology, 110*, 1458–1502.

Epstein, J. L. (2001). *School and family partnerships: Preparing educators and improving schools.* Boulder, CO: Westview Press.

Fry, R. (2004). *Latino youth finishing college: The role of selective pathways.* Washington, DC: Pew Hispanic Center.

Fry, R. (2007). Are immigrant youth faring better in U.S. schools? *International Migration Review, 41*(3), 579–601.

Fuller, B., Bein, E., Bridges, M., Halfon, N., Jang, H., Kuo, A., & Rabe-Hesketh, S. (2009). The health and cognitive growth of Latino toddlers: At risk or immigrant paradox? *Maternal and Child Health Journal, 13*(6), 755–768.

Galindo, C. (2010). Language minority students' math and reading achievement in early childhood. In E. E. Garcia & E. Frede (Eds.), *Young English-language learners: Current research and emerging directions for practice and policy* (pp. 42–59). New York: Teachers College Press.

Galindo, C., & Fuller, B. (2010). The social competence of Latino kindergartners and growth in mathematical understanding. *Developmental Psychology, 46*(3), 579–592.

Galindo, C., & Sheldon, S. (2012). School and home connections and children's Kindergarten achievement gains: The mediating role of family involvement. *Early Childhood Research Quarterly, 27*(1), 90–103.

Gándara, P. (1999). Telling stories of success: Cultural capital and the educational mobility of Chicano students. *Latino Studies Journal, 10*, 38–54.

Gándara, P., Rumberger, R., Maxwell-Jolly, J., & Callahan, R. (2003). English learners in California schools: Unequal resources, unequal outcomes. *Education Policy Analysis Archives, 11*(36), 1–54.

García, E. (2001). *Hispanic education in the United States: Raices y alas.* New York: Rowman and Littlefield.

García Coll, C., & Marks, A. (2009). *Immigrant stories: Ethnicity and academics in middle childhood.* New York: Oxford University Press.

Glick, J. E., & Hohmann-Marriott, B. (2007). Academic performance of young children in immigrant families: The significance of race, ethnicity, and national origins. *International Migration Review, 41*(2), 371–402.

Glick, J. E., & White, M. J. (2003). The academic trajectories of immigrant youths: Analysis within and across cohorts. *Demography, 40*, 759–783.

Hirschman, C. (2001). The educational enrollment of immigrant youth: A test of the segmented-assimilation hypothesis. *Population Association of America, Demography, 38*, 317–336.

Kao, G., & Tienda, M (1995). Optimism and achievement: The educational performance of immigrant youth. *Social Science Quarterly, 76*, 1–19.

Kewal Ramani, A., Gilbertson, L., Fox, M. A., & Provasnik, S. (2007). *Status and trends in the education of racial and ethnic minorities.* Washington, DC: National Center for Education Statistics, U.S. Department of Education.

Kindler, A. (2002). *Survey of the states' limited English proficient students and available educational programs and services: 2000-2001 Summary Report* (No. C ED-00-CO-0113). Washington, DC: National Clearinghouse for English Language Acquisition and Language Instruction Educational Programs.

Krashen, S. (1999). *Condemned without a trial: Bogus arguments against bilingual education.* Portsmouth, NH: Heinemann.

Lareau, A. (2003). *Unequal childhoods: Class, race, and family life.* Berkeley, CA: University of California Press.

Lichter, D. T., Qian, Z., & Crowley, M. (2005). Child poverty among racial minorities and immigrants: Explaining trends and differentials. *Social Science Quarterly, 86*, 1037–1059.

Lowell, L., & Suro, R. (2002). *The improving educational profile of Latino immigrants.* Washington, DC: Pew Hispanic Center.

Martin, P., & Midgley, E. (2006). Immigration: Shaping and reshaping America. *Population Bulletin, 58*(3), 3–42.

Massey, D. (1999). Why does immigration occur? A theoretical synthesis. In C. Hirschman, P. Kasinitz, & J. DeWind (Eds.), *The handbook of international migration: The American experience* (pp. 34–52). New York: Russell Sage Foundation.

Murr, A. (1998). English spoken here—or else. *Newsweek, 131*(17), 65.

National Center for Education Statistics (NCES). (2003). *User's manual for the ECLS-K third grade restricted-use data file and electronic codebook (NCES 2003-003).* Washington, DC: U.S. Department of Education, Office of Educational Research and Improvement.

Ogbu, J. U., & Simmons, H. D. (1998). Voluntary and involuntary minorities: A cultural-ecological theory of school performance with some implications for education. *Anthropology and Education Quarterly, 29*(2), 155–188.

Padrón, Y., Waxman, H., & Rivera, H. (2002). *Educating Hispanic students: Obstacles and avenues to improve academic achievement* (CREDE Report No. 8). Santa Cruz: Center for Research on Education, Diversity & Excellence.

Pew Research Center. (2009). *Hispanics of Mexican origin in the United States, 2007.* Washington, DC: Pew Hispanic Center.

Pong, S.-L., Hao, L., & Gardner, E. (2005). The roles of parenting styles and social capital in the school performance of immigrant Asian and Hispanic adolescents. *Social Science Quarterly, 86*(4), 928–950.

Porter, R. P. (1999). Educating English language learners in U.S. schools: Agenda for a new millennium. In J. E. Alatis & A. Tan (Eds.), *Georgetown University roundtable on language and linguistics: Language in our time* (pp. 128–138). Washington, DC: Georgetown University Press.

Portes, A., & Rumbaut, R. G. (2001). *Legacies: The story of the immigrant second generation.* Berkeley, CA: University of California Press.

Reardon, S. F., & Galindo, C. (2009). The Hispanic-White achievement gap in math and reading in the elementary grades. *American Educational Research Journal, 46,* 853–891.

Rock, D., & Pollack, J. (2002). *Early Childhood Longitudinal Study-Kindergarten class 1998-99 (ECLS-K): Psychometric report for Kindergarten through third grade.* Washington, DC: U.S. Department of Education.

Roscigno, V., & Ainsworth-Darnell, J. (1999). Race, cultural capital and educational resources: Persistent inequalities and achievement returns. *Sociology of Education, 72,* 158–178.

Rouse, C. E., Brooks-Gunn, J., & McLanahan, S. (2005). Introducing the issue in school readiness: Closing racial and ethnic gaps. *The Future of Children, 15,* 5–14.

Rumberger, R., & Larson, K. (1998). Toward explaining differences in educational achievement among Mexican American language-minority students. *Sociology of Education, 71*(1), 68–92.

Saracho, O. N., & Marinez-Hancock, F. (2007). The culture of Mexican-Americans: Its importance for early childhood educators. *Multicultural Perspectives, 9*(2), 43–50.

Schmid, C.L. (2001). Educational achievement, language-minority students, and the new second generation. *Sociology of Education, 74,* 71–87.

Valencia, R. (2002). Current realities of the Chicano schooling experiences. In R. Valencia (Ed.), *Chicano school failure and success: Past, present and future* (pp. 1–2). New York: Routledge.

Valenzuela, A. (1999). *Subtractive schooling: U.S.-Mexican youth and the politics of caring.* Albany, NY: SUNY Press.

Wojtkiewicz, R. A., & Donato, K. M. (1995). Hispanic educational attainment: The effects of family background and nativity. *Social Forces, 74*(2), 559–574.

Appendix: Estimated Standardized Gaps: ECLS-K Standardized Math Achievement Gaps, by Mexican Subgroup and Wave

	Fall K	Spring K	Fall 1st	Spring 1st	Spring 3rd	Spring 5th
Black, native	-.725	-.778	-.735	-.804	-.866	-.881
	(.040)	(.044)	(.078)	(.054)	(.045)	(.052)
Generational Status						
First generation	-1.022	-.974	-1.248	-.810	-.769	-.422
	(.081)	(.089)	(.182)	(.124)	(.150)	(.219)
Second generation	-1.101	-1.039	-.927	-.729	-.786	-.726
	(.044)	(.047)	(.084)	(.049)	(.044)	(.051)
Third-plus-generation	-.460	-.343	-.190	-.206	-.266	-.248
	(.059)	(.061)	(.127)	(.052)	(.060)	(.081)
Socioeconomic Status						
Quintile 1 (low)	-1.203	-1.147	-1.096	-.842	-.890	-.777
	(.040)	(.044)	(.080)	(.050)	(.050)	(.069)
Quintile 2	-.951	-.826	-.664	-.573	-.587	-.514
	(.075)	(.081)	(.170)	(.073)	(.079)	(.090)
Quintile 3	-.737	-.570	-.424	-.381	-.475	-.431
	(.085)	(.091)	(.169)	(.088)	(.093)	(.113)
Quintile 4	-.211	-.082	-.020	.040	-.103	-.184
	(.096)	(.091)	(.139)	(.088)	(.118)	(.122)
Quintile 5 (high)	-.073	-.132	-.026	.148	.061	.282
	(.148)	(.122)	(.205)	(.124)	(.124)	(.151)

Appendix: Estimated Standardized Gaps: ECLS-K Standardized Math Achievement Gaps, by Mexican Subgroup and Wave (continued)

	Fall K	Spring K	Fall 1st	Spring 1st	Spring 3rd	Spring 5th
Within socioeconomic status						
Mexican/ Quintile 1 (low)	-.380	-.378	-.160	-.018	-.089	.128
	(.070)	(.077)	(.127)	(.103)	(.082)	(.132)
Mexican/ Quintile 2	-.634	-.586	-.349	-.292	-.278	-.116
	(.094)	(.091)	(.180)	(.084)	(.086)	(.105)
Mexican/ Quintile 3	-.649	-.498	-.361	-.363	-.438	-.397
	(.090)	(.095)	(.187)	(.095)	(.100)	(.124)
Mexican/ Quintile 4	-.330	-.193	-.125	-.089	-.235	-.361
	(.102)	(.098)	(.146)	(.096)	(.127)	(.137)
Mexican/ Quintile 5 (high)	-.506	-.515	-.544	-.249	-.391	-.265
	(.156)	(.125)	(.201)	(.120)	(.125)	(.156)
Language-minority, English proficiency						
Not language- minority (LM)	-.562	-.476	-.192	-.298	-.396	-.346
	(.058)	(.053)	(.102)	(.048)	(.058)	(.068)
LM, English- proficient	-.759	-.630	-.789	-.513	-.438	-.431
	(.071)	(.084)	(.165)	(.097)	(.085)	(.103)
LM, not English- proficient	-1.33	-1.262	-1.180	-.913	-.989	-.835
	(.045)	(.054)	(.089)	(.058)	(.055)	(.077)

Note: Gaps were based on standardized Item Response Theory rescaled in 5th grade. Reference group=native White students. Survey design corrected standard errors are in parentheses. Standard errors were significantly bigger for fall of 1st-grade estimates given the reduced sample size.

Part II

MEXICAN ORIGINS

For too long school trajectories for Mexican American children have been analyzed and interpreted without considering the educational opportunities and experiences of their parents and relatives in Mexican communities of origin. For many children, this means understanding what schools are like in rural Mexican communities. In this part, the authors provide recent analyses of school quality in different Mexican settings. Both chapters grapple with the rapid expansion of school enrollments for rural and poor Mexican children, on the one hand, while coming to terms with unequal resources and inadequate school quality, on the other. They make the case that schooling of Mexican American children cannot be fully understood without coming to terms with the basic though pervasive infrastructural problems faced by thousands of teachers and students in Mexican schools. In Chapter 5, Ernesto Treviño discusses the quality of learning opportunities for indigenous students in Mexico, identifying some of the sources of deep social inequity. And in Chapter 6 María Guadalupe Pérez Martínez, Guadalupe Ruiz Cuéllar, and Benilde García Cabrero contrast the rapid growth of preschool access in Mexico with the unequal distribution of resources between communities.

Learning Inequality Among Indigenous Students in Mexico

Ernesto Treviño

Educational inequality is one of the main global challenges, and poor education quality particularly affects the world's most marginalized societal groups. Strong evidence of this phenomenon can be observed in Mexico, the country with the second-highest level of economic inequality in the Organisation for Economic Co-operation and Development (OECD).

Mexico's indigenous people are found at the tail end of the population in practically all aspects related to socioeconomic well-being. They have a greater probability of living in poverty and being geographically isolated compared to their non-indigenous counterparts. With regard to education, children of indigenous families attend school for fewer years and have lower levels of academic achievement compared to the rest of the Mexican population.

When indigenous families migrate across the Mexican-U.S. border, the children of these families are classified as either Mexican or Latino. However, in Mexican schools they were regarded as indigenous. Once in the United States, these children need specific educational supports to overcome the overwhelming cultural transitions and educational disadvantages they face. It is only with knowledge of the children's indigenous background that U.S. educational policies, schools, and teachers can provide the necessary culturally appropriate support. With this chapter my goal is to provide information about indigenous schooling in Mexico that could be useful to U.S. educators.

First, I want to point out that in my research I use the term *indigenous* as defined by the Mexican Census, which considers a person to be indigenous if he or she speaks a language of indigenous origin as his or her mother language. While this definition employs an objective characteristic, it excludes those who define themselves as belonging to an indigenous group but do not speak the native language.

In order to provide context for the study discussed in this chapter, I briefly describe the organization of primary education in Mexico, a complex nation of 32 states. Although the states have sovereignty over some aspects of primary education, the federal government retains the authority to prescribe a mandatory national curriculum and to determine the different types of schools that can be established. In addition, the federal government funds significant portions of the state educational budgets.

Mexican primary education served approximately 15 million children during the 2011–2012 school year, according to figures from the *Instituto Nacional para la Evaluación de la Educación*. The primary education system includes three types of schools:

- Regular schools: Spanish-only public and private schools that are located either in urban (more than 2,500 inhabitants) or rural (less than 2,500 inhabitants) communities. Urban schools serve 73% of the total primary enrollment, and rural schools serve 21%.
- Community courses: Aimed at reaching geographically dispersed populations, these courses are highly structured and taught by high school graduates who serve as community educators. Due to the small number of students in these communities, the classes often comprise children in different grade levels. Only 1% of the students enrolled in primary education attend community courses.
- Indigenous schools: Schools focused on serving one of the almost 60 different ethnic groups living in Mexico. These schools are located in places with high concentrations of indigenous peoples, typically rural communities. The mission of these schools is to provide bilingual and culturally relevant education to indigenous children in order to promote both indigenous and mainstream cultures and languages. The enrollment in indigenous schools is 6% of the total enrollment in Mexico.

Traditionally it has been suggested that indigenous education—bilingual and culturally appropriate—is the best school alternative for indigenous children (Hernandez-Zavala, Patrinos, Sakellariou, & Shapiro, 2006). I examine this proposition throughout this chapter and place my findings in a broader context by discussing other research findings on indigenous education.

This chapter looks at the learning outcomes of indigenous children, comparing results between those attending indigenous schools and Spanish-only regular public schools. I take into account students' socioeconomic characteristics and community characteristics, and examine whether the indigenous school model provides the opportunities indigenous children and their families expect in order to improve social mobility. I explore what happens in schools labeled "indigenous" in an effort to identify shortcomings and suggest improvements. At no point do I necessarily suggest that rural public schools are better for indigenous children than "indigenous" schools. Rather, I compare indigenous pupil performance across school types to find out ways to improve models to enhance learning opportunities and performance of this underserved population.

I organized the chapter into the following five sections. The first section describes the social and educational context for indigenous students in Mexico. The second presents an analysis of indigenous student academic performance in primary school. The third section interprets these findings, and the fourth offers some conclusions and recommendations. In the final section I draw policy implications.

SOCIAL AND EDUCATIONAL CONTEXT OF INDIGENOUS STUDENTS

The population speaking indigenous languages in Mexico[1] comprises 6.7% of the country's total population (Instituto Nacional de Estadística y Geografía, 2010). After Peru, Mexico has the largest indigenous population in Latin America (Hirmas, Hevia, Treviño, & Marambio, 2005). Indigenous groups in Mexico are diverse. Official national data list 62 different languages spoken among Mexican indigenous groups (INEGI, 2010). About 85% of the indigenous population is bilingual (speaking both their indigenous language and Spanish); the remaining 15% are monolingual in their language, as shown in Table 5.1.

Mexico's indigenous groups are the most marginalized segment of the population. Approximately 35% of the indigenous population is classified as "highly marginalized," whereas only 2% of the non-indigenous population falls into this category (Borja-Vega, Lunde, & García Moreno, 2007). The inequalities between Mexico's indigenous and non-indigenous groups are evident when comparing the numbers living in poverty and extreme poverty. National data show that the indigenous population is four times as likely to live in extreme poverty as the non-indigenous population (see Table 5.2).

Indigenous populations in Mexico also suffer from segregation and geographic isolation. Table 5.3 shows that two out of three indigenous people live in communities of less than 2,500 inhabitants, while only one out of four non-indigenous people inhabit these areas. This isolation is associated with limited access to different household services, such as drinking water, electricity, telephone, and Internet.

The marginalization of indigenous groups in Mexico is reproduced in the schools. Compared to other student subgroups in Mexico, school enrollment is the lowest among indigenous students. As shown in Table 5.4, in 2010 11% of Mexican indigenous children age 6–14 did not attend school, compared to 6% of the total population of the same age. However, a point of progress is that school enrollment among indigenous girls has improved in recent years. In 2000, indigenous girls had a 4% lower enrollment than indigenous boys, compared to 1% in 2010.

Spanish literacy rates among indigenous groups are low compared to the general Mexican population. The estimated national literacy rate is 92%, compared to 72% for the indigenous population (see Table 5.5). This difference, however, is steadily declining. Nonetheless, indigenous and non-indigenous women alike continue to demonstrate lower overall literacy levels than men. This gender disparity is larger among indigenous populations.

ACHIEVEMENT OF INDIGENOUS STUDENTS IN PRIMARY SCHOOL

The distribution of learning results for 6th-grade primary students in Mexico reflects a series of inequalities: urban private schools achieve the highest scores, followed by urban public, then rural public, and at the bottom are indigenous schools with the poorest results on the Excale test. As shown in Table 5.6, the gap for Spanish literacy (or language arts) results between urban and indigenous schools is abysmal— an entire standard deviation difference. Students attending indigenous schools perform worse than those in all other school settings, including, though to a lesser degree, rural public schools.

There is a 15-point difference (one-fifth of a standard deviation) in Spanish literacy performance between indigenous children in each type of school, where those attending rural public schools perform higher, on average, than those attending indigenous schools. It might be easier to think of these achievement differences in terms of proficiency levels. As shown in Table 5.7, 44% of indigenous children in rural schools perform at the "below basic" level, compared to nearly 50% of indigenous students attending indigenous schools. Moreover, 48.7% of indigenous students in rural schools achieve at the "basic" level, compared to 45% in indigenous schools. Finally, only 7% of indigenous students in rural schools and 5% in indigenous schools achieve expected levels or higher.

Thus, broad inequalities in learning opportunities exist for Mexican students across school types. Those attending indigenous schools tend to fare the worst. It is important to note that the achievement gap between indigenous students attending rural versus indigenous schools is relatively small compared to the overall inequalities between, for example, indigenous and urban private schools. However, comparing learning outcomes of indigenous students in rural and indigenous schools allows us to analyze the impact of different school models designed for Mexico's most disadvantaged student groups, and to test the hypothesis that these differences result from discrepant resources available across school types.

ANALYSIS OF LEARNING OUTCOMES

In the following analysis[2] I only include students whose primary language is indigenous, and those who attended either indigenous or general rural schools in the Mexican states of Chiapas, Hidalgo, Oaxaca, Puebla, San Luis Potosí, and Yucatán. In selecting the schools, I used the following criteria:

- schools were located in rural areas;
- students within schools had similar socioeconomic status; and
- schools were located in the states with the highest proportion of indigenous populations.

The states were selected because they account for the greatest number of indigenous students in rural schools participating in the Excale national exam, conducted by the *Instituto Nacional para la Evaluación de la Educación*, and because they face similar challenges in delivering indigenous and bilingual education. Student sample details are found in Table 5.8.

Comparing Resources across School Types

Comparing the results of indigenous children across school types is a useful way to assess basic school policy effectiveness for the indigenous students in Mexico because 61.4% of Mexico's indigenous live in rural settings (INEGI, 2010), and families tend to send their children to one of the two types of schools. The variables used in this analysis are described in the Appendix to this chapter. Again, analyses in this chapter use the Mexican Census definition of "indigenous" (INEGI, 2000, 2005), including only those who reported their native language as indigenous. There are other ways, however, of classifying indigenous populations, such as cultural tradition or self-identification (McEwan, 2004a).

For indigenous 6th-grade students there was an overall 15-point difference in Spanish performance between rural and indigenous schools; the same gap in mathematics is 19 points (see Table 5.9). Below I explain these learning inequalities as a function of students' socioeconomic characteristics and the resource disparities between rural and indigenous schools.

Table 5.9 shows that there are inequalities in socioeconomic characteristics between indigenous students attending rural and indigenous schools. On average, indigenous students in rural schools have a higher socioeconomic status than those attending indigenous schools. The cultural capital of students is slightly higher in rural schools as well. Indigenous students in indigenous schools use their mother tongue more frequently than those in rural schools. However, there are a similar number of students who receive *Oportunidades* financial support (a conditional cash transfer program in Mexico [Reimers, da Silva, & Treviño, 2006]) in both types of school. Receipt of the *Oportunidades* grant can also be considered an estimate of student socioeconomic status.

Children attending indigenous schools, in contrast to those attending rural schools, live in smaller and more isolated localities, with a greater concentration of indigenous people living in the community. Those attending indigenous schools also live in communities where households tend to have less access to basic public services (see Table 5.10).

Both rural and indigenous schools are situated in communities with only basic resource access. However, there are important differences in human resources and materials between rural and indigenous schools, favoring rural schools and their students. Table 5.11 shows that rural schools in the sample have teachers with more formal training (preservice and in-service training), and indigenous schools have fewer classroom resources than rural schools. Indigenous schools also have a greater proportion of teachers acting as principals, which suggests that indigenous schools are more likely to be understaffed. In terms of reported teaching quality, there were no significant differences between the two school types. Overall, rural schools demonstrated more favorable conditions than indigenous schools.

Student Characteristics, School Resources, and Learning Outcomes

Next I examined whether disparate student learning outcomes across school types could be explained (statistically speaking) by student characteristics or by the school resources mentioned. To do so, I conducted two types of analyses. In the first I identified indigenous students with similar socioeconomic characteristics across rural and indigenous schools in order to compare mean differences in academic performance. This way we can understand how school types contribute differently to the performance of students with the same socioeconomic status (SES). Second, I conduct a regression analysis using "propensity score matching" (a statistical method to estimate "unbiased" effects of treatment variables) to compare students who were statistically similar in observed characteristics. This way I test the hypothesis that differences in student achievement between indigenous students in rural and indigenous schools can be explained by school resource discrepancies.

Once indigenous student samples across school types were matched by family SES, descriptive analyses showed there were no significant differences in family characteristics or the communities in which they live (see Table 5.12). Importantly, however, matching did not eliminate the performance gap. Indigenous students attending rural schools continued to achieve higher scores in Spanish language arts and mathematics than their peers in indigenous schools (see Table 5.12). Thus, it can be assumed with some confidence that the indigenous achievement gaps across schools are not due to family SES of students. We can assert that indigenous students in rural schools perform better academically than those attending indigenous schools.

An analysis of the school resources suggests that rural schools have an important advantage in terms of classroom resources, as shown in Table 5.13. In terms of resources for indigenous students within the same SES strata, however, rural and indigenous schools are quite similar.

The above analyses suggest that differences in learning outcomes between indigenous students in rural and indigenous schools are not explained by disparities in family SES. It is plausible that learning inequalities can be explained, at least in part, by school resource disparities, which slightly favor rural schools. I examine this hypothesis in the analyses that follow, using a multiple regression approach to determine relationships between the Spanish test scores of indigenous students and school resources over and above family SES. The socioeconomic strata were estimated using propensity score matching.

Overall, regression analyses indicate that some measured processes within the school were associated with indigenous student achievement. "Teacher quality" was a particularly important variable. Taken together, however, school resources were not able to explain the achievement gap for students between school types. The first of the regression models, shown in Table 5.14, shows once again that there is an average performance difference of 15 points between 6th-grade students in rural and indigenous schools. Socioeconomic strata variables were able to explain only a small part of performance differences—less than 3%, as shown in Model 2. Teacher quality as a school resource carried the greatest weight in explaining achievement differences, with a coefficient of 18 points, observed in Model 3. The same model also shows that greater classroom resources and the participation of teachers in professional development (i.e., *Carrera Magisterial*) were positively associated with higher achievement scores. Also, a teacher serving as the principal had a negative effect on academic performance, suggesting that these schools are very small and/or lack sufficient personnel.

Some school resource variables interacted with one another to influence student performance as well. Teacher quality interacted with indigenous schools, meaning that having "poor teacher quality" in indigenous settings had a greater effect on performance than it did in rural public schools. Finally, these regression models also indicated that state-level differences in indigenous student achievement were significant over and above the effects of school and family resources analyzed. Indigenous students from Chiapas and the Yucatan had significantly lower scores than their counterparts in Oaxaca (which serves as the "reference category" in the reported regression models).

In summary, even when we compare Mexican indigenous students whose families possess the same socioeconomic resources, who attend schools with comparable resources, and who live in similar communities, those who attend rural schools have, on average, a 17-point (roughly one-fifth of a standard deviation) academic achievement advantage over students attending rural indigenous schools. In other words, school resource differences were not able to explain performance gaps between indigenous students attending different school types. In part, this could be because of the limited overall variation in resources available to indigenous students regardless of school type.

More classroom resources, schools with a designated principal, and teacher participation in professional development (*Carrera Magisterial*) are features that benefit learning outcomes for indigenous students in Mexico. School resources, however, have little impact on the variation of Spanish language arts performance. These results are consistent with other research findings showing relationships between school resources and student outcomes to be weak (Coleman et al., 1966; Figlio, 1999; Hanushek, 1995, 2003, 2005; Mosteller & Moynihan, 1972; Murnane, Willett, Bub, & McCartney, 2006). Still, it is important to consider that the schools compared in the present analysis are quite similar in terms of both student characteristics and school resources. Students attending both school types are very disadvantaged compared to other student groups in Mexico.

Of all school resources analyzed in this study, teacher quality had the highest impact on student achievement. This effect was stronger in indigenous than rural schools. Again, teacher quality refers to the basic tasks of teaching such as arriving on time, attending class, treating pupils with respect, and offering clear explanations to students (see the Appendix to this chapter). This finding suggests that one way to support student learning, particularly in indigenous schools, is to improve these basic elements of teacher quality.

Indeed, the impact of teacher quality on student performance is consistent. It should be a central policy focus to improve learning opportunities for indigenous students in Mexico. In Figure 5.1 we observe how students in indigenous schools with better-quality teachers demonstrate higher academic performance. We see how a substantial increase in teaching quality, as measured in the current study, could close the performance gap between indigenous students across rural and indigenous schools. (In Figure 5.1 the gap is closed at the point where the two lines intersect.)

CONCLUSIONS AND RECOMMENDATIONS

Results in this chapter suggest that Mexican indigenous students who attend rural schools perform better than those who attend indigenous schools. And they show that this performance gap is not explained by student socioeconomic disparities or differences in school resources. "Teaching quality," however, was found to be associated with the academic performance of indigenous students. Thus, enhancing teacher quality appears to offer the greatest potential for improving indigenous student performance. These findings are consistent with other research

Figure 5.1. Estimated Spanish Language Arts Performance for
Indigenous Students Across Teacher Quality Scores, by School Type

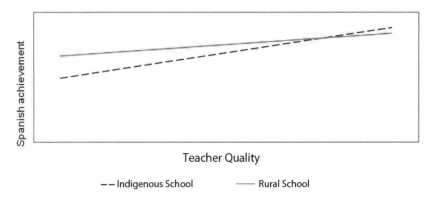

evaluating compensatory programs, which shows that students in indigenous schools demonstrate poorer performance than those in regular public schools (Paqueo & López-Acevedo, 2003; Shapiro & Moreno Trevino, 2004).

The literature conclusively shows that indigenous students in Mexico demonstrate the poorest academic performance among the student population, and that these differences are principally related to the socioeconomic inequalities between indigenous and non-indigenous families. However, these studies are limited to performance comparisons between indigenous and non-indigenous students (Cueto & Secada, 2004; García Aracil & Winkler, 2004; Hernandez-Zavala et al., 2006; Kudo, 2004; McEwan, 2004a, 2004b; Wu, 2000). They do not address performance differences among indigenous students or the factors within schools that may explain these differences.

In contrast, in this chapter I sought to answer a different question: How do indigenous children perform academically in rural compared to indigenous schools? My objective was to determine whether indigenous schools were in fact providing expanded educational opportunities for indigenous children. The results suggest that they are not. Indigenous children in rural schools surpass the achievement level reached by their counterparts who attend indigenous schools. In trying to find the factors that explain this achievement gap, I have shown that improving teacher quality could significantly diminish academic learning inequalities between indigenous children attending rural and indigenous schools.

Studies about school efficacy and factors associated with student performance show that teaching quality (Backhoff et al., 2006; Hanushek,

2005; Wenglinsky, 2002)—particularly in indigenous contexts (Cueto & Secada, 2004)—and teacher training initiatives are important factors to improve student learning (Acevedo, 1999; Brunner & Elacqua, 2003; Fuller & Clarke, 1994; Greenwald, Hedges, & Lain, 1996; LLECE, 2001; Scheerens, 2000; Treviño & Treviño, 2004). Indeed, teacher training has a positive and significant relationship to the performance improvements of students at indigenous schools in Mexico (Treviño & Treviño, 2004). Teacher professional development is particularly important in indigenous schools because teacher preparation in these settings tends to be poor, with requirements that differ from other school types. Teachers in indigenous schools may enter the profession with only a high school diploma *(bachillerato)*, and then receive certification through distance education while they work as teachers (Schmelkes, 2004; Treviño et al., 2007). This professional training does not include coursework in teaching Spanish as a second language, which is essential for their work in multilingual school settings.

If learning inequalities between indigenous students in rural and indigenous schools are not explained by socioeconomic differences or by school resource disparities, we need to know more about the factors behind this inequality. This question is particularly relevant because it appears to be common sense that students learn more when they utilize their mother tongue. Yet this study fails to support this assertion.

One important aspect to take into consideration is that indigenous education is not synonymous with bilingual or culturally relevant education. Research in the United States has shown that bilingual programs are more effective than English-only programs when systematically offered, carefully structured, and facilitated by well-trained teachers. This finding has been replicated over and again in evaluations of bilingual education programs for Spanish speakers learning English (Center for School District Improvement, 2004; Gándara, 1997; Rolstad, Mahoney, & Glass, 2005; Slavin & Cheung, 2003), and some evidence also exists to support the idea that "culturally relevant" teaching can improve academic learning for indigenous student groups in the United States (Demmert & Towner, 2003).

In Mexico, available evidence shows that indigenous schools employ a wide variety of instructional models in bilingual classrooms (Dietz, 1999; Hamel, 2001), from lesson design to implementation. So it is probably misleading to think of indigenous education as a consistent group of actions, because in reality there are many approaches to bilingual education employed within classrooms of indigenous schools. Studies in other Latin American countries have found that indigenous schools do not implement the intended curriculum because they lack materials and trained teachers (e.g., proficient in the native tongue of the children; Cueto & Secada, 2004). One study in Mexico showed that greater implementation of the intended bilingual/intercultural curriculum in schools was actually associated with poorer student learning (Yonker & Schmelkes, 2005). This finding was attributed to the fact that indigenous schools are not truly bilingual and do not engage in culturally relevant practices. The indigenous language is used principally as a tool to teach Spanish (Schmelkes, Águila, Magaña, Rodríguez, & Ojeda, 2007). Thus, under the umbrella of indigenous education in Mexico, there are an unknown number of teaching models, including some that contradict principles of bilingualism in order to provide Spanish-only instruction to indigenous children. More systematic observational research is needed to draw stronger conclusions for improvement.

Research evidence is mixed regarding the influence of indigenous school participation on school access and persistence of indigenous students. Three studies suggest that participation in indigenous education reduces school enrollment and attainment gaps between indigenous and non-indigenous students (Bando, Lopez-Calva, & Patrinos, 2005; Parker et al., 2003, 2005), as well as the negative effects of family monolingualism (Parker et al., 2005). In contrast, more recent research shows that general primary schools have lower rates of grade retention than indigenous schools (Schmelkes et al., 2007). This apparent contradiction requires more research as well.

Again, this chapter shows that indigenous children consistently perform better in Spanish language arts when they attend rural schools rather than indigenous schools, and that school resource inequalities cannot explain this difference. This finding requires contextualization in order to draw policy conclusions, especially since there could be school resources associated positively with student performance that I failed to measure in this study. Furthermore, I compared two types of schools in Mexico that, in actuality, both tend to be underresourced. It could be that the homogeneity of resource distribution across school types precluded a statistical explanation for student performance differences.

Finally, these findings should not necessarily be interpreted as proof that bilingual or culturally responsive education is less effective than regular Spanish language coursework using universal pedagogical methods. Available research shows that bilingual programs can be quite effective when they are adequately and consistently implemented in schools. Programs must be implemented with fidelity to make these comparisons. In Mexico a wide range of pedagogical models are implemented, from Spanish-only education to additive bilingualism. So it appears—at least in practice—that the indigenous school model in Mexico is far from uniform.

In this analysis, teaching quality is the most consistent educational resource associated with improved learning outcomes for indigenous students, especially for those who attend indigenous schools. Teachers who attend their classes, arrive on time, and create an intellectually challenging learning environment contribute to higher student academic achievement. These should be minimal requirements for teachers. This finding could be an indication that many teachers of indigenous students are not meeting basic standards, which in turn contributes to student underperformance. On the other hand, teachers in rural schools have higher teacher pre-service training requirements, as well as greater opportunities for in-service training, compared to teachers in indigenous schools. The poor preparation of teachers in indigenous schools and the failure of some to meet basic standards suggest that these teachers may be far from understanding and implementing culturally relevant teaching practices. In summary, teaching capacities in both rural and indigenous schools are very low, but they seem to be lower in indigenous schools.

Finally, I have shown that indigenous children attending schools where the principal is also a teacher demonstrate lower academic achievement. These schools face serious challenges because of their institutional fragility. It is likely that many of these schools are small, multigrade sites, which can be complex environments where it is difficult to teach effectively.

POLICY IMPLICATIONS

This chapter raises several school policy questions for Mexico. First, we need to seriously review whether indigenous education is fulfilling its mandate: to offer bilingual and culturally suitable education for indigenous students. Second, we must improve the quality of teachers in indigenous schools. Teachers' attendance should be enforced. Pre-service teacher training should require a university-level degree. Training initiatives should prepare teachers to use the indigenous language for instruction, and to teach Spanish as a second language. Teachers should be able to fluently speak the language of the community where they work. Research initiatives should be funded to complement and sustain these efforts.

Third, educational policy should acknowledge that more resources are needed to address the language and socioeconomic needs of children in indigenous communities. Greater resource investments are needed, particularly to improve teaching quality. The challenges facing school improvement for indigenous students in Mexico are enormous. To meet these challenges, further development, research, and evaluation work should identify the elements needed for informed policy making. These elements should address how the intended school curriculum is implemented, by examining classroom pedagogy, teacher content knowledge, instructional time in class, and attention to the range of student learning needs.

As this chapter demonstrates, indigenous children in Mexico are different from non-indigenous children, not only in their cultural, ethnic, and linguistic backgrounds, but also in the educational and socioeconomic challenges they face. The findings of this study are crucial to understand and provide educational opportunities to indigenous children who move across the Mexico-U.S. border. States, districts, schools, and teachers should understand this situation in order to design and implement effective educational and social interventions for indigenous children.

First, indigenous children carry with them a burden of social and cultural inequalities that are greater than that of non-indigenous Mexican children. This means that they may require additional social services and educational assistance. Secondly, indigenous children attending both indigenous and rural school types are afforded very low levels of academic learning opportunities. Although indigenous children in rural schools achieve slightly higher learning outcomes than those in indigenous schools, all indigenous children, on average, attain low levels of learning compared to the rest of the population. Such low achievement in both indigenous and rural schools may, in part, be due to the cultural discontinuities between the indigenous ways of learning and the ways of learning in schools. Despite the heterogeneity of indigenous cultures in Mexico, there is evidence that they have key differences with mainstream Mexican culture (Treviño, 2006). In general, indigenous cultures share a collective notion of work and performance. The work is done in groups where all members share the responsibility for results. Therefore, indigenous children may find individual evaluations of their performance counterintuitive, and they also may expect that teachers take responsibility for their students' results. Third, indigenous people learn by observation and immediate practice, and language it is not the main vehicle for teaching and learning. By contrast, Mexican schools rely principally on language to convey concepts, and opportunities for observation and immediate practice occur infrequently.

Fourth, a salient feature of indigenous cultures is that in the process of learning there is room for mistakes without social or individual sanctions or performance praise. In these cultures grades may not play a culturally relevant role. Partial evaluations of performance and grade assignment may not provide culturally relevant information for children or their families on how they are faring at school and what to do to improve.

Fifth, indigenous cultures have a holistic view of reality, very different from the analytical approaches that are taught in mainstream education systems. For example, in some cultures when children are faced with the subtraction problem, "If you have five apples and then eat one, how many apples are left?" They may respond, "I am missing one." This is because they see the set of apples as an integrated whole that is missing one of its parts. These cultural differences may produce communication problems in which teachers interpret a culturally relevant and correct answer of indigenous children as wrong, when they are using a different cultural framework and are unaware of this fact. And finally, indigenous children may not speak Spanish, or may be only partially fluent in the language. The implication is obvious. In this case, the provision of additional support in Spanish may be of very little use.

NOTES

I wish to thank Felipe Godoy Ossa, researcher at the Center for Comparative Educational Policy (*Centro de Políticas Comparadas de Educación*) in Santiago, Chile, for his assistance in the final versions of this chapter. I would also like to thank Anthony D. Tillett for his timely translation and Kate Place for her editorial assistance.

1. This research uses the definition of *indigenous* as defined by the Census, which considers a person to be indigenous if he or she speaks a language of indigenous origin as his or her mother language. While this definition employs an objective characteristic, it excludes those who define themselves as belonging to an indigenous group but do not speak the native language.

2. This section examines only the performance of indigenous children in rural and indigenous schools to improve reading levels, so that the terms "child" and "student" refer only to those who speak an indigenous language.

Table 5.1. Percentage of the Indigenous Population in Mexico That Is Bilingual and Monolingual, 1950 to 2010*

Indicator	1950	1960	1970	1990	2000	2005	2010
Indigenous % of total population (i.e., speaking an indigenous language)	11.2	10.4	7.8	7.6	7.2	6.7	6.7
Percentage of indigenous population who are bilingual	67.5	63.5	72.4	83.5	83.1	87.7	85.3
Percentage of the population who are monolingual	32.5	36.5	27.6	16.5	16.9	12.3	14.7

Sources: INEGI, Population and Housing Census (*Censos de Población y Vivienda*) from 1950 to 2010; INEGI, II Population and Housing Count, 2005.

*All figures refer to the population ages 5 years and older, and the totals do not include unidentified cases.

Table 5.2. Percentage of Population Living in Poverty by Region, 2002

Population	Extreme Poverty (%)	Poverty (%)
National	22.8	54.3
Indigenous/Native American	59.4	78.4
Non-Indigenous	15.4	44.2
Urban	14.5	50.1
Indigenous	49.4	68.1
Non-Indigenous	13.5	42.6
Rural	34.0	66.5
Indigenous	61.1	80.1
Non-Indigenous	18.7	51.8

Source: Borja-Vega et al., 2007.

Table 5.3. Percentage of Indigenous and Non-Indigenous Population by Locality Size—2000-2010*

Locality size	% of Indigenous Population			% of Non-Indigenous Population		
	2000	*2005*	*2010*	*2000*	*2005*	*2010*
Less than 2,500	61.7	62.3	61.4	25.4	23.5	20.4
2,500–14,999	19.4	19.9	20.1	13.6	13.7	13.9
15,000 or more	18.9	17.8	18.5	61.0	62.8	65.7

Sources: INEGI, Population & Housing Census, 2000 to 2010 and INEGI, II Population and Housing Count, 2005.

*All calculations based on population ages 5 years and older, and the totals exclude undefined cases.

Table 5.4. Percentage of Population Ages 6–14 Enrolled in School, 2000–2010

	2000			2005			2010		
	Total	*Boys*	*Girls*	*Total*	*Boys*	*Girls*	*Total*	*Boys*	*Girls*
Indigenous population	83.5	85.2	81.7	88.7	89.7	87.8	88.6	89.0	88.2
Total population*	93.8	93.9	93.8	96.1	96.1	96.1	94.0	93.8	94.2

Sources: INEGI, Population and Housing Census 2000 to 2010, and INEGI, II Population and Housing Count 2005.

*The population data refer to the ages 6–12 for 2000 and 2005 and 5–14 for 2010.

Table 5.5. Literacy Rates in Mexico Among Total and Indigenous Populations Ages 15 Years and Older, 2000–2010

	2000			2005			2010		
	Total	*Men*	*Women*	*Total*	*Men*	*Women*	*Total*	*Men*	*Women*
Indigenous population	66.2	76.1	56.8	68.3	76.7	60.2	72.1	79.7	64.9
Total population	90.5	92.5	88.6	91.4	93.0	90.0	92.3	93.6	91.1

Sources: INEGI, Population and Housing Census, 2000 to 2010, and INEGI, II Population and Housing Count, 2005.

Table 5.6. Excale Mean and Standard Errors (SE) for Spanish Literacy Achievement for 6th-grade Students in Mexico by School Type, 2005 & 2007

Type of primary school	Spanish literacy achievement					
	2005		2007		2005–2007 Difference*	
	Mean	*SE*	*Mean*	*SE*	*Mean*	*SE*
Urban public	512	2.1	523	3.4	**11**	4.1
Rural public	466	2.2	482	3.3	**16**	3.8
Indigenous education	417	3.1	426	3.4	**10**	4.9
Private	603	3.0	609	3.6	5	4.2
National (total)	500	1.4	516	2.3	**16**	2.7

Source: Instituto Nacional para la Evaluación de la Educación (2009).

*Statistically significant differences are in **bold**.

Table 5.7. Academic Proficiency Levels of Indigenous Students by School Type, 2005

Proficiency level	Rural School		Indigenous School	
	N	*%*	*N*	*%*
Below basic	103	44.4%	632	49.8%
Basic	113	48.7%	570	45.0%
Average	15	6.5%	61	4.8%
Advanced	1	0.4%	5	0.4%
Total	232	100%	1268	100%

Source: Ernesto Treviño's calculations from Excale data, 2005.

Table 5.8. Student and School Sample Sizes from Excale 2005 Used in Present Analyses

School Type	# of Schools	# of Indigenous Students
Indigenous	180	1,268
Rural	51	232
Total	231	1,500

Source: Ernesto Treviño's calculations from Excale data, 2005.

Table 5.9. Student Indicators in Rural and Indigenous Schools

Indicators		School Type		Total
		Rural	*Indigenous*	
Socioeconomic status	*N*	232	1,268	1,500
	Mean	0.27	-0.05	0.00
	SD	0.81	1.02	1.00
Language use	*N*	232	1,268	1,500
	Mean	-0.40	0.07	0.00
	SD	0.93	1.00	1.00
Cultural capital of family	*N*	232	1,268	1,500
	Mean	0.05	-0.01	0.00
	SD	0.80	1.03	1.00
Receives *Oportunidades** grant	*N*	229	1,251	1,480
	Mean	0.90	0.89	0.89
	SD	0.30	0.31	0.31
Spanish score	*N*	232	1,268	1,500
	Mean	423.66	408.36	410.73
	SD	75.03	70.00	70.99
Math score	*N*	232	1,268	1,500
	Mean	443.53	424.11	427.12
	SD	79.78	75.02	76.07

Source: Ernesto Treviño's calculations based on Excale 2005.

*Formerly *Progresa*, *Oportunidades* is a federal social assistance program in Mexico for low-income families. It provides cash payments to families in exchange for regular school attendance and health maintenance.

Table 5.10. Socioeconomic Characteristics of Communities Where Sample Schools are Located

Community Characteristic		Type of School		Total
		Rural	Indigenous	
Total community population	N	16	79	95
	Mean	1041.39	869.69	898.61
	SD	521.36	914.70	861.28
Proportion of houses with drinkable water	N	16	79	95
	Mean	0.54	0.38	0.41
	SD	0.40	0.37	0.38
Proportion of houses with electricity	N	16	79	95
	Mean	0.74	0.69	0.70
	SD	0.35	0.31	0.32
Proportion of houses with sewage	N	16	79	95
	Mean	0.14	0.10	0.11
	SD	0.20	0.21	0.20
Proportion of the population 5 years and older who speak an indigenous language	N	16	79	95
	Mean	.84	.91	.90
	SD	.33	.19	.22

Source: Author's calculations on the basis of XII General Census of the Population and Housing, INEGI, 2000.

Table 5.11. School Resources for Indigenous and Rural Educational Centers

Resource Indicators		Type of School		Total
		Rural	Indigenous	
Teacher quality*	N	232	1,268	1,500
	Mean	-0.03	0.01	0.00
	SD	0.91	1.02	1.00
Teacher as principal**	N	51	180	231
	Mean	0.73	0.66	0.68
	SD	0.45	0.48	0.47
Classroom resources	N	51	180	231
	Mean	0.37	-0.11	0.00
	SD	0.85	1.02	1.00
Teachers with degree (licenciatura)	N	51	180	231
	Mean	0.73	0.63	0.65
	SD	0.45	0.49	0.49
Teachers who participate in professional development (Carrera Magisterial)	N	51	180	231
	Mean	0.49	0.37	0.40
	SD	0.51	0.49	0.49

Source: Author's calculations using Excale 2005.
*The teacher quality indicator is calculated using information supplied by the students about their teachers' characteristics and actions. For this reason, the sample number is equivalent to the number of students.
**Variables corresponding to school/room/teacher were calculated using information from the 231 sample schools.

Table 5.12. Mean Socioeconomic Characteristics and T Tests between Indigenous Students in Rural and Indigenous Schools

	School Type	
Student variables	Rural *n=117*	Indigenous *n=592*
	Mean	
Socioeconomic status	0.09	0.08
Indigenous language use	-0.14	-0.10
Family cultural capital	0.03	0.01
Father education index	0.02	-0.04
Spanish score	426.55**	405.11**
Math score	451.01***	421.46***
Community variables		
Total population	1,903	1,924
Proportion of illiterate population 15 years or older	0.38	0.38
Proportion of the population that speaks indigenous language, ages 5 years or older	0.96	0.97
Proportion of houses with drinking water	0.48	0.50
Proportion of houses with electricity	0.78	0.76
Proportion of houses with drainage	0.29	0.28

**p<.01, ***p<.001

Table 5.13. Average of School Resources and T Tests for Differences between Rural and Indigenous Schools

	School Type	
School Resources	*Rural n=117*	*Indigenous n=592*
Classroom resources	0.52***	0.08***
Teacher with degree (*licenciatura*)	0.62	0.67
Teacher participate in professional development (*Carrera Magisterial*)	0.38	0.36
Teacher is principal	0.34	0.29
Teaching quality	-0.01	-0.04

***p<0.001

Table 5.14. Adjusted Regression Models with Robust Standard Errors for School Resources that Predict Learning Outcomes in Spanish for Indigenous Students Attending Either Rural or Indigenous Schools

Predictors	Model 1			Model 2			Model 3		
	Coef	*SE*	*p*	*Coef*	*SE*	*p*	*Coef*	*SE*	*p*
Indigenous school	-15.3	9.85		-19.4	10.1	~	-17.72	9.93	~
Socioeconomic stratum 2				-16.95	25.88		-9.49	25.77	
Socioeconomic stratum 3				-52.17	11.36	***	-32.5	13.68	*
Socioeconomic stratum 4				-39.3	10.78	***	-22.75	13.31	~
Socioeconomic stratum 5				-24.17	11.73	*	-9.33	14.01	
Classroom resources							5.47	3.15	~
Teacher quality							18.07	2.38	***
Teacher as principal							-11.31	6.66	~
Teacher has degree (*licenciatura*)							3.45	6.6	
Teacher participates in professional development (*Carrera Magisterial*)							12.57	6.44	~
Classroom resources * indigenous school									
Teacher quality * indigenous school									
Teachers as principal * indigenous school									
Degree (*licenciatura*)* indigenous school									
Professional development (*Carrera Magisterial*)* indigenous school									
Chiapas									
Hidalgo									
Puebla									
San Luis Potosi									
Yucatan									
Intercept	423.66	9.09	***	464.14	5.4	***	442.49	12.69	***
Squared	*0.006*			*0.027*			*0.112*		

~p<0.1, *p<0.05, **p<0.01, ***p<0.001

n=232 children in rural schools and 1,268 children in indigenous schools.

Table 5.14. Adjusted Regression Models with Robust Standard Errors for School Resources that Predict Learning Outcomes in Spanish for Indigenous Students Attending Either Rural or Indigenous Schools (continued)

Predictors	Model 4			Model 5		
	Coef	*SE*	*p*	*Coef*	*SE*	*p*
Indigenous school	-17.28	10.08	~	-17.32	9.62	~
Socioeconomic stratum 2	-14.7	24.58		-26.66	24.43	
Socioeconomic stratum 3	-38.57	13.33	**	-44.10	14.24	**
Socioeconomic stratum 4	-28.67	12.79	*	-35.00	14.08	*
Socioeconomic stratum 5	-15.48	13.5		-22.79	14.53	
Classroom resources	5.52	3.14	~	4.97	3.28	
Teacher quality	8.58	5.65		7.31	5.46	
Teacher as principal	-10.96	6.66		-12.84	6.45	*
Teacher has degree (*licenciatura*)	3.15	6.6		8.68	6.57	
Teacher participates in professional development (*Carrera Magisterial*)	12.66	6.41	*	14.14	6.27	*
Classroom resources * indigenous school						
Teacher quality * indigenous school	10.86	6.2	~	12.17	6.00	*
Teachers as principal * indigenous school						
Degree (*licenciatura*)* indigenous school						
Professional development (*Carrera Magisterial*)* indigenous school						
Chiapas				-22.82	9.47	*
Hidalgo				-7.25	10.83	
Puebla				-11.78	11.14	
San Luis Potosi				6.23	11.18	
Yucatan				-18.61	10.15	~
Intercept	448.12	11.05	***	461.55	13.79	***
Squared	*0.115*			*0.135*		

The children are grouped into 51 rural and 180 indigenous schools.

Appendix. Variables Used in the Analysis

Variable	Definition
Student variables	
Socioeconomic status	Standardized measure of household characteristics; access to services and household consumer goods (Mean = 0 & S.D. = 1)
Family cultural capital	Standardized measure of 7 variables that measure access to cultural goods and education of father (Mean = 0 & S.D. = 1)
Index of parents' education	Standard measure that summarizes the variables of education and literacy of parents (Mean = 0 & S.D. = 1)
Indigenous language use	Standardized measure that measures knowledge and indigenous language used as first language in home and school (Mean = 0 & S.D. = 1)
Spanish score	Standardized measure of performance in the Excale Spanish examination with a national average of 500 and a standard deviation of 100
Math score	Standardized measure of math performance in Excale examination with a national average of 500 and a standard deviation of 100
Community variables	
Total population	Number of inhabitants in community where school is located
Proportion of illiteracy of those 15 years plus	Proportion of illiterates of 15 years or more in the locality where the school is located
Proportion of inhabitants with indigenous mother tongue age 5 years or older	Proportion of the population age 5 years or more who speak their indigenous language in the community where the school is located
Proportion of houses with electricity	Proportion of houses with electricity in the community where the school is located
Proportion of houses with drinking water	Proportion of houses with drinking water in the community where the school is located
Proportion of houses with drainage	Proportion of houses with drainage in the community where the school is located

Appendix. Variables Used in the Analysis (continued)

Variable	Definition
School resources	
Classroom resources	Standardized measure of 13 variables that measure the availability of pedagogic resources, such as audiovisual equipment, computer programs, & equipment to use them (Mean = 0 & S.D. = 1)
Teacher quality	Standardized measure for 6 variables that measure student perceptions of teacher quality such as attendance, punctuality, and teaching (Mean = 0 & S.D. = 1)
Teachers who participate in professional ndevelopment (*Carrera Magisterial*)	Dichotomous variable with the values 1= participates and 0 = does not participate
Teachers with first degree (*licenciatura*)	Dichotomous variable with the values 1 = degree and 0 = no degree
Teacher as principal	Dichotomous variable with values 1 = principal and 0 = not principal

REFERENCES

Acevedo, G. (1999). *Learning outcomes and school cost-effectiveness in Mexico: The Pare Program*. Washington, DC: The World Bank.

Backhoff, E., Andrade, E., Sánchez, A., Peon, M., & Bouzas, A. (2006). *El aprendizaje del español y las matemáticas en la educación básica de México: Sexto de primaria y tercero de secundaria*. México, DF: Instituto Nacional para la Evaluación de la Educación.

Bando, G. R., Lopez-Calva, L. F., & Patrinos, H. A. (2005). *Child labor, school attendance, and indigenous households: Evidence from Mexico* (No. 3487). Washington, DC: The World Bank.

Borja-Vega, C., Lunde, T., & García Moreno, V. (2007). Economic development and indigenous peoples in Latin America: Mexico. In H. A. Patrinos & E. Skoufias, and T. Lunde (Eds.), *Economic opportunities for indigenous peoples in Latin America* (pp. 2–8). Washington, DC: The World Bank.

Brunner, J. J., & Elacqua, G. (2003). Factores que inciden en una educación efectiva: Evidencia internacional. In R. Hevia (Ed.), *La educación en Chile, hoy* (pp. 1–11). Santiago: Ediciones Universidad Diego Portales.

Center for School District Improvement. (2004). *English language learner (ELL) programs*. Portland, OR: Northwest Regional Education Laboratory.

Coleman, J. S., Campbell, E. Q., Hobson, C. J., McPartland, F., Mood, A. M., & Weinfeld, F. D. (1966). *Equality of educational opportunity*. Washington, DC: U.S. Government Printing Office.

Cueto, S., & Secada, W. (2004). Oportunidades de aprendizaje y rendimiento en matemática de niños y niñas Aimara, Quechua y Castellano hablantes en escuelas bilingües y monolingües en Puno, Perú. In D. R. Winkler & S. Cueto (Eds.), *Etnicidad, raza, género y educación en América Latina* (pp. 393–408). Santiago, Chile: Programa de Promoción de la Reforma Educativa en American Latina y el Caribe (PREAL).

Demmert, W. G., & Towner, J. C. (2003). *A review of the research literature on the influences of culturally based education on the academic performance of Native American students*. Portland, OR: Northwest Regional Education Laboratory.

Dietz, G. (1999). Indigenismo y educación diferencial en México: Balance de medio siglo de políticas educativas en la región purhépecha. *Revista Interamericana de Educación de Adultos, 21*(1), 35–60.

Figlio, D. N. (1999). Functional form and the estimated effects of school resources. *Economics of Education Review, 18*, 241–252.

Fuller, B., & Clarke, P. (1994). Rising school effects while ignoring culture? Local conditions and the influence of classroom tools, rules and pedagogy. *Review of Educational Research, 94*(1), 119–157.

Gándara, P. (1997). *Review of research on the instruction of limited English proficient students*. Santa Barbara, CA: University of California Linguistic Minority Research Institute.

García Aracil, A., & Winkler, D. R. (2004). Educación y etnicidad en Ecuador. In D. R. Winkler & S. Cueto (Eds.), *Etnicidad, raza, género y educación en América Latina* (pp. 55–92). Santiago, Chile: Programa de Promoción de la Reforma Educativa en American Latina y el Caribe (PREAL).

Greenwald, R., Hedges, L., & Lain, R. (1996). The effects of school resources on student achievement. *Review of Educational Research, 66*(3), 361–396.

Hamel, R. (2001). Políticas del lenguaje y educación indígena en México: Orientaciones culturales y estrategias pedagógicas en una época de globalización. In R. Bein & J. Born (Eds.), *Políticas lingüísticas: Norma e identidad* (pp. 143-170). Buenos Aires: Universidad de Buenos Aires.

Hanushek, E. A. (1995). Interpreting recent research on schooling in developing countries. *The World Bank Research Observer, 10*(2), 227–246.

Hanushek, E. A. (2003). The failure of input-based schooling policies. *The Economic Journal, 113*, F64–F98.

Hanushek, E. A. (2005). The economics of school quality. *German Economic Review, 6*(3), 269–286.

Hernandez-Zavala, M., Patrinos, H., Sakellariou, C., & Shapiro, J. (2006). *Quality of schooling and quality of schools for indigenous students in Guatemala, Mexico and Peru* (No. 3982). Washington, DC: The World Bank.

Hirmas, C., Hevia, R., Treviño, E., & Marambio, V. (2005). México. In C. Hirmas, R. Hevia, E. Treviño, & V. Marambio (Eds.), *Políticas educativas de atención a la diversidad cultural: Brasil, Chile, Colombia, México y Perú* (pp. 405–495). Santiago, Chile: UNESCO-Santiago.

Instituto Nacional de Estadísticas y Geografía (INEGI). (2000). *XII Censo General de población y vivienda, 2000*. Aguascalientes, Mexico: Author.

Instituto Nacional de Estadísticas y Geografía (INEGI). (2005). *Censo General de población y vivienda*. Aguascalientes, Mexico: Author.

Instituto Nacional de Estadísticas y Geografía (INEGI). (2010). *Censo de población y vivienda 2010*. Aguascalientes, Mexico: Author.

Jencks, C., & Meredith, P. (Eds.). (1998). *The black-white test score gap*. Washington, DC: Brookings Institution Press.

Kudo, I. (2004). La educación indígena en el Perú: Cuando la oportunidad habla una sola lengua. In D. R. Winkler & S. Cueto (Eds.), *Etnicidad, raza, género y educación en América Latina* (pp. 93-132). Santiago, Chile: Programa de Promoción de la Reforma Educativa en American Latina y el Caribe (PREAL).

Laboratorio Latinoamericano de Evalución de la Calidad de la Educación (LLECE). (2001). *Segundo Informe del Primer Estudio Internacional Comparativo sobre lenguaje, matemática y factores asociados, para alumnos del tercer y cuarto grado de educación básica*. Santiago and Bogotá: UNESCO-OREALC Ministerio de Educación Nacional de Colombia.

McEwan, P. J. (2004a). The indigenous test score gap in Bolivia & Chile. *Economic Development & Cultural Change, 53*, 157–190.

McEwan, P. J. (2004b). La brecha de puntajes obtenidos en las pruebas por los niños indígenas en Sudamérica. In D. R. Winkler & S. Cueto (Eds.), *Etnicidad, raza, género y educación en América Latina*. Santiago, Chile: PREAL.

Mosteller, F., & Moynihan, D. (1972). *On equality of educational opportunity*. New York: Random House.

Murnane, R., Willett, J., Bub, K., & McCartney, K. (2006). *Understanding trends in the black-white achievement gaps during the first years of school*. Washington, DC: Brookings-Wharton Papers on Urban Affairs.

Paqueo, V., & López-Acevedo, G. (2003). *Supply-side school improvement and the learning achievement of the poorest children in indigenous and rural schools: The case of PARE* (No. 3172). Washington, DC: The World Bank.

Parker, S., Rubalcava, L., & Teruel, G. (2003). Language barriers and schooling inequality of the indigenous in Mexico. In J. R. Behrman, A. Gaviria, & M. Székely (Eds.), *Who's in and who's out: Social exclusion in Latin America* (pp. 145–177). Washington, DC: InterAmerican Development Bank.

Parker, S., Rubalcava, L., & Teruel, G. (2005). School inequality and language barriers. *Economic Development and Cultural Change, 54*(1), 71–94.

Reimers, F., da Silva, C., & Treviño, E. (2006). *Where is the "education" in conditional cash transfers in education?* Montreal, Canada: UNESCO Institute for Statistics.

Rolstad, K., Mahoney, K., & Glass, G. V. (2005). The big picture: A meta-analysis of program effectiveness research on English language learners. *Education Policy, 19*(4), 572–594.

Scheerens, J. (2000). *Improving school effectiveness* (Vol. 68). Paris: UNESCO, Internatonal Institute for Educational Planning.

Schmelkes, S. (2004). La política de la educación intercultural bilingüe en México. In I. Hernaiz (Ed.), *Educación en la diversidad: Experiencias y desafíos en la educación intercultural bilingüe* (pp. 185–196). Buenos Aires: UNESCO, Internatonal Institute for Educational Planning.

Schmelkes, S., Águila, G., Magaña, R., Rodríguez, J., & Ojeda, V. (2007, March). Estudio cualitativo del impacto del Programa Oportunidades sobre la educación de la población indígena. Presented at the Biennial Meeting of the Congreso Nacional de Investigación Educativa, Mérida de Yucatán, México.

Shapiro, J., & Moreno Trevino, J. (2004). *Compensatory education for disadvantaged Mexican students: An impact evaluation using propensity score matching* (No. 3334). Washington, DC: The World Bank.

Slavin, R., & Cheung, A. (2003). *Effective reading programs for English language learners: A best-evidence synthesis* (CRESPAR Report No. 66). Baltimore, MD: Center for Research on the Education of Students Placed At Risk, John Hopkins University.

Treviño, E. (2006). Evaluación del aprendizaje de los estudiantes indígenas en América Latina: Desafíos de medición e interpretación en contextos de diversidad cultural y desigualdad social. *Revista Mexicana de Investigación Educativa, 11*(28), 225–268.

Treviño, E., Pedroza, H., Martínez, G., Ramírez, P., Ramos, G., & Treviño, G. (2007). *Prácticas docentes para el desarrollo de la comprensión lectora en primaria.* México, DF: Instituto Nacional para la Evaluación de la Educación

Treviño, E., & Treviño, G. (2004). *Estudio sobre las desigualdades educativas en México: La incidencia de la escuela en el desempeño académico de los alumnos y el rol de los docentes.* México, DF: Instituto Nacional para la Evaluación de la Educación

Wenglinsky, H. (2002). The link between teacher classroom practices and student academic performance. *Education Policy Analysis Archives, 10*(12). Retrived online: http://epaa.asu.edu/ojs/article/view/291

Wu, K. B. (2000). Education and poverty in Peru. In F. Reimers (Ed.), *Unequal schools, unequal chances* (pp. 376–399). Cambridge, MA: Harvard University Press.

Yonker, M., & Schmelkes, S. (2005). *Análisis de la implementación de las políticas interculturales bilingües en México.* México: Coordinación General de Educación Intercultural Bilingüe.

CHAPTER 6

Challenges to Improving Preschool Quality in Mexico

María Guadalupe Pérez Martínez,
Guadalupe Ruiz Cuéllar,
and Benilde García Cabrero

Preschool has long been recognized as a mechanism to improve educational opportunities for children throughout their lives, especially for children living in poverty. The benefits of preschool, however, are only as good as its quality, which includes structural conditions (materials, infrastructure, classroom and school organizational norms and characteristics, financial resources) and the processes (e.g., instruction, classroom assessment, student grouping, teacher supervision, professional development) conducive to student learning.

Recognizing the benefits of preschool, several countries are beginning to offer universal access to preschool programs. In Mexico, schooling for children ages 3 to 5 years was declared compulsory and universal nationwide in 2002, though the law has only been implemented for 4- and 5-year-old children. Plans are under way to extend coverage for 3-year-old Mexican children in the near future, reflecting a priority of the Mexican government to expand preschool access. Policy discussions with regard to preschool *quality*, however, have not been seriously considered.

This chapter reviews some results from a recent study of preschool quality in Mexico called *Condiciones de la Oferta Educativa en Educación Preescolar en México* (Conditions in Preschool Offerings in Mexico)—referred to hereafter as the COEP study—developed by the three of us together with the *Instituto Nacional para la Evaluación de la Educación* (Pérez Martínez et al., 2010). The purpose of this study was to understand the conditions under which preschool education is provided in Mexico and how these conditions vary across preschool types (i.e., modalities), in order to guide policy decisions targeting improvement.

The COEP study was based on the understanding that the quality of educational services entails inputs, processes, and outputs of the contexts in which schooling occurs (Pérez Martínez et al., 2010). Previous to COEP, studies have addressed preschool outputs (e.g., student achievement with respect to curricular aims) and analyzed the context of this educational service (e.g., population characteristics). The COEP study was designed as the first major effort to advance our knowledge base of some of the processes that underlie preschool quality.

It is important to mention that we see studying preschool quality as compatible with the notion of education and a civil right. Simply accessing educational systems in and of itself is not sufficient to achieve educational objectives. In the addition to access, educational services need to be *acceptable*, which means that school resources and processes should be consonant with the intended purposes of school and related needs of school-age children (Tomaševski, 2001).

In what follows we provide a rationale for the COEP study, discuss its design, share key results, and end with a series of conclusions and recommendations for preschool improvements in Mexico. Data we present were gathered in May 2008. Informants included teachers, principals, and parents (or guardians). The study sample included 1,892 schools and 4,675 teachers.

RATIONALE FOR THE COEP STUDY

The COEP study was based on two underlying considerations: (a) the importance of preschool to the learning and development of young children, and subsequent benefits throughout students' school careers and life opportunities, on the one hand; and (b) the present state of preschool in Mexico, on the other.

Importance of Preschool

A host of research studies have demonstrated over and again that children's learning and learning ability are much more intensive during the first 5 years of life. This is because infancy and early childhood constitute stages of rapid neurological development characterized by greater plasticity and synaptic conception. As a result, the first 5 years constitute a huge window of opportunity for children to develop key cognitive, linguistic, social, and emotional competencies (Bowman, Donovan, & Burns, 2001).

The first 5 years of life also constitute a period of deep dependence on adults, particularly parents. Adults are the providers of children's needs, and children's relationships with adults provide the means through which competencies can be developed. Consequently, inadequate nurturing on the part of adults can have permanent effects on children that extend throughout their lives (UNESCO, 2006).

Preschool programs, thus, are important because they intervene during a period when children have a natural disposition to learn and develop through stimulating interactions with adults and other children. Benefits of preschool participation are both educational (or academic) and social. They include greater school persistence, greater academic performance, less grade retention, lower levels of school dropout, and reduction in socioeconomic inequality (UNESCO, 2006).

Importantly, children from low-socioeconomic status (SES) families and communities benefit the most from preschool participation (Center for Mental Health in Schools, 2006; Curry, 1997; Espinosa, 2002; Yoshikawa et al., 2006). Low-SES children, from birth or earlier, often demonstrate cognitive delay, which is why early intervention initiatives are so important—both to overcome early inequalities and to prevent inequality growth. For example, the High/Scope Perry School Project, a study that explored the short- and long-term effects of preschool participation for U.S. children living in poverty, found that program participation contributed to social and cognitive gains, school success, and greater economic integration and a lower propensity toward antisocial behaviors later in life (Schweinhart et al., 2005).

For these benefits to take shape, however, preschool programs should maintain a caliber of quality, which includes both structural (e.g., provision of human, material, and organizational resources) and process (e.g., classroom quality) variables designed to address children's learning needs at various developmental stages. Based on the findings of previous international research and the aims of the INEE, it was clear that in order to have a deeper understanding of preschool quality we needed to explore the structural conditions and processes carried out inside Mexican preschools.

State of Preschool in Mexico

Given the rapid expansion of preschool programs in Mexico—and corollary pressures placed on states, schools, and practitioners—there are two reasons for investigating the quality of preschool in Mexico: (a) the national decree made in 2002 to make preschool compulsory for children ages 3 to 5 years, and (b) the curricular reform associated with preschool expansion.

Compulsory preschool means that all states within the Mexican Republic provide preschool coverage for all young children. Parents are legally obligated to send their young children to preschool as a requirement for entering elementary school (at age 6). The compulsory mandate has been enforced in stages: for 5-year-old children during the 2004–2005 school year and 4-year-old children during the 2005–2006 school year; for 3-year-olds the intention was to enforce preschool attendance during the 2008–2009 school year, but the measure was deferred and has not yet been applied.

Mandates for compulsory preschool attendance have placed immense and growing pressures on the Mexican educational system. It is important, therefore, to understand how local conditions associated with preschool quality fare in response to these pressures, particularly as the system prepares to expand access to 3-year-old children.

Moreover, preschool curricular reform, initiated in 2002, was designed to improve educational programs–and the equity across programs–for children ages 3 to 5. This reform led to the *Programa de Educacion Preescolar 2004* (Early Childhood Education Program of 2004; PEP 2004), the national preschool curriculum. Reflecting the centralized tradition of curricular development in Mexico, PEP 2004 aimed to: a) provide a high-quality preschool experience to all children through activities that develop children's emotional, social, and cognitive competencies, in ways that respond to children's developmental abilities; and b) articulate a preschool agenda that contributes to subsequent schooling by establishing clear objectives that correspond with the stated purposes of elementary school. These aims correspond to all three levels of the preschool system (for children ages 3, 4, and 5 years).

The PEP 2004 curriculum is organized in terms of six skill domains:

1. personal and social development,
2. language and communication,
3. mathematical thinking,
4. world exploration and knowledge,
5. artistic expression and appreciation, and
6. physical development and health.

These domains constitute the conceptual basis for preschool teacher training and evaluation. Unlike other curricular programs in Mexico, however, PEP 2004 does not specify content. It is an "open curriculum," where teachers are responsible for designing learning activities that address the development of specific skills within the aforementioned domains, based on the individual and group needs of students. The goals and unique curricular approach of Mexican preschools provide yet another reason to understand how quality conditions might vary from site to site. This includes understanding how teacher practice, preschool management and organization, and curricular compliance vary.

DESIGN OF THE COEP STUDY

As mentioned, the main objective of the COEP study was to identify the conditions of quality through which preschool services are provided throughout Mexico. Conditions selected for the COEP study were based on a preschool quality literature review. Most of the studies reviewed recognized that preschool participation should foster children's developmental outcomes (e.g., Peisner-Feinberg et al., 2001), contribute to school readiness, and enhance children's academic trajectories over time. Thus, our review was focused on understanding school conditions that provided greater gains in developmental outcomes. Structural conditions reviewed refered to human, infrastructure, financial, and organizational resources of schools and classrooms. Many studies emphasized the importance of human resources, particularly teacher characteristics such as educational attainment and teaching experience. And process variables addressed several dimensions of teacher-children interactions in the classroom.

In the COEP study, we decided to explore both variable types (i.e., structural conditions and processes). We selected the variables according to the importance they had in the implementation of the current preschool curriculum and the extent to which variables were modifiable by educational policies. The selection of the variables required a consultation process with scholars specializing in preschool education; policymakers; and particularly those involved in designing, implementing, and evaluating the current curriculum. Selection was also influenced by our capacity to measure the variables with available instruments, mostly surveys. We wound up categorizing study variables by resources (infrastructure, materials, and organization), personnel (teacher and head teacher characteristics), and processes (teacher-children interactions). We also wanted to assess quality differences across school types, communities, and family SES, due to the importance of preschool education for children from low-SES families.

To meet these objectives, we designed a multilevel, large-scale study intended to provide representative information by preschool type:

- Public urban–schools located in communities with more than 2,500 inhabitants.
- Rural unitary–schools located in communities with fewer than 2,500 inhabitants, with only one teacher who has twofold responsibilities, to teach children and to be in charge of the school, as the head teacher.
- Rural non-unitary–schools located in communities smaller than 2,500, where two or more teachers work in the schools; in these cases, there might be a head teacher appointed to be in charge of the school or one of the teachers might have both responsibilities (see Chapter 9 in Pérez Martínez et al., 2010).
- Indigenous unitary–public schools where multicultural, bilingual curricula are implemented by one teacher at the school.
- Indigenous non-unitary–multicultural, bilingual curricula implemented by more than one teacher.
- Community schools–very rural school sites, administered by the *Consejo Nacional de Fomento Educativo* (National Council for Educational Development [CONAFE]), too remote to adequately implement national curricula.
- Private schools–schools located mostly in urban communities, financed by private funds.

We should also mention that once data were gathered, the urban public preschool type was divided into two groups–lower-family SES and higher-family SES–in order to better understand the heterogeneity among this large group of children. Information about family SES was obtained in the COEP study through a parent (or guardian) questionnaire, which allowed us to develop an SES index (e.g., Internet access, automobile access, household income, parent education). (Low-SES urban schools' index varied from 3.52 to 5.10; high-SES urban schools' index varied from 5.11 to 6.75.)

Study informants were principally schoolteachers and principals, or others in charge of administration at preschool sites. Teachers included instructors from extremely rural or CONAFE preschools, whose credentials require much less formal training. Teachers also conducted structured interviews with parents to gather information about family SES characteristics. In all, 4,675 teachers and 23,370 parents participated, and the total number of preschools in the sample was 1,892. The sample distribution of preschool sites, teachers, and parents by school type is provided in Table 6.1.

Table 6.1. COEP Sample of Schools, Teachers, and Participating Parents

School Type		Population						Sample		
		Schools	%	Teachers	%	Enrolled Children	%	Schools	Teachers	Parents or Legal Guardians
CONAFE Preschool		15526	19.4	15526	7.8	126635	2.8	328	327	1597
Indigenous	Unitary	5509	6.9	5509	2.8	124057	2.7	214	214	1053
	Non-unitary	3758	4.7	10528	5.3	255817	5.6	74	213	1067
Rural	Unitary	14403	18.0	14403	7.3	276166	6.1	281	279	1417
	Non-unitary	9291	11.6	23982	12.1	549011	12.1	211	526	2646
Urban	Low-SES	18954	23.7	88427	44.6	2532671	55.8	305	1320	6633
	High-SES							163	850	4243
Private		12679	15.8	39950	20.1	678302	14.9	316	946	4714
Total		80120	100	198325	100	4542659	100	1892	4675	23370

A series of surveys and interviews for school administrators, teachers, and parents were designed to gather data on quality factors and associated conditions. These conditions were derived from the empirical literature of preschool quality. Rather than attempting to establish an exhaustive list of quality conditions, we selected those most relevant and feasible given our research design–a very large sample, limited to surveys and highly structured interviews. The 13 conditions selected were organized by the three dimensions described earlier: (a) resources, (b) personnel, and (c) school and classroom processes (see Table 6.2).

SELECTED COEP RESULTS

Instead of presenting data on all 13 quality conditions from the COEP study, we focus our discussion here on three (shown in bold in Table 6.2): (a) financial resources are provided for school operation; (b) classroom composition (e.g., size) allows teachers to address individual and collective needs of students; and (c) length of school day is sufficient to address student, family, and societal needs. We selected these three because they are considered fundamental, upon which the other quality conditions rest. These were also selected because they are particularly sensitive to family SES differences, and because they are directly relevant to public policy (e.g., class size, length of school day).

Financial Resources for School Operation

Of course, adequate financial resources are necessary to operate high-quality preschools–to address children's learning and development. Adequate financial support allows preschool sites to meet their basic obligations to provide conditions that affect teaching and learning activities. These obligations include things like electricity, basic building infrastructure, and the provision of learning materials (e.g., texts, paper, writing utensils). Without these basic resources it is difficult, if not impossible, to operate a preschool, address teacher and student well-being, or engage curricular goals meaningfully. Without these basic resources, teachers and others in the community (including parents) are compelled to focus their efforts on resource accumulation in lieu of educationally significant tasks.

In the COEP study we wanted to identify who was involved in supporting the operation of preschools throughout Mexico, and to specify ways parents contributed. We focused our analysis on public preschools,

Table 6.2. Quality Factors and Associated Conditions Investigated in COEP Study

Quality Factors	Conditions
Resources (infrastructure, materials, organization)	1. **Financial resources are provided for school operation.**
	2. Educational infrastructure guarantees child well-being and contributes to competency development.
	3. Classrooms are equipped with various, accessible materials.
	4. **Classroom composition (e.g., size) allows teachers to address individual and collective needs of students.**
	5. Classroom space and trained personnel are dedicated to serving children with special needs.
Personnel (Teachers and Principals)	6. Contractual conditions are adequate for a high-quality teacher workforce.
	7. Teachers have adequate training and experience.
	8. Teacher beliefs are consistent with curricular orientations.
	9. Opportunities for teacher professional learning and development are provided.
	10. School administrators have adequate training and experience.
Process	11. **Length of school day is sufficient to address student, family, and societal needs.**
	12. Interactions between teachers and children are optimal for learning and development.
	13. Opportunities are provided for children to work individually and in small groups.

Bold refers to the quality conditions discussed in the text below.

since it is assumed that operation costs at these sites would be absorbed by the states, as outlined in the Mexican Constitution (Bracho, 1995; Bracho & Zamudio, 1997). We wanted to know whether in practice the state actually covered all operation costs and, if not, from what sources (public or private) additional financial support was given.

This is an important consideration not only because the involvement of additional donors to support preschool operation helps meet the needs of a community, but also because it promotes shared respon- sibility and, thus, increased transparency in the use of school resources (Saavedra & Suárez, 2002). On the other hand, outside financial con- tributions also create a certain amount of problematic dependency be- cause ongoing support in the long term is uncertain. At the same time, however, wealthier donors (like parents) can afford to give larger sums, in which case donation is not as frequently needed.

Examining preschool operation costs is fundamental to the provi- sion of rich learning environments for children, and the issue had not been studied systematically in previous research. Some evidence sug- gests it is a timely topic in Mexico (e.g., Jensen, 2005). The COEP study sought to gauge the financial contributions of parents to preschools for two reasons. First, other research on public school operation costs in Mexico shows that a substantive portion of public school budgets comes from parent fees, which represent a significant expense for families. Bra- cho and Zamudio (1997), for example, found that school-related ex- penses represented, on average, 10% of overall family expenses among those studied. Enrollment fees alone represented 12% of the minimal family salary. With these fees, parents are able to influence school deci- sions associated with their children's education. Yet when parent fees are not paid–a very real predicament for low-SES families in Mexico– preschool enrollment and attendance could be jeopardized, or a child might be forced to transfer to a preschool of lesser quality. Second, we examined parent financial contributions because we wanted to know the extent to which they varied across preschool type, which could re- sult in differentiated preschool investments and in effect perpetuate so- cial and educational inequalities by family SES (Bracho, 1995).

To identify external financial support to preschools, we specified contributions by expenditure items:

a. basic utilities (electricity, water, gas, telephone, Internet),
b. infrastructure improvements (construction of classrooms, wall repair, window protection, etc.),
c. furniture purchase and repair (shelves, bookcases, tables, chairs),
d. equipment purchase (tape recorders, computers, televisions), and
e. payment of support staff (to teach physical education, art, computer classes, and English).

The COEP study identified five groups who contributed financially to school operations:

- parents,
- state authorities,
- *Programa Escuelas de Calidad* (PEC), a federal program designed to improve student performance through the implementation of strategic educational management and the provision of additional resources to advance meeting educational goals) (Pérez Martínez, 2005; Reimers & Cardenas, 2007),
- county authorities, and
- others (including civil associations and companies).

Results showed overall that parents were the largest provider of financial resources to preschools. As shown in Figure 6.1, about half of preschools surveyed indicated that parents were the principal source of financial support to cover basic utilities, and more than half of schools indicated that parents were the principal source to pay costs associated with infrastructure, furniture, and equipment. The state was reported to be the second most important financial contributor for preschool operation. A majority of preschools studied (82.5%) indicated that the state was the principal source to pay for staff expenses.

It is important to note that financial contributions from parents are articulated in *La Ley General de Educación* (General Education Law) as social subsidies that under no condition should be construed as trade-offs for educational services. According to Section II of Article 67 in *La Ley General*, parents are permitted to "work together for better integration of the school community, participate in school improvement, and help school authorities on a voluntary basis within their means, either financially or through community work." In other words, educational services should not depend in any way on the financial contributions of parents.

To determine the variation in parent financial support across preschool types, we gathered information on the amount of parent contributions given annually as well as monthly. We then totaled these contributions to estimate the annual monetary sum parents contributed. Of course, these figures do not include non-financial contributions parents made for preschool operations, including free labor or donated building materials.

Table 6.3 shows that across all public preschools, 71.5% received financial contributions from parents. These data also show a relationship between family SES and the percentage of preschools receiving this support: preschools enrolling children from higher-SES families received greater financial contributions from parents. Across preschools,

Figure 6.1. Principal Sources of Financial Support for Preschool Operation, by Expenditure

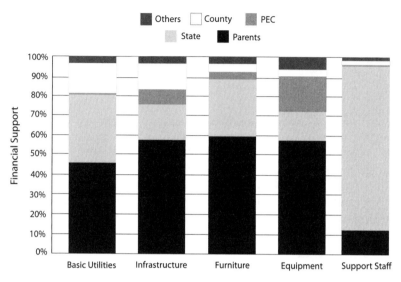

Table 6.3. Percentage of Preschools Receiving Financial Support from Parents and Total Annual Contributions

Preschool Type		% Receiving Financial Contributions from Parents	Annual Parent Contribution (in Mexican pesos)
Average public		71.5%	$272
Community (CONAFE)		28.0%	$144
Indigenous	*Unitary*	53.6%	$81
	Non-unitary	59.6%	$57
Rural	*Unitary*	84.0%	$249
	Non-unitary	93.5%	$235
Urban	*Lower-SES*	92.8%	$423
	Higher-SES	97.7%	$689

annual contributions averaged $272 MXN (roughly equivalent to $25 USD at the time) per child. These totals varied widely across preschool types. Parents of children in higher-SES urban preschools paid $689 MXN on average, compared to parents of children attending non-unitary indigenous preschools, who paid $57 MXN. These differences are attributed to wide discrepancies in family purchasing power across Mexican communities.

In sum, it is clear that parent financing in the current system is important to the basic operation of preschools in Mexico. A problem with this scenario is that parent support is unequally distributed across the preschool types mentioned. This creates a public preschool system that not only perpetuates existing educational and social inequalities among Mexican children, but quite possibly exacerbates those differences (Bracho, 1995; Saavedra & Suarez, 2002). These results demonstrate the need to reorient education finance policy for preschools in Mexico so that learning opportunities for children from lower-SES families are not hindered by their parents' inability to pay for basic school operation costs. Simply stated, public financing alone should cover the costs of utilities, building infrastructure, furniture, equipment, and extracurricular staff support.

Classroom Composition

Preschool children require basic classroom conditions to develop and learn key competencies. These conditions should provide children with sufficient individual time and attention from adults to address their basic social, emotional, and academic needs (Bowman et al., 2001; Seefeldt & Wasik, 2005). Indeed, studies have found that young children demonstrate stronger learning outcomes when they are provided adequate opportunities to work individually and in small groups, and when interactions with teachers are continuous, emotionally supportive, and cognitively challenging (Hamre & Pianta, 2001). For these conditions to occur in the preschool classroom, teachers must be continually available to interact with children either individually or in small groups (Seefeldt & Wasik, 2005).

In the COEP study we addressed the adequacy of classroom composition for student learning by measuring class size (i.e., number of children per classroom) and calculating student-teacher ratios. Indeed, the number of preschoolers per teacher affects the amount of time and attention she or he is able to give each child, which in turn can influence the quality and frequency of learning opportunities. Several studies demonstrate that student-teacher ratio is an important indicator of quality interactions between teachers and students in the classroom (Seefeldt & Wasik, 2005). Fewer children per teacher allow for more consequential teacher-student interactions (Munton et al., 2002).

There are different recommendations for class sizes and student-teacher ratios in preschool settings. The National Association for the Education of Young Children (NAEYC) provides perhaps the strictest ratio recommendation. They suggest that for children ages 4 and 5 years old, the maximum ratio should be 10 students per teacher, and that no more than 20 children should attend a single classroom. The NAEYC recognizes, however, that these ratios can change based on curricular demands, the inclusion of children with special needs in the classroom, and the time of day children attend preschool (Munton et al., 2002).

Figure 6.2 demonstrates class sizes by the preschool types described earlier; the unit of analysis of class size was at the classroom rather than the school level. Nationally, nearly one-fifth of preschool classrooms had classes with more than 30 students. This far exceeds the most conservative recommendation. Not surprisingly, the largest class sizes were concentrated in urban preschools, especially those in lower-SES communities. Indeed, more than a third of lower-income urban preschool classrooms had more than 30 students. It is also important to highlight that even many rural and indigenous classrooms were overpopulated and/or understaffed. Nationally, about 4 in 10 preschool classes met the NAEYC recommendation to have no more than 20 students per class (though this does not necessarily address the ratio issue). Again, this was less the case in public urban preschools, particularly in lower-SES communities, where fewer than 1 in 6 classrooms satisfied the recommendation.

Another way to look at class size data by preschool type is using statistical averages, shown in Figure 6.3. Here we see that nationally the average class size of preschools in 2008 was 20 children. Again, we see significant differences across various preschool types. The largest class sizes were found in lower-SES urban preschools, followed by higher-SES public preschools. The smallest class sizes are found in private and CONAFE preschools. Private preschool settings simply have more financial overhead to maintain smaller class sizes, and CONAFE preschools tended to be very small because of their extremely remote locations. Rural and indigenous preschools averaged about 20 children per classroom.

In addition to class size, we also assessed student-teacher ratios in preschool classrooms (see Figure 6.4). These figures were simply calculated by dividing the number of students by the number of teachers and teachers' assistants within each preschool classroom. (We asked

Figure 6.2. Distribution of Class Sizes by Preschool Type

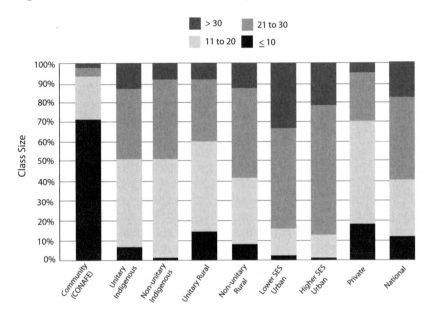

Figure 6.3. Average Class Sizes by Preschool Type, 2008

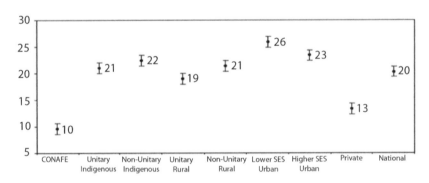

teachers to report if there was another adult in charge of the group regularly. Teacher assistants were mainly reported in private preschools, though some public preschools reported having them as well.) Note comparisons with Figure 6.3, which analyzed class sizes. Distributions from class size to student-teacher ratios did not change for CONAFE, indigenous, or unitary rural schools, suggesting that virtually none of the classrooms in these preschool settings had more than one teacher.

Figure 6.4. Distribution of Student–Teacher Ratios by Preschool Type

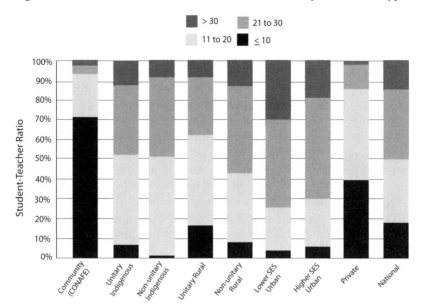

Distributions changed for urban preschools, more for higher-SES than lower-SES settings. Indeed, 30% of lower-SES urban preschools had more than 30 students per teacher.

No matter how you cut the data, we see that Mexican children in less favorable socioeconomic conditions are more likely than their peers in more favorable conditions to attend preschools with overcrowded, understaffed classrooms. This situation presents a host of problems for children who arguably need high-quality preschool the most. Thus, preschool as it is currently practiced in Mexico may be more of an obstacle to—or even have adverse effects on—the learning and development of young, at-risk children (Myers, 2004).

Length of School Day

Internationally, duration of the school day as a means for improving children's learning opportunity has been discussed at length. These deliberations have revolved around three core issues:

a. the benefits of full- versus half-day preschool attendance,
b. the compensatory benefits of full-day preschool participation for children from low-SES families, and

c. the academic, social, and economic impacts different durations
    have on children (Lee, Burkham, Ready, Honigman, &
    Meisels, 2006).

Outside of Mexico, extensive research has addressed these issues (e.g.,
NCES, 2004). Several have shown that full-day preschool programs
benefit teachers, children, and parents. A longer school day gives teachers more time to identify children's needs, individualize teaching, assess
student progress, and provide small-group learning activities. It also allows teachers to explore the curriculum in greater depth, and to develop
more meaningful relationships with parents. Full-day programs benefit
children by providing them with more formal learning experiences, including small-group and independent learning time. Working parents
who would otherwise seek out child care also benefit (Lee et al., 2006).

In the COEP study we found that virtually no preschool program is
available for Mexican children with a school day longer than 5 hours.
As shown in Figure 6.5, the length of the school day for more than half
of Mexican preschools nationally is 3 hours or less. Roughly a third of
preschools have a 4-hour schedule, and another 11%, 5 hours. In other
words, for 9 out of 10 preschool programs across Mexico, the school day
is half as long or less than a regular workday.

Figure 6.5. Distribution of School Day Length by Preschool Type

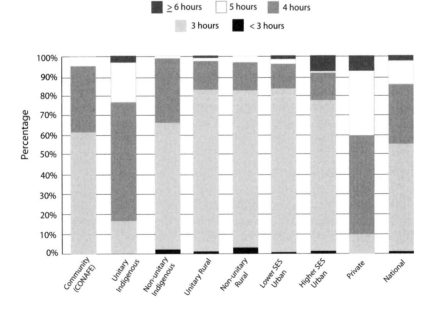

Among public preschools, indigenous and CONAFE programs reported the longest school days. For more than 4 out of 5 of the other public preschool programs, the school day lasted 3 hours or less. Three out of 5 of CONAFE preschools had a 4-hour school day, compared to 1 in 3 for indigenous schools and less than 1 in 7 for urban public schools. Ironically, the school day was shorter in urban areas where the rate of female employment was higher (Instituto Nacional de las Mujeres, 2008).

These data differ greatly from the length of the school day in other countries. In the United States, 57% of public preschool programs, 78% of private programs, and 63% of Catholic programs are full-day (NCES, 2004). Preschools found in urban areas are more likely to be full-day programs, whereas about 50% of preschool programs in suburban and rural areas are full-day (NCES, 2004).

Thus, results from the COEP study reveal that the length of the school day in Mexican preschools is inadequate, both for children's learning and development, and to accommodate the schedules of working parents. Given pressures on families to have two parents working full-time outside of the home, this situation could weaken Mexico's economic competitiveness and affect gender equality (OECD, 2005).

CONCLUSIONS

Preschool quality in Mexico is crucial for children's present and future development. Several research studies in different countries and diverse settings have established over and over again that high-quality preschooling boosts children's cognitive, emotional, motor, and social development. This is because the neurological development of young children is very rapid, unlike any other developmental stage in life. The competencies developed during this short period benefit children through adulthood. Comparative studies suggest that the developmental needs of young children are universal, and that they are largely shaped by the quality of environmental stimuli.

The importance of early learning environments to later school and life opportunities has deep implications for national and interactional policies associated with early education initiatives. These programs should be well connected with family and community initiatives designed to provide children with a holistic development (Schneider, Ramirez, Gomes-Paiva, & Almeida, 2009). Indeed, it is important to underscore the role of community factors where preschools are located so that human, material, and institutional resources are used to optimize children's learning and development. As indicated by Brazelton and Greenspan (2002), education should instill in children a sense of respect for their cultural heritage, on the one hand, while providing them with the academic competencies they will need to succeed in society, on the other. This requires education policies to find ways to encourage safety, trust, and social cohesion within the communities where preschools are found.

The early stages of children's development certainly provide a huge window of opportunity to prepare future Mexican citizens. The potential benefits of taking advantage of early developmental stages, however, are mediated by the quality of learning opportunities provided by children's day-to-day settings. Preschool is a principal setting for young children. And we have argued that the benefits of preschool depend on its quality.

The COEP study addressed 13 conditions of preschool quality. National and international studies have coalesced around these conditions as imperatives to providing a high-quality preschool program. In this chapter we have focused on three of these conditions: financial resources, classroom composition, and length of the school day. A major conclusion from the COEP study was that the structural inequalities of Mexican preschools prevent many children from receiving a quality education. These inequalities directly affect teachers' working conditions, children's learning, and, therefore, the realization of Mexico's stated objectives for early education programs.

Our analysis of financial resources for operation costs showed that preschools depend heavily on parent contributions. A major problem with this finding is that many Mexican parents simply cannot afford to give preschools the support they need to meet basic operational costs, particularly parents whose children need high-quality programs the most. Children whose parents have greater incomes, therefore, attend better equipped, more functional preschools. This certainly could contribute to widening opportunity gaps between young Mexican children rather than diminishing them. Although indigenous and rural preschools, in comparison with public urban preschools, tended to have slightly longer school days with smaller student-teacher ratios, this is not enough to compensate for low financial contributions from rural parents.

High student-teacher ratios were found across Mexican preschools, especially in public urban settings. This was especially the case in lower-SES urban preschools, where nearly a third of classrooms had more than 30 children per teacher. Reducing these ratios is imperative to improving the quality of teacher-child interactions, particularly for low-SES children. A way to do this is bringing another adult (e.g., teacher assistant, parent, volunteer) into the classroom to support the teacher.

In summary, the COEP study showed that current conditions in Mexican preschools are inadequate to provide children and families with high-quality learning opportunities. Moreover, expanding preschool services under the current model could worsen existing inequalities rather than diminish them. We found, for example, that class sizes and student-teacher ratios are much too large. Only a small portion of preschools meet international recommendations in this regard. This decreases opportunities for meaningful teacher-student interactions, peer collaborations, and individualized support. In many cases, large class sizes lead to poor use of classroom space, insufficient materials, and excessive time spent on behavior management. These findings beg further research and deep policy changes in Mexico to improve preschool quality for our most disadvantaged children. Further study is needed to understand more complex dimensions of preschool quality, particularly learning processes within preschool classrooms.

We believe that these findings have implications beyond the Mexican context. For educators and policymakers working with children of Mexican migrants in the United States, our findings can help them understand the contexts the children come from, the educational and organizational practices children and parents are used to, and how their previous experiences might frame their dispositions to learn and participate in the school community. This should inform parent-teacher collaborations and family outreach initiatives like family literacy programs.

It is certainly clear that preschool in Mexico is different from preschool in the United States. Teachers, principals, and other school personnel should be careful with their assumptions about Mexican-origin children's experiences prior to preschool, or that parents share an understanding about the infrastructure and organization of U.S. educational institutions. Proper steps should be taken to ensure that Mexican-origin parents and children understand how the educational services are rendered, what is expected of them, and what they can expect from their peers, other families, and the school staff. Supports might be rendered as well to help children and families adjust to the lengthy school day.

Preschool educators working with Mexican-origin children and families should also be proactive to help parents interact appropriately with the school. Though some research shows Mexican parents believe child learning is the shared responsibility of the school and home (e.g., Slate & Jones, 2007), many are not familiar with curricular learning objectives, and their collaborations with schools (in Mexico) tend to be limited to economic donations, cleaning and repairing of facilities, or event organization. Preschool teachers and administrators should systematically work with parents of Mexican-origin children to understand children's developmental potential, and to support parents so that their children acquire the knowledge, skills, and attitudes that are consistent with academic success. These efforts should build on the relative strengths of Mexican American parents, including high parental expectations (Lara-Alecio, Irby, & Ebener, 1997), high aspirations (Valencia & Black, 2002), and high interest in and care for their children (Morrow & Young, 1997).

REFERENCES

Bracho, T. (1995). Gasto privado en educación: México, 1984-1992. *Revista Mexicana de Sociología*, 91–119.

Bracho, T., & Zamudio, A. (1997). El gasto privado en educación: México, 1992. *Revista Mexicana de Investigación Educativa*, 323–347.

Bowman, B., Donovan, M., & Burns, S. (2001). *Eager to learn: Educating our preschoolers.* Washington, DC: National Academy Press.

Brazelton, T. B., & Greenspan, S. (2002). *As necessidades essenciais das criancas.* Porto Alegre, Brazil: Artmed.

Center for Mental Health in Schools. (2006). *Preschool programs: A synthesis of current policy issues* (Report Brief). Los Angeles, CA: University of California, Los Angeles.

Curry, J. (1997). *Pre-k best practices review 1996-1997.* Austin, TX: Austin Independent School District, Office Program Evaluation.

Hamre, B., & Pianta, R. (2001). Early teacher-child relationships and the trajectory of children's school outcomes through eighth grade. *Child Development, 72*(2), 625–638.

Instituto Nacional de las Mujeres. (2008). *Mujeres y hombres en México*, p. 326.

Jensen, B. (2005). Culture and practice of Mexican primary schooling: Implications for improving policy and practice in the U.S. *Current Issues in Education* [Online], *8*(25). Available: http://cie.asu.edu/volume8/number24/index.html

Lee, V., Burkam, D., Ready, D., Honigman, J., & Meisels, S. (2006). Full-day versus half-day Kindergarten: In which program do children learn more? *American Journal of Education, 112*, 163–208.

Munton, T., et al. (2002). *Review of international research on the relationship between ratios, staff qualifications and training, group size and the quality of provision in early years and child care setting.* Norwich, UK: Queen's Printer.

Myers, R. (2004). *In search of quality in programmes of Early Childhood Care and Education* (ECCE). EFA Global Monitoring Report. Paris, France: UNESCO.

NCES. (2004). *Full-day and half-day Kindergarten in the United States: Findings from the Early Childhood Longitudinal Study, Kindergarten class of 1998-99.* Washington, DC: Department of Education, Institute of Education Sciences.

OECD. (2005). *¿Mi bebé o mi jefe? Cómo reconciliar la vida familiar con el trabajo.* México: Organisation for Economic Co-operation and Development.

Peisner-Feinberg, E. S., Burchinal, M. R., Clifford, R. M., Culkin, M. L., Howes, C., Kagan, S. L, & Yazejian, N. (2001). The relation of preschool child-care quality to children's cognitive and social developmental trajectories through second grade. *Child Development, 72*(5), 1534–1553.

Pérez Martínez, M. G. (2005). Bringing individuals back into impementation: A case study of an intergovernmental educational policy in Mexico– Programa Escuelas de Calidad. Unpublished doctoral dissertation. York, UK: University of York.

Pérez Martínez, M. G. et al. (2010). *La educación preescolar en México: Condiciones para la enseñanza y el aprendizaje.* México: Instituto Nacional para la Evaluación de la Educación.

Reimers, F., & Cardenas, S. (2007). Who benefits from school-based management in Mexico? *Prospects, 37*(2), 37–56.

Saavedra, J., & Suárez, P. (2002). *El financiamiento de la educación pública en el Perú: El rol de las familias.* Lima, Perú: Grupo de Análisis para el Desarrollo.

Schneider, A., Ramirez, V. R., Gomes-Paiva, M. G., & Almeida, L. (2009). The better early development program: An innovative Brazilian public policy. *Current Issues in Comparative Education, 11,* 24–32.

Schweinhart, L., Montie, J., Xiang, Z., Barnett, W., Belfield, C., & Mores, M. (2005). *Lifetime effects: The Highscope Perry preschool study through age 40.* Ypsilanti, MI: Highscope Press.

Seefeldt, C., & Wasik, B. (2005). *Preescolar: Los pequeños van a la escuela.* México: Secretaría de Educación Pública.

Slate, J. R., & Jones, C. H. (2007). Mexican parents' and teachers' views of effective elementary schools. *International Journal for Leadership in Education, 11,* 1–12.

Tomaševski, K. (2001). *Human rights obligations: Making education available, accessible, acceptable and adaptable.* Lund, Sweden: Raoul Wallenberg Institute of Human Rights and Humanitarian Law.

UNESCO. (2006). *Strong foundations: Early childhood care and education.* EFA Global Monitoring Report 2007. Paris, France: Author.

Yoshikawa, H., Weisner, T., & Lowe, E. D. (2006). *Making it work: Low-wage employment, family life, and child development.* New York: Russell Sage Foundation.

Part III

TRANSNATIONAL REALITIES

In addition to a common border, Mexico and the United States also share students and a multitude of interrelated schooling and migratory processes. While U.S. schools have long educated students with previous schooling experiences in Mexico, an increasing number of Mexican schools now serve students who have previously attended U.S. schools, especially as return migration to Mexico has increased since the 2008 economic recession. There are also many students in Mexico—though never having migrated themselves—who are directly impacted by migration in ways both beneficial and detrimental to their schooling. Much more needs to be done to understand and improve the educational well-being of students living within the web of transnational realities that link the United States and Mexico. In Chapter 7, Regina Cortina, Ivania de la Cruz, and Carmina Makar compare the secondary schooling opportunities of Mexican immigrants in New York City with those in their communities of origin in the states of Guerrero, Puebla, and Oaxaca. Víctor Zúñiga and Edmund Hamann, in Chapter 8, summarize their survey research on the responses of Mexican schools to U.S.-born children who return to their parents' country of origin. And Adam Sawyer, in Chapter 9, provides a case study of schooling experiences of youth impacted by migration in southern Mexico and the ways in which absent migrant parents continue to support their education from afar.

CHAPTER 7

School Trajectories for Mexican Immigrant Youth in New York City

Regina Cortina, Ivania de la Cruz, and Carmina Makar

> Two years ago, Oscar Chico entered the New York City public school system knowing, at best, a few words of English. At 15 and newly arrived in the United States, he was part of the wave of young Mexicans who have swept New York City during the past decade. (Teachers College, Columbia University, 2009, p. 14)

When questioned about his experience in learning English and his arrival in the United States, Oscar was certain about one thing: His teachers had supported him through the learning process. Although Oscar embodies the many challenges faced by Mexican immigrant students upon arrival, he was lucky enough to find a network of support that was sensitive to his prior learning experiences and native culture. Indeed, teachers who know about their students' trajectories and transnational identities are inclined to design culturally sensitive and educationally effective pedagogues for them.

To promote an understanding of the school trajectories across countries of transnational students, this chapter examines the educational challenges and achievements of Mexican students in New York City. We identify as Mexican students both those who migrated from Mexico and those who are U.S.-born, even though we are aware that most Mexican children in the lower grades are U.S.-born, while those students in high school and beyond are predominantly Mexico born. We refer to Mexican students in New York City as transnational because their social capital and the support they receive from relatives, mentors, and friends derive from their community of origin. We are informed by Coleman's (1988) definition of social capital as "the ability to gain access to resources by virtue of membership in social networks" (as cited by Portes & Rumbaut, 2001, p. 353). In the case of Mexican communities in the United States, social networks are central to their survival.

Our purpose in this chapter is to identify factors from students' education and family life in Mexico—including their acquisition of literacy and other academic skills, and their social and cultural background—that can help explain their later schooling trajectories in the United States and inform the provision of relevant achievement-oriented in-school support. Key elements include the grade level students completed before migrating, the quality and type of education they received in their communities of origin, and their family's average years of schooling before they migrated to the United States.

Several Mexican, United States, and New York City sources provided data for this chapter. To describe the demographic patterns of Mexican immigration to New York, we drew on statistics from the *Instituto de los Mexicanos en el Exterior* (Institute for Mexicans Abroad; IME) of the *Secretaría de Releciones Exteriores* (Ministry of Foreign Affairs of Mexico, Secretaría de Relaciones Exteriores [SRE]) regarding information about Mexicans who request services at the *Consulado General de México* (Mexican General Consulate in New York). The data provided by IME included information on the average years of schooling for women and men coming from the three states we considered: Puebla, Oaxaca, and Guerrero. In addition, data collected by several other agencies of the Mexican government furnished complementary information about the education of students from these states. These data provided the educational indicators for our investigation: years of schooling and levels of education for both adolescents and their parents. We appraised the quality of schooling the adolescents received based upon whether they graduated from formal schooling in contrast with distance learning education—known in Spanish as *Telesecundaria*, a schooling alternative with a core curriculum taught through television with the assistance of one or two teachers per school.

Building upon previous research on Mexican students by Cortina (2009a), this chapter argues that transnational factors, particularly the social networks and the average years for schooling of the families before they migrate to the United States, contribute to an explanation of the schooling patterns of the Mexican population in U.S. schools.

The chapter has six sections. The first provides information about the Mexican population in New York City overall and in the city's schools. The second section discusses the educational attainment of Mexican immigrants, and the third section addresses the quality of schooling in their home communities. It is followed by sections on the experiences of Mexican youth in New York City schools. Last, the chapter makes recommendations and draws conclusions related to opportunities for collaboration between the United States and Mexico to create improved educational strategies and teaching practices for the benefit of Mexican students.

THE MEXICAN POPULATION IN NEW YORK CITY

The Mexican population in New York City has dramatically increased: by 57.7% between 2000 and 2007. According to Census data, by 2007 there were 289,629 people of Mexican origin in the city (U.S. Census Bureau, 2007). The population growth—27% from 2005 to 2007 alone—is a result of the continuing arrival of migrants as well as the high birth rate of Mexican women already living in the city (Bergad, 2008). Over the past two decades, New York City has become a destination for Mexican families, and they are the fastest-growing group within the overall population of Caribbean and Latin American origin, which consists mainly of Dominicans and Puerto Ricans (Cortina, 2009b). On average, the Mexican population is very young and approximately one-third are school age. Based on U.S. Census Bureau data compiled by Cortina (see Cortina & Gendreau, 2003), in 2008 the median age of Mexicans in New York City was 26, and approximately 60% of the Mexican population in the city was younger than age 29 (see Table 7.4). Given these demographic patterns, it is important to consider the educational implications and address the potential educational challenges for the Mexican population.

Two analyses, conducted in 1999 and 2007, respectively, of the services provided by the Consulate show that the three most important Mexican states sending immigrants to New York City were Puebla, Oaxaca, and Guerrero. These states include many rural communities where people speak several indigenous languages and exhibit high levels of poverty. They also are the three states with the largest number of indigenous students in their rural secondary system and with schools where the language of instruction is not Spanish but one of several indigenous languages spoken in the region. The Mexican census defines children as indigenous if their mother speaks an indigenous language other than Spanish. In 2010 Oaxaca was the Mexican state with the largest indigenous population—34% of those 5 and older spoke an indigenous language. Guerrero is the state with the fourth-largest indigenous population, with 15% of those 5 and older speaking an indigenous language. Puebla is the state with the seventh largest indigenous population, with almost 12% of children ages 5 and older speaking an indigenous language (INEGI, 2010a).

Puebla has been the state of origin for the greatest number of Mexican immigrants in New York. By the year 2000 more migrants from its poor southern region lived in New York City than in any other place where *Poblanos* had previously migrated, including Mexico City (Cortés, 2003, p. 196). One striking feature is the youthfulness of most immigrants, since 70% of immigrant women from the state of Puebla and 68% of men come to the United States between the ages of 15 and 24 (Cortés, 2003, p. 235). Statistics on gender and educational attainment of young people arriving in the city are available for two points in time, 1999 and 2007, from the database of Mexicans requesting government identification at the Mexican Consulate in New York City. In 2007, the Consulate issued 30,053 *matrículas consulares*, the identification card provided to Mexicans in New York regardless of their migration status. Sixty percent were women, and 40 percent were men (IME, 2007). Of the total, 13,121 (44%) were for immigrants from Puebla; 3,579 (12%) were for immigrants from Oaxaca; and 2,689 (9%) were for immigrants from Guerrero.

A similar analysis done by the Mexican Consulate earlier shows that between 1995 and 1999 51% of Mexicans who requested a passport came from Puebla, 6.5% from Oaxaca, and 5.8% from Guerrero. The 2000 report, which contains data from 1997, includes the number of *matrículas consulares* and passports requested by Mexicans in New York City, while the 2007 report only includes the *matrículas consulares* that were issued (Mexican Consulate in New York City, 2000).

While Puebla has continued to provide the largest number of Mexican immigrants to New York City, the number of immigrants from Oaxaca and Guerrero has grown, which demonstrates a trend of increasing migration coming from these states since 1995 (Mexican Consulate in New York City, 2000). Women were also a significant number of those who migrated in 2007, representing 40% of the migrants from Puebla and 38% from Oaxaca and Guerrero (IME, 2007).

The continual arrival of immigrants from these three states is having significant effects on the New York City schooling system, not only because immigrants themselves enroll in schools, but also because their children are becoming part of the educational system of the city.

THE EDUCATIONAL ATTAINMENT OF YOUTH IN MEXICO

In Mexico, compulsory basic education consists of nine years of schooling: 6 years of elementary education plus 3 of *secundaria* (middle school). On October 2011 the Mexican Congress passed a constitutional amendment that makes high school a compulsory schooling level. The law became effective in August 2012.

National statistics from the *Instituto Nacional de Evaluación Educativa* (National Institute of Educational Evaluation [INEE], 2008) show that in 2007 roughly 60% of the Mexican youth ages 15–29 had not completed basic education before migrating to the United States, while 33% had reached this educational level. The remaining 7% of Mexican immigrants had at least completed high school. The corresponding figures for immigrants from Puebla show the same educational attainment: 33% completed *secundaria* before arriving in the United States in 2007. Only 27% of immigrants from Oaxaca and 24% of immigrants from Guerrero came to the United States with *secundaria* completed in 2007.

As Table 7.1 shows, the educational attainment of immigrants can be seen in the information about Mexicans requesting government services at the Mexican Consulate in New York City. In 2007, 82% of those coming from Puebla had completed *secundaria*. The figures for immigrants from Guerrero and Oaxaca were 82 and 83%, respectively (IME, 2007). Compared with the national statistics shown in the previous paragraph, the immigrants arriving in the United States from these three sending states had levels of education above the Mexican national average upon arrival. Interviews in the state of Puebla corroborate this information (Cortés, 2003). The migrants arriving from these three states were young and better educated than the national average. This high educational attainment of immigrants can partly be explained by the massive enrollment of students in *telesecundarias*, a distance education system taught through television.

One noteworthy finding from the data shown in Table 7.1 is that approximately 82% of the migrants from the three states arrived in New York after finishing middle school, which is the equivalent of the 9th grade in the United States. We were not surprised by this finding, since it was confirmed by the statistics of the Department of Education in New York City. Most of these students enrolled in the city high schools, but because of their lack of knowledge of academic English, among other reasons, they were not able to stay long in the schools.

In October 2009, four recently emigrated students from Mexico stood before an audience of students and faculty of Teachers College (Columbia University) and city educators to discuss their experience in schools. Their stories echoed the challenges of many students, some struggled because they were undocumented: others endured segregation within their schools, and many experienced unchallenging academic programs. Their personal stories put a face to the numbers and provided an understanding about the constraints that such students face.

Table 7.1. Educational Attainment of Mexicans in New York City, According to Consulate

Level of Education	Number of Matrículas	Percentage of Matrículas
Average of Three States for Secundaria (Middle School):		82
Puebla		
Less than Elementary	89	0.81
Elementary	978	8.95
Basic Education	**8,930**	**81.74**
Technical Degree	51	0.47
High School	738	6.76
Some College	75	0.69
College	64	0.59
Total	10,925	100
Oaxaca		
Less than Elementary	39	1.3
Elementary	239	7.95
Basic Education	**2,498**	**83.07**
Technical Degree	9	0.3
High School	191	6.35
Some College	15	0.5
College	16	0.53
Total	3,007	100
Guerrero		
Less than Elementary	34	1.52
Elementary	174	7.79
Basic Education	**1,820**	**81.47**
Technical Degree	8	0.36
High School	164	7.34
Some College	12	0.54
College	22	0.98
Total	2,234	100

Bold for Basic Education denotes the years of compulsory school in Mexico according to national law.

Source: Information compiled by the authors, based on reports of the Instituto de los Mexicanos en el Exterior, SRE (2007).

Despite these constraints, some students highlighted the teachers' supportive roles. In the words of a student: "Our teachers motivate us. . . . My teachers always tell me they believe in me, and you start believing in yourself and want to move forward" (Teachers College, 2009, p. 14). Indeed, with adequate support, teachers can connect their transnational students' experience both in Mexico and the United States, for the lively relationship of mentorship and guidance between teachers and their students is one that shapes students' educational trajectories.

SCHOOLING SYSTEMS IN STUDENTS' MEXICAN COMMUNITIES OF ORIGIN IN PUEBLA, OAXACA, AND GUERRERO

The educational attainment of Mexican students in their communities of origin shapes their possibilities for continuing their education in their communities of destination. As indicated above, a high proportion of youth leave Mexico when they complete basic education and arrive in the United States with the hope of entering high school. This section provides more detailed information on the type and quality of education, including literacy and other academic skills, which Mexican students received in middle school in Puebla, Oaxaca, and Guerrero. We did not track individuals who migrated, which means we cannot argue that each and every one of the Mexican immigrants in New York City was enrolled in the type of education we described for Puebla, Guerrero, and Oaxaca. However, learning about the school systems in the communities of origin is a first step toward identifying the educational assets of Mexican students.

We portray the quality of education received by these Mexican immigrants through three indicators: the type of schools and the availability of schooling, a quality indicator of the schools; student scores on a national test in Mexico; and the educational attainment of parents.

The Nature and Extent of the Schooling

We used two indicators to assess the quality of schooling in the sending states. One was the incidence of *primarias indígenas*, or indigenous elementary schools, in each. The second indicator was the availability of education through formal schooling or only via distance education.

Indigenous elementary schools. In 2008 there were 9,881 indigenous schools in Mexico, and the states with highest enrollments were

Oaxaca, Guerrero, and Puebla, along with Chiapas and Veracruz. Approximately 75% of indigenous children attended indigenous elementary schools in these five states (Dirección General de Educación Superior para Profesionales de la Educación, 2004). At the end of AY 2008–2009, Oaxaca, Guerrero, and Puebla were among the five Mexican states with the highest number of indigenous elementary school graduates. A total of 21,783 indigenous students graduated from indigenous elementary schools in Oaxaca, 10,299 in Puebla, and 12,992 in Guerrero (INEGI, 2010b). Teachers in these schools had high turnover rates and lacked updated training in the teaching of Spanish to indigenous students. The fact that they were teaching in such remote rural communities meant that they had only recently graduated and thus lacked teaching experience.

In Mexico indigenous children attend elementary schools managed by the states or the federal government. In the school year 2007–2008, 838,700 indigenous students attended *primarias indígenas* (indigenous elementary schools), which are administered by the *Subsecretaría de Educación Básica* (Sub-Secretariat of Initial Education) through the *Dirección General de Educación Indígena* (General Directorate of Indigenous Education, DGEI). DGEI was the agency in charge of education in indigenous elementary schools at the national and state levels, and its main responsibilities included professional development of teachers who worked in indigenous elementary schools; the design of curricula that incorporated indigenous cultures, practices, and knowledge; and the coordination of national and local educational policies for indigenous students (Secretaría de Educación Pública [SEP], 2009).

A smaller percentage of indigenous children attended schools through *Cursos Comunitarios* (community courses), which were part of the *Consejo Nacional de Fomento Educativo* (National Council of Educational Development, CONAFE). These community courses were given by itinerant teachers called *instructores comunitarios* (community instructors) who circulated among villages in rural areas. CONAFE´s community instructors are not trained teachers, but middle school or high school graduates who teach for 1 or 2 years in communities where the population is too small to have an elementary school. After completing their community service, CONAFE instructors receive funding to cover their high school or college expenses. In the school year 2007–2008 this system had 11,234 schools and served 110,200 students in small communities without schools or access to distant education (Presidencia de la República, 2008).

Distance education. One significant finding of our research is the high percentage of students in the three states whose only option to finish basic education was through distance education. Of all the middle schools in the states, more than half were *telesecundarias*, a distance education alternative with a core curriculum taught through television. The model had three basic components: teachers, TV programming, and texts and lesson plans. All the programs were designed to teach basic concepts in an effective way, and the teachers were present to support the TV programming and engage the students in discussion. Schools could have one teacher, or two or three. Classes were held in small buildings with a satellite dish overhead. In the morning, an average of 20 students would arrive and begin by watching the first 15-minute television program, followed by a 35-minute teacher-student discussion on topics related to that program. The teacher was responsible for programming logistics and guiding the students with the accompanying text. *Telesecundarias* served thousands of students in the three states who lived in communities with 2,500 or fewer residents.

The number of young adolescents migrating with completed basic schooling has increased in recent years because of the fast expansion of the distance education system in rural areas. In the state of Puebla, in 2007 39% of students attended *telesecundaria*, which represented 65% of all middle schools in the state. In Oaxaca, distance education represented 70% of all middle schools in the state, and 39% of all students who graduated from basic education attended a *telesecundaria*. Finally, in Guerrero only 22% of students attended a *telesecundaria*, but this type of school represented 54% of all middle schools in the state (INEE, 2007a). The accelerated expansion of the system of *telesecundarias* created additional access to schooling for a greater number of students at a low cost. Evaluations done by INEE make clear, however, that the students getting this form of education show lower levels of academic achievement than those learning in other types of schools.

The Quality of the Schooling

As a quality indicator, we used the results of the 2005 Excale, a national test for all students enrolled in the 3rd year of *secundaria*. As Table 7.2 shows, the quality of education in *telesecundarias* was below average. Half of the students of *telesecundaria* taking the Excale received scores that showed their knowledge of Spanish was below the basic level of proficiency. Similarly, their knowledge of writing and math was below the lowest "acceptable" level (INEE, 2007a). Results of the PISA (Programme for International Student Assessment) study in 2003 show that 89% of *telesecundaria* students did not acquire basic literacy skills. In contrast, in public and private middle school in Mexico, the percentage

Table 7.2. Percentage of Students Enrolled in the 3rd Year of *Secundaria* (Middle School) Who Obtained Scores Below the Basic Level of Performance by Subject on Excale 2005

Type of Secundaria	Spanish	Writing	Math
Private	8.1	25.9	23.7
Public (General)	29.7	54.9	50.5
Public (Technical)	31.1	56.7	52
Telesecundaria	51.1	69.5	62.1
National	32.7	56	51.1

Source: INEE, 2007a.

of students without basic literacy skills is smaller (58%), which confirms that *telesecundaria* students show lower levels of academic achievement than students learning in formal school settings. Moreover, PISA 2003 reports that 94% of students who attended *telesecundarias* had insufficient math skills (INEE, 2007a).

Our examination of the school characteristics in Puebla, Oaxaca, and Guerrero aimed to contrast the educational system that immigrants experienced in their communities of origin with the system they encountered after their arrival in the United States. There were some similarities between the systems, such as the lack of adequate resources and the poor quality of instruction, as reported in assessments conducted by INEE in Mexico and school report cards in the United States. It can be argued that the systems in both countries, particularly for students of indigenous background, did not provide a clear and well implemented strategy for learning an additional language, Spanish when they were in Mexico and English when they arrived in the United States. In both of these settings immigrant students were part of a linguistically, ethnically, and economically segregated population. In Mexico, segregation was a result of the historical marginalization of indigenous communities that represented an important percentage of the population in these states. In the United States, immigrant students were part of the urban segregated communities where they were economically and linguistically at a disadvantage (Cortina, 2009a). The need for access to better schools, teachers, and curricula and to higher-quality resources was common to the communities of origin and destination alike.

Parents' Educational Attainment and Support of their Children

Educational attainment in Mexico. Researchers who study the impact of the level of parents' education on the school attainment and performance of their children have found that educated parents tend to have habits and practices that contribute to the better school performance of their children, such as the use of sophisticated vocabulary, access to technology, and help with assignments, among other support strategies (Suárez-Orozco, Suárez-Orozco, & Todorova, 2008). Also, educated parents tend to have books and other resources that improve their children's literacy skills. Even though all children might acquire literacy skills at school, those with educated parents have better opportunities to build up such skills (August & Shanahan, 2006).

In 2005, for Puebla, Oaxaca, and Guerrero, the percentage of school-aged children (ages 3–14) whose parents did not complete basic education was 26.4%, 35.3%, and 35.1%, respectively (INEE, 2007b). The averages for the three states were higher than the national average of 18.5%. Despite significant improvements in basic literacy over recent decades, the percentage of illiterate parents in the three states was above the national average. In 2005 the national average of illiterate parents was 13%, while in Puebla it was 21%; in Oaxaca, 29%; and in Guerrero, 32.6% (INEE, 2007b). The limited educational attainment of mothers whose children attended indigenous schools demonstrates the long-standing educational inequality that indigenous groups have experienced. As Table 7.3 shows, the highest percentage of mothers at the national level with less than basic education are mothers of children attending community courses or indigenous elementary schools.

In addition, the national statistics regarding educational attainment of the parents of students who attended *telesecundaria* show that 13.4% of mothers and 11.4% of fathers whose children attended a *telesecundaria* never attended school. Moreover, 66% of mothers and 63% of fathers whose children attended a *telesecundaria* only completed elementary school (INEE, 2007a).

Family support. Parents in the rural areas of Mexico tend to have only a few years of education but still get involved in the educational experiences of their children. In rural areas some teachers were members of the community, and even if they were not, they had frequent interaction with parents outside school. The smaller size of rural towns in Mexico allowed for more opportunities to discuss a child's performance in school.

Table 7.3. The Education of the Mothers of 3rd-Grade Students by Type of School, 2005 (Percentage)

Education Level	Community Courses	Indigenous Elementary School	Rural School	Public urban school	Private School	National Average
Less than Basic Education	77.3	64.5	51.7	22.9	4.7	30.1
Basic Education	17.1	19.9	27.6	27.6	12	25.7
High School	2.8	7	8	14.3	14.7	12.5
College	2.8	8.7	12.7	35.2	68.7	31.7

Source: INEE, 2007.

Immigrant parents have high educational aspirations for their children regardless of their own level of education, and they positively influence their children's academic performance (Portés & Rumbaut, 2001). Research shows that Mexican immigrant parents in particular have high educational aspirations for their children, motivate them to stay in school, provide constant moral support, and stress the importance of merit and hard work.

Several researchers argue that despite the aspirations of Latino parents, they often lack specific means and resources to help their children understand and navigate the schooling system. Moreover, the education of immigrant parents took place in remarkably different circumstances, resulting in unfamiliarity with the characteristics of the schooling systems in U.S. communities (Suárez-Orozco et al., 2008).

The difficulties that Mexican immigrant parents face in supporting their children are not related to a lack of effort and interest on their part, but rather are a result of structural impediments to their successful involvement in the education of their children in the U.S. education system. Some Mexican parents admit that their perceived isolation, undocumented status, lack of English proficiency, and demands of a low-wage job limit their capacity to assist their children with schoolwork. This is where social capital plays a role, understood as the networks established by family members and extended family.

Among the social resources that relatives provide are institutional support, moral guidance, discipline, emotional resiliency, and social networks. Immigrant Mexican families encourage students by giving advice (*consejos*); they tell their children to make the most of the opportunities afforded them. Immigrants also discuss with their children the hardships of working at unskilled jobs, as a way of encouraging them to get a good education that will lead to better-paying and more rewarding jobs.

Parental involvement in rural communities in Mexico is part of the commitment that these communities have to improving educational opportunities for their children. Such involvement to support the education of their children in their communities of origin is an important part of the background of Mexican immigrants in New York. In Mexico, parents and children often provide many of the maintenance services that the school needs, from painting to cleaning to participating in construction projects. Through these daily rituals parents are present in the schools, meet the teachers and principal, and are effectively supporting the education of their children.

Schools are beginning to take into account the nature of these social networks and are encouraging greater parental involvement, but they need to continue to promote programs to help Mexican immigrant parents understand the type of participation that is expected from them for the educational success of their children. Many schools across New York City attempt to include parents by reaching out through parent coordinators, who serve as important liaisons between the school and recently arrived families. With improved communication between schools and families, Mexican immigrant parents will have a better understanding that the school system relies significantly on their advocacy and participation.

MEXICAN YOUTH IN NEW YORK CITY SCHOOLS

As noted, many Mexican adolescents migrate to New York City by the time they have completed the 9th grade in Mexico, which is considered basic education. Once in New York, they are usually required to repeat the 9th grade, however. The combination of low economic status, the quality of the education provided to Mexican youth upon their arrival in the United States, and the challenges of the high school system as it is structured in the United States contribute to what scholars refer to as downward assimilation, which means that children of immigrants experience the opposite of upward mobility when they learn new cultural patterns and attempt to join United States social networks (Portés & Rumbaut, 2001, p. 59).

Further, students usually live in impoverished households where parents have no access to social welfare programs and where several working adults pool their wages to pay rent and send remittances to Mexico. Table 7.4 shows that in 2008 almost half of the Mexican population in New York City was younger than 24 years of age. Their numbers are rapidly increasing; these are the children of men and women from Mexico who came in search of better economic opportunities. Given these demographic patterns, it is important to consider their implications for educational practices in the city and to address the potential educational challenges for the Mexican population. While it is generally accepted that access to quality education is essential to help immigrants graduate from high school and improve their life chances, in fact the Mexican population in New York has the lowest average level of education among all the Latin American and Caribbean immigrant groups. The high school dropout rate in NYC for children of Mexican descent was 41% in 2009 (U.S. Census Bureau, 2011). Without doubt, the educational pathways for this population are characterized by a wide range of challenges.

Table 7.4 School-Age Mexican Children as a Percentage of Mexican Population in New York City, 1999 and 2008

Age Group	1999	2008
5 or younger	12.1	11.3
6 to 14	13.5	15.3
15 to 19	6.9	7.0
Total School Age	**32.5**	**33.5**
20 to 24	14.5	12.7
25 to 29	14	15.1
30 to 34	13.4	13.2
35 to 39	10.1	9.0
40 to 44	5.8	6.8
45 to 64	8.4	8.7
65 and older	1.3	1.2
Mean	25.4	25.3
Median	25	26

Source: Information compiled by Cortina, based on U.S. Census Bureau (1999 and 2008).

Placement and Persistence

Mexican immigrant students are tracked and often segregated in programs in New York City schools that lack relevant academic content. The tracking systems based on English-language proficiency promote a monolithic culture; exclude students' histories, experiences, and values; and place them into programs that limit their access to academic content courses (Cortina, 2009b). Students are provided with an education that will not allow them to navigate the mainstream society. Moreover, the students' background is usually ignored. Ángela Valenzuela (1999) argues that American schools tend to divest Mexican students of their culture and language, eroding rather than enhancing their chances to succeed.

Policies and Standards

The accountability policy in the high school system contributes in significant ways to the poor educational achievement of Mexican immigrant youth. Their educational aspirations are facing a new roadblock with accountability policies implemented in 1996 by the New York State Board of Regents to create standardized measures of educational achievement: students must now pass five Regents examinations to graduate and earn a high school diploma. Their test scores on the state's Regents exams determine the type of diploma that students can receive. Students who score within the 55–64 range in specific content areas receive a Local Diploma, those scoring between 65 and 84 qualify for a Regents Diploma, and those scoring above 85 qualify for an Advanced Regents Diploma. In addition to the yearly assessments required under the federal No Child Left Behind Act (NCLB), within New York State these new examinations work to the disadvantage of immigrant students who are making a transition into U.S. society. The high-stakes accountability regime has resulted in a spike in dropout rates, particularly noticeable in the dramatic exit of students in 10th grade when they are required to take the Regents examinations (De Jesús & Vasquez, 2005).

Beyond the impact of these state and federal educational requirements, the characteristics of the schools that immigrant children attend constrain their chances of educational success. At the beginning of the 2003–2004 school year, 3,681 Mexican students were registered in the 10 high schools with the largest Mexican enrollment in New York City (Cortina, 2009a). They did not take classes in the general education track, but in auxiliary services programs, and 83% of them became school dropouts before the end of the academic year (Cortina, 2009a,

p. 124). While in school, they attended class with other students from minority backgrounds, had no access to the most qualified teachers in the school, and lacked peer networks that could support their academic work. Also, students of Mexican origin were not taught in their native language, which means they did not experience a smooth transition to education in English. Most Mexican students were tracked into English Language Learner (ELL) courses, which isolated them from the rest of the school and removed them from academic courses.

As Table 7.5 shows, the education system in Mexico contributes to the education of the labor force in the United States. In the case of the transnational students, both educational systems are shaping a shared future. Their low level of education and limited labor market skills upon arrival keep Mexican immigrants concentrated in service occupations; a quarter of them work in restaurants and food services. Approximately four-fifths of the Mexican population is in the service sector overall, concentrated in the lowest-paid occupations in construction, restaurants, dry cleaners, janitorial services, and so on.

Table 7.5. Occupations of Mexicans in New York City, 1999 and 2008

Occupation	1999	2008
Non-service Occupation		
Managers/Professionals	6.8	7.5
Technical, Sales, & Administrative Support Occupations	12.5	15.9
Service Occupation		
Private Household	5.5	2.3
Protective	0.9	1.3
Food Preparation/Service	22.6	25.8
Health Services	1.8	3.0
Cleaning & Building Occupations	4.1	10.8
Personal	1.4	1.1
Precision, Production, Crafts, & Repair Occupations	8.2	11.2
Operators, Fabricators, Laborers, Machine Operators, Assemblers, & Inspectors	18.4	14.7
Transportation & Material Moving Occupations	6.7	7.0
Handlers, Equipment Cleaners, Helpers, & Laborers	10.8	3.9

Source: Information compiled by Cortina, based on the U.S. Census Bureau (1999 and 2008).

In sum, the resources available to Mexican parents and students are lacking and do not reinforce their school performance. These conditions harden, and even block, access to and completion of high school and college. For New York City, previous research by Cortina (2009a) on the graduation rate of the high school cohort of 1995–2002 shows that only 36% of the Mexican-born students who entered high school in 1995 were able to graduate after 7 years. When they moved to the next academic level, the community college, they were not better off. Community colleges serving the Latino population predominantly offer remedial education that delays students' possibilities of graduation. Clearly, school abandonment and dropout rates are serious challenges facing the Mexican community in the city.

RECOMMENDATIONS FOR COLLABORATION BETWEEN THE UNITED STATES AND MEXICO AND FOR IMPROVED EDUCATIONAL PRACTICE

In this chapter we discussed the schooling background of immigrants from the Mexican states of Puebla, Oaxaca, and Guerrero to identify the challenges that students face when attempting to succeed in schools in the United States. The differences between their sending and receiving community include the type and extent of parental involvement in their education, which we mentioned earlier, an urban compared with a rural setting, the language of instruction, teaching practices, and the programs available to them in United States schools. If adequate preparations are not made through policy and educational practice, the differences between the two countries can have a negative impact on the ability of these students to fulfill their academic aspirations.

For example, many immigrant students from Puebla, Oaxaca, and Guerrero migrate from rural areas to urban schools in New York City. Once in the United States, parents, as a result of their low literacy levels, might have limited ways to assist their children with schoolwork and with the challenges presented by such a different schooling system in a city like New York. American schools also need to be aware that some Mexican immigrant students from rural areas are not native Spanish speakers; Spanish is the second language in many indigenous communities in Mexico.

The quality of schools in these three Mexican states, and the fact that immigrants from the rural towns within them most probably finished middle school through distance education, make it clear that these students did not attend the best schools in Mexico. As we have shown, students in *telesecundarias,* a distance education alternative, tend to obtain the lowest scores on Mexico's standardized tests. Despite these problems, Mexican students are taught to be respectful toward adults and teachers, and they learn to value education and tend to have high educational aspirations for themselves (Valenzuela, 1999). Once they arrive in the United States, students enter schools that lack adequate resources and offer poor-quality instruction.

It is necessary for policymakers in Mexico and the United States to design and implement education programs that effectively assist transnational students. In New York City and other locations where immigrants constitute a large proportion of the student population, the education system needs to invest in the professional development of teachers and provide them with the instructional resources they need to build on the strengths of these students and help them with the transition to the American school system.

In the United States, Mexican immigrant students are likely to attend a school whose environment is unsafe, with negative effects on them ranging from psychological distress to racial, linguistic, and economic discrimination. Newcomer immigrant children are also unlikely to encounter innovative English language learning strategies (Cortina, 2009a; Suárez-Orozco et al., 2008). Therefore, schools that work with Mexican students need to provide social supports—such as counseling, mentoring, and a positive school climate—to help students overcome academic challenges. In addition, providing teachers with information about the strengths of the Mexican culture and habits, and of those of other countries of origin, can diminish the low academic expectations that some of them might have. School administrators and teachers need to realize that most Mexican youth in high school also have jobs that are close to full-time. Education policy needs to promote flexible ways of supporting their school completion while they work, since their family's economic circumstances do not allow them to forgo employment.

There is also a need in United States schools to consider a broader definition of family, recognizing the extended family as a social network available to Mexican and other Latino children. These networks are strong support systems for immigrant students as they maintain valuable connections to their culture through the way they organize their experience in the U.S. Extensive participation within their networks gives students agents for support, and schools may benefit from considering these relationships as an extension of efforts to involve parents in school.

A roundtable of educational experts on how poor immigrants are negotiating the European educational systems in comparison with the U.S.' system was held at Teachers College in [2009]. Although scholars investigated different countries, there was ultimately unanimous agreement around the impediments to a high-quality education for immigrants and ineffective educational practices to counterbalance them (see Alba & Waters, 2011, for findings from the study).

Immigrant students are well aware that language differences have become language hierarchies that deeply affect them. They feel marginalized, alienated, and unchallenged by academic offerings. Schools can implement a variety of changes to foster their achievement and assimilation. Our recommendations below are well aligned with the goals of this current volume.

Bi-National Collaboration

Bi-national collaboration is an effective strategy to increase the knowledge and exposure of everyone involved in the education of transnational students. Existing programs such as PROBEM, a bi-national program between Mexico and the United States that focuses on important goals such as teacher exchanges, help to ease the transitions from one school system to the other. To better serve transnational students, schools, nongovernmental organizations (NGOs), and researchers need to disseminate resources about school enrollment and completion as well as culture and pedagogy in both countries. An example of an effective resource is *The Handbook for Educators Who Work with Children of Mexican Origin*, a CD with practical advice and relevant background information on Mexican schools for educators in the U.S. (2009).

Institution of an Integrated and Relevant Curriculum

Using a relevant curriculum is effective because it provides a space for students to recognize their own voices and gives them tools to develop meaningful resources from their learning experiences. When students are exposed to content that mirrors something familiar, they are better able to make sense of subject matter, especially when it makes visible connections to their own backgrounds. In thinking about critical approaches to curriculum, educators are likely to be more attuned to those whose voices are being privileged and whose history is taught, but all students are collaborators in the educational system and they must be allowed to help build their own learning goals.

Implementation of an Equitable School Structure

We discussed above the implications of having a school structure that leads to tracking and segregation. Structures that favor programs such as English pullout programs, where students are taken away for large periods of class and taught English in often isolated settings, are largely responsible for the lack of rigorous education the participants receive. New school configurations, where students learn side by side with their peers, and dual-language programs, which serve both native English and native Spanish speakers, have proven to be effective not only in raising academic performance but in legitimizing students' native culture. There is evidence that structural features of schools make a difference for immigrant students. Studies on comparative scores of PISA report that the disadvantages in achievement among immigrant children are significant across countries (Alba & Waters, 2011, p. 15).

Development of Innovative School Partnerships

New York City is a great laboratory for schools to partner with their communities. Connections with museums, cultural centers, NGOs, and grassroots movements are common strategies in some schools that are striving to provide wider opportunities for their students to integrate into the local social and cultural environment. A science program at the American Museum of Natural History, for example, provides middle school students with the opportunity to work at the museum for a whole year while learning from curators and educators and creating connections with their science modules at school. These partnerships need not happen in New York City only, for the foundation of their success rests largely in schools' interest in providing learning opportunities for their students that go beyond the classroom and bring relevant, dynamic questions and experiences to their lives.

Creation of a Caring School Climate

Students have frequently emphasized the role that their teachers play in encouraging or discouraging them in their studies. Indeed, the difficulties that students face when coming from Mexico to a new country, described in this chapter, can be largely ameliorated by a caring school climate. A caring climate makes a powerful difference in the way immigrant students can manage their transition, especially because in Mexico students' relationships with teachers tend to be close, often driven by teachers' strong sense of vocation to protect vulnerable populations. A caring school climate starts with the interest of principals, teachers, and staff in supporting all students and providing resources to help their families become involved and participate in their children's educational development.

Implementation of Resourceful Multimodal Academic Assessment

In the current climate of standardized testing, students are lost in a system that tries to capture their learning in a manner that doesn't completely reveal the progress they make, particularly for those who are learning a new language. Multimodal assessments call for a variety of measures in assessing student learning, for example, integrated portfolios in which students display their body of work; directed products, such as documentaries, photography exhibitions, and podcasts; and even involvement in community projects. All these nontraditional types of assessment provide opportunities to assess the way these students are making connections and bringing content into their own lives and experience.

CONCLUSION

In sum, we argue that teachers who are aware of the cultural backgrounds and previous academic experiences of their students can build on those assets, and on their social networks, to improve their performance in school. Linking the content of the curriculum in U.S. schools with the knowledge and practice of the teachers in Mexican immigrants' original community can significantly improve their ability to learn in their new community. This connection is the basis for an effective binational approach, established through a dialogue between both nations that will best address the educational challenges of these transnational communities. We suggest that effective pedagogies for children of Mexican origin share a common core of knowledge, skills, and dispositions: knowledge of second-language acquisition theory and pedagogy, use of culturally relevant curricula, and validation of the students' home language and culture, among others. Understanding how educational systems assist with the transition of students may help both countries define success for their shared populations.

Oscar, the teenage student quoted at the beginning of this chapter, told his story about coming to the United States with courage and dignity. He was proud to report the efforts of his teachers and peers to support him through his education. For every Oscar who has been supported and guided by his teachers, thousands of students are struggling alone every day to make sense of their new environment in school and at home. The task at hand is clear. Teachers and policymakers, schools and parents: everyone must be held accountable for providing an inclusive, effective, and academically challenging setting for immigrant students. These students have been considered underachievers for far too long. If adequately challenged, they can demonstrate brilliance in every American classroom.

REFERENCES

Alba, R. D., & Waters, M. C. (Eds.) (2011). *The next generation: Immigrant youth in a comparative perspective.* New York: NYU Press.

August, D., & Shanahan, T. (2006). *Developing literacy in second-language learners: Report of the National Literacy Panel on Language-Minority Children and Youth.* Mahwah, NJ: Lawrence Erlbaum Associates.

Bergad, L. W. (2008). *Mexicans in New York City, 2007: An update.* New York: Graduate Center, City University of New York.

Coleman, J.S. (1988). Social Capital in the Creation of Human Capital. *American Journal of Sociology, 94,* S95–S120.

Cortés, S. (2003). Migrants from Puebla in the 1990s. In R. Cortina & M. Gendreau (Eds.), *Immigrants and schooling: Mexicans in New York.* New York: Center for Migration Studies.

Cortina, R. (2009a). Immigrant youth in high school: Understanding educational outcomes for students of Mexican origin. In T. Wiley, J. S. Lee, & R. Rumberger (Eds.), *The education of language minority immigrants in the United States* (pp. 113–135). Clevedon, UK: Multilingual Matters.

Cortina, R. (2009b). *The education of Latinos in Northern Manhattan schools.* NYLAR net (Policy Paper). Albany, NY: State University of New York.

De Jesús, A., & Vasquez, D. W. (2005). *Exploring the Latino education profile and pipeline for Latinos in New York State.* Albany, NY: State University of New York.

Dirección General de Educación Superior para Profesionales de la Educación. (2004). *Los Retos de la Formación Docente en la Educación Básica: La Atención Educativa con Pertinencia Cultural y Lingüística de la Población Indígena en Primaria.* Ciudad de México: Secretaría de Educación Pública. Retrieved from http://www.dgespe.sep.gob.mx/planes/leprib/campos

Instituto para Mexicanos en el Exterior (IME). (2007). Retrieved from: http://www.ime.gob.mx/

INEE. (2007a). *La educación para poblaciones en contextos vulnerables. Informe Anual.* México, DF: Instituto Nacional para la Evaluación de la Educación.

INEE. (2007b) *Panorama Educativo de México. Indicadores del Sistema Educativo Nacional 2007. Informe Anual.* México: Instituto Nacional para la Evaluación de la Educación. Retrieved from: http://www.inee.

edu.mx/images/stories/Publicaciones/Panorama_educativo/2007/Partes/panorama200706.pdf

Instituto Nacional para la Evaluación de la Educación (INEE). (2008). *Panorama Educativo Mexicano 2008. Reporte General.* México: Author.

INEGI. (2010a). *Censo de población y vivienda 2010.* Retrieved from: http://www.inegi.org.mx/sistemas/olap/

INEGI. (2010b). *Mapa temático: Alumnos egresados en Primaria Indígena.* Mexico: Author.

Instituto para Mexicanos en el Exterior (IME). (2010). *Estadísticas de Mexicanos en el Exterior.* Retrieved from: http://www.ime.gob.mx/

Mexican Consulate in New York City. (2000). *Características de la comunidad Mexicana en Nueva York.* Informe General. New York: Author.

Portés, A., & Rumbaut, R. G. (2001). *Legacies: The story of the immigrant second generation.* Berkeley: University of California Press.

Presidencia de la República. (2008). *Segundo informe de gobierno.* Retrieved from: http://segundo.informe.gob.mx/anexo_estadistico/pdf/estadisticas_nacionales/igualdad_de_oportunidades/2_3.pdf

Secretaría de Educación Pública (SEP). (2009). *Documento rector de la Dirección General de Educación Indígena: Para concebir el futuro en el presente.* Mexico: Author. Retrieved online: http://basica.sep.gob.mx/dgei/pdf/inicio/conocenos/documentoRector.pdf

Suárez-Orozco, C., Suárez-Orozco, M., & Todorova, I. (2008). *Learning a new land: Immigrant students in American society.* Cambridge, MA: Harvard University Press.

Teachers College, Columbia University. (2009). *The voices of NYC Mexican Youth. Inside TC, 4,* 14–15. Retrieved from: http://www.tc.edu/news.htm?articleId=7250

University of North Carolina. (2009). *The handbook for educators who work with children of Mexican origins,* (4th ed.). Chapel Hill, NC: Author.

U.S. Census Bureau. (1999). New York City Housing and Vacancy Survey. Retrieved from: http://www.census.gov/hhes/www/housing/nychvs/nychvs.html

U.S. Census Bureau. (2007). American Community Survey. Table S0201. Selected Population Profile in the United States, New York City, New York (Mexican). Washington, DC: Author.

U.S. Census Bureau. (2008). New York City Housing and Vacancy Survey. Retrieved from: http://www.census.gov/hhes/www/housing/nychvs/nychvs.html

U.S. Census Bureau. (2011). *American Community Survey.* Retrieved from: http://factfinder2.census.gov/faces/nav/jsf/pages/index.xhtml

Valenzuela, A. (1999). *Subtractive schooling: U.S.-Mexican youth and the politics of caring.* Albany, NY: SUNY Press.

CHAPTER 8

Understanding American
Mexican Children

Victor Zúñiga and Edmund T. Hamann

In 1997, when we first met while independently conducting field work in Whitfield County, Georgia, and its county seat, Dalton, we heard from local principals and teachers that Latino students sometimes "disappeared" from the schools. Most of these who disappeared were immigrant students from Mexico and other Central American countries, students who had arrived suddenly in local schools while accompanying their parents who found jobs in the carpet and poultry mills of the area (Hamann, 2003; Hernández-León & Zúñiga, 2000; Zúñiga & Hernández-León, 2009). The "disappearances" led one of us (Hamann, 2001) to develop a concept–the sojourner student–and draw from it various pedagogical/ political conclusions. Using a few empirical facts–like the reported "disappearances" and survey results showing that about a quarter of Mexican newcomer parents were not confident that they would still be living in northwestern Georgia 3 years hence–but mainly conjecturing from a range of literature on transnational migration, Hamann hypothesized that, akin to the presence of students in the United States with prior Mexican school experience, there might be students in Mexican schools with prior U.S. school experience. Very few scholars in the United States and none in Mexico previously reported that issue. One exception was Trueba (1999), who pointed out that some Mexican parents living in the United States decided to send their adolescent sons and daughters to Mexico to avoid some real or hypothetical risks associated with high school dynamics in the United States. Also, Mahler (1998) asked about the transnational experiences of international migrants' children. Thus, the fact and recognition that American schools host sojourner students in their classrooms was the starting point of what became a larger and still ongoing research project in Mexican schools a few years after our Georgian experience.

Fourteen years have passed since our first peripheral encounters with the students who were moving transnationally from one school system to another. Now we believe we have a better and more complicated idea of student movement between the United States and Mexico than we could articulate in that first sojourner student article (Hamann, 2001). The purposes of this chapter are, first, to sketch this more detailed picture of "American Mexican" students encountered in Mexican schools, and second, to summarize some of our main findings on that emergent schooling process. Finally, we will identify the most important, but not necessarily obvious, educational challenges that teachers, school officials, and educational policymakers have to face in the present and the near future in both the American and Mexican schools if they are to be responsive to these transnationally mobile students.

GATHERING DATA

The "disappeared" students from the U.S. schools were later found (or at least many of them were). We found them in Mexico by conducting surveys on representative samples of schools and students in four Mexican states. With support from the *Consejo Nacional de Ciencias y Tecnologia* (CONACYT) and later the *Secretaría de Educación Pública*, we began in Nuevo León (2004), continued in Zacatecas (2005), then Puebla (2009), and most recently conducted surveys in Jalisco in 2010. In each state, surveys were conducted in November or December through visits to classrooms.

Collectively, in these four states, the *educación básica* (1st to 9th grades) enrollment was approximately 3,300,000 students attending about 21,000 schools. Our four representative samples tallied 53,998 students. Most sampled students responded to a written questionnaire, except the younger ones (1st to 3rd grades). Given the fact that the younger ones would have less skill reading and writing and thus could not reliably respond to written questionnaires, we decided to organize a kind of collective oral interview for students in these grades that began with the following question: Who has studied in a U.S. school?

Complementing this quantitative approach, we conducted on-location observations at more than 100 schools from our quantitative sample, where we interviewed more than 140 students and 40 teachers. Typically these returns for observation and interviews were carried out in the spring months just after the November/December surveying.

Most of these interviews were transcribed, resulting in over 1,000 pages of qualitative data to review and code. The quantitative surveys, our in-depth interviews with students and teachers, and our on-site observations constitute the sources of data we present in this chapter.

As a final introductory note, we should add that our research projects, first in Georgia, then in those four states in Mexico, have always used an inductive approach. We have learned from our interviews, surveys, observations, and discussions with educational actors step by step. In contrast to this step-by-step growth, the following sections offer a synthesis of our investigative journey.

SOME MAIN FINDINGS

From Sojourner Students to Transnational Children

The transnationally dislocated (and dislocatable) sojourner students do exist. We found them attending classrooms in Mexican schools. They told us they had attended U.S. schools in Arizona, Arkansas, California, Georgia, Nebraska, New York, Oregon, Texas, and 31 other states. We found 982 students with school experience in American schools who represented 1.8% of our sample. As a result, we estimated that there were about 69,500 students with U.S. school backgrounds in the four Mexican state school systems we sampled. Correlating the proportions of transnational students with the classification of international migration density that Mexico's census system already calculates at the *municipio* (county) level, we were then able to estimate that 420,000 transnational students were enrolled in Mexico's national *educación básica* system (1st to 9th grades) as the second decade of the 21st century began.

Almost 4 out of 10 of those students with transnational school experiences were born in the United States, the rest, in Mexico. Simplifying the trajectories (and momentarily ignoring some revealing detail), we can say that most of the students born in the United States began their schooling in the United States and then they went to Mexico. The opposite happened with those who were born in Mexico. Most started in Mexican schools; then they attended American ones before returning to Mexican schools.

How should we refer to these students? Referencing the long-standing settler-versus-sojourner debate that has transpired in migration studies over the last decades, Hamann (2001) had identified them as *sojourners*. By doing this, he wanted to emphasize that biographically responsive schooling with these students would emphasize their past experiences and likely future need to not only code-switch (between languages) but to "culture switch" (Clemens, 1999), from one type of literacy to another, from one social context to another. His concern was to alert American educators to the special pedagogical condition of transient students who have particular needs (e.g., to be bilingual, to develop multiple literacies, and to negotiate geographically dislocated lives). Ultimately, sojourners "are neither 'here' nor 'there' but at once *both* 'here' and 'there'" (Smith, 1994, p. 17). The first analysis developed by Hamann had the purpose of discussing the common belief of American teachers that immigrant students are always and undoubtedly permanent settlers and, in consequence, what they need is to be prepared for a future life, as adults, in that specific local society where they are newly living. Critiquing those beliefs as sometimes misplaced, Hamann pointed out the paradoxical responsibility American teachers have when they recognize the fragmented trajectories of some of their students (i.e., the possibility that they would continue their schooling in the country of origin of their parents). The dilemma for the American teachers was fascinating: how should they educate students who were attending American schools to be successful if/when they continued their education in Mexico (or other Central American countries), as a hard-to-identify portion surely would? More abstractly, how should the schooling provided *here* pertain to a student's future navigation of *there*, with *there* perhaps referencing more than one locale, more than one country, and more than one life phase?

From our first encounters in 2004 and 2005 with "sojourner students" in Nuevo León and Zacatecas, particularly when we had personal contacts with them, we witnessed that often they were bilingual and had deep experiences in being educated in American schools. Many felt as attached to the Mexican community where we had encountered them as to one or more locales in the United States. Most (75%) wished to return to continue their education in the United States. An important proportion of them (36%) identified themselves as "Mexican Americans," around 20% for those born in Mexico and 60% for those born in the United States (Hamann & Zúñiga, 2011). *Sojourner* may have described the biography of many of them, but it captured the cosmology of these students less well. So we decided a more neutral descriptive label was *transnational students* (Zúñiga & Hamann, 2009; Zúñiga et al., 2008). These students had moved transnationally, and that fact had implications for how they had and would continue to negotiate school. While it was important earlier to emphasize the hazards of imagining these students as "settled," the label *transnational* was, we hoped, less charged.

A recent analysis of our databases and interviews showed us the significance of three conditions that affect the lives, and school trajectories, of transnational children.

Legal status. The first condition (and the one we examined least) was the legal status of their parents and themselves while they lived in the United States. Our survey intentionally did not ask for the legal status of the respondents when they lived in the United States. However, we included one question that allows us indirectly to approach that issue: *Why did you and your family decide to return to Mexico?* Nonetheless, during interviews we had some transnational students who volunteered that immigration enforcement actions in the United States explained their returns to Mexico.

U.S. immigration enforcement had substantial consequences on some transnational students' vision of the past and their definition of their future (Zúñiga & Hamann, forthcoming). Transnational students who experienced legal restrictions on themselves and/or on their parents were more prone to develop pessimistic visions of their future lives; they were less sure how to use for their own benefit what they learned and the competencies they acquired from American schools. That was particularly true for those who suffered, directly or indirectly, incarceration or deportation of their parents.

More complex was the situation of students born in the United States whose parents (both or one of them) were undocumented migrants still living in the United States. When we encountered them in Mexico, such students usually lived with grandparents and/or one of their parents, while the other parent, siblings, and/or extended family continued to labor in the United States. These students knew they were citizens in the United States (because of birthplace), knew they would have rights there as adults, but also knew their parents (or one of them) were at risk of being deported. Such students faced an odd sense of welcome/unwelcome in relation to the United States (Gitlin et al., 2003). The country that might play a key role in their future opportunities (and that may have been a crucial economic lifeline through remittances) was also the cause of the geographic bifurcation of their family. Particularly in Puebla we heard accounts from U.S.-born students (who ostensibly had the protection of American citizenship) who had been sent to Mexico to protect them from possible traumas that could be associated with their parents' detention and/or deportation (Sánchez García, Hamann, & Zúñiga, in press). Such students experientially overlap with the "left behind" children whom Dreby (2010) has so evocatively described–students who live with grandparents or extended family in Mexico while their parents (and sometimes younger siblings whom they have never met) live in the United States.

Not all U.S.-born transnational students whose parents lacked U.S. documentation were in Mexico because of enforcement regimes, however. Some children had neither a direct experience with deportation nor a fear related to an absent parent's legal vulnerability in the United States. Like U.S.-born transnational students' whose parents illegally worked or had worked in the United States, this subcategory could often aptly be referred to as "double national." For this type of transnational student, it made sense to be (or aspire to be) bilingual, to have spent years in the United States, and to appreciate several traits of their American experience. They could count on a network spread across two countries (of aunts, uncles, cousins, friends, etc.). They felt they belonged to a "transnational community" (Guerra, 1998), a territory and a society divided by national border, but that transcended that border, too, as they could cross when they (or their parents) decided to. Such students seemed more capable than their transnational Mexican peers (students born in Mexico who had lived in the United States without authorization before returning to Mexico) to negotiate the bi-national opportunity structures and prospects for affiliation and attachment.

Early school experiences. The second salient condition concerned the country in which transnational students began their schooling, as the first school years became a hallmark and a reference for the following phases of the schooling process (Hamann & Zúñiga, 2011). Early school experiences were associated with the affiliation chosen by transnational students. In our two first surveys (Nuevo León and Zacatecas school systems) we asked the students to self-identify with one of three alternatives: (a) Mexican, (b) Mexican American, or (c) American. Then, for the Puebla and Jalisco surveys, we added indigenous identities to our list of possibilities. Especially in the case of Puebla, one of these identities–i.e., Mixteco–proved particularly popular.

Table 8.1 shows the relationship between early school experience and the identity affiliation selected by the students. Four findings should be highlighted. One is the existence of a few exceptional cases of students who started their schooling in Mexican schools but still declared themselves "American." Second, the hyphenated Mexican American identity is well accepted even for the students who started the school in Mexico. Third, the American affiliation was more frequent for the students who began school in the United States, but even for them, it is exceptional.

Finally, we have the case of students who declare themselves to be Mixtecos (or Indians). This affiliation was much more frequent for Puebla students who were born in the United States and less commonly selected by those born in Puebla. Perhaps for those transnational students an ethnic identity that did not correspond with a nation-state (and with a school system that did not expect or accommodate their biography) was particularly appealing.

Years of U.S. schooling. A third salient factor was the amount of time spent in the United States. Some of the students in our sample attended only 1 or 2 school years in American schools, while others had spent almost all their school life in the United States. We present the distribution of the percentage of U.S. schooling years of transnational students from our four samples in Figure 8.1. Overall, a majority of the students in our sample of transnational students had spent more than a quarter of their school careers in one or more U.S. schools.

As expected, the percentage of schooling spent in the United States is associated with the student's self-reported native language. For instance, in Jalisco, where we met the largest number and proportion of transnational students, we compared the students with a high percentage of their school years in the United States (75% or more) with those who spent less than one-quarter of their school life in the United States. Only 23% of the first group stated that Spanish was their first language versus 67% for the latter group.

From Transnational Students to American Mexican Children

As already noted, through our surveys we met 982 transnational students; 122 of them were 1st-, 2nd-, and 3rd-graders, while the other 860 were attending 4th to 9th grades. Additionally, we encountered 460 students who had never attended school in the United States but who were born there. Let's listen to one of those children, Karla, whom we interviewed (in Spanish) in Lagos de Moreno, Jalisco, in February, 2011. She was enrolled in 7th grade (i.e., the first year of *secundaria*):

> *Interviewer 1*: When did you come to Lagos, Karla?
> *Karla*: I came here when I was almost four.
> *Interviewer 1*: Wow, when you were very young!
> *Karla*: Then I went back to Los Angeles when I was seven. I stayed there only for three months just before I got to the elementary school here in Lagos. I was there just to visit my uncles, aunts, and cousins. I did not go to the school in Los Angeles.

Table 8.1. Affiliation by the School System Where the Transnational
Students Started Education

Started School	Mexican	Mexican American	American	Mixteco/ Other Indigenous	Total
In Mexico	68%	27%	1%	4%	100% (187)
In the U.S.	48%	39%	7%	6%	100% (516)
Total	53%	36%	5.5%	5.5%	100% (703)

Source: Nuevo León (2004), Zacatecas (2005), Puebla (2009), and Jalisco (2010) surveys. Universidad de Monterrey databases of transnational students attending 4th to 9th grade in Mexican schools (*n* = 860).

Figure 8.1. Four State Student Sample Distribution of Total Years
in U.S. Schools

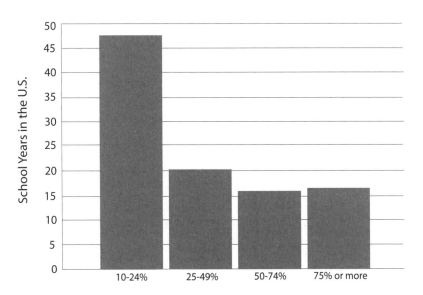

Source: Nuevo León (2004), Zacatecas (2005), Puebla (2009), and Jalisco (2010) surveys. Universidad de Monterrey databases of transnational students attending 4th to 9th grade in Mexican schools (*n* = 860).

Interviewer 1: So, you never attended school in the U.S., did you?

Karla: No, I didn't.

Interviewer 2: But you were born there, weren't you?

Karla: Yes.

Interviewer 1: So, all of your schooling has been here in Lagos.

Karla: Yes.

Interviewer 1: And your parents, where are they?

Karla: Here, in Lagos.

————————————

Interviewer 1: How many members are in your family?

Karla: My dad, my mom, two sisters, and I.

Interviewer 2: And were your sisters born in Los Angeles, too?

Karla: No, I'm the only one who was born in Los Angeles.

Interviewer 1: How do you feel? Do you feel Mexican or American?

Karla: No, Mexican!

Interviewer 1: Oh yeah? Why?

Karla: Because I've been living all my life here.

Interviewer 1: Do you speak English?

Karla: No.

————————————

Interviewer 2: Do you ever want to study in the U.S.?

Karla: Yes.

Interviewer 1: Are you sure? What would you want to study there?

Karla: Tourism or hotel management.

Interviewer 1: Do you have an idea where you want to study in the U.S.?

Karla: I would like, well, I've been in Los Angeles, I would like to study in Los Angeles or in Las Vegas.

Interviewer 1: In Las Vegas . . . do you have members of your family in Las Vegas?

Karla: Uncles. There are my father's cousins. I also have other uncles, my mother's brothers. But they are in Chicago. I also have my cousins in Los Angeles.

Interviewer 2: Do you visit regularly with your family in Los Angeles?

Karla: No . . . because when I was little I could do this, but now I don't think I can because I don't have a Mexican passport. I have an American passport, so I can go there, but then I couldn't come back.

Interviewer 1: No, you can enter [to Mexico] as an American. Or you can get the Mexican passport.

Karla: Well, my godmother, who lives there [Los Angeles], wants me to go next summer for vacation, and she told me she is going to get my passport (from Mexico).
Interviewer 1: Do you know the nationalities you have?
Karla: Nationalities? How?
Interviewer 1: You are American, aren't you?
Karla: Yeah.
Interviewer 2: Because you were born there. Are you also Mexican?
Karla: Yes, because my father and my mother are Mexicans.
Interviewer 1: So, you know it very well!
Karla: Yep.
Interviewer 1: Where will you want to live when you grow up?
Karla: There, in the United States, in Los Angeles.

Whereas Karla had not been socialized in U.S. schools as were her transnational peers at her school, the United States formed an important part of her imagined (or future) social world. We had decided to interview her because the principal thought Karla was one of the transnational students at the school, though Karla did not speak any English. She had spent less than 4 years of her life in Los Angeles, nearly all as a young child, other than the 3 months she spent visiting her extended family. Even so, it was very clear to Karla that she was legally an American and, consequently, that she had the right to reside in the United States.

Paradoxically, it was unclear to her, before our interview, that she was also a legal Mexican (though she immediately identified culturally as a Mexican). She even thought that she would have trouble getting back into Mexico because she lacked a Mexican passport, until the interviewers explained to her that she had the right to also have a Mexican passport. She knew she had two nationalities. Although she identified as Mexican, she anticipated an adult life in the United States, which sets up two long-standing questions of our research: How well do Mexican schools prepare students for adult life in U.S. society? And how *should they* do so?

Our surveys found 460 students born in the United States without school experience in the American schools. In addition, we encountered 366 other U.S. citizens by birthplace who had spent several years in the American schools. Together they represent 1.5% of our sample. We estimate that as of this writing (late 2011) there are approximately 50,000 children in Jalisco, Puebla, Zacatecas, and Nuevo León imagining their futures as adults in the United States like Karla did. The total tally of U.S. citizens (by birth) might be around 330,000 students in the whole

Mexican school system. These students are double nationals, and many know how profitable/helpful that could be.

The case of Karla is not exceptional. She only reminded us (thanks to the principal's mix-up) what we had already observed before in Puebla, Zacatecas, and Nuevo León. Double national children are often aware of their rights. They more readily imagine themselves doing their vocational or professional studies in U.S. colleges and know well that they can count on their parents', grandparents', uncles', aunts', or cousins' support for achieving this goal. Those findings explain another terminological change on our part: why we have supplemented our *transnational students* label with a partially overlapping one: *American Mexican children*. The latter encompass a new generation of Americans who are being socialized in Mexican schools. Many of these American Mexican children do not culturally identify as Americans (there is little in their Mexican schooling that would reinforce such an identification); still, they are aware of their legal identity and its ensuing implications for their future economic security and place of residence.

(IN)VISIBLE EDUCATIONAL CHALLENGES

Transforming from Invisibility to Visibility

From our earliest field work in Georgia and then in Nuevo León, we have learned just how invisible the geographies and cosmologies of these *sojourner-transnational-American-Mexican* students are. In American schools they automatically become *English Learners, English as Second Language Students, Limited English Proficient Students,* and/or whatever other linguistic label du jour is applied that obscures much of the rest of who they are. Sometimes, these students also get counted as *Latinos* or *Hispanics*. Sometimes, if their parents are involved in American food production, they are (in the United States) labeled as *Migrant students*, but this references a particular federal program that is a synonym for poverty and mobility more than for transnationalism. Rarely are they seen as *Mexican American* or *American Mexican* children.

Thus, we understand the principal's reaction in a North Carolina school when one of us visited in March 2005. It experienced a sudden demographic transformation over just 2 years. In that community, the turkey-processing industry had attracted thousands of Latino workers and their families. The principal did not know what to do. When we visited we saw a school with more than 40% of students speaking Mexican Spanish in the cafeteria, but the only language aide the school had found was a teacher who came from Spain as part of an agreement signed by one Spanish university and the school district. As expected, the young teacher from Spain did not have much of an idea as to what to do. She had never been to Mexico. The Mexican American students had fun hearing the Spanish and the English accent of their unique bilingual teacher in the school. When one of us told the principal that some of their students likely would return to Mexico, she admitted that she had never thought of that. Immediately, she sent an e-mail to her staff telling them not to prohibit the use of Spanish by students. In a modest but real way, our side comment made the invisible visible. She had discovered that ELL students might be transnational students, and that changed the calculus of what they needed to know.

The situation in Mexican schools for transnational students is similar–i.e., they are invisible–but for other reasons. The returnees' children seem to have few differences with their peers in the schools. They have the same surnames; they speak Mexican Spanish (often less well). Acknowledging the physiological heterogeneity of any population, they nonetheless "look Mexican." As we found transnational students during our school visits, we often encountered teachers who revealed their surprise when they saw their student converse ably in English. They did not realize they had that kind of student in their classrooms. Only in the small towns with a long history of international migration (e.g., in Jalisco) did teachers and principals know well who the *alumnos migrantes* (transnational students) were. They were aware of it because they knew their parents and other family members. By revealing these invisibilities, our projects have had one particularly important outcome: announcing that such students exist.

Training Teachers

Certainly, evidence matters. Transnational, American Mexican children exist and are attending Mexican and American schools. However, teachers both in the United States and in Mexico have frequently told us that they have little of the necessary training for working with these emergent realities. In Zacatecas, when we were interviewing teachers, we learned a valuable lesson: teachers told us they wanted to help. They wanted to support and be useful to transnational students, but did not know what to do. The teachers recognized they never had the opportunity to visit American schools (and likely would not) and that they did not speak, read, and write English. They felt unprepared to imagine how their students had fared during their education in the United States.

In one of our last visits to Puebla, that state's Secretary of Education asked one of us what kind of training the teachers of Puebla needed to understand and address the needs of transnational students. With limited time, we responded, "Teachers in Puebla need to acquire some knowledge they usually lack. This includes: (a) knowing American schools–their foundations, dynamics, evaluation practices, moral and pedagogical practices; (b) learning basic English, including speaking, reading, and writing; (c) designing a transitional period for newcomers/returnees; and (d) welcoming the school biography and background of their transnational students." Of course, this is easier said than done. Almost all Mexican teachers are monolingual. They know little about American schools. It is difficult for them to comprehend the educational experiences of their students in the United States, and Mexican schools strongly communicate nationalistic views in their curriculum and instructional practices (Rippberger & Staudt, 2003). This reality makes it difficult for teachers in Mexico to appreciate and welcome the identities and learning of their American Mexican students (Zúñiga & Hamann, 2008).

Similar statements might be said about U.S. teachers. Generally, they know little about what Mexican schools are like and, with exceptions, see little need to learn more (Hamann, 2003). Because of this stance, American teachers often underestimate the *funds of knowledge* (Gonzalez, Moll, & Amanti, 2005) their transnational students bring to the schools. These teachers are also almost always monolingual, even those who are responsible for the ESL programs. Their nationalism perhaps manifests itself differently than that of those we observed in Mexican schools (Rippberger & Staudt, 2003), but for them, too, the premise that schooling should account for a student living in another country, in the past and/or future, does not seem to fall within their realm of concern.

Encountering Multiple Literacies and Localities

What became clear for us through this research is that standardized schooling is not appropriate for the educational needs of children who are moving between locales and nations. Many have contested the premise of one-size-fits-all, but we would argue that this is particularly poorly suited for transnational students. Our point is not only to defend the values of preserving language competencies that American Mexican students develop. Certainly, we met several kids who fear they will forget their English, though some continue using English with their brothers, sisters, friends, aunts, and grandmothers. But from our perspective, bilingualism is not the primary issue.

Literacy, as Guerra (1998) pointed out, is not only the ability to be proficient in one written language, it is also the capacity to read contexts and to engage effectively in a variety of social practices. For instance, bilingual kids of Mexican or Central American parents in the United States develop interpretation skills in adult interactions, as Valdés (2003) and Orellana (2009) have shown in their groundbreaking studies on young children. Equally, American Mexican children of rural parents, when they return (or come for the first time in their lives) to Mexico, develop the ability to understand rural community dynamics they could not imagine when they lived in metropolitan Atlanta, New York, or Los Angeles. Moreover, and more generally, these kids have to master two different national histories, two different political organizations, two different symbolic geographies, and so on. And very often they have to develop such abilities and knowledge while being members of working-class families who possess very little cultural capital and have a history of limited school experience.

From the beginning of our field work in Mexican schools, we learned from the American Mexican students that many faced troubles in transitioning from English literacy to Spanish literacy. In other words, they had problems in reading and writing Spanish with cognitive academic language proficiency, a problem obscured usually by their basic interpersonal communication skills learned at home and in the community. Mexican schools had no standardized test for evaluating the students' needs in acquiring the necessary skills for reading and writing Spanish in those children. The mix-up is, in this case, almost perfect. Given the fact that transnational children speak Mexican Spanish almost like their peers in the school, teachers believe that they read and write Spanish like their peers. Sometimes, the teachers found that transnational students do not read well and make several mistakes while writing. But this performance data did not produce particularly appropriate actions from the teachers, being misunderstood, for example, as proof that a student was slow, quiet, or inattentive.

Recently, Panait (2011) followed three junior high school students in a small town in Nuevo León to observe their literacy "transitions" from English to Spanish. She discovered there were no "transitions," but rather ruptures and contradictions. The students (who spent half of their school year in Minnesota and the other half in Nuevo León) not only faced several obstacles in reading Spanish, but more important, they did not understand the basic rules of Spanish grammar and orthography. For instance, the vowel "a" in Spanish—given the vastly different pronunciation from its English counterpart—constitutes a colossal challenge for them while the consonant "h" is viewed almost as absurd sign because it is a useless letter in Spanish, and so on.

CONCLUSIONS

As a result of these findings, we are developing and recommending to school officials in several states in Mexico that they use evaluation guides, transitional programs, and short training activities that we have designed for supporting teachers and principals in the schools with higher concentrations of returnees' children (Sánchez García et al., 2011). Our purpose is to raise awareness of the existence of American Mexican children, to argue for schooling that is more responsive to mobility (particularly transnational mobility), and to facilitate the literacy transitions of those American Mexican children. Fortunately, American Mexican students are not randomly dispersed in the geography of Mexico, but instead are concentrated in the *municipios*–regions similar in size and governance to U.S. counties–already identified as having higher participation in international migration. There are specific places where making American Mexican children more visible and arguing for seeing their backgrounds as assets to be built upon would be particularly advantageous.

Raising Mexican teachers' awareness of American Mexican students is an important step, but hardly the only one necessary if Mexican and American educational systems are going to catch up to the demographic realities of mobility between the two countries. The American task for the binationally mobile student can no longer be rationalized as purely assimilative (if it ever could have been), because it is not a foregone conclusion that the Mexican American/American Mexican student being taught will come to adulthood and stay in the locale or even the country of their current schooling. The task for Mexico and the United States is bigger than just becoming aware of the fact that several hundred thousand such students exist. In a 21st century that will be marked by continued economic globalization and mobility, these transnational students are prospectively parts of a transformational bi-national, bilingual, bicultural, cosmopolitan vanguard, but for this opportunity to be realized, teacher preparation, curricula, and other targets of educational policies will need to be rethought. The facts on the ground are changing, and so, too, should the schools (*de aquí y de allá.*).

REFERENCES

Clemens, E. S. (1999). From society to school and back again: Questions about learning in and for a world of complex organizations. In E. C. Lagemann & L. S. Shulman (Eds.), *Issues in education research: Problems and possibilities, pp.* 105–120. San Francisco: Jossey-Bass.

Dreby, J. (2010). *Divided by borders: Mexican migrants and their children.* Berkeley: University of California Press.

Gitlin, A., Buendia, E., Crosland, K., & Doumbia, F. (2003). The production of margin and center: Welcoming-Unwelcoming of immigrant students. *American Educational Research Journal, 40*(1), 91–122.

Gonzalez, N., Moll, L., & Amanti, C. (Eds.). (2005). *Funds of knowledge: Theorizing practices in households and classrooms.* Mahwah, NJ: Lawrence Erlbaum Associates.

Guerra, J. C. (1998). *Close to home: Oral and literate practices in a transnational Mexicano community.* New York: Teachers College Press.

Hamann, E. T., (2001). Theorizing the sojourner student: (With a sketch of appropriate school responsiveness). In M. Hopkins & N. Wellmeier (Eds.), *Negotiating transnationalism: Selected papers on refugees and immigrants, Vol. IX,* (pp. 32–71). Arlington, VA: American Anthropology Association

Hamann, E. T. (2003). *The educational welcome of Latinos in the New South.* Westport, CT: Praeger.

Hamann, E. T., & Zúñiga, V. (2011) Schooling, national affinity(ies), and transnational students in Mexico. In S. Vandeyar (Ed.), *Hyphenated selves: Immigrant identities within education contexts,* pp. 57–72. Amsterdam, Netherlands: Rozenberg: .

Hernández-León, R., & Zúñiga, V. (2000). "Making carpet by the mile": The emergence of a Mexican immigrant community in an industrial region of the U.S. historic South. *Social Science Quarterly, 81*(1), 49–66.

Mahler, S. J., (1998). Theoretical and empirical contributions toward a research agenda for transnationalism. In M. P. Smith & L. E. Guarnizo (Eds.), *Transnationalism from below* (pp. 64–100). New Brunswick, NJ: Transaction Publishers.

Orellana, M. F., (2009). *Translating childhoods: The cultural roots of standards reform in American education.* New Brunswick, NJ: Rutgers University Press.

Panait, C. (2011). *Cuentos de mis escuelitas: La princesa y el hombre de hojalata. Transiciones, rupturas e identidades lingüísticas en alumnos con escolaridad circular.* (Master's dissertation). Monterrey, Mexico: Universidad de Monterrey.

Rippberger, S., & Staudt, K. (2003). Pledging allegiance: Learning nationalism at the El Paso-Juárez border. New York: Routledge Falmer.

Sánchez García, J., Hamann, E. T., & Zúñiga, V. (2012). What the youngest transnational students have to say about their transition from U.S. schools to Mexican ones. *Diaspora, Indigenous, and Minority Education, 6,* 157–171.

Sánchez García, J., Zúñiga, V., Hamann, E. T., Dorantes, I., Castellanos, M., Martínez, M. G., & Ayala, N. (2011) *Guía didáctica, alumnos transnacionales, las escuelas mexicanas frente a la globalización.* Mexico: Programa de Educación Básica sin Fronteras, Subsecretaría de Educación Básica, Secretaría de Educación Pública.

Smith, M. P. (1994). Can you imagine? Transnational migration and the globalization of grassroots politics. *Social Text, 39,* 15–33.

Trueba, E. T. (1999). The education of Mexican immigrant children. In M. Suárez-Orozco (Ed.), *Crossings: Mexican immigration in interdisciplinary perspective* (pp. 253–275). Cambridge, MA: Harvard University, David Rockefeller Center for Latin American Studies.

Valdés, G. (2003). *Expanding definitions of giftedness.* Mahwah, NJ: Lawrence Erlbaum Associates.

Zúñiga, V., Hamann, E. T., & Sánchez García, J. (2008). *Alumnos transnacionales: Las escuelas mexicanas frente a la globalización.* Mexico: Secretaria de Educación Pública. http://digitalcommons.unl.edu/teachlearnfacpub/97

Zúñiga, V., & Hamann, E. T. (2008). Escuelas nacionales, alumnos transnacionales: La migración México/Estados Unidos como fenómeno escolar. *Estudios Sociológicos, XXVI*(76), 65–85.

Zúñiga, V., & Hamann, E. T. (2009). Sojourners in Mexico with U.S. school experience: A new taxonomy for transnational students. *Comparative Education Review, 53*(3), 329–353.

Zúñiga, V., & Hamann, E. T. (forthcoming). Volviendo a visitar la noción de transnacionalidad: Comunicación transfronteriza y redes diaspóricas en alumnos migrantes internacionales en las escuelas de México. En J. J. Olvera y B. Vázquez (Eds.), *Procesos comunicativos y migración.* Tijuana, Mexico: El Colegio de la Frontera Norte.

Zúñiga, V., & Hernández-León, R. (2009). The Dalton story: Mexican immigration and social transformation in the carpet capital of the world. In M. E. Odem & E. Lacy (Eds.), *Latino immigrants and the transformation of the U.S. South* (pp. 34–50). Athens, GA: University of Georgia Press.

CHAPTER 9

The Schooling of
Youth Impacted by Migration:
A Bi-National Case Study

Adam Sawyer

During the international migration boom of the late 20th century and the early years of the 21st, migration from Mexico to the United States stood out as one of the globe's most intensive population flows. At its height in the 1990s and first part of the 2000s, roughly 500,000 Mexicans migrated each year for either permanent or temporary settlement (Passel & Cohn, 2010). Currently more than 11.7 million Mexican-born people live in the United States, representing nearly a third of the nation's foreign-born population (Passel, 2011).

While the impact of this massive movement of people on the economic, political, social, and cultural life of the United States has received extensive attention from scholars and policymakers, how this migration has reconfigured the same domains in Mexican society has received relatively scant notice. Preliminary scholarship into the cultural, social, economic, and political shifts occurring in Mexico due to this demographic transformation suggests that migration has brought both costs and benefits to the communities from which migrants depart and the nation as a whole. While outmigration can entail human capital loss, community and family breakdown, and the exacerbation of existing inequalities, it can also bring enhanced social networks, human capital, and income to needy Mexican migrant-sending communities (Cornelius & Sawyer, 2008; Fitzgerald, 2008; Smith, 2006). Though these initial accounts have been extremely helpful in mapping out the implications of outmigration for Mexico's migrant-sending communities, there nevertheless remains much to be learned about the extent and complexities of the changes wrought by migration to the United States.

In this chapter I share findings on the effect of financial remittances—the money migrants send back to their communities of origin—on schooling processes and outcomes for those who remain behind in one prominent migrant-sending community in southern Mexico. I have chosen to examine this phenomenon in regard to education due to the prominent role schooling can play in contributing to social equality, the formation of human capital, and the provision of skills necessary for democratic citizenship. Financial remittances provide a useful independent variable with which to study the overall impact of this phenomenon, as they are one of the most concrete and tangible manifestations of outmigration and one that is hypothesized—based upon both direct and indirect evidence—to boost educational opportunity within migrant-sending communities.

Using data from the University of California, San Diego's Mexican Migration Field Research and Training Project (MMFRP), which was obtained from the migrant-sending community of San Miguel Tlacotepec, Oaxaca, my work builds on previous studies by presenting qualitative case studies of four remittance-receiving youth enrolled in the town's sole upper secondary school during the 2007–2008 school year. The portraits of these students and their families provide a detailed illustration of how the background attribute of maternal education level—found to be the most powerful mediator of a remittance effect on educational outcomes—shapes the schooling pathways of these remittance-receiving youth. Through these examples, I discuss how other factors such as "social remittances" from absent family members, school-based processes, gender, and social constructions of migration also figure into the schooling lives of these students.

MIGRATION AND SCHOOLING IN SAN MIGUEL TLACOTEPEC: A COMMUNITY ON THE MOVE

The case studies I illustrate in this chapter are drawn from the prominent southern Mexican migrant-sending community of San Miguel Tlacotepec, Oaxaca. (For a more extensive discussion of the migratory and educational context of San Miguel Tlacotepec, see Cabrera et al., 2009; Cornelius & Sawyer, 2008; Sawyer, 2010b.) Tucked away within the mountainous and rugged landscape of southern Mexico's Mixteca Baja, this rural indigenous municipality of 1,696 people is classified by the

Mexican government as a "highly intensive" migrant-sending community (Consejo Nacional de Población [CONAPO], 2007). Tlacotepec, as
its residents call it, has very few economic opportunities for its citizens
and now loses most of its working-age population to migration. According to government statistics, nearly 1,100 Tlacotepenses departed for the
United States between 1995 and 2004, most settling in or around the
community of Vista, California, near San Diego.

Similar to communities described in other accounts (see Cornelius,
Fitzgerald, & Lewin-Fischer, 2007; Levitt, 2001; Smith, 2006), migrants
from San Miguel Tlacotepec living in the United States retain strong
transnational ties to their home community. One of the most tangible
manifestations of this relationship is the large amounts of money migrants send back to Tlacotepec. In 2008, 72% of the town's U.S.-based
migrants reported sending financial remittances to family members in
Tlacotepec, with an average of $350 U.S. dollars per month. Meanwhile,
47% of the town's current residents–and 81% of those with migrant
family members–said they received money from the United States (Cornelius, Fitzgerald, Díaz, & Borger, 2009). As a result of this exchange,
San Miguel Tlacotepec's economy is increasingly dependent upon remittances sent from the United States.

Persisting Barriers to Educational Opportunity

Situated in one of the poorest areas of one of Mexico's most impoverished states, educational indicators in San Miguel Tlacotepec are,
unsurprisingly, low in comparison to state and national averages (see
Table 9.1).

There have been signs of progress in the town, however, and young
Tlacotepenses are increasingly completing their compulsory schooling
(grades 1-9), when it once was quite rare to do so (see Figure 9.1). In
addition to its public preschool (pre-Kindergarten and Kindergarten),
two primary schools (grades 1–6), and lower secondary school (grades
7–9), the town recently saw the opening of an upper secondary school
(grades 10–12), which has raised hopes that educational attainment in
the municipality will continue to increase (Sawyer, Keyes, Velásquez,
Lima, & Bautista, 2009).

Transition to post-compulsory schooling can be financially prohibi-
tive for many Tlacotepec youth. While no tuition is charged at the basic
education levels (primary and lower secondary school) and the costs of
books and supplies are at least partially met through government programs, attending upper secondary school is much more expensive. In

Table 9.1. Selected Educational Indicators, Population 15 Years and Older, 2005

Indicator	Mexico	Mexico City	Oaxaca	San Miguel Tlacotepec
Literacy rate	90.5	97.0	80.6	68.2
Percent attended school	91.6	97.0	93.6	87.0
Percent incomplete primary	14.3	6.5	20.6	57.0
Average years of schooling attained	8.1	10.5	6.4	6.7

Sources: Instituto Nacional de Estadística y Geografía (INEGI), CONAPO.

Figure 9.1. Schooling Attainment by Age and Gender in San Miguel Tlacotepec

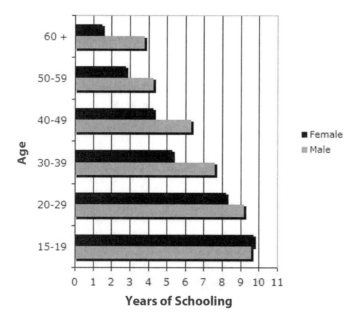

Source: Mexican Migration Field Research and Training Project 2007–2008 Survey.

addition to tuition expenses (though merit-based scholarships are available), families must fully meet the costs of books and other materials and supplies (Sawyer & Keyes, 2008).

As formal credit markets are mostly unavailable in rural Mexico, cash-strapped Tlacotepense families possess few alternatives for meeting the costs of unsubsidized schooling. Some participate in the shadowy world of private education loans, entities reputed to open and close their operations at a moment's notice, sometimes with the hard-earned deposits of families attempting to save for educational expenses (Sawyer & Keyes, 2008). For migrant families, on the other hand, remittances have become an increasingly viable option, and 33% of remittance receivers reported using this income toward educational expenses, the third most common use of this resource behind food and shelter (Sawyer et al., 2009).

Transnational Communities and Remittances

In Mexico, where maintenance of transnational communities is facilitated by geographic proximity and circular migration patterns, remittances represent a significant contribution to the national economy. This financial source, which reached $24.7 billion in 2008, is the third most numerous source of foreign trade—trailing only tourism and petroleum—and represents a full 3% of the nation's GDP (Banco Nacional de México [Banamex], 2008). Studies on the impact of remittances in Mexico are in their infancy and have yielded mixed results. Remittances seem to be beneficial in their ability to finance household expenses, business creation, public works projects, and the costs of schooling (Orozco, 2009; Ratha, 2003). On the other hand, they also appear in some cases to increase existing inequalities and come with the cost of family separations and human capital loss (Dreby, 2010; Global Exchange, 2008; Menjivar & Abrego, 2009).

It is important to note that remittances are not just financial in nature. Migrant-sending communities—such as those in Mexico—are also transformed by social interactions non-migrants have with departed migrants through visits (either in the sending or receiving community), phone calls, letters, emails, blogs, and other media (Levitt & Lamda-Nieves, 2010). This phenomenon, known as "social remittances," has received limited scrutiny from scholars, but has been speculated to have cultural, political, and scholastic implications (Levitt, 2001; Levitt & Lamda-Nieves, 2010). For example, it is believed that as sending community residents interact with migrants—who themselves are transformed by their new environments—their ideas regarding such matters as gender roles, democracy, and schooling can be altered (Levitt, 2001; Levitt & Lamda-Nieves, 2010).

Remittances and Educational Opportunity

As pointed out earlier, in rural Mexico, finances can pose a significant barrier to students persisting in school, especially at the higher grade levels (Reimers, 2002; Santibañez, Vernez, & Razquin, 2005). Within San Miguel Tlacotepec, for example, only 17% of the population has completed upper secondary school, while a mere 7.5% has attended college. For these reasons, it has been hypothesized that financial remittances can help remittance-receiving households spend more on the schooling of their dependents, which in turn can increase the opportunity they have to progress through the educational system and complete their schooling (Hanson, 2002; Kandel & Kao, 2001; Sawyer, 2010b).

Very few studies have directly studied the relationship between financial remittances and educational opportunity in Mexico. There are, however, several nationally representative and multisite studies that have gotten at the question indirectly by comparing students from migrant families to those from non-migrant households along a range of educational indicators related to educational aspirations and attainment. The findings from these studies have been somewhat murky, as some have found apparent scholastic benefits for migrant household members (Hanson, 2002; Hanson & Woodruff, 2003; Kandel & Kao, 2001); others have unveiled negative findings (Kandel & Massey, 2001; McKenzie & Rapoport, 2006; Miranda, 2007), while still others have found both positive and negative associations (Kandel & Kao, 2001). These studies, however, shed little light on the impact of remittances in this equation and the underlying mechanisms behind these relationships.

I directly explored the relationship between remittances and educational opportunity within San Miguel Tlacotepec (Sawyer, 2010b). In my studies, remittance-receiving households were compared to non-remittance receivers in terms of family educational spending, parent and student aspirations, total educational attainment, and completion of the lower secondary and upper secondary school cycles. While remittance income was not found to effect household educational spending, youth educational attainment, likelihood of lower secondary completion for youth, or upper secondary enrollment, it was found to be related to higher levels of schooling aspirations for youth and parents with relatively low levels of maternal education and to greater likelihood of upper secondary completion for those with *higher* maternal education levels (Sawyer, 2010a). In sum, while these findings provide evidence that remittances *can* help students in migrant-sending communities with their educations, they also suggest that their ability to do so depends upon more than just receiving money.

Other Impacts of Migration: Parent-Child Separations, the "Culture of Migration," and Gender Differences

Aside from maternal education levels, there are other individual, household, and contextual factors that may affect the schooling pathways of remittance-receiving students in migrant-sending communities. For one, the receipt of remittances almost always necessitates the separation of children and youth from at least one parent. Such separations have been found in some studies to impact the mental well-being of children and youth, which can hinder schooling motivation and engagement (Dreby, 2010; Menjívar & Abrego, 2009; Sawyer et al., 2009).

Similarly, in such contexts where outmigration becomes a community norm—especially for young men—schooling in the higher grade levels may be interrupted or terminated in favor of international migration (Cornelius, 1990; Fitzgerald, 2008; Kandel & Massey, 2001; Sawyer, 2010a). As participation in this "culture of migration" is dominated by males during the school-age years, it has been hypothesized that females might benefit more from remittances in the higher grade levels such as upper secondary than males, given the greater likelihood females have to still be enrolled in school (Kandel & Massey, 2001; Sawyer, 2010a). In fact, the receipt of remittances in and of itself signals the presence of a kin network in the United States, which can increase the prospects that would-be adolescent migrants (typically males) have of realizing these intentions to migrate (Kandel & Massey, 2001). Despite anecdotal evidence to support a gender-specific effect in terms of remittances and educational persistence, empirical evidence in this regard is still inconclusive.

COLLECTION OF DATA

Data for my study were collected as part of a bi-national "ethno-survey" designed and carried out by the 2007–2008 Mexican Migration Field Research and Training Project, a partnership between the University of California, San Diego's Center for Comparative Immigration Studies and the *Instituto de Investigaciones Sociológicas* at the *Universidad Autónoma Benito Juárez de Oaxaca* (For more information, see http://www.polisci.ucsd.edu/cornelius/). Part of a bi-national team of

30 researchers, I spent 2 weeks in San Miguel Tlacotepec, Oaxaca, in December 2007, where I participated in the administration of a 158-item survey to all residents aged 15 to 65 in the community. We also conducted 49 semi-structured interviews with school administrators, teachers, parents, and students and collected extensive observational field notes based upon time spent in households, community gathering places, and all five of San Miguel Tlacotepec's schools, as well as those attended by Tlacotepenses in San Diego County in the United States.

In the semi-structured interviews, all respondents were asked to describe their perceptions of migration's impact on schooling in the community; teachers and administrators were specifically asked for vignettes about particular students impacted in one way or another by migration; parents were asked to describe aspirations for their children, and how decisions about allocation of resources for education were made; and students were prompted to describe the role of schooling in their lives, their perception of the educational opportunities available to them, their intentions regarding international migration, and their aspirations for future attainment.

Positionality and Validity

Our bi-national (United States and Mexico) research team was composed of expert academic faculty and both graduate and undergraduate students, most with previous experience conducting research on the nexus of migration and social development. The U.S. researchers (myself included) were mainly middle-class Anglophone (though all competent second language speakers of Spanish) U.S. nationals of both White (non-Hispanic) and Latino/a heritage. Hence, despite there being some linguistic and cultural commonalities between us and our research participants, there were also considerable barriers between us and they that were likely exacerbated by the great disparity between us in terms of formal education levels and social class.

While these factors have inevitably impacted the lens by which I have approached and described the present research, we also took several steps in both data collection and analysis to address the ways that these linguistic and cultural barriers might pose a threat to the validity (Maxwell, 2005) of our research. For one, on two occasions our complete team (from both universities) met to discuss survey items and critically reflect upon the meaning of each question and the adequacy of its wording. During these bi-national summits, our Mexican colleagues (all of whom had extensive research experience in San Miguel Tlacotepec) provided critical advice on the wording and appropriateness of various

survey and protocol items and tips on culturally relevant ways to establish rapport and trust (Seidman, 1998). Additionally, once in San
Miguel Tlacotepec, our team met for an hour each day to discuss issues
with the survey, interview, and observation protocols and other dilemmas in the field and adjustments were made as necessary to our data
collection instruments and strategies.

As a result, despite our many challenges in regard to validity, we
believe that our methods were quite successful overall. The members of
our research team felt confident, and the feedback we received from the
participating families—who on balance seemed relaxed and welcoming
to our presence—made us believe that the information we got from them
was accurate and detailed.

VOICES FROM TLACOTEPEC: THE COMPLEX INTERPLAY OF REMITTANCES AND SCHOOLING

Here I present case studies of four students from San Miguel Tlacotepec's high school to illustrate the complex and double-edged nature of
remittances and their impact on educational processes. The cases of
Mercedes Gómez, Héctor Padilla, Isabella Galindo, and Carlos Villareal demonstrate first and foremost—in line with previous work in this
area—the central role of remittance-recipient mothers in mediating the
schooling of their children.

These case studies also reveal the importance of the departed
migrant parent in the schooling pathways of youth from remittance-
receiving households, a factor not observed in previous quantitative
studies. The communication that these youth have—or do not have—
with their migrant parent has important implications for their persistence and success in school.

Mercedes and Isabella: Support for School at Home and from "El Norte"

Mercedes Gómez. A 16-year-old 10th-grader at Tlacotepec's high
school, Mercedes lives in a colorful and well-maintained adobe dwelling
in the relatively affluent downtown of San Miguel Tlacotepec with her
mother, Ana, and three younger siblings. Their finely carved wooden
furniture, tiled floors, and large color television all suggest the trappings
of a comfortable middle-class life. Mercedes's father, Pedro, has lived
and worked in Northern California as a construction worker for over 10
years and according to Ana sends money to the family every month, and

calls at least once a week. Mercedes and her three brothers and sisters (ages 13, 10, and 8) are still in school, and according to Ana Gómez, this is made possible by the remittance income received from her husband:

> He works, sends money, and from that I have what I need for the week and for supplies to complete the school assignments we do on the weekends.

This statement suggests two important ingredients, seen throughout the interviews, for remittances to make a difference in the schooling of the young who remain behind. For one, the Gomez family has enough income left after meeting basic costs of subsistence to use the roughly 385 USD per month of remittance income toward meeting the costs of education. As seen in our surveys, families typically ranked education as a secondary use of remittances after food and shelter. Thus, the fact that Ana Gómez is able to use remittances toward educational expenses is suggestive of a relative economic comfort even aside from the remittance income. Second, Ana is obviously committed to her children's schooling and perhaps most importantly—thanks to her relatively high 8th-grade education—is able to help them with their schoolwork:

> I visit their schools and talk to their teachers as much as I can. Every night we work on the homework together. They are not to watch television until all of their assignments are finished. On the weekends, I try to take them different places so that they can learn outside of school and we read books together.

Given this high level of support, it is not surprising that all of Ana's children appear to be doing well in school, and teachers at the high school all concur that Mercedes is at the top of the 10th-grade class and is seen as being college-bound. In a visit to the high school, I talk to Mercedes about her schooling, and she professes to greatly enjoy school and discusses her aspirations of going to college and becoming a doctor or astronaut someday. I ask about her father in California, and what they talk about. Mercedes tells me that she speaks to her father weekly and he frequently inquires into her schoolwork. According to Mercedes: "He tells me to work hard at school, so 'you don't have to migrate like me.'" The frequency and nature of Mercedes' interaction with her father illustrates another important element of how remittances interact with schooling. Not only does Pedro Gómez support Mercedes' schooling through the sending of financial remittances, but he also provides the "social remittance" of reinforcing the message transmitted by Ana at home as to the importance of schooling–a notion likely informed in part by this experience as a low-wage migrant laborer in the United States. As such, he gives caution that life in the United States is no easy answer and recommends the alternative path of getting a good education back in San Miguel Tlacotepec.

While the remittance income Pedro Gómez sends from the United States, alongside his continued involvement in the education of his children, appears instrumental to the academic success of his daughter Mercedes, his absence is not without a severe trade-off. As his wife, Ana, puts it:

> Living here alone as a mother with my kids, it's hard, but one does whatever possible to help the kids move forward. My husband can't be here because he has to go work, to earn money so that the kids have, not even a good life, but a decent life. Because if he were here, we would all be happy because we'd be together, but we'd be in a bad situation economically.

Thus Ana's words demonstrate the painful bargain faced by families in San Miguel Tlacotepec. In order to attain such aspirations as providing post-compulsory schooling for their children, many must send family members to the United States to provide added income through the sending of remittances. The departure of a family member, however, comes with the painful side effect of being separated from a loved one, which sometimes hinders academic engagement.

Isabella Galindo. On my 1st day at the town high school, I ask the principal to introduce me to his top students. One of the four students he brings me is a bright-eyed, bubbly, and articulate 11th-grader named Isabella Galindo. As I get to know her, Isabella speaks glowingly of her classes at the high school and how much she likes her teachers. Her eyes light up further when discussing her future plans:

A.S.: What do you want to be when you grow up?
Isabella: A doctor. I am between two–doctor and studying
    international relations.
A.S.: So, you want to go to college?
Isabella: Yes, in Acapulco. There they have the major I want to
    study, International Relations. It is important to continue
    studying, to be at the vanguard of all the frequent changes that
    are happening in the world.
A.S.: Will you and your family be able to pay for college?

> *Isabella*: Yes, we've saved. I'm going to have to apply, ask for medical records, after I have to go to a (test preparation) course, and then take a test to see if I can get in.

From her words, it is clear not only that Isabella has high aspirations for her schooling, but also a great deal of information at her disposal to help make attending college a reality. Probing more into her background, I learn that Isabella is the youngest of four children and lives in one of the communities outlying the county seat in San Miguel Tlacotepec. She lives there with two older sisters and her mother, while her older brother and father are working together in the southern California farming town of Temecula. At home, similar to Mercedes, she receives a great deal of support from her mother, who completed 7th grade, a relatively high level for women of her age in the community. Speaking of her mother, Teresa, Isabella says: "Each weekend we sit down together and review the work the teachers give me that I have to turn in." On top of this concrete help with schoolwork received from her mother, Isabella receives encouragement from her two older sisters, who were unable to continue studying past lower secondary school and are confined to low-wage domestic labor in the neighboring city of Juxtlahucaca: "My sisters, they tell me, 'Study, work real hard, because we didn't have the same opportunity to study as you, make the most of it, do something rewarding with your life. Work very hard!'" Isabella also tells me about two college-going cousins who have served as role models for her, and presumably serve as at least a partial source of her knowledge of college admissions: "I have a [female] cousin who is studying Administration in Oaxaca City. I have another [male] cousin who is studying at the university in Oaxaca City."

Speaking of her migrant father, Julián, Isabella informs me that he is a documented worker, and as such receives higher wages (as compared to an undocumented worker). According to Isabella, he sends $400 per month of this income back to his family in the form of remittances. Similar to Mercedes, Isabella speaks to her father frequently, and given his legalized status, he is able to visit his family once or twice a year. Julián Galindo, similar to Pedro Gómez, reinforces the support provided to Isabella's studies at home by her mother and sisters not only with his U.S. dollars, but also his words. According to Isabella: "He tells me, 'I send money so that you can buy books and the things you need so that you can keep studying.'" The importance of school is also bolstered by her older brother, Davíd, who is now working in the United States and wishes that he had stuck with his schooling in Mexico: "He [Davíd] sometimes tells me, 'Work hard, take advantage now, I was stupid to not take advantage of when my parents supported me, but now I regret it.'"

In sum, both Mercedes Gómez and Isabella Padilla are thriving in school not only thanks to the remittance income their families receive from the United States, but in the way having this financial source interacts with other aspects of their backgrounds. Both young women have relatively well-educated mothers who support their schooling through the allocation of financial resources, encouragement, and assistance with school assignments. Mercedes and Isabella also both enjoy regular communication with their U.S.-based fathers, who socially remit a school positive message to the girls.

Carlos and Héctor: Money is Not Enough

Not all remittance-receiving youth in San Miguel Tlacotepec possess the background advantages enjoyed by Mercedes and Isabella. In the ensuing cases of Carlos Villareal and Héctor Padilla, I demonstrate how simply having this financial resource available to support schooling is not enough to ensure schooling success and persistence.

Carlos Villareal. During the final days of our field work in San Miguel Tlacotepec, we were invited by a concerned Civics teacher at the high school to give a talk to his 11th-grade class on the perils of migration and the reality of life working in the United States for Mexican migrants. The teacher, Raúl, a 33-year-old originally from the state capital of Oaxaca City, had become alarmed by the large number of boys at the school who dropped out over the course of their studies to migrate. He had taken on what he described as a "losing battle" to keep these kids at school and wanted to take advantage of the presence of so many U.S. researchers in town to provide firsthand information that might dissuade youth at the school from seeing their future solely as migrants to the United States.

I spoke to Raúl to gain a better sense of what he perceived to be the dynamics that led so many of the young men to want to leave San Miguel Tlacotepec for the United States. Beyond the obvious limitations of the local economy, Raúl felt that the adolescent boys were drawn to an image of U.S. life that exemplified a romanticized ideal of masculinity:

They are seduced by the images of the United States—the cars, the big houses, the blondes in bikinis. This is what they see from the movies and the exaggerations spun by those that come back [returned migrants][. . .] They think that they will go work in the North, then come back here with the nicest shoes and clothes and lots of money and be big shots.

To give me a sense of the power this social force held over these adolescent boys, Raúl took me to the playground at the end of the school day to observe a group of 10th- and 11th-grade males. He quickly pointed out a young man with hip, slicked-back hair and a confident strut as the ringleader:

Carlos is the leader of the pack, whenever he talks the others listen—wherever he goes the others follow. His father is working in the United States and sends him money. One time he came back here and bought him that hot-rod *vochito* (Mexican term for a VW bug), and ever since then all the other boys want to be just like him.

Watching this group of boys over the course of the lunchtime break, it seemed that Raúl's assessment was spot-on. Seeing the youth circle together, Carlos was without doubt the center of attention. As he spoke, the others seemed to hang on his every word. When he moved, the others followed. From his confident body language and the compliant actions of the others, it was clear that Carlos was used to leading, and the others were similarly accustomed to following.

According to Raúl, Carlos—equipped with his souped-up *vochito*—had become a single-handed purveyor of the *culture of migration*—the social norm by which migration becomes an expected rite of passage—at the school and, as such, representative of everything he sought to fight against as a teacher in this migrant-sending community:

The sad thing is that aside from the money and exaggerated view of life in the North, he gets nothing else from his father. So the money comes, the gifts come, but he receives no guidance. His mother tries at home, but she never studied so cannot do very much. Really, all he aspires to is to be like his father and work in the United States and it will be easier because his dad is already there. In the meantime, he barely tries in school and his grades are low.

On my last day at the high school, I was able to catch up with Carlos. I chatted with him about his home life and schooling aspirations:

A.S.: Do you receive money from the United States?

C.V.: Yeah, man, my dad lives there and makes big bucks. He sends me money, so I can buy things like my cool *vochito*.

A.S.: Do you use this money for school expenses?

C.V.: I don't know, man. Maybe my mom does, but me, I use that money to do fun things after school.

A.S.: What do you usually do after school?

C.V.: I mostly like to drive around in my *vochito* with my homies. Sometimes we stop at the kiosk (community center) and play video games. You know, fun things.

A.S.: I know that you are given a lot of homework at the high school, when do you find time to do it if you are doing so many fun things after school?

C.V.: The homework doesn't matter so much to me. My mother sometimes scolds me, and tells me to do my work, but I usually just throw it away.

A.S.: Why do you throw your homework away?

C.V.: Because school here doesn't matter. I'm going to go to the North. There my dad has lots of work and drives a truck. There's no work here in Tlacotepec, to be a man you have to go to California.

Héctor Padilla. The Padilla family lives on the northern periphery of San Miguel Tlacotepec near the entrance for the state highway. Here they have carved out a very modest homestead within the remains of a long-closed pool hall and discothèque. Entry into their dwelling can only be managed by physical contortion through a narrowly torn opening in a chain-link fence surrounding the condemned property. Once inside, one can see that despite the modesty of its surroundings, the home is nevertheless equipped with proper concrete floors, electricity, a functioning gas stove, and a television.

Héctor Padilla, a 17-year-old 10th-grader at the high school, lives in this house with his mother, Esthér, and his three siblings: a 16-year-old boy, a 12-year-old girl, and a 7-year-old boy. Héctor and his oldest brother both attend the local high school, while the two youngest attend the middle school and elementary school. Esthér, a morose 42-year-old woman whose glazed looks and sunken posture are suggestive of depression, tells me that her husband, Pablo, left for the United States 8 years ago with promises of returning to San Miguel Tlacotepec with the money to build the family a nice new house. Apparently this dream never manifested itself, as she tells me:

At first he sent money and called every week, but little by little he started calling less and only sometimes sending money … Eventually, the calls and money stopped all together and I haven't heard even a word from him for two years. . . . He always was a drunk and womanizer, so I guess that's what became of him in the North.

Despite no longer receiving financial help from her husband, Esthér tells me that she receives frequent remittances from two sisters living in California totaling about 300 USD per month, which allows her to buy food and clothing for her family and to send her two oldest sons, Héctor and Tómas, to the high school. When asked about how Héctor and Tómas are doing as students, Esthér describes them as being only mediocre students because "they are both very lazy. Luckily the younger one [Tómas] has the [music] band, but the older one [Héctor] is trouble." Ésthér's assessment—at least in terms of the educational trajectories of her sons—is somewhat confirmed by her sons and their teachers at the high school. The high school Civics teacher describes both boys as doing the minimum to get by in class and suspects that they do not receive much help at home, and notes that Esthér only completed 2nd grade in her own education. He also describes Tómas as having the semblance of a future through his music, but senses that Héctor is a migration dropout risk.

In my discussions with Héctor, the teacher's assessment is corroborated. He tells me that he has no real desire to finish high school and instead hopes to migrate to the United States to work as soon as he can: "I hope to go to the United States . . . I don't want to stay because there aren't any jobs." I probe further into Héctor's desire to go to the United States, and ask him what he plans to do there when he arrives. He tells me that he intends to find his father, so that he can work with him. Remembering what Esthér has told me about the father's estrangement from the family, I ask Héctor if his father is aware of his plans. Pausing for a moment, and looking slightly askance, he tells me: "No, not yet, but when I get there he will want me to work with him." I ask Héctor to tell me more about his long-range plans. Once again, he pauses for a moment before responding:

What I will do is work for a while in the United States until I learn English well. Then I will come back here and teach English. That is a problem we have here. We don't speak English well and our English teachers are no good. I will come back here and fix that.

Throughout the remainder of my conversations with Héctor, his strong aspiration to migrate alongside unformed ideas of how he would make this a reality continued to present themselves. As we discussed such themes as his schooling, life in San Miguel Tlacotepec, perceived life in the United States, and soccer, he would stop me every once in a while to gather the type of information he knew that I was well equipped to provide. For example, he asked: "When you go through the border, what do you have to show to *la migra* (border agents)? If you work without papers, do you have to give fake ones to the boss?" Along with a clear determination to fulfill his dream was an accompanying, though heartbreakingly unfounded, belief that his father would be there to guide him in his new life in the United States.

DISCUSSION OF THE FINDINGS

These four case studies both corroborate and expand upon previous findings on this topic. In line with previous work, I find that remittances, while potentially helpful for schooling performance and attainment, are alone not enough to boost educational outcomes. As in Sawyer (2010b), I find that the role of a youth's remittance-receiving mother is indispensable in mediating these outcomes. The ability of mothers to aid their children with school-related tasks–usually as a result of relatively high educational attainment in their own right–appears to make the difference in ensuring schooling success and the promise of future levels of schooling.

This study also illustrates factors not seen in previous work. Most prominently, these four case studies demonstrate the importance of social remittances, the values transmitted both explicitly and implicitly by absent migrant family members. Whereas for Mercedes and Isabella, the values transmitted are encouragement of schooling persistence and success, Carlos and Héctor–both through direct and indirect channels–are provided romanticized ideals of migrant life that trump efforts to engage these youth in school by their mothers and school personnel.

In considering the cases of Mercedes, Isabella, Carlos, and Héctor, it is important to note the possibility that gender-based dynamics may also be at work in regard to their schooling pathways. As such, the findings from previous work on the relationship between outmigration and schooling support the notion that girls tend to stay in school longer than boys in migrant-sending communities, especially compared to boys with migrant family members (Kandel & Massey, 2002; McKenzie & Rapoport, 2006; Miranda, 2007). As we also know, it is the case in San Miguel Tlacotepec that females–while migrating in ever-higher numbers–tend to outmigrate at an older age (usually after 18) than males, who begin to migrate in large numbers at age 15, the traditional start of upper secondary school.

It is also important to consider how school-related factors figure into the schooling trajectories of these students. In terms of student support, I found no evidence of after-school programs, study halls, parent-education efforts, or any other initiative targeted for struggling students like Héctor or Carlos who lacked parental support at home (Field Notes, December 16, 2007). In terms of the migration phenomenon, the school and national curriculum do little to attend to the matter in relevant ways for students. Teachers confessed that the issue was rarely if ever discussed during class time, and where textbooks touched upon the topic, it was discussed in general and global terms with no mention of the intensive migration flows out of Mexico to the United States (Field Notes, December 16, 2007).

CONCLUSION

Migration to the United States has become a necessary way of life for individuals and families throughout Mexico. While outmigration of family members can entail painful separations for those who remain behind, they can also benefit materially and sometimes scholastically from the money family members send back from *el Norte*. As this chapter has shown, however, remittances–even when applied to educational expenses–don't necessarily guarantee enhanced performance or persistence in school. In fact, in cases where youth receive little academic support at home or from their absent migrant parent, remittances can reinforce widely held perceptions for youth that migration can provide a glamorous improvement to one's living conditions and a preferable alternative to schooling attainment in Mexico.

For schooling to be an attractive and viable alternative to migration for the youth of Mexico's migrant-sending communities, efforts must be made within Mexico to provide academic support to struggling students and their families, nonromanticized and relevant depictions of migration must surface more prominently in the curriculum, and access to higher education must be expanded. Furthermore, given the potential role of U.S.-based migrants in supporting the schooling persistence of their Mexico-based children, U.S. actors should consider steps that can be taken through immigration and education policy as well as strategic bi-national programmatic initiatives with Mexico to help support migrant parents to continue supporting the education of their children remaining in Mexico. Without such steps, youth in communities such as San Miguel Tlacotepec will be denied a true choice to remain in school and, ultimately, the right to stay home.

REFERENCES

Banco Nacional de México (Banamex). (2008). *Review of the economic situation of Mexico*, Vol. LXXXIV. Mexico City, Mexico: Author

Cabrera, B., Hildreth, E., Rodríguez, A., & Zárate, V. (2009). San Miguel Tlacotepec as a community of emigration. In W. A. Cornelius, J. Hernández Dia, & S. Borger (Eds.), *Migration from the Mexican Mixteca: A transnational community in Oaxaca and California*, (pp. 1–30). San Diego, CA: Center for Comparative Immigration Studies, University of California, San Diego.

CONAPO (Consejo Nacional de Población). (2005). *Migración México-Estados Unidos: Panorama regional y estatal*. Mexico: Author.

CONAPO (Consejo Nacional de Población). (2007). *Migración México-Estados Unidos: Panorama regional y estatal*. Mexico: Author.

Cornelius, W. (1990). *Labor migration to the United States: Development outcomes and alternatives in Mexican sending communities*. Working Paper No. 38. Washington, DC: U.S. Commission for the Study of International Migration and Cooperative Economic Development.

Cornelius, W., Fitzgerald, D., Hernández-Díaz, J., & Borger, S. (2009). Migration from the Mexican mixteca: A transnational community in Oaxaca and California. San Diego, CA: Center for Comparative Immigration Studies, University of California, San Diego.

Cornelius, W., Fitzgerald, D., & Lewin-Fischer, P. (2007) *Mayan journeys: The new migration from Yucatán to the United States*. San Diego, CA: Center for US-Mexico Studies, University of California, San Diego.

Cornelius W., & Sawyer, A. (2008). *Does migration impact educational mobility?: Evidence from a Oaxacan sending community and its U.S. satellites*. Paper presented at the 2008 Annual Meeting of the American Educational Association, New York, NY.

Dreby, J. (2010). *Divided by borders: Mexican migrants and their children*. Berkeley, CA: University of California Press.

Fitzgerald, D. (2008). *A Nation of emigrants: How Mexico manages its migration*. Berkeley, CA: University of California Press.

Global Exchange. (2008). *The right to stay home: Alternatives to mass displacement and forced migration in North America*. San Francisco, CA: Global Exchange.

Hanson, G. (2002). *Emigration and educational attainment in Mexico.* University of California, San Diego, Working Paper.

INEGI. (2005). *Censo general de población y vivienda.* Aguascalientes, Mexico: Author.

Kandel, W., & Kao, G. (2001). The impact of temporary labor migration on Mexican children's educational aspirations and performance. *International Migration Review, 35*(4), 1205–1231.

Kandel, W., & Massey, D. S. (2002). The culture of Mexican migration: A theoretical and empirical analysis. *Social Forces, 80*(3), 981–1004.

Levitt, P. (2001). *The transnational villagers.* Berkeley: University of California Press.

Levitt, P. & Lamda-Nieves, D. (2010). *"It's not just about the economy stupid"– Social remittances revisited.* Washington, DC: Migration Information Source, Migration Policy Institute.

Maxwell, J. (2005). *Qualitative research design: An interactive approach* (2nd ed.). Thousand Oaks, CA: Sage.

McKenzie, D., & Rapoport, H. (2006). *Can migration reduce educational attainment? Evidence from Mexico.* Washington, DC: World Bank Working Papers.

Menjivar, C., & Abrego, L. (2009). Parents and children across borders: Legal instability and intergenerational relations in Guatemalan and Salvadoran Families. In N. Foner (Ed.), *Family ties: Intergenerational dynamics in immigrant families,* (pp. 160–189). New York: New York University Press.

Miranda, A. (2007). *Migrant networks, migrant selection, and high school graduation in Mexico.* IZA Discussion Paper No. 3204. Available online at http://www.iza.org/conference_files/amm2007/miranda_.pdf

Orozco, M. (2009). *Understanding the continuing effects of the economic crisis on remittances to Latin America and the Caribbean.* Washington, DC: Inter-American Development Bank, Multilateral Investment Fund.

Passel, J. (2011). Demography of immigrant youth: Past, present, and future. *Immigrant Children, 21*(1), 19–42.

Passel, J., & Cohn, D. (2010). *U.S. unauthorized immigration flows are down sharply since mid-decade.* Washington, DC: Pew Hispanic Center.

Ratha, D. (2003). Worker remittances: An important and stable source of external development finance. In *Global Development Finance 2003,* (pp. 157–175). Washington, DC: World Bank.

Reimers, F. (2002). *Unequal schools, unequal chances.* Cambridge, MA: Harvard University, David Rockefeller Center for Latin American Studies.

Santibañez, L., Vernez, G., & Razquin, P. (2005). *Education in Mexico: Challenges and opportunities.* Santa Monica, CA: Rand Corporation.

Sawyer, A. (2010a). *In Mexico, mother's education and remittances matter in school outcomes.* Washington, DC: Migration Information Source,

Migration Policy Institute. Retrieved at: http://www.migrationinformation. org/Feature/display.cfm?ID=775

Sawyer, A. (2010b). *Money is not enough: Remittances and other determinants of youth educational attainment in a Southern-Mexican migrant-sending community.* Cambridge, MA: Harvard Graduate School of Education Doctoral Dissertation.

Sawyer, A., & Keyes, D. (2008). *Going to school, going to the U.S.A.: The impact of migration on the education of Oaxacan students.* Presented at the Center for Comparative Immigration Studies Research Seminar Series, San Diego, CA.

Sawyer, A., Keyes, D., Velásquez, C., Lima, G., & Batista, M. (2009). Going to school, going to *el norte*: The impact of migration on the education of Oaxacan students. In W. A. Cornelius, D. Fitzgerald, J. Hernández Díaz, & S. Borger (Eds.), *Migration from the Mexican Mixteca: A transnational community in Oaxaca and California,* (pp. 123–164). San Diego: Center for Comparative Immigration Studies, University of California, San Diego.

Seidman, I. (1998). *Interviewing as qualitative research: A guide for researchers in education and the social sciences.* New York: Teachers College Press.

Smith, R. C. (2006). *Mexican New York: The transnational lives of new immigrants.* Berkeley: University of California Press.

Part IV

ASSETS ORIENTATIONS

To "regard *educación*" is to identify and esteem the individual and interpersonal abilities nurtured in traditional Mexican households. Chapters in this section specify these abilities, how they develop, and why they are important to school success.

In Chapter 10, Leslie Reese demonstrates ways by which cultural values and practices persist following migration to the United States, compared with the ways Mexican communities of origin are also being shaped by migration and other international phenomena. Gabriela Livas Stein, Cynthia García Coll, and Nadia Huq, in Chapter 11, summarize the research literature on how family and cultural competencies of Mexican American youth develop in cultural settings and, in particular, how these competencies relate with school outcomes. And in Chapter 12 Francisco Gaytan discusses how, at the community level, Mexican American youth in New York City leverage their social networks to persist through secondary school, despite inadequate efforts of educators to create bridges between home and school social capital.

CHAPTER 10

Cultural Change and Continuity in U.S. and Mexican Settings

Leslie Reese

In the town of Concepción in west-central Mexico, as in other towns in the region, it is the custom that the festival of the patron saint include a mass and pilgrimage by the *hijos ausentes* (literally "absent children"), who are townspeople who no longer reside in town but return for the festival. The great majority of *hijos ausentes* live in the United States. Having moved to the United States for better opportunities—economic and educational opportunities for themselves and their children being among the forefront—many of the *hijos ausentes* continue to draw upon home-country values and experiences as they raise their children in the United States. However, immigrant families do not simply transport home-country values and practices to the tasks of raising children and making a living in a new cultural and linguistic environment. Rather, they adapt their values to challenges that they encounter in U.S. settings. Many yearn for the healthier and simpler way of life that they experienced before immigration, experiencing nostalgia for the life left behind in a profound manner imbued with moral values.

At the same time, the "life left behind" in Mexico is in the process of adaptation and transformation as well, as families respond to increasing globalization, demands of transnational business (both legal and illegal), and expectations for higher levels of schooling. This chapter draws on data from 25 years of longitudinal studies of Mexican immigrant parents and children in California schools and communities, as well as data from studies of children and families in Mexico, to examine transnational changes in family daily routines and practices, and the values that inform these practices. One of the focal issues in all of these studies was documentation of the ways in which parents support their children's schooling and learning, and the understandings that guide their practices. Accommodations that parents and children make, guided by home-country values and constrained by structural and environmental forces in their new environment, have consequences for students' academic and post-school outcomes.

Children's experiences outside of school–including activities and interactions in the home and community–have the potential to impact learning in the classroom. A substantial body of research has examined the differences between home and school expectations, values, and discourse patterns that may place minority, working-class, and/or immigrant children at a disadvantage in American schools (see for example Foster, 1995; Lareau, 1989; Valdés, 1996). However, within a framework that highlights home-school differences, the continuities and compatibilities that exist between home and school are often overlooked. In addition, "cultural differences" are often assumed to be constant over time and for all members of a group.

In our studies of children's experiences outside of school, and the cultural values that shape these experiences, we have sought to understand not only differences but also compatibilities between immigrant Latino homes and the schools that educate their children, and have documented changes in cultural practices and values over time as schools and parents interact. We have examined the following:

- Parents' aspirations and expectations for their children (Goldenberg, Gallimore, Reese, & Garnier, 2001; Reese, 2001; Reese, Gallimore, Goldenberg, & Balzano, 1995)
- Home reading practices (Reese, 2009; Reese & Gallimore, 2000; Reese, Gallimore, & Goldenberg, 1999; Reese, Goldenberg, Loucky, & Gallimore, 1995)
- Immigrant students' academic trajectories in American schools (Reese, Gallimore, & Guthrie, 2006; Reese, Garnier, Gallimore, & Goldenberg, 2000; Reese, Kroesen, & Gallimore, 2000)
- Concepts of ethnic identity (Reese, Gallimore, & Zarate, 2003; Zarate, Bhimji, & Reese, 2005)

In the present chapter, I will not attempt to summarize findings from each of the studies. Rather, I reflect on some of the things that we have learned about cultural change and continuity in U.S./Mexican contexts, and how these understandings can inform research and instruction of Mexican children in American schools.

SOURCES OF DATA

Over the years, I have had the good fortune to participate in several longitudinal studies of language and literacy development and home-school connections among immigrant Latino families in California and Texas and with Mexican families in Jalisco, Mexico. The 15-year UCLA Latino Home-School Project began in 1989 and followed 120 Spanish-speaking English Language Learners from Kindergarten through high school. Initially parents of the children participated in interviews and surveys; by high school, the students themselves were the major participants. Themes of interest in this project included parents' aspirations and expectations for their children's academic achievement, home reading practices, students' academic trajectories, and concepts of ethnic identity.

In 2001, we began a 4-year study of bilingual and biliteracy development of Spanish-speaking children, grades K–2, in California and Texas. The study included over 1,400 children and families in 35 schools and communities in urban and border Texas and in the greater Los Angeles area. Data collection included surveys of all parents and twice-yearly interviews with a subset of 144 parents, classroom observations, community observations, and focus group interviews and surveys of teachers. Themes of interest in this project included literacy practices in the home and community influences on home literacy experiences.

During the summer of 1997, I had the opportunity to interview and spend time with 12 families residing in Mexico who were relatives of case-study families in the UCLA Latino Home-School Project. The parents were siblings of the parents participating in the UCLA study with children of the same age as project participants but who had not chosen to immigrate to the United States. Themes of interest in this study included parents' aspirations and expectations for their children and ways in which parents' childrearing strategies are adapted to the demands of life in different environments.

Finally, current work is concluding on a 4-year study of language and literacy development among 360 children in grades 1–3 in Guadalajara, Jalisco, Mexico. This project parallels the California/Texas study, collecting data from parent surveys and interviews, teacher surveys, classroom observations, and community observations. Themes of interest examined to date in this study include literacy practices of the home and home-school connections.

AN ECOLOGICAL/CULTURAL APPROACH

Our work has examined the lives of immigrant Latino families as they carry out the tasks involved in raising children through the lenses of sociocultural and ecocultural theories. By this we mean that family actions are not conceived of only in individual terms, nor are they entirely determined by the conditions—social, economic, physical—in which the family resides; rather, family activity within a daily routine is situated within the sociocultural context. Ecological/cultural theory (hereafter ecocultural) draws on evidence from anthropological and cross-cultural human development research (Super & Harkness, 1986; Weisner, 1984, 1997, 2002; Whiting & Edwards, 1988). From the perspective of ecocultural theory, a family's routine is constructed of sustainable activities that are partly determined by the surrounding environment and partly constructed by the families in accordance with personal and cultural schemas and values.

Daily Activities

These daily activities and the settings in which they occur are observable manifestations of the balance that families seek between what they desire and what their structural constraints permit. Of particular importance in our work is the fact that these everyday settings create opportunities for children to learn and develop through modeling, joint production, apprenticeship, and other forms of mediated social learning embedded in goal-directed interactions (Rogoff, 1990, 2003; Tharp & Gallimore, 1988). In other words, children learn through social interactions in settings that are in part shaped by the values and understandings that participants bring to the interactions and in part by the resources available to participants in the settings in which they find themselves.

Family activities are shaped not only by the local conditions in which families live, but also by national and transnational forces. While greatly constrained by the socioeconomic and political structure, individuals and families are not passive victims of overwhelming structural forces. Just as they must accommodate structural constraints, families also consider personal and cultural values in the active construction of daily routines. The daily routine that families work to construct is simultaneously, in Giddens's (1987) words, an instantiation of the social order that constrains families and a medium of human agency.

Local Setting

The ecological niche (Weisner, 1984), or local setting in which many of the immigrant Latino families in the Los Angeles studies reside, consists of working-class neighborhoods characterized by gang activity and viewed as relatively dangerous by the inhabitants. Most of the parents work at service or factory jobs outside of the immediate neighborhood, often working long hours for low pay, without benefits or much in the way of job stability. Approximately 40% of the mothers (in both the UCLA and California/Texas studies) work outside the home, and families often accommodate schedules so that one parent goes to work early and is home in time to pick up children from school, while the other works a later schedule and is available to get children ready in the morning and take them to school. While the stores and businesses directly serving the community often conduct business in Spanish, most contact with institutions in the larger society, other than the school, is in English. Most parents interviewed have described situations, either on the job, in searching for housing, or in institutional contacts, in which they have experienced discrimination as limited-English-speaking Latinos (Reese, Kroesen, & Gallimore, 2000).

Cultural Model of *Educación*

Parents bring cultural values and beliefs to the task of creating a meaningful and sustainable daily routine. In raising their children, the immigrant parents in our studies uniformly espoused the values of respect for parents and family unity, what we have called the cultural model of *"educación."* Cultural models are shared and internalized patterns of thought that mediate the interpretation of experiences (D'Andrade & Strauss, 1992); in other words, models are understandings of how things work in the world and, thus, how one should behave that are shared by a group of people. Latino parents express a common understanding of what a child who is *bien educado,* or well brought up, is, as well as what the responsibilities are for parents in raising such a child. *Educación* encompasses the values that LeVine and White (1986) characterized as part of an agrarian model of childrearing: obedience to and respect for parents and elders, family unity, and correct behavior. The dominant culture, as experienced through the media and in the news, is perceived by parents to be characterized by a freedom for children that undermines these values and that some parents refer to not as liberty but *"libertinaje,"* or libertine behavior. Home is the source of support and safety, while *"la calle"* (literally "the street" but referring more generally to outside of the home) is a source of danger to children. Danger comes not only in the form of actual violence but also in the form of *malas amistades* ("bad friends") who will lead children astray. These attitudes about the home and the street have parallels in descriptions of small towns in Mexico (Ingham, 1986, pp. 56–61).

"Estudios" Schema

Thus the term *educación* refers to the raising of a well-behaved child. Studying and staying in school are seen by parents as part of *educación;* spending time on the streets with *malas amistades* is definitely not part of *educación.* When referring to formal academic education—usually the referent for the word "education" in English—parents typically use the words *"estudios"* (study) or *"preparación"* (Reese, Balzano, Gallimore, & Goldenberg, 1995). Another common cultural model or schema we have documented is one that we have called the *"estudios"* schema. Derived from the oft-heard expression *"con más estudios mejor está uno"* (the more study that you have, the better off you are), this schema expresses the assumption that staying in school and attaining the highest level of schooling that one can are valued activities. Parents repeatedly remark that schooling is the avenue by which their children will be able to get a good job and "be someone." As one parent succinctly expressed it, *"Se necesitan estudios para obtener un buen trabajo, de otra manera no se puede"* ("You need to study in order to get a good job, otherwise you can't").

Thus, when children begin school, parent aspirations for their educational attainment are uniformly high, with over 90% of parents aspiring to university completion for their children. This cultural schema has been documented with working-class families in Mexico (Martin, 1990), as well as with immigrants in the Midwest (Carger, 1996). Not only the parents but also the high school students, higher and lower achievers alike, expressed support for the *estudios* schema. An academically low-performing male stated, "If you go to school every day, when you grow up you will get a better job"–a statement echoed by two-thirds of the students interviewed.

Our studies, therefore, have focused on understanding the cultural schemas, or models that inform human activity. Geertz (1983) has referred to cultural patterns as not only models "of the world," that is, understandings of the world and how things operate in the world, but also models "for the world," informing participants about how they should behave. But these cultural models are not timeless and unchanging.

Rather, they are influenced by the settings in which they are employed. Thus, understanding the ecological characteristics and constraints of the communities in which families live and raise children is another key component in our studies.

CULTURE IN A STATE OF FLUX

Assessments from the field of anthropology have critiqued ethnography as largely ahistorical in nature, describing a timeless present in which self-contained traditional cultures exist as they "always" have (Keesing, 1994). An example of adaptations made by families resulting in changes in cultural models is found in the area of literacy development. In 1989, at the beginning of the UCLA study, when children entered Kindergarten, 27% of the parents reported reading aloud to their children; of these, half reported starting when the child was 5 years old, and only 14% began as early as 2 years old. Many parents felt that below the age of 5 children would not be able to understand what was read to them, and most felt that reading before age 2 was just too young. When asked how they would explain American mothers' reading to very young children, Manuel's mother offered the explanation that *"debe ser una costumbre que ellos tienen"* ("must be a custom that they have"). Noemi's mother was less generous: *"Les leen porque no tienen otra cosa que hacer"* ("[Americans] read to them because they don't have anything else to do") (Reese & Gallimore, 2000, p. 115).

Maricela's mother was one who stated that she read to her oldest son when he began Kindergarten. Maricela, age 2 at the time, was not included because *"apenas tenía dos años y no estaba tan atenta porque estaba chiquita"* ("she was just two years old and wasn't so attentive because she was small"). Her mother began reading to Maricela when she entered preschool. The older brother, at this point participating in the home reading club at his school, kept asking his mother for books, but she reported answering him, *"Ay, ¿por qué quieres tantos libro?"* ("What do you want so many books for?") However, she later did begin to buy children's books and to visit the library regularly. By the time Maricela was in 1st grade, reading aloud to her and her younger sister was a regular occurrence. Their mother noted this time that the youngest sibling, a 2-year-old boy, was also attentive. She stated that the littlest boy *"se interesa porque ve más la bola. Todos están conmigo en la cama y quienes están arriba y uno por un lado y otro por el otro, y él ve y le llama la atención"* ("He's interested because he sees the whole group. Everyone's with me in bed and some are on top and one on one side and the other on the other, and he sees and is interested.") Whereas earlier she believed that 2-year-old Maricela was too little to attend to stories, now she sees that her 2-year-old son loves to listen. Thus, the mother's response to school-initiated home reading resulted in changes over time in her perceptions of the nature and value of the task of reading aloud (Reese & Gallimore, 2000, pp. 123–124).

Not only do we see changes in cultural models as families adapt to new settings and demands, we can also observe changes in the settings themselves over time. One way in which settings have changed for the immigrant families in our studies has been in the area of state and federal policies directing educational programs of instruction for English Language Learners. For example, the UCLA study began when state education policies mandated bilingual instruction for English Language Learners, with transitional bilingual programs being the most common forms of bilingual instruction. It is likely that parents interviewed for the UCLA study would be more likely to understand the homework that their children brought home and be able to communicate with their children's teachers (at least in the early elementary school years) than parents in California today. Currently, more restrictive language policies are in place as a result of the passage of Proposition 227, which sought to eliminate bilingual education in California (Gándara et al., 2010). It is possible that generalizations about parental involvement in schooling and help with homework from a study completed under policies favoring primary language use may not be as applicable under current conditions.

PLACE MATTERS

Use of an ecocultural approach compels us to take seriously the local settings in which our studies take place, because of the influence of ecology on the families' construction and sustaining of a daily routine of activities. Often the ways in which the setting may be shaping activities in the daily routine is not apparent until comparisons are made. Our work over the years has permitted a variety of comparative studies. One such comparison occurred during the UCLA longitudinal study as students were interviewed regarding their performance and interest in high school.

High School Settings

By the time students in the UCLA study were in high school, 30% of the students had moved away from their original neighborhoods. Those students who remained in the original neighborhoods attended three high schools, all of which were categorized by state accountability measures as being in the lowest-performing decile statewide. These "decile 1 schools" were large, overwhelmingly minority (averaging fewer than 3% White students), had large numbers of English Language Learners (33% on average per school), and were characterized by relatively high numbers of teachers with emergency credentials and without full certification (25% on average per school). Many of the students who had moved away found themselves in higher-ranking schools.

The students themselves described differences in their school settings that influenced both the quality of instruction that was offered as well as their own engagement in school and interest in their studies. In 90% of the Decile 1 schools that students attended, safety concerns were reported by students. Adriana described her attempts to stay out of trouble with girls in a crew who taunted and pushed her at her neighborhood school: "They say that I walk around like I'm the big thing at school. I was like I just walk. Mind my own business. Go to class. Get it over with. I just want the day to end. And that's it. That's just my main concern." By contrast, students in the higher-achieving (higher-decile) schools often described their schools as "calm" and "peaceful," and none reported incidents of fighting, stealing, or harassment (Reese, 2002).

Students in Decile 1 schools were also more likely to report having substitute teachers rather than regular teachers, or being unable to take books home because one set was shared among all periods. In addition, classes at the Decile 1 schools were more likely to be described by students as "easy," and only 40% of these students reported receiving homework on a daily basis. Carlos, a low achiever, explained, "All we had to do was go to class, show up, do our work, and that was our grade; 90% of the work was done in class. We didn't get homework for nothing." Evidence points to the conclusion that Decile 1 schools were more likely to produce or foster lower levels of engagement on the part of the students, and students themselves notice this difference (Reese, 2002). Emilia had gone to Hudson, her neighborhood high school, for a couple of months during her freshman year. She commented on the difference between her new school in a more upscale suburban neighborhood. "It's a bit harder. They give you more work to work on and it's harder. They challenge you more."

Thus, instructional settings that fail to engage students are more likely to be found in the schools in the Decile 1 range of academic performance. Although no differences between the two groups of students (those attending Decile 1 schools and those attending higher-ranking schools) were observed on literacy tests upon entrance to Kindergarten or on standardized tests of reading and math at the end of grade 1, by the time students were in high school students at Decile 1 schools had lower levels of engagement in school as well as lower levels of performance.

Settings in Mexico and Southern California

When children in the UCLA study finished middle school, a subset of students' parents (21 families) were asked if they had brothers or sisters in Mexico with children of about the same age as the study participants, and if they would be willing to contact their siblings to see if they would be willing to participate in interviews similar to those we carried out in the Los Angeles area. Twelve families met the criteria and agreed to participate. Parents and students were asked about their school experiences, their daily activities, and their aspirations and expectations for the future.

As families described their daily routines, a major difference that emerged between the two settings was the degree of perceived safety of the neighborhoods in which families resided. A theme that permeated interviews in Los Angeles was the danger that parents felt surrounded their children, both in a physical sense from gang violence and drug sales and in a moral sense in the form of *"malas amistades"* that could lead their children astray. The school itself was often reported to be the locale in which children were exposed to undesirable peer influences. Families responded by closely monitoring children's activities, keeping them inside the house or playing in sight of the parent. For example, kindergartner Carol received extra homework that her mother devised, in an effort to keep her occupied inside their small apartment. By contrast, Freddy's home had an enclosed driveway where he often played, and he was not kept inside and occupied with literacy activities (Reese, Goldenberg, Loucky, & Gallimore, 1995).

In the small towns and *ranchos* (isolated rural dwellings) where many of the families in the Mexican sample resided, however, parents reported having few of these concerns. They knew the families and children with whom their children associated, and were confident that neighbors would keep an eye out for all children. Parents were comfortable sending children as young as 4 to buy milk at a local store on their own. Young adolescents stayed out with their friends until 10 or 11 p.m. in the summer, and parents often did not know exactly where their children were during the day. Even in the major cities, where there was a greater level of concern and perception of danger in the environment, it was far from the level expressed by parents in Los Angeles. Interestingly, one of the small-town school principals interviewed felt that the very safety of the community led to what he saw as *"descuido,"* or lack of care on the part of the parents, which was reflected in lack of focus on academic pursuits.

It is not surprising, therefore, that children in the Mexico sample rated their parents as less strict than did children in the Los Angeles sample. In both urban and more rural settings in Mexico, there was a greater degree of control exercised over girls than boys. One of the boys in the Mexico study, a 14-year-old who had just finished *secundaria* (junior high), visited his relatives in Los Angeles during the summer following the study. He was reported to be bored staying home as much as his cousins did, and he could not understand why his aunt would not let them go to the local mall on their own. Thus, although parental values, level of education, and childhood experiences were similar between the two groups of families, the level of perceived danger in the U.S. environments resulted in parental accommodations that were much more controlling and limiting for children than the more relaxed controls over some aspects of children's activities and friendships in safer environments in Mexico. This was particularly true for boys, less so for girls as they entered adolescence (Reese, 2001).

MÉXICO AND EL OTRO MÉXICO

Keesing (1994) has contended that "anthropologists have disciplinary vested interests in construing cultural diversity in more extreme terms than our ethnographic evidence justifies" (p. 304). Studies in education that make use of concepts of culture and ethnicity often fall into similar characterizations of the values, beliefs, and behaviors of immigrants' "home country culture," casting the culture in terms of difference from the (imagined) U.S. culture and assuming cultural continuity over time. Our work in communities in Jalisco over the past decade has documented cultural changes taking place in Mexico that may result in conditions quite different from the ones experienced and remembered by immigrant parents as they grew up 2 or 3 decades ago (Reese, 2002; Reese & Gallimore, 2000).

The stories of the families in our studies, both those in Mexico as well as those now residing in the United States, can be viewed as part of a process of decision making within families that has been unfolding over generations. For example, the semirural and densely populated region of Los Altos de Jalisco, where the majority of families in the Mexico study resided, is an area that has experienced massive migration to the United States beginning as far back as the latter part of the 19th century (Orozco, 1992). López Castro (1986) notes that it is uncommon to find in western Mexico a family without at least one immigrant among its members. At the same time, the large-scale migration of undocumented immigrants from Mexico that has characterized the last 3 decades is on the decline, and evidence suggests that changes in Mexico itself—including expanding economic and educational opportunities and smaller family size—are contributing to lower rates of overall Mexican migration to the U.S. (Cave, 2011).

Heavy and sustained migration to the United States has contributed to the growth of migratory knowledge on the part of families that not only facilitates increased migration but also serves to transform the sending communities in the home country. As immigrant families in the United States adapt to American settings and school expectations, so, too, are families in Mexico in the process of adapting to changing settings. Culture change is not a one-way process, and life in villages, towns, and cities in Mexico is increasingly influenced by American styles, habits, commodities, and behaviors. The results of work in *el norte* (literally the north, referring to the United States) are seen in the form of clothes, appliances, CDs, and vehicles purchased in the United States and in the form of houses built with remittances from *el norte*. Drawing in the term *el norte* to refer to the United States in general, Alarcón (1988) referred to this cultural change phenomenon as the "northernization" of Mexico. Northernization includes not only the impact of American popular culture and the investment in Mexican communities of capital from work in the United States, but also the tendency toward a matrifocal lifestyle, as the wife of the migrant worker assumes greater responsibility at home for the domestic economy and the raising and educating of the children. An increase in absent working-age males has resulted in an increase of both women and children in the workplace in Mexico as well as problems with adolescent male children as women cope with raising their sons without a male figure present (Mummert, 1988).

Writing of growing up with family contacts on both sides of the Arizona border, Vélez-Ibáñez (1996) describes himself as born *"con un pie en cada lado"* ("with a foot on each side"). Even outside of the immediate border region, differences between México and the United States are increasingly blurred, as northernization occurs in the south and Latinization occurs in the north. For example, families in Guadalajara take their laundry to the Quick Wash, while in Los Angeles others buy records at the Discotienda (see Figure 10.1).

Children in a Guadalajara elementary school include jack-o-lanterns (associated with Halloween in the U.S.) in their illustrations of the celebration for the Day of the Dead (*Día de Muertos*), which is at the beginning of November (see Figure 10.2).

Figure 10.1. Images of "Northernization" in Guadalajara (a)
and "Latinization" in Los Angeles (b)

Life in *el norte* is being transformed through immigration. In California today, 27% of the population was born outside the United States (U.S. Census, 2010). In a neighborhood near the port of Los Angeles, a morning pilgrimage on the feast day of the patron saint of Mexico attracts little attention from commuters as residents walk along a major thoroughfare behind a newly painted image of the *Virgen de Guadalupe,* with a large arch of blue and white balloons swaying overhead. Bundled in sweatshirts and jackets against the chill, parents hold the hands of small children. Teenagers walk along with their families, some carrying poinsettia plants to be placed in the church. With a voice raw with emotion, a short woman in jeans and hooded sweatshirt leads chants, exhorting the group to join her in cries of *"Viva la Virgen de las Américas"* and *"Viva México."* And just as these transformations are occurring in the north, transformations are occurring in the immigrants' home country as well.

Figure 10.2. Jack-o-lanterns Included in Children's *Día de los Muertos* Art in Guadalajara and the U.S. Southwest Depicted as "Amexica"

On the same day in the town of Concepción in Jalisco, another procession begins in honor of the town's patron saint. The *Virgen de Guadalupe* is carried through the streets of the town in a procession that includes allegorical floats created by different organizations and clubs in the town. As described at the beginning of this chapter, there is a pilgrimage of the *"hijos ausentes"* (or absent children), townspeople who no longer reside in the town but who return for the town fiesta. On the cover of a book documenting the history of Concepción, written by the director of the local high school, remembrance of the home town is compared to remembrance of Jerusalem by the Jews in captivity in Babylon: *"Que la lengua se me pegue al paladar, si no me acuerdo de ti"* ("May my tongue cling to the roof of my mouth if I do not remember you").

A common theme in the U.S./Mexico study, as residents of Concepción talked of life in *"el norte,"* was the oft-repeated refrain that *"allá la gente se echa a perder"* (or "people spoil," in the same sense that food goes bad if left out too long). This moral ruin occurs because there is too much temptation and too much liberty. One of the allegorical floats in the procession compared the tranquil and family-centered life in Concepción with scenes from life in Chicago, complete with realistically portrayed vices of smoking and shooting up drugs. The allure of *el norte* is economic opportunity; it is the land where *"el dinero rinde más"* ("money is worth more"). But the allure of the home town is its moral safety, its commitment to traditional values.

And yet this reassuring image is not quite accurate either. Residents point to spacious and modern two-story homes that have been built recently in newer parts of town. Some homes and small businesses are funded by *hijos ausentes* who send money from their wages in the United States to relatives in their hometown; others are acknowledged to be homes of *narcos* (drug dealers or *narcotraficantes*) who ship drugs for sale in the United States. The drug trade, although recognized as an evil, was viewed with some ambivalence in Concepción, where *narcos* had made contributions to the local school and town fiesta. A local construction worker described the town's elite as treating their social inferiors *"con la punta del pie"* ("as if touching them with the tip of their toe"), while a well-known *narco* was more generous and egalitarian, on occasion inviting all the men in the bar to a drink.

Akhtar (1999) describes the immigrant's nostalgia as a mechanism resulting in an idealization of the past, in which everything from that past "acquires a glow" (p. 125). The home town is the place where one builds a home in expectation of retirement. Second-generation children residing in the United States plan weddings and *quinceañeras* (celebrations of a girl's 15th birthday) in their parents' hometowns.

As a consequence of a long history of contact, conquest, and migration, the families in our Los Angeles studies live in an American metropolis that hosts the third-largest Mexican population in the world. They join a Mexican-descent population that includes other recent immigrants, grandchildren of those who fled Mexico during the Revolution, and descendants of the original settlers and landowners of the 18th and 19th centuries. They join English-speaking Americans buying Mexican-style fast food at Taco Bell or eating at restaurants featuring the cuisine of Mexico and decorated in a style that is indistinguishable from establishments in many parts of Mexico. Residing in a state in which close to 40% of the population is Latino, Mexican immigrants live in an area that was once Mexico and is now "un-Mexico," a region politically separate yet retaining historical and cultural links with their homeland, a region sometimes referred to as *"el otro México,"* or the other Mexico (Anzaldúa, 1987).

IMPLICATIONS FOR RESEARCH AND PRACTICE

Gallimore and Goldenberg (2001) claim that the concept of culture can be of greater practical use in educational research and practice through use of the concepts of cultural models and cultural settings. They contend that "researching the features of culture using these ideas produces the kind of details most needed to address the linked problems of underachievement and school reform" (p. 47). The ecocultural approach utilized in our studies of immigrant Latino families in the United States and families in Mexico provides us with a unit of analysis—the routine of daily activity—that includes both the cultural models that inform and guide activity as well as the ecological niche within which the activities occur. Through shared activity, cultural models are continually reinforced and re-created and, at times, reshaped.

We have seen that parents' cultural models guide what they do with children and why they carry out the activities that they do. For example, when parents believe that children under the age of 5 are too young to understand stories that are read to them, they are not likely to read to preschool-aged children. Similarly, we have seen that local settings make a difference in how activities are carried out as well. For example, families in unsafe urban neighborhoods may share cultural values of *educación* and *estudios* with families in safer small towns in Mexico, and yet they may act on these values differently, keeping children inside and tightly monitored in one setting and not in another.

For practitioners, one of the questions becomes how to obtain the detailed information about parents' beliefs and understandings, as well as details about children's everyday lives, that will help them understand how best to engage children and how best to involve parents in their children's education in ways that are meaningful and strategic. The "funds of knowledge" approach described by Gonzalez, Moll, and their colleagues is one way in which teachers can obtain this information firsthand (Gonzalez, Moll, & Amanti, 2005). This approach involves teachers making visits to children's homes and engaging in conversations with parents in the role of learner rather than teacher. In this way, teachers obtain information not only about children's interests and activities, but also about the kinds of learning experiences the child participates in outside of the home. These experiences may include helping the family sell items at the local swap meet, using herbal remedies for everyday health conditions, and listening to sayings and refrains that encapsulate cultural knowledge. Other teachers develop surveys with their students about various aspects of home life, and use the findings from these surveys to inform social studies lessons, illustrate concepts, or create math problems. Still other teachers make use of the traditional parent conference to find out about students' home experiences as well as to share with parents the child's classroom performance (Amanti, 1995).

The ways in which teachers incorporate students' home and cultural experiences to enhance student comprehension and engagement are varied. Students' lives can form the basis of narrative and poetry writing (Atkin, 1993; Christensen, 2000), as well as forming the basis from which to engage in critical analysis (Bigelow, 2001; Lyman, 2001). Kindergarten teachers in a pilot project in the Central Valley of California (Reese, Jensen, & Ramirez, under review) chose to transform weekly homework to include interactive projects between parents and children to enhance children's understanding of the themes from their language arts program. For example, for a unit on transportation, children constructed a model of a mode of transportation they had experienced on a family trip and recounted a narrative of the trip for the class, with trips varying from a trip to the supermarket by bus to a flight to visit families in Mexico.

In addition, the changes taking place in Mexico call into question generalizations about students' "home country" or about "Mexican culture" that are often heard in U.S. schools. It is common for parents and teachers who are themselves second- and third-generation immigrants to assume that the experiences of their parents and grandparents continue to hold true for children being educated in Mexico today. Recent immigrants may not know or have participated in traditional celebrations of *Día de los Muertos,* but instead may have celebrated by chanting *"queremos Halloween"* (we want Halloween) on the eve of the Day of the Dead (November 1–2) instead. Investigating with students and families what the students' actual cultural practices and experiences are, and not assuming familiarity with an idealized traditional culture, is recommended.

Finally, for researchers, the challenge is to go beyond a description of the setting or of the sample in one's study, and seek out ways in which aspects of the setting may be influencing findings. For example, to what extent are findings from a study carried out with immigrant Latino students in "the new South" (Hamann, 2003) applicable to students in areas such as Los Angeles with long histories of immigration from Mexico? Posing these questions is likely to result in more cautious generalizations than are often the case in educational research.

REFERENCES

Akhtar, S. (1999). *Immigration and identity: Turmoil, treatment, and transformation.* Lanham, MD: Rowman and Littlefield Publishers, Inc.

Alarcón, R. (1988). El proceso de "norteñización": Impacto de la migración internacional en Chavinda, Michoacán. In T. Calvo & G. Lopez (Eds.), *Movimientos de población en el occidente de México* (pp. 337–357). Zamora, Mexico: El Colegio de Michoacán.

Anzaldúa, G. (1987). *Borderlands-La frontera: The new mestiza.* San Francisco, CA: Aunt Lute.

Atkin, S. B. (1993). *Voices from the fields.* Boston: Little, Brown & Company.

Bigelow, B. (2001). The human lives behind the labels: The global sweatshop, Nike, and the race to the bottom. In B. Bigelow, B. Harvey, S. Karp, & L. Miller (Eds.), *Rethinking our classrooms, Volume 2.* Williston, VT: Rethinking Schools.

Carger, C. (1996). *Of borders and dreams: A Mexican-American experience of urban education.* New York: Teachers College Press.

Cave, D. (2011, July 6). Better lives for Mexican cut allure of going north. *New York Times.*

Christensen, L. (2000). *Reading, writing, and rising up: Teaching about social justice and the power of the written word.* Milwaukee, WI: Rethinking Schools.

D'Andrade, R., & Strauss, C. (Eds.). (1992). *Human motives and cultural models.* New York: Cambridge University Press.

Foster, M. (1995). African American teachers and culturally relevant pedagogy. In J. Banks & C. McGee Banks (Eds.), *Handbook of research on multicultural education.* New York: Macmillan.

Gallimore, R., & Goldenberg, C. (2001). Analyzing cultural models and settings to connect minority achievement and school improvement research. *Educational Psychologist, 36*(1), 45–56.

Gándara, P., Losen, D., August, D., Uriarte, M., Gómez, C., & Hopkins, M. (2010). Forbidden language: A brief history of U.S. language policy. In P. Gándara & M. Hopkins (Eds.), *Forbidden language: English learners and restrictive language policies* (pp. 20–36). New York: Teachers College Press.

Geertz, C. (1983). *Local knowledge.* New York: Basic Books.

Giddens, A. (1987). *Social theory and modern sociology.* Stanford, CA: Stanford University Press.

Goldenberg, C., Gallimore, R., Reese, L., & Garnier, H. (2001). Cause or effect? A longitudinal study of immigrant Latino parents' aspirations and expectations and their children's school performance. *American Educational Research Journal, 38*(3) 547–582.

Gonzalez, N., Moll, L., & Amanti, C. (Eds.) (2005). *Funds of knowledge: Theorizing practices in households and classrooms.* Mahwah, NJ: Lawrence Erlbaum Associates.

Hamann, E. T. (2003). *The educational welcome of Latinos in the New South.* Westport, CT: Praeger.

Ingham, J. (1986). *Mary, Michael, and Lucifer: Folk Catholicism in Central Mexico.* Austin: University of Texas Press.

Keesing, R. (1994). Theories of culture revisited. In R. Borofsky (Ed.), *Assessing cultural anthropology.* New York: McGraw-Hill.

Lareau, A. (1989). *Home advantage.* New York: Falmer.

LeVine, R. A., & White, M. I. (1986). *Human conditions: The cultural basis of educational development.* New York: Routledge & Kegan Paul.

López Castro, G. (1986). *La casa dividida: Un estudio de caso sobre la migración a Estados Unidos en un pueblo michoacano.* Zamora, Mexico: Colegio de Michoacán.

Lyman, K. (2001). The trial: How one teacher explores issues of homelessness. In B. Bigelow, B. Harvey, S. Karp, & L. Miller (Eds.), *Rethinking our classrooms, Volume 2* (pp. 140–143). Williston, VT: Rethinking Schools.

Martin, C. (1990). To hold one's own in the world: Issues in the educational culture of urban working class families in West Mexico. *Compare, 20*(2), 115–139.

Mummert, G. (1988). Mujeres de migrantes y mujeres migrantes de Michoacán: Nuevos papeles para las que se quedan y para las que se van. In T. Calvo & G. Lopez (Eds.), *Movimientos de población en el occidente de México* (pp. 281–297). Zamora, Mexico: El Colegio de Michoacán.

Orozco, J. L. (1992). *El negocio de los ilegales: Ganancias para quién.* Guadalajara, Mexico: Instituto Tecnológico y de Estudios Superiores de Occidente (ITESO).

Reese, L. (2001). Morality and identity in Mexican immigrant parents' visions of the future. *Journal of Ethnic and Migration Studies, 27*(3), 455–472.

Reese, L. (2002a). Parental strategies in contrasting cultural settings: Families in México and "el norte." *Anthropology and Education Quarterly. 33*(3), 30–59.

Reese, L. (2002b, April). *Interest and engagement in school among second generation Latina/o adolescents.* Paper presented at the Biennial Meeting of the Society for Research on Adolescence, New Orleans, April 2002.

Reese, L. (2009). Literacy practices among immigrant Latino families. In G. Li (Ed.), *Multicultural families, home literacies, and mainstream schooling* (pp. 129–152). Charlotte, NC: Information Age Publishing.

Reese, L., Balzano, S., Gallimore, R., & Goldenberg, C. (1995). The concept of *educación*: Latino family values and American schooling. *International Journal of Educational Research, 23*(1), 57–81.

Reese, L., & Gallimore, R. (2000). Immigrant Latinos' cultural model of literacy development: An evolving perspective on home-school discontinuities. *American Journal of Education, 108*(2), 103–134.

Reese, L., Gallimore, R., & Goldenberg, C. (1999). Job-required literacy, home literacy environments, and school reading: Early literacy experiences of immigrant Latino children. In *Negotiating power and place at the margins: Selected papers on refugees and immigrants, Vol. VII*. Washington, DC: American Anthropological Association.

Reese, L., Gallimore, R., Goldenberg, C., & Balzano, S. (1995). Immigrant Latino parents' future orientations for their children. In R. Macias & R.G. Ramos (Eds.), *Changing schools for changing students*. UC Linguistic Minority Research Institute Publication.

Reese, L., Gallimore, R., & Guthrie, D. (2006). Impact of transition from Spanish to English instruction on the reading trajectories of immigrant Latino students. *Bilingual Research Journal, 29*, 679–698.

Reese, L., Gallimore, R., & Zarate, E. (2003). To be an American: Ethnic identity, biculturalism, and citizenship among second-generation immigrant Latino youth. *Kolor: Journal on Moving Communities, 3*(1), 3–14.

Reese, L., Garnier, H., Gallimore, R., & Goldenberg, C. (2000). A longitudinal analysis of the ecocultural antecedents of emergent Spanish literacy and subsequent English reading achievement of Spanish-speaking students. *American Educational Research Journal, 37*(3), 633–662.

Reese, L., Goldenberg, C., Loucky, J., & Gallimore, R. (1995). Ecocultural context, cultural activity, and emergent literacy of Spanish-speaking children. In S. W. Rothstein (Ed.), *Class, culture and race in American schools: A handbook*. Westport, CT: Greenwood Press.

Reese, L., Jensen, B., & Ramirez, D. (Under Review). Emotionally supportive classroom contexts for young Latino children in rural California. *Elementary School Journal*.

Reese, L., Kroesen, K., & Gallimore, R. (2000). Agency and school performance among urban Latino youth. In R. Taylor & M. Wang (Eds.), *Resilience across contexts: Family, work, culture and community*. Mahwah, NJ: Lawrence Erlbaum Associates.

Rogoff, B. (1990). *Apprenticeship in thinking: Cognitive development in social context*. Oxford, UK: Oxford University Press.

Rogoff, B. (2003). *The cultural nature of human development*. Oxford, UK: Oxford University Press.

Super, C., & Harkness, S. (1986). The developmental niche: A conceptualization at the interface of child and culture. *International Journal of Behavior Development, 9*, 1–25.

Tharp, R., & Gallimore, R. (1988). *Rousing minds to life: Teaching, learning, and schooling in social context.* New York: Cambridge University Press.

U.S. Census Bureau. (2010). *State and county QuickFacts.* (Data derived from Population Estimates, American Community Survey, Census of Population and Housing, State and County Housing Unit Estimates, County Business Patterns, Nonemployer Statistics, Economic Census, Survey of Business Owners, Building Permits, Consolidated Federal Funds Report.) Retrieved online: http://quickfacts.census.gov/qfd/states/06000.html

Valdés, G. (1996). *Con respeto: Bridging the distances between culturally diverse families and schools: An ethnographic portrait.* New York: Teachers College Press.

Vélez-Ibáñez, C. (1996). *Border visions.* Tucson: University of Arizona Press.

Weisner, T. S. (1984). Ecocultural niches of middle childhood: A cross-cultural perspective. In W. A. Collins (Ed.), *Development during middle childhood: The years from six to twelve.* Washington, DC: National Academy of Sciences.

Weisner, T. S. (1997). The ecocultural project of human development: Why ethnography and its findings matter. *Ethos, 25*(2), 177–190.

Weisner, T. S. (2002). Ecocultural understanding of children's developmental pathways. *Human Development, 45,* 275–281.

Whiting, B., & Edwards, C. (1988). *Children of different worlds: The formation of social behavior.* Cambridge, MA: Harvard University Press.

Zarate, E., Bhimji, F., & Reese, L. (2005). Ethnic identity and academic achievement in a Latino community. *Journal of Latinos and Education, 4,* 95–114.

CHAPTER 11

Fostering Resilience in Mexican American Youth Through Cultural and Family Assets

Gabriela Livas Stein,
Cynthia García Coll, and Nadia Huq

Mexican-origin students, referring to both Mexican immigrant youth as well as Mexican American youth born in the United States, along with their families, possess many assets that teachers and other school personnel can build on to promote resilience and positive academic outcomes. In this chapter we highlight ongoing research to examine some of the current trends in the cultural and developmental assets literature on Mexican-origin youth and their families. While our chapter is not exhaustive, it provides readers with an understanding of emergent issues regarding the cultural assets and developmental competencies of Mexican-origin youth that have applicability to schooling and public policy. Cultural assets are broadly conceptualized familial and individual factors that promote the adaptive development of Mexican-origin youth. Developmental competencies entail positive academic, psychological, and emotional outcomes for Mexican-origin youth that lead to adaptive functioning in the face of multiple stressors (García Coll et al., 1996). We examine current research on cultural strengths that lie within the child such as ethnic identity and biculturalism as well as familial and contextual factors that influence positive development, such as ethnic socialization, familism, and Mexican-American parenting. These factors have been studied in reference to school outcomes such as grades, performance on achievement tests, school motivation, attachment, and persistence. And we argue that they can also promote healthy social and psychological development among Mexican-origin youth.

Immigrant and ethnic minority youth's developmental path results in psychological, academic, and social competencies that are found universally across youth, but it also entails the development of unique competencies that are necessary to combat multiple sociopolitical and economic risk factors present in the lives of these youth (García Coll & Marks, 2009). For Mexican-origin youth in particular, the development of a positive ethnic identity and an ability to navigate between multiple cultural contexts are essential to becoming successful, well-adjusted students. Yet these competencies do not develop in a vacuum. Families, teachers, school personnel, and community members active in the lives of these youth are key socializing agents who promote and foster these competencies. This occurs as these agents provide messages regarding ethnicity and cultural values, nurture the connection to Mexican values, and help students understand the multiple worlds they inhabit.

INDIVIDUAL ASSETS

Ethnic identity and biculturalism are important to Mexican-origin students' sense of belonging and general well-being, in school and in other settings. Research shows this is especially true through middle childhood and adolescence (García Coll & Marks, 2009), when psychosocial development is rapid and often haphazard. We review representative research below, including emergent findings about the roles of ethnic identity and biculturalism in Mexican-origin students' academic well-being.

Ethnic Identity

Ethnic identity has emerged over the past 2 decades of developmental research as a key asset. It is more than a sense of belonging or attachment to a specific ethnic group. Ethnic identity is a "multidimensional, dynamic construct that develops over time through a process of exploration and commitment" (Phinney & Ong, 2007, p. 271). It entails ethnic behaviors and values, beliefs about how one and others view the ethnic group (i.e., private and public regard), exploration of one's identity, and the salience of one's ethnicity in relation to other aspects of identity (Phinney & Ong, 2007). Typically, ethnic identity is measured by asking youth to rate their level of agreement with sentences describing different aspects of identity (e.g., "I have a lot of pride in my ethnic group" or "I have spent time trying to find out more about my ethnic group, such as history, traditions, or customs"). Theorists argue that a strong sense of ethnic identity protects Mexican-origin youth (and other ethnic

minorities) against negative stereotypes, discrimination, and other ethnic stressors that youth face by providing them with a positive sense of
self and belonging and by highlighting the positive aspects of their ethnic group (e.g., Shelton, Yip, Eccles, Chatman, Fuligni, & Wong, 2005).
Latino youth who feel more connected to their group exhibit higher
self-esteem (e.g., Romero & Roberts, 2003), greater academic motivation (Fuligni, Witkow, & Garcia, 2005), and better school performance
(e.g., Supple, Ghazarian, Frabutt, Plunkett, & Sands, 2006) than those
without as much of an ethnic identity.

Research on ethnic identity in adolescence has focused particularly
on its association with discrimination. Not surprisingly, Mexican-origin
youth who feel connected to their ethnic group experience fewer negative psychological outcomes, such as depression or low self-esteem,
when they encounter discrimination (e.g., Romero & Roberts, 2003).
Though this work has emphasized psychological rather than academic
outcomes, it is important to note that schools are one of the primary
contexts where children and youth experience ethnic stereotypes and
discrimination (Quintana & McKown, 2008). Thus, promoting a strong,
positive ethnic identity may be an avenue for schools to help combat the
negative effects of discrimination. Teachers and school personnel can
help foster positive ethnic identity by encouraging students to appreciate ethnic group differences, which in turn can reduce discrimination
toward Mexican-origin youth.

In a similar vein, ethnic identity may be particularly important to
inoculate youth against stereotyped messages of academic failure and to
motivate youth to overcome academic challenges. In fact, Latino high
school students who are connected to their ethnic group and view their
ethnic identity as tied to their academic achievement maintain higher
GPAs compared to youth who are less connected to their identity (Alt-
shcul, Oyserman, & Bybee, 2006). This suggests that schools and teachers can promote increased academic performance by linking student
ethnic identity with school membership and academic excellence.

In addition to overcoming stereotypes and discrimination, ethnic
identity can help youth face other stressors as well. In a study of Mexican-
origin youth, those who held positive ethnic beliefs were better protected
against the stress of schoolwork and peer demands. Youth with strong
ethnic identity reported greater daily happiness when confronted by these
stressors than those with weak ethnic identity (Kiang, Yip, Gonzales-
Backen, Witkow, & Fuligni, 2006).

Although many people believe identity issues are restricted to adolescence, ethnic identity actually emerges during middle childhood
(Cooper, García Coll, Bartko, Davis, & Chatman, 2005; García-Coll &

Marks, 2009). Additionally, ethnic identity continues to change over the course of adolescence and into young adulthood (e.g., French, Seidman, Allen, & Aber, 2006). Thus, schools can begin to support the links between ethnic identity and academic achievement in the elementary years and should continue these supports through high school.

Finally, the social context of an individual's ethnic identity may also determine how ethnic identity impacts outcomes. One of the most important contexts may be the ethnic composition of neighborhoods. A strong sense of ethnic identity may be especially valuable when Mexican-origin youth constitute a minority of the student population in their school. In this case, they may be more likely to face discrimination and other ethnic stressors yet lack the social connectedness associated with an ethnic enclave (García Coll et al., 1996). Some research, however, suggests that Mexican-origin youth in schools with fewer Latinos report more positive ethnic identity than at schools where they make up a larger percentage of the student body (Umaña-Taylor, 2004). Additionally, among Latino college students (country of origin not reported), there was no relationship between ethnic belonging and self-esteem for youths living in California, where Latinos make up a large portion of the population. In the Midwest, where there are many fewer Latinos, greater ethnic belonging was related to greater self-esteem for Latino youth (Umaña-Taylor & Shin, 2008). Thus, it could be that the development and maintenance of ethnic identity is especially critical for Mexican-origin youth in communities with fewer co-ethnics. This consideration is important given existing migration patterns where Mexican-origin families are settling in states where they form a small minority of the overall population (e.g., North Carolina, Wisconsin).

Biculturalism

Generally defined as the maintenance a culture of origin while incorporating the values, beliefs, and practices of another, biculturalism is another individual competency that promotes psychological and academic well-being (Schwartz & Unger, 2010). It implies that the individual is and feels competent in disparate cultural settings. Though ethnic identity and biculturalism are related, the latter uniquely addresses how youth incorporate disparate values of two cultural worlds. Ethnic identity and biculturalism might even be orthogonal, as you can be high in one and low in the other. In a study of immigrant youth in 26 countries, a bicultural orientation was associated with greater life satisfaction, greater self-esteem, fewer depressive and anxious symptoms, fewer behavior problems, and improved school adaptation (Berry, Phinney,

Sam, & Veeder, 2006). A bicultural orientation is also the most common type (compared to straight assimilation to the host country or
separation from the majority culture). For U.S. Latinos, biculturalism
has also been associated with improved psychological adjustment (e.g.,
less depression, improved self-esteem), better quality of life, cognitive
flexibility, greater adaptability, less family conflict, and less likelihood
of dropping out of school (Bacallao & Smokowski, 2009).

A next step in this research is to understand the explanatory mechanisms that link biculturalism to positive developmental outcomes—particularly academic outcomes such as academic persistence and school
adaptation. In a recent qualitative study of student resilience (Campa,
2010), Mexican-origin college students highlighted the importance of
biculturalism to academic success. They attributed their academic persistence to the struggle and sacrifice of their parents as well as the larger
struggle of their community—suggesting an orientation to Mexican values of familism and collectivism. They understood that their resilience
was based on their ability to navigate the school system and interact
effectively with other ethnic groups. They mentioned their knowledge
of the unwritten rules of academia as well as building their social capital through relationships with professors who could help them obtain
scholarships, write letters of recommendation, and provide guidance.
This type of research points to important explanatory mechanisms such
as familism, collectivism, social capital, and knowledge of U.S. systems
to understand how biculturalism leads to positive academic outcomes
(see Chapter 12, this volume). It also points to the importance of early
opportunities for Mexican-origin students to acquire competencies to
successfully navigate disparate cultural settings.

An important question that remains to be answered is how cultural
maintenance can serve as a protective mechanism for Mexican-origin
youths of later immigrant generations. This question emerges in part from
the "immigrant paradox" finding, where first- and second-generation
immigrant children demonstrate greater psychological and academic
resilience than those of later generations (García Coll & Marks, 2011).
Theorists posit that this paradox results because Mexican immigrant
youth maintain their connection to natal cultures while at the same time
assimilating to U.S. culture, whereas third- and fourth-generation Mexican Americans tend to lose the cultural values and practices of their
grandparents. Thus, later generations are less likely to draw on protective
factors in pursuit of academic success. Another way to understand how
biculturalism leads to positive outcomes is to clarify *how* the maintenance
of cultural values and identity is actually protective.

One avenue through which biculturalism protects youth may be through native language (i.e., Spanish) maintenance. Bilingual children and adolescents—especially those in the second generation—report higher self-esteem and higher educational and occupational aspirations, and are less likely to drop out of high school compared to English-monolingual Latinos (Bacallao & Smokwoski, 2009; Portés & Rumbaut, 2001). In fact, native language maintenance is associated with better academic achievement and school effort in Mexican-origin youth (Hao & Bonstead-Burns, 1998; Kim & Chao, 2009). So at least part of the protective effects of Mexican American biculturalism against undesirable outcomes stems from native language maintenance, associated with cultural socialization.

Of course, biculturalism is not achieved without the incorporation of U.S. values and norms (in conjunction with cultural maintenance); thus it is important to understand how acculturation to the host culture occurs. Whereas there is no monolithic U.S. culture, some researchers posit that the culture to which immigrant groups assimilate has significant ramifications for their educational and occupational status (Portés & Zhou, 1993). The theory of *segmented assimilation* proposes that an immigrant youth can assimilate either to White middle-class culture or to a culture of the U.S. underclass (associated with low socioeconomic and minority status). This controversial position argues that disengagement from majority norms and institutions while at the same identifying with impoverished minority groups places immigrant communities at risk for continued poverty and poor academic outcomes (Portés, 2003).

It is important to note, however, that the effects of this affiliation often depend on the characteristics of the ethnic enclave (García Coll & Marks, 2011). In fact, only 10% of immigrants demonstrate this pattern of acculturation, and many immigrant youth in these low-SES communities do quite well in school (García Coll & Marks, 2011; Stepick & Stepick, 2010). Not surprisingly, it is through the retention of the values of the country of origin *and* the social capital associated a close-knit immigrant community that provide access to resources Mexican-origin youth need to develop resilience in the face of barriers like racism, segregation, low-quality schools, and poor neighborhoods (García Coll et al., 1996; Portés & Zhou, 1993; Stepick & Stepick, 2010).

Certainly, further research is needed to understand optimal patterns of biculturalism. Padilla (2006) defines biculturalism as "an individual who possesses two social persona and identities. The person is equally at ease with members of either ethnic culture and can easily switch from one cultural orientation to the other" (p. 472). While useful, this definition does not take into account whether identities associated with each culture are separate or integrated. An integrated bicultural identity would mean that regardless of contrasts, the individual possesses a cohesive sense of self that incorporates both cultures, whereas a separate identity refers to individuals who maintain two different cultural sets (Schwartz & Unger, 2010). Little research has examined whether one is more strongly associated with psychological and academic outcomes than the other. One study found that Mexican-origin adolescents who demonstrated integrated biculturalism were more likely than separate biculturals to report positive attitudes toward other ethnic groups and to take pride in the accomplishments of their co-ethnic peers (Phinney & Devich-Navarro, 1997). Separated biculturals, however, were more likely to be bilingual, view their languages as two separate parts of themselves, and be less connected to their U.S. identity than integrated biculturals. Separated biculturals reported identity shifts associated with the changes in their environmental contexts—consistent with Padilla's (2006) definition of *social flexibility*.

Research with Asian populations has also documented these two patterns of biculturalism on cognitive tasks, finding that integrated biculturalism leads to greater cognitive fluidity than a separated biculturalism (Benet-Martinez, Leu, Lee, & Morris, 2002). Therefore, some compelling research suggests that these two patterns of biculturalism may lead to different outcomes. Schools might inadvertently foster separated biculturalism, as students may feel the need to behave in ways more consistent with U.S. culture at school while demonstrating a different cultural set at home. Schools and families may be able to work together to foster a sense of integration across the home and school settings to amalgamate cultural values and identity that can ultimately lead to positive academic outcomes.

FAMILY ASSETS

Further research on the developmental assets of ethnically diverse populations has focused on the family as the unit of analysis. Obviously, social forces beyond the family influence children and youth. Particularly for Mexican-origin students (Fuligni, Witkow, & Garcia, 2005; Gamble & Modry-Mandell, 2008), however, the family is a critical institution for the development of individual assets mentioned above. The research literature points to ethnic-racial socialization, "familism," and parenting practices as important processes associated with psychosocial and, increasingly, academic well-being for Mexican-origin children and youth.

Ethnic-Racial Socialization

In order to understand the cultural values and strengths of Mexican-origin families, we need to examine the process through which Mexican-origin children and youth learn about their cultural heritage. The literature has used both the terms *racial* and *cultural socialization* to describe parenting practices associated with teaching children about cultural values, living in a racialized society, and coping with discrimination (Hughes et al., 2006). We use the term adopted by other investigators, *ethnic-racial socialization,* which attempts to integrate across diverse literatures. A majority of this research has focused on four family practices:

- Cultural socialization—practices parents use to teach children about their ethnic heritage and cultural customs, and to promote ethnic/racial pride
- Preparation for bias—parental messages of potential ethnic/racial discrimination, in conjunction with messages about effective coping mechanisms to deal with this bias
- Promotion of mistrust—the ways parents warn their children to be wary of intercultural interactions, emphasizing the barriers to success ethnic minorities often encounter
- Egalitarianism—messages from parents that promote a color-blind approach, emphasizing the universalities among ethnic groups (Hughes et al., 2006)

For Mexican-origin families, most research on ethnic-racial socialization has focused on cultural socialization, the most common type among ethnic groups. Eighty-eight percent of Mexican-origin parents report using cultural socialization (Phinney & Chavira, 1995), and Mexican-origin youth report receiving more frequent messages of cultural socialization from their parents than European American students report receiving from their parents (Huynh & Fuligni, 2008). Cultural socialization leads to a more positive ethnic identity and self-esteem in ethnic minority youth (e.g., Rodriguez, Umaña-Taylor, Smith, & Johnson, 2009). Less research, however, has been dedicated to understanding how cultural socialization relates to child outcomes. Some studies show that cultural socialization may be linked to academic self-efficacy and school engagement (Hughes et al., 2006). Indeed, Mexican-origin students who report greater cultural socialization also report stronger intrinsic motivations, greater personal value, and higher perceived utility of school content (Huynh & Fuligni, 2008).

One reason cultural association may be linked to academic well-being is that academic messages can be embedded in messages of cultural socialization (Hughes et al., 2006). That is, parents may socialize their children to see academic success as an avenue to move out of poverty in a racially stratified society by acquiring higher-wage employment. In interviews with Mexican-origin parents, half reported providing these types of messages to their children (Phinney & Chavira, 1995). Immigrant parents in general have high academic and career expectations for their children (García Coll & Marks, 2009).

Fewer studies have examined the other aspects of ethnic-racial socialization (i.e., preparation for bias, promotion of mistrust, and egalitarianism) in Mexican-origin families. Phinney and Chavira (1995) found 58% of the Mexican-origin parents discussed discrimination with their children, supporting the notion that bias preparation is an important aspect of ethnic-racial socialization in Mexican-origin families. It is not clear, however, how bias preparation relates to psychological and academic well-being for Mexican-origin children and other ethnic minority groups. One study found no statistically significant relationships between the two for Mexican-origin youth (Huynh & Fuligni, 2008), and studies with other ethnic groups have documented negative relationships with academic outcomes (Hughes et al., 2006).

Familism and Family Obligation

Familism is considered one of the most important cultural values among Mexican-origin families (Marin, 1993). Compared to other ethnic groups, familism among Mexican Americans is particularly high (Fuligni & Pedersen, 2002; Phinney, Ong, & Madden, 2000). Familism "involves an individual's strong identification with and attachment to his or her nuclear and extended families and strong feelings of loyalty, reciprocity, and solidarity" (Lugo Steidel & Contreras, 2003, p. 314). Filial obligation, defined as "the extent to which family members feel a sense of duty to assist one another and to take into account the needs and wishes of the family when making decisions" (Fuligni & Pedersen, 2002, p. 856), is an important aspect of familism. Compared with Euro-Americans, Mexican-origin adolescents and their parents demonstrate greater levels of filial obligations, including current family assistance and expected support in the future (Fuligni, Tseng, & Lam, 1999; Tseng, 2004). Familism and filial obligations remain constant cultural values, even for Mexican-origin youth who have acculturated or who are children or grandchildren of immigrants (Fuligni, Tseng, & Lam, 1999; Fuligni & Pedersen, 2002; Tseng, 2004).

It is hypothesized that greater familism among Mexican-origin youth is associated with greater respect toward parents, in addition to fewer problem behaviors (Germán, Gonzales, & Dumka, 2009). Some propose that familism promotes higher academic achievement because success in school is important for family honor. Familism has been linked to many positive psychological outcomes in Mexican-origin youth, including increased self-esteem and fewer internalizing symptoms (e.g., depression, anxiety, withdrawal) (e.g., Gonzales, Deardoff, Formoso, Barr, & Barrera, 2006), and fewer conduct problems like aggression (German et al., 2009). In terms of academic achievement, in a sample of Latino adolescents (40% Mexican-origin), familism was related to fewer missed classes, greater academic motivation, and higher GPA (for those whose mothers had limited formal schooling) (Esparza & Sánchez, 2008). In a younger Mexican-origin sample, familism strengthened the relationship between maternal warmth and closeness and positive preschool functioning (Gamble & Modry-Mandell, 2008), suggesting that familism is associated with positive development across age groups.

Theorists posit that greater levels of filial obligations help immigrant youth succeed in school because their parents tend to have high educational aspirations for their children (Stepick & Stepick, 2010). On the other hand, others have argued that greater filial obligations undermine study time and college attendance (Fulgini & Pedersen, 2002). Although there is some evidence that high levels of filial obligations interfere with academic functioning, moderate levels are associated with greater motivation and valuing of education (Fuligni et al., 1999). In the transition to adulthood, greater filial obligations have been found to promote college attendance in youth with lower GPAs (Fuligni & Pedersen, 2002).

Language brokering–or language interpretation for a family member–is a type of filial obligation that has been examined a little more closely. Some have argued that this practice helps Mexican-origin youth communicate more effectively, navigate their social environment, and feel the satisfaction of helping their family (Love & Buriel, 2007). Others argue that language brokering increases stress associated with responsibility and obligation (e.g., Martinez, McClure, & Eddy, 2009). To date, the research is not clear one way or the other. Some studies document greater stress and poorer academic functioning associated with language brokering (Martinez et al., 2009), whereas others find language brokering to be protective in certain situations (e.g., with greater responsibility in the home, in closer parent-child relationships, when youth report greater ethnic identity) (Love & Buriel, 2007; Villanueva & Buriel, 2010; Weisskirch, 2005, 2006).

In terms of academic well-being, language brokering is thought to improve children's cognitive flexibility and language development (Dorner, Orellana, & Li-Grining, 2007; Orellana, 2009). Some studies show that language brokering is associated with higher GPA and reading performance for Mexican-origin students (Buriel, Perez, de Ment, Chavez, & Moran, 1998; Dorner et al., 2007; Orellana, 2009). In addition, language brokering may help to foster natal language maintenance, ethnic identity, and the preservation of important cultural values (Love & Buriel, 2007).

Mexican-Origin Parenting

Several years of research show that Mexican-origin parents tend to value obedience (Delgado-Gaitan, 1993) and respectful behavior (Arcia & Johnson, 1998) from their children. Indicators of respect and obedience include children politely greeting guests, sitting quietly among adults, not interrupting, respecting elder authority, showing proper manners, and, most importantly, keeping within your expected family role (Delgado-Gaitan, 1993; Valdés, 1996).

Along with obedience and respect, Mexican-origin parents value children's good moral upbringing and proper comportment. Well-behaved, moral children are deemed *bien educados* (well educated) because they exhibit *buenos modales (*good manners), and they know right from wrong (Goldenberg & Gallimore, 1995). Misbehaving children need to be set on the *buen camino* (the right path) (Reese, Balzano, Gallimore, & Goldenberg, 1995) through moral molding. *Educación* helps children not only to behave within their social spheres, but to succeed in school (Reese et al., 1995).

Traditional Mexican-origin parenting goals are accompanied by practices that promote respect and *educación* from young childhood through adolescence. Indeed, Mexican-origin parents report high levels of monitoring, parental control, parental decision making (vs. child autonomy), psychological control, and giving *consejos* (advice) (see Halgunseth, Ispa, & Rudy, 2006, for a review). Of course, the goals and practices of Mexican-origin parents are not static. They depend on acculturation levels and exposure to the U.S. school system. Further research is needed to understand how parenting goals and practices within Mexican-origin families change across generations following immigration (Halgunseth et al., 2006; Livas-Dlott et al., 2010).

Despite corollary risk factors (e.g., poverty, low parental education, language barriers), these parenting practices are associated with better academic performance among Mexican-origin students. Indeed, parental supportiveness, acceptance, involvement, and monitoring are related to higher GPA and achievement scores among Mexican-origin youth (DeGarmo & Martinez, 2006; Keith & Litchtman, 1994; Rodriguez, 2002; Ruiz, 2009; Updegraff, McHale, Whiteman, Thayer, & Crouter, 2006). Parental involvement, communication, support, and monitoring also predict greater school engagement and motivation and higher educational aspirations in Mexican-origin youth (Mireles-Rios & Romo, 2010; Plunkett & Bámaca-Gómez, 2003; Plunkett, Henry, Houltberg, Sands, & Houltberg, 2008). Moreover, Mexican-origin parenting interacts with teacher variables in school settings to influence student outcomes. For example, student perceptions of teacher support predicted academic motivation, satisfaction, and GPA of Mexican-origin students (Plunkett et al., 2008), where more support was associated with improved outcomes.

In addition to promoting positive academic outcomes specifically, Mexican parenting also provides youth with socioemotional advantages that may be critical to the successful academic adaptation of Mexican-origin youth. Overall, research has found that social competence of young Mexican-origin children is quite strong (Galindo & Fuller, 2010). Moreover, Mexican American kindergartners with greater social competence demonstrated greater growth in math skills throughout the school year. Supporting the notion that bilingualism is protective, the study also found that students from English-dominant homes where some Spanish was spoken showed more robust math skills than Mexican-origin students from English-only homes (Galindo & Fuller, 2010). Thus, it appears that current parenting practices within Mexican-origin communities support social development of Mexican youth and that these practices can be retained in ways that lead to improved academic performance. Specifically, practices related to maintaining cultural ties and Spanish language are essential and should be encouraged in Mexican-origin families.

However, other studies show that traditional Mexican-origin parenting is not enough to make needed improvements to students' academic performance (Aud, Fox, & Kewal-Ramani, 2010; Crosnoe, 2006). As Claudia Galindo shows in Chapter 4 of this volume, Mexican-origin students continue to lag substantially behind their White, non-Hispanic peers in academic achievement. These findings in later childhood are juxtaposed with emerging research that suggests that young Mexican-origin children actually begin life with particular advantages compared to other ethnic groups in the United States (Padilla, Hamilton, & Hummer, 2009). For example, Mexican-origin newborns–particularly those with immigrant parents–are less likely than White, non-Hispanic newborns to be underweight or born prematurely. Mexican-origin children have a lower mortality rate despite the fact that they are more likely to be living in poverty (e.g., Fuller, Bridges, Bein, Jang, Jung, et al., 2009; Hummer, Powers, Pullum, Gossman, & Frisbie, 2007). This robust research finding has been linked to healthier maternal prenatal practices of Latina mothers compared to White mothers (see Padilla et al., 2009), suggesting that cultural practices may provide Mexican-origin children with healthy advantages that may have long-term implications for development.

More recently, researchers have been attempting to understand how positive birth outcomes extend to toddlers and preschool children. In examining health outcomes, it appears that the birth advantages dissipate over time—especially for second-generation youth (Fuller et al., 2009; Padilla et al., 2009). By 24 months Mexican-origin children demonstrate slower cognitive growth compared to White children when accounting for SES and parenting practices. More research is needed to understand how to support the cognitive development of Mexican-origin infants to maintain the positive advantages they demonstrate at birth. Perhaps low levels of maternal education and poverty in Mexican-origin families serve as barriers to parents providing the optimal environment to promote cognitive growth (Fuller et al., 2009). A recent study found that Mexican-origin mothers who pursued more education were more likely to be involved in their children's schooling (Crosnoe & Kalil, 2010). This finding suggests that providing parents with educational opportunities can change parenting practices. Similarly, in the study by Fuller et al. (2009), middle-class Mexican-origin toddlers did not significantly differ from their White peers in terms of cognitive development—highlighting the role of SES in these outcomes. Both of these studies support the notion that positive changes in the socioeconomic context relate to parenting practices in ways that support the cognitive growth of Mexican-origin children, even though academic performance differences between Mexican-origin and White, non-Hispanic students tend to persist beyond the effect of family SES (Galindo, Chapter 4, this volume).

Overall, Mexican-origin parents appear to differ from other ethnic groups in their parenting goals and practices. Much research shows that these goals and practices lead to positive child and adolescent outcomes, and thus should be viewed as assets that support the growth of developmental competencies in Mexican-origin youth. It is imperative, however, to understand how Mexican-origin parenting can better support their children's language and cognitive development to succeed in U.S. society. Moreover, it appears that parenting goals can be enhanced through educational opportunities that build on natal practices rather than attempt to replace them. This objective should bear in mind that many Mexican-American parents highly value and want to support their children's academic success, though they may lack the resources to do so.

CONCLUSIONS

We have highlighted the unique cultural and familial assets of Mexican-origin youth–especially as they relate to academic outcomes. Though there has been a great increase in the amount of research examining these assets, many questions remain unanswered. It is particularly important to understand how multiple factors work synergistically to promote the developmental competencies of Mexican-origin youth. How do ethnic identity, biculturalism, and language brokering interact to promote self-esteem and academic competence? In addition, research needs to elucidate the optimal contexts that foster a positive ethnic identity and retention of cultural values. Why do some Mexican-origin youth retain a connection to culture of origin while others do not? What are the important values from both Mexican and U.S. culture that promote resilience?

Second, whereas the research we reviewed in this chapter was conducted with preschoolers to college students of Mexican-origins, little is known about the importance of these assets throughout development. We conjecture that the relative importance of some assets versus others changes as children develop. More longitudinal studies are needed to answer how cultural practices and values change through time, and also to detail their developmental influence in different contexts.

RECOMMENDATIONS FOR PRACTITIONERS

Though many questions remain unanswered, the extant literature is sufficient to guide teachers and schools toward practices that take advantage of the cultural and family assets of Mexican-origin students. We suggest that school practitioners promote ethnic identity and biculturalism among Mexican-origin students, and support cultural socialization and educational opportunities for their parents. Teachers and curriculum committees should emphasize the history and literature of Mexican-origin peoples from elementary through high school. This would have multiple benefits in terms of students' ethnic identity. First, it increases Mexican-origin students' knowledge of the deep Mexican-American legacy. Youth growing up in immigrant families may not know the rich history of Mexican populations in the United States. Second, teaching ethnic-oriented content communicates to Mexican-origin students that their teachers and schools value the contributions of their ethnic group, thereby improving their perception of how others view their ethnic group. And third, students of other ethnic groups will also increase their knowledge of Mexican-origin people, which can serve to counter negative stereotypes. This curriculum should not be limited to Hispanic Heritage Month or done in a cursory manner, but thoughtfully integrated with other school content. States and school districts (e.g., Tuscon Unified School District No. 1) prohibiting ethnic studies should come to terms with the psychosocial and academic restraints these policies place on their students.

As mentioned, teachers and schools should seek to link students' ethnic identity with academic achievement and excellence. Whereas Mexican-origin families tend to highly value academic success and parents communicate these messages to their children, Mexican-origin students may be discouraged by the lack of visible Latino role models that help increase self-efficacy for academic success. When students are exposed to co-ethnic role models, they increase their interest in and persistence toward academic performance while nourishing ethnic pride and knowledge. These role models can be older students in the district, local college students, community leaders, local business owners, and/ or school personnel. To positively influence students' self-efficacy, role models should share as many individual and family characteristics with students as possible. Schools can collaborate with local Latino professional societies, college and university clubs, and parents to locate potential role models. Needed resources should be allocated to support stable, long-term mentorships.

Parents and teachers should collaborate to support biculturalism and a strong ethnic identity. Teachers should be aware that for many Mexican-origin parents, their respect for teachers may lead them to view academics as the school's responsibility alone (see Chapter 6, this volume), whereas the obligation of morality and character-molding belongs to the family in the home. Thus, teachers may need to invite parents to participate in academic activities that foster the socialization goals of respect and obedience within the school. Teachers should start the school year by eliciting the academic and social goals that parents have for their children in order to develop home and school activities that support these goals. Home visits at the beginning of the academic year are especially helpful to establish personal partnerships between schools and families. For some families, particularly monolingual Spanish-speaking, teachers and school personnel should provide guidance to parents with regard to homework completion in English. In these conversations, teachers can also assess students' language brokering or familial obligations. Teachers can help parents understand how filial obligations support their child's education and vice versa.

Finally, cultural and family assets research points to larger school policies and practices to help teachers provide a culturally enriching and supportive environment for their pupils and families. Native language maintenance is essential to the success of Mexican-origin students, so schools should promote bilingualism (rethinking restrictive language policies in states like Arizona, California, and Massachusetts). In so doing, schools, offering professional development as needed, can encourage biculturalism and thus communicate to students and families that their ethnicity is valued. Schools should also provide avenues for parents to communicate with one another and build a supportive network around their Mexican-origin student body. In this way children are linked to a wider community of Latinos who can provide positive ethnic messages, model success, and support their academic needs. Schools should also provide teachers with the freedom to incorporate into the curriculum history, art, and literature content that addresses the rich backgrounds of multiple U.S. ethnic groups.

REFERENCES

Altschul, I., Oyserman, D., & Bybee, D. (2006). Racial-ethnic identity in mid-adolescence: Content and change as predictors of academic achievement. *Child Development, 77,* 1155–1169.

Arcia, E., & Johnson, A. (1998). When respect means to obey: Immigrant Mexican mothers' values for their children. *Journal of Child and Family Studies, 7,* 79–95.

Aud, S., Fox, M., & Kewal-Ramani, A. (2010). *Status and trends in the education of racial and ethnic groups* (NCES 2010-015). U.S. Department of Education, National Center for Education Statistics. Washington, DC: U.S. Government Printing Office.

Bacallao, M. L., & Smokowski, P. R. (2009). Entre dos mundos/Between two worlds: Bicultural development in context. *The Journal of Primary Prevention, 30*(3-4), 421–451.

Benet-Martínez, V., Leu, J., Lee, F., & Morris, M. (2002). Negotiating biculturalism: Cultural frame-switching in biculturals with "oppositional" vs. "compatible" cultural identities. *Journal of Cross-Cultural Psychology, 33,* 492–516.

Berry, J. W., Phinney, J. S., Sam, D. L., & Vedder, P. (2006). Immigrant youth: Acculturation, identity, and adaptation. *Applied Psychology, 55*(3), 303–332.

Buriel, R., Perez, W., de Ment, T.L., Chavez, D.V., & Moran, V.R. (1998). The relationship of language brokering to academic performance, biculturalism, and self-efficacy among Latino adolescents. *Hispanic Journal of Behavioral Sciences, 20(3),* 283–297.

Campa, B. (2010). Critical resilience, schooling processes, and the academic success of Mexican Americans in a community college. *Hispanic Journal of Behavioral Sciences, 32*(3), 429–455.

Cooper, C. R., García Coll, C. T., Bartko, W. T., Davis, H., & Chatman, C. (Eds). (2005). *Developmental pathways through middle childhood: Rethinking contexts and diversity as resources.* Mahwah, NJ: Lawrence Erlbaum Associates.

Crosnoe, R. (2006). *Mexican roots, American schools: Helping Mexican immigrant children succeed.* Stanford, CA: Stanford University Press.

Crosnoe, R., & Kalil, A. (2010). Educational progress and parenting among Mexican immigrant mothers of young children. *Journal of Marriage and Family, 72*(4), 976–990.

DeGarmo, D. S., & Martinez, C. R. Jr. (2006). A culturally informed model of academic well-being for Latino youth: The importance of discriminatory experiences and social support. *Family Relations, 55,* 267–278.

Delgado-Gaitan, C. (1993). Research and policy in reconceptualizing family-school relationships. In P. Phelan & Ann Davidson (Eds.), *Cultural diversity and educational policy and change* (pp. 139–159). New York: Teachers College Press.

Dorner, L. M., Orellana, M. F., & Li-Grining, C. P. (2007). "I helped my mom," and it helped me: Translating the skills of language brokers into improved standardized test scores. *American Journal of Education, 113*(3), 451–478.

Esparza, P., & Sánchez, B. (2008). The role of attitudinal familism in academic outcomes: A study of urban, Latino high school seniors. *Cultural Diversity and Ethnic Minority Psychology, 14*(3), 193–200.

French, S. E., Seidman, E., Allen, L., & Aber, J. (2006). The development of ethnic identity during adolescence. *Developmental Psychology, 42*(1), 1–10.

Fuligni, A. J., & Pedersen, S. (2002). Family obligation and the transition to young adulthood. *Developmental Psychology, 38*(5), 856–868.

Fuligni, A. J., Tseng, V., & Lam, M. (1999). Attitudes toward family obligations among American adolescents with Asian, Latin American, and European backgrounds. *Child Development, 70*(4), 1030–1044.

Fuligni, A. J., Witkow, M., & Garcia, C. (2005). Ethnic identity and the academic adjustment of adolescents from Mexican, Chinese, and European backgrounds. *Developmental Psychology, 41,* 799–811.

Fuller, B., Bridges, M., Bein, E., Jang, H., Jung, S., Rabe-Hesketh, S., Halfon, N., & Kuo, A. (2009). The health and cognitive growth of Latino toddlers:

At risk or immigrant paradox? *Maternal and Child Health Journal, 13*, 755–768.

Galindo, C., & Fuller, B. (2010). The social competence of Latino kindergartners and growth in mathematical understanding. *Developmental Psychology, 46*(3), 579–592.

Gamble, W. C., & Modry-Mandell, K. (2008). Family relations and the adjustment of young children of Mexican descent: Do family cultural values moderate these associations? *Social Development, 17*(2), 358–379.

García Coll, C., Crnic, K., Lamberty, G., Wasik, B. H., Jenkins, R., García, H. V., & McAdoo, H. P. (1996). An integrative model for the study of developmental competencies in minority children. *Child Development, 67*, 1891–1914.

García Coll, C., & Marks, A. K. (2009). *Immigrant stories: Ethnicity and academics in middle childhood.* New York: Oxford University Press.

García Coll, C., & Marks, A. K. (2011). *The immigrant paradox in children and adolescents: Is becoming an American a developmental risk?* Washington, DC: American Psychological Association.

García Coll, C., Germán, M., Gonzales, N. A., & Dumka, L. (2009). Familism values as a protective factor for Mexican-origin adolescents exposed to deviant peers. *The Journal of Early Adolescence, 29*, 16–42.

Goldenberg, C. N., & Gallimore, R. (1995). Immigrant Latino parents' values and beliefs about their children's education: Continuities and discontinuities across cultures and generations. In P. Pintrich & M. Maehr (Eds.), *Advances in motivation and achievement* (pp. 183–227). Greenwich, CT: JAI Press.

Gonzales, N. A., Deardorff, J., Formoso, D., Barr, A., & Barrera, M. J. (2006). Family mediators of the relation between acculturation and adolescent mental health. *Family Relations: Interdisciplinary Journal of Applied Family Studies, 55*(3), 318–330.

Halgunseth, L. C., Ispa, J. M., & Rudy, D. (2006). Parental control in Latino families: An integrated review in the literature. *Child Development, 77*(5), 1282–1297.

Hao, L., & Bonstead-Bruns, M. (1998). Parent-child differences in educational expectations and the academic achievement of immigrant and native students. *Sociology of Education, 71*(3), 175–198.

Hughes, D., Rodriguez, J., Smith, E. P., Johnson, D. J., Stevenson, H. C., & Spicer, P. (2006). Parents' ethnic-racial socialization practices: A review of research and directions for future study. *Developmental Psychology, 42*, 747–770.

Hummer, R. A., Powers, D. A., Pullum, S. G., Gossman, G. L., Frisbie, W. P. (2007). Paradox found (again): Infant mortality among the Mexican-origin population in the United States. *Demography, 44*(3), 441–457.

Huynh, V. W., & Fuligni, A. J. (2008). Ethnic socialization and the academic adjustment of adolescents from Mexican, Chinese, and European backgrounds. *Developmental Psychology, 44*(4), 1202–1208.

Keith, P. B., & Lichtman, M. (1994). Does parental involvement influence the academic achievement of Mexican-American eighth graders? Results from the national education longitudinal study. *School Psychology Quarterly, 9*(4), 256–273.

Kiang, L., Yip, T., Gonzales-Backen, M., Witkow, M., & Fuligni, A. J. (2006). Ethnic identity and the daily psychological well-being of adolescents from Mexican and Chinese backgrounds. *Child Development, 77,* 1338–1350.

Kim, S., & Chao, R. K. (2009). Heritage language fluency, ethnic identity, and school effort of immigrant Chinese and Mexican adolescents. *Cultural Diversity and Ethnic Minority Psychology, 15*(1), 27–37.

Livas-Dlott, A., Fuller, B., Stein, G. S., Bridges, M., Mangual Figueroa, A., & Mireles, L. (2010). Commands, competence, and cariño: Maternal socialization practices in Mexican American families. *Developmental Psychology, 46*(3), 566–578.

Love, J.A., & Buriel, R. (2007). Language brokering, autonomy, parent-child bonding, biculturalism, and depression: A study of Mexican American adolescents from immigrant families. *Hispanic Journal of Behavioral Sciences, 29*(4), 472–491.

Lugo Steidel, A. G., & Contreras, J.M. (2003). A new familism scale for use with Latino populations. *Hispanic Journal of Behavioral Sciences, 25,* 312–330.

Marin, G. (1993). Influence of acculturation on familism and self-identification among Hispanics. In M. E. Bernal & G. P. Knight (Eds.), *Ethnic identity: Formation and transmission among Hispanics and other minorities* (pp. 181–196). Albany, NY: State University of New York Press.

Martinez Jr., C.R., McClure, H.H., & Eddy, M. (2009). Language brokering contexts and behavioral and emotional adjustment among Latino parents and adolescents. *The Journal of Early Adolescence, 29*(1), 71–98.

Mireles-Rios, R., & Romo, L. F. (2010). Maternal and teacher interaction and student engagement in math and reading among Mexican American girls from a rural community. *Hispanic Journal of Behavioral Sciences, 32*(3), 456–469.

Orellana, M. F. (2009). *Translating childhoods: Immigrant youth, language, and culture.* Piscataway Township, NJ: Rutgers University Press.

Padilla, A.M. (2006). Bicultural social development. *Hispanic Journal of Behavioral Sciences, 28*(4), 467–497.

Padilla, Y. C., Hamilton, E. R., & Hummer, R. A. (2009). Mexican American health in early childhood: Is the health advantage at birth sustained? *Social Science Quarterly, 90*(5), 1072–1088.

Phinney, J. S., & Chavira, V. (1995). Parental ethnic socialization and adolescent coping with problems related to ethnicity. *Journal of Research on Adolescence, 5,* 31–53.

Phinney, J. S., & Devich-Navarro, M. (1997). Variations in bicultural identification among African American and Mexican American adolescents. *Journal of Research on Adolescence, 7,* 3–32.

Phinney, J., & Ong, A. (2007). Conceptualization and measurement of ethnic identity: Current status and future directions. *Journal of Counseling Psychology, 54*(3), 271–281.

Phinney, J. S., Ong, A. D., & Madden, T. (2000). Cultural values and intergenerational value discrepancies in immigrant and non-immigrant families. *Child Development, 71*(2), 528–539.

Plunkett, S. W., & Bámaca-Gómez, M. Y. (2003). The relationship between parenting, acculturation, and adolescent academics in Mexican-origin immigrant families in Los Angeles. *Hispanic Journal of Behavioral Sciences, 25*(2), 222–239.

Plunkett, S.W., Henry, C.S., Houltberg, B.J., Sands, T., & Abarca-Mortensen, S. (2008). Academic support by significant others and educational resilience in Mexican-origin ninth grade students from intact families. *Journal of Early Adolescence, 28*(3), 333–355.

Portés, A., & Zhou, M. (1993). The new second generation: Segmented assimilation and its variants. *Annals of the American Academy of Political and Social Science, 530,* 74–93.

Portés, A., & Rumbaut, R.G. (2001). *Legacies: The story of immigrant second generation.* Berkeley: University of California Press.

Portés, A. (2003). Ethnicities: Children of migrants in America. *Development, 46,* 42–52.

Quintana, S. M., & McKown, C. (2008). Introduction. In S. M. Quintana & C. McKown (Eds.), *Race, racism, and the developing child* (pp. 1–15). Hoboken, NJ: John Wiley & Sons.

Reese, L., Balzano, S., Gallimore, R., & Goldenberg, C. (1995). The concept of educación: Latino family values and American schooling. *International Journal of Educational Research, 23*(1), 57–81.

Rodriguez, J. L. (2002). Family environment and achievement among three generations of Mexican American high school students. *Applied Developmental Science, 6*(2), 88–94.

Rodriguez, J. L., Umaña-Taylor, A. J., Smith, E. P., & Johnson, D. (2009). Cultural processes in parenting and youth outcomes: Examining a model of racial-ethnic socialization and identity. *Cultural Diversity and Ethnic Minority Psychology, 15*(2), 106–111.

Romero, A. J., & Roberts, R. E. (2003). The impact of multiple dimensions of ethnic identity on discrimination and adolescents' self-esteem. *Journal of Applied Social Psychology, 33*(11), 2288–2305.

Ruiz, Y. (2009). Predictors of academic achievement for Latino middle schoolers. *Journal of Human Behavior in the Social Environment, 19*(4), 419–433.

Schwartz, S. J., & Unger, J. B. (2010). Biculturalism and context: What is biculturalism and when is it adaptive? *Human Development, 53*(1), 26–32.

Shelton, J. N., Yip, T., Eccles, J. S., Chatman, C., Fuligni, A. J., & Wong, C. (2005). Ethnic identity as a buffer of psychological adjustment to stress. In G. Downey, J. S. Eccles, & C. M. Chatman (Eds.), *Navigating the future: Social identity, coping and life tasks* (pp. 96–113). New York: Russell Sage Foundation.

Stepick, A., & Stepick, C. D. (2010). The complexities and confusions of segmented assimilation. *Ethnic and Racial Studies, 33*(7), 1149–1167.

Supple, A. J., Ghazarian, S. R., Frabutt, J. M., Plunkett, S. W., & Sands, T. (2006). Contextual influences on Latino adolescent ethnic identity and academic outcomes. *Child Development, 77,* 1427–1433.

Tseng, V. (2004). Family interdependence and academic adjustment in college: Youths from immigrant and U.S.-born families. *Child Development, 75,* 966–983.

Umaña-Taylor, A. J. (2004). Ethnic identity and self-esteem: Examining the role of social context. *Journal of Adolescence, 27*(2), 139–146.

Umaña-Taylor, A. J., & Shin, N. (2007). An examination of ethnic identity and self-esteem with diverse populations: Exploring validation by ethnicity and geography. *Cultural Diversity & Ethnic Minority Psychology, 13,* 178–186.

Updegraff, K. A., McHale, S. M., Whiteman, S. D., Thayer, S. M., & Crouter, A. C. (2006). The nature and correlates of Mexican-American adolescents' time with parents and peers. *Child Development, 77*(5), 1470–1486.

Valdés, G. (1996). *Con respeto: Bridging the distances between culturally diverse families and schools: An ethnographic portrait.* New York: Teachers College Press.

Villanueva, C. M., & Buriel, R. (2010). Speaking on behalf of others: A qualitative study of the perceptions and feelings of adolescent Latina language brokers. *Journal of Social Issues, 66*(1), 197–210.

Weisskirch, R.S. (2005). The relationship of language brokering to ethnic identity for Latino early adolescents. *Hispanic Journal of Behavioral Sciences, 27*(3), 286–299.

Weisskirch, R.S. (2006). Emotional aspects of language brokering among Mexican American adults. *Journal of Multilingual and Multicultural Development, 27*(4), 332–343.

CHAPTER 12

Social Capital and the Academic Resources of Mexican Youth in New York City

Francisco X. Gaytan

The educational outcomes of the U.S. Mexican-descent population are a concern for the United States as a whole because of the size and relative youth of this group. In New York City Mexicans are the fastest-growing immigrant group (Cortina & Gendreau, 2003), so the educational success of the group in this area is a particular concern. In 2007, the Mexican-descent population of New York City swelled to 288,629 individuals (U.S. Census Bureau, 2007). Due to low participation in the Census by undocumented Mexicans (Smith, 2005), Rivera-Batiz (2004) calculated that a more accurate estimate of New York City's Mexican-origin population in the year 2000 would have been between 275,000 and 300,000, compared to the official number of 186,872. Extrapolating from those estimates, the 2007 population would likely be between 385,000 and 465,000. Population increases in New York's Mexican-origin population due to migration have also been augmented by relatively high birth rates among Mexican immigrant women. There were nearly 29,000 births to Mexican mothers between 1990 and 1996, the third-highest number of births to an ethnic group behind Dominicans and Jamaicans. The trend of rapid growth has continued to the present, with births to Mexican mothers representing the largest to any ethnic group in New York City in 2005 (Bernstein, 2007). In addition to this large American-born Mexican population, there were over 11,000 Mexican-born students enrolled in the New York City public schools as recently as 2004 (New York City Department of City Planning, 2004). The significant number of Mexican-descent children thus represents an important consideration for the New York City public schools. Looking at the multiple contexts and interpersonal influences in the lives of this group is an important step in gaining a holistic understanding of their academic adaptation (Bronfenbrenner, 1977).

Despite a rapid growth in New York City, there has been little systematic investigation of the school-age portion of this population. The experiences of Mexican youth in the United States have typically been documented in areas such as California, Texas, and the Southwest. Research on Mexican immigrants in New York City is important because of their relative newcomer status in a city with a large presence of other large Latino, Spanish-speaking immigrant groups, namely those from the Dominican Republic and Puerto Rico. While evidence suggests that Mexican immigrants in New York have tightly knit communities that engage in transnational political practices, religious practices, and local community activities (Smith, 2005), the connections they have to the larger society and access to mainstream institutions are not very strong.

Immigrant groups come to the United States with varying levels of economic and human capital, such as financial assets, information, education, and cultural knowledge (i.e., language, norms, and customs) that aid or hinder their adaptation. In addition to these individual resources, their social capital, or the relationships that provide them with support and resources, before, during, and after their arrival to the new country will lead to different pathways of adaptation (Portes & Zhou, 1993). Access to these resources comes from one's position and status within a social network, according to social capital theory (Bourdieu, 1986), rather than resulting solely from individual capacity or effort. With respect to education, immigrant students who have more educated parents, who understand the intricacies of the U.S. educational system, who have the ability to communicate in English, and who have access to systems of social support and power will fare better than immigrant students who does not have these resources (Suárez-Orozco, Suárez-Orozco, & Todorova, 2008). The benefits of social capital generated through supportive relationships with teachers include a significantly lower probability of high school dropout, particularly for youth from socially disadvantaged backgrounds (Croninger & Lee, 2001). Unfortunately, Mexican immigrants and their descendants have low levels of social capital in terms of parental education and occupational status, with few connections to teachers who might supplement parental support (Stanton-Salazar, 2001; Valenzuela, 1999).

Simple connections through proximity, regular contact, institutional organization, and social events, as some social capital theorists have posited as sufficient for aiding social functioning and individual well-being

(Coleman, 1988; Putnam, 2000), are not enough; for minority and immigrant students, the *quality* of these connections is paramount. Studies of Mexican immigrant youth in Texas and California reveal that genuine, caring connections to informal mentors and respect for culture, or discriminatory and "subtractive" approaches toward Mexican-descent youth on the part of school staff, can affect educational outcomes. The findings of Valenzuela (1999) and Stanton-Salazar (2001) confirm the view that the neighborhoods and social contexts that immigrants settle in and the contact they have with other ethnic minority groups can be instrumental in the production of social capital (Noguera, 2004). The options available to immigrants are constrained by personal background (i.e., language, geographic location, personal preferences) and by constraints that others impose (i.e., discrimination and geographic isolation). Constraints in social network composition can thus be self-perpetuating and can limit socioeconomic opportunities for certain groups by hindering the generation of positive social capital. Wacquant (1998) terms this reliance on social networks that lead to limited or downward socioeconomic mobility "negative social capital." Conversely, Granovetter (1973) argued that access to those with power and information, even through a single social network member, can greatly enhance life opportunities. So while an immigrant group, such as Mexicans in living in an urban ethnic enclave, may have "bonding social capital" (Woolcock & Narayan, 2000) or social support provided within the immigrant family and community, "bridging social capital," or relationships outside the family that connect their immigrant world to the dominant culture and socioeconomic opportunities, may be scarce and thus limit opportunity and mobility (Woolcock & Narayan, 2000).

This chapter thus explores how Mexican immigrant youth in New York City are able to generate social capital, given their socioeconomically disadvantaged backgrounds, through relationships with individuals within and outside their families and communities. I examine the existence of social connections and support (i.e., social capital), as well as the generation and the specific nature of that support.

APPROACH TO RESEARCH

Both quantitative and qualitative methods were utilized in this study. A mixed-methods approach in this project was useful for several reasons. First and foremost, this study was an examination of a particular group of students in a real-world context, and mixed methods lend themselves well to this type of research (Tashakkori & Teddlie,

1998). Relationships are naturally complicated and complex, so it is beneficial to utilize more than one approach to thoroughly examine this topic. A mixed-methods approach offered a pragmatic way to capture the effects of relationships on the educational experiences of Mexican-descent youth in a nuanced way. The quantitative data precisely captured the different types of academic support provided by social networks. The qualitative data complemented these findings by capturing the meaning students made around the adults in their lives and the process of how social networks provided support (Maxwell, 1996). Collecting both quantitative and qualitative data also allowed for stronger conclusions to be drawn through triangulation, or the corroboration of findings (Tashakkori & Teddlie, 1998).

I was at once an insider and an outsider in this study. My own background as a researcher and second-generation Mexican American aided recruitment and allowed for the establishment of quick rapport with the participants. At the same time, my status as an adult with a high level of education distanced me from my participants. Thus I had a unique perspective into the lives of the study participants. I refrain from judgments as to whether my pragmatic perspective is better or worse than either a more objective/quantitative study or a more phenomenological/subjective study; rather, I make my values and experiences explicit here to show how they add both validity and limitations to the findings.

I used a snowball method to recruit students for participation in this study. The specificity of the sample and the difficulty of reaching out to an immigrant community that could be suspicious of research projects such as this one made this approach necessary in order to get a large enough sample to complete the investigation. There are several indications that a diverse sample of youth participated in the study. The students in the sample attended 42 different schools, lived in 21 zip codes, and came from all 5 boroughs of the city. One hundred and seven Mexican-descent youth living in New York City and attending public middle or high schools during the 2007–2008 school year participated in this study. Participants ranged in age from 12 to 19 years (mean = 14.81, s.d. = 1.80). The total sample was 49.5% male ($n = 53$) and 50.5% female ($n = 54$).

No students who met the selection criteria of being born in Mexico (first-generation) or born in the United States to two Mexican immigrant parents (second-generation) were excluded. First-generation students comprised 23.4% ($n = 25$) of the sample and second-generation students represented 76.6% ($n = 82$) of the sample. The 25 first-generation students had spent between 4 and 17 years in the United States (mean = 10.62, s.d. = 3.42), suggesting that many of them were actually generation

1.5 (arriving before 12 years of age) or generation 1.75 (arriving before 6 years of age). The fact that there were very few students over the age of 12 in the sample was not surprising, given that many adolescents who arrive from Mexico enter directly into the labor force rather than school (Fry, 2004).

SURVEY DATA

First let us look at the quantitative data generated by the survey I administered to the 107 students in my sample. I assisted students in completing a measure that assessed the composition and function of their social networks. I first asked the students to generate a list of "the important people" in their lives, which we wrote down together. These people were then categorized by their relationship to the student: family, peers, adult community members and adults at school. The latter two categories comprised the larger non-relative adult category. Students then characterized these people by several factors including their language use, educational status, country of origin, and frequency of contact, which were annotated. Students also completed a written checklist of whether or not these individuals had provided them with a list of 16 emotional and academic resources (e.g. "Who tells you about college?" "Who makes you feel respected?" etc.) in the past year.

Social Network Size and Composition

There was a wide range in the reported size of students' networks (see Table 12.1). Students reported social networks with a size ranging from 1 to 20 individuals, with an average size of about 7.

When looking at the size of network membership by the type of relationship they had to the student, we see that family members were represented in the highest numbers, on average, with a mean size of

Table 12.1. Social Network Descriptives

	Minimum	Maximum	Mean	SD
Total Family	0	17	4.49	2.95
Total Peers	0	9	1.77	2.24
Total Non-Rel. Adult	0	4	0.43	0.90
Total Network	1	20	6.71	3.95

Source: Survey conducted by Francisco X. Gaytan under the auspices of New York University's IRB.

4.49, followed by peers with a mean size of 1.77 and finally non-relative adults, with fewer than 1 in each student's network on average (mean = .43).

Given the unequal distribution of the data, I created dichotomous categories (i.e., "at least 1" vs. "none") that were used in network analyses from this point forward. Examining the data categorically, describing networks in terms of those who had at least one member from a particular relationship category (i.e., family, peer, non-relative adult), I found the following:

- 95.3% named at least one family network member ($n = 102$)
- 57.0% named at least one peer ($n = 61$)
- 25.2% named at least one non-relative adult ($n = 27$)

The educational status of social network members was examined next. Among the parents of the youth in the sample, 18.7% ($n = 20$) had mothers who had completed 12 years of schooling, and 11.2% ($n = 12$) of the youth reported having fathers who had completed 12 years of schooling. Looking more broadly at the educational status of all social network members, 65.4% ($n = 70$) of students named no college graduates in their networks (see Figure 12.1). In terms of college-educated non-relative adults, 21.5% ($n = 23$) of students named a network member in that category; 13.1% ($n = 14$) of students named a family member who was a college graduate. Of note is that all of the students who had a family member who was a college graduate also had non-relative college graduates in their social network. This suggests that having more educated family members may generate more social capital in terms of access to college-educated individuals outside the family.

Students' social networks were comprised largely of co-ethnics, with 50.5% ($n = 54$) of students reported having only Mexican individuals in their social networks, leaving roughly the other half of students with non-Mexican-descent individuals named as important network members. Looking at the pan-ethnic category of Latino, including all individuals of Latin American origin, 29% ($n = 31$) of students reported having at least one non-Latino individual in their social networks. Thus the overwhelming compositions of these students' social networks included individuals of Latino descent (71%; $n = 76$).

The students in the sample reported the following about their household-language usage:

- 4.7% ($n = 5$) spoke Spanish exclusively in their homes
- 26.2% ($n = 28$) spoke more Spanish than English

Figure 12.1. Percentage of Students with at Least 1 College-Educated Network Member in Selected Categories

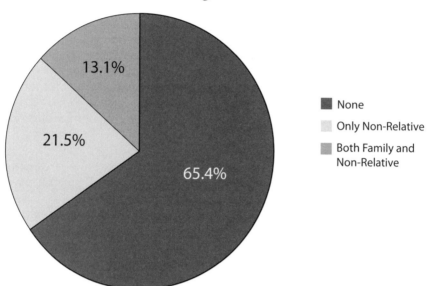

Legend:
- **None**
- Only Non-Relative
- Both Family and Non-Relative

13.1%

21.5%

65.4%

- 47.4% ($n = 51$) used both languages equally
- 21.5% ($n = 23$) spoke more English than Spanish
- None spoke English exclusively

In addition to the student reports of their own language use and the language use of those in their social networks, several unintended pieces of language data emerged during the student interviews. First, the overwhelming majority of students preferred that the surveys and interviews be conducted in English. Some intermittently mingled Spanish words in their conversations (Spanglish), but the recorded interviews and surveys were primarily in English. When students were asked about their home language, a significant number asked if they could disaggregate their language use by the person with whom they were speaking. Students clarified either on their own or with my probing that they typically only spoke Spanish to their parents and English to their siblings. Among those students who spoke Spanish, the transcribed interviews revealed a large number of grammatical errors. Together, this information suggests the contextual nature of language use generally, and the likelihood that among this largely second-generation sample, English was a stronger preference than the home language survey indicated.

Academic Support

To gauge different types of tangible academic supports, students were asked:

1. Whether a network member had ever provided information about college
2. Whether a member had ever helped the student study for an exam
3. If a member had ever helped the student with a homework assignments

Students named family members as providing support more frequently than peers, and peers providing academic support more frequently than non-relative adults.

Overall, 77.6% ($n = 83$) of youth reported receiving information about gaining access to college from some source, whereas 22.4% ($n = 24$) of youth did not receive this information from anyone in their social networks. Nearly 64% ($n = 68$) of students reported that a family member was the source of college information; these students had at least one family member who told them about college access. Only 16.8% ($n = 18$) had at least one non-relative adult in their social network who provided this kind of information. Another 21.5% ($n = 23$) turned to peers as they considered college choices (see Figure 12.2).

More than one-fourth (28%, $n = 30$) of students said that they had no one in their social network who helped them study for an exam; 72% ($n = 77$) of the participants had someone to turn to for help as they prepared for exams, however. Only 14% ($n = 15$) of students reported receiving assistance in studying for an exam from a non-relative adult, whereas 75.7% ($n = 81$) reported receiving this assistance from a family member and 28% ($n = 30$) received this help from peers (see Figure 12.3).

Turning to homework help, 10.3% ($n = 11$) of students reported that no one provided help with homework, compared to 89.7% ($n = 96$) of students who reported receiving help in this area. Among the youth receiving help, 16.6% ($n = 18$) received help with homework from non-relative adults, compared to 35.5% ($n = 38$) who reported receiving this help from peers, and 75.7% ($n = 81$) who received it from a family member (see Figure 12.4).

Figure 12.2. College Information by Source

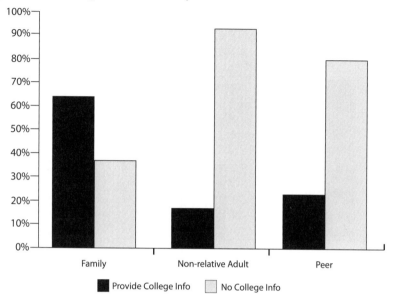

Figure 12.3. Help Studying for Exam by Source

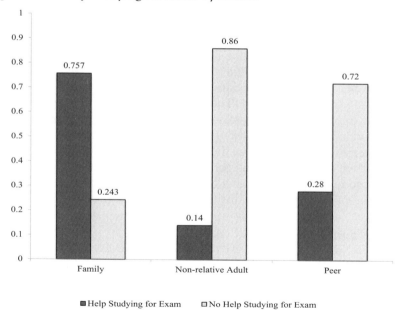

Source (Figures 12.2 & 12.3): Francisco X. Gaytan

Figure 12.4 Homework Help by Source

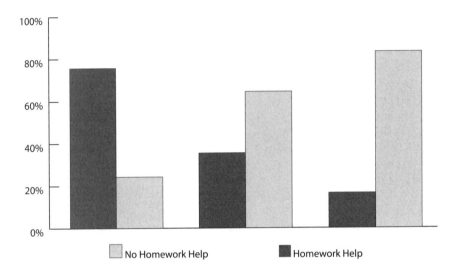

Source: Survey conducted by Francisco X. Gaytan under the auspices of New York University's IRB.

INTERVIEW DATA

The semi-structured qualitative data revealed some themes that helped provide specific examples of the types of support students reported receiving in the quantitative survey data as well as expanding upon the meaning they made from this support. The data were analyzed both deductively, building upon the survey questions and existing theories of social capital and academics, and inductively, using a grounded theory approach to find emerging themes. Some of the support that was described by students was particular to certain categories of network members (i.e., parents, peers, and teachers), while other themes of support were provided across the different significant relationships students reported.

Encouraging Academics

Descriptions of general encouragement to do well in school were very common in the qualitative data and were described by the students in much the same way regardless of the source. For example: a 16-year-old male describes his parents' advice: "They just say that I have to study a lot to go to college." Another description of general encouragement from a mother around grades comes from the following 15-year-old fe-male: "Like when I get low grades, which is most of the time, she keeps on telling me that I shouldn't be getting low grades and she gives me speeches." A 19-year-old female who was a senior in high school re-ceived the following message from her mother:

> *Student*: She tells me that since I'm the only, like, it's only me and my brother, so she hopes that both of us could go through college and become a better person.
> *Interviewer*: Did she go to college?
> *Student*: No.
> *Interviewer*: OK. Did she tell you anything in particular about how to get into college or anything like that?
> *Student*: No, she just tells me to do good in school, to get good grades, and just keep up with my work.

General academic support and encouragement were not limited to parents. An 18-year-old male stated that teachers "always told me to have good grades." A 14-year-old boy similarly described support he re-ceived from teachers when he said that they "just tell me to do all my work and like to study more and to do better on my quizzes and my tests." Another 14-year-old male described a similar sentiment from a teacher he quoted as saying, "Oh, you should try hard and try to get a good job and don't ever give up if you're not sure on something, just try, try, try." Although the quantitative data showed that family mem-bers were the most frequent sources of academic support, the qualita-tive data show how rare it was for students to receive specific advice about what to do to achieve academic success (e.g., help with actually completing a homework assignment or assistance in finding someone to provide specific homework help). A key issue here is that these are student perceptions of the support they received, and may not reflect whether the support was actually provided or available. It may be that students were only able to receive encouragement because their own baseline level of understanding was at a level too low to comprehend much beyond the basics or because they did not feel connected to teach-ers. Nonetheless, it was apparent in the data that few adults in the lives of these youth were gauging how or whether this general support was being translated into positive academic outcomes.

The significance of tangible support was nonetheless seen among some students. I will next explore how the different types of social net-work members, family, non-relative adults, and peers, each provided concrete forms of academic support to the participants in this sample.

Academic support from family. A 16-year-old female student de-scribed the tangible academic support she received from her father: "He loves to study. He'll sit me down and read to me and influence me. He has a big Spanish dictionary and we'll translate things." A male student, age 13, describes his mother's support: "Sometimes she helps me with math. Like she remembers what she used to do and she teaches me. If I don't understand a problem she helps me." Notable is that this support comes in the area of math, which does not necessarily require English language skills, and the fact that the student is in middle school, a level of education of the average parents in this sample. A 14-year-old male described another occurrence of tangible parental support, displaying the proactive involvement of his mother.

> *Interviewer*: Is there anybody else that influences you to be a
>   certain type of student?
> *Student*: My mother.
> *Interviewer*: What does she say?
> *Student*: She's really, really supportful [*sic*]. Like she's really, really
>   into my school and she's into almost everything I do. She's like
>   nosy, I guess in a way, but nosy in the good way.
> *Interviewer*: Like what does she do?
> *Student*: She talks to all my teachers. She gives them her cell
>   phone number to call them just in case I don't do the
>   homework.
> *Interviewer*: And how often does she talk to your teachers?
> *Student*: Every marking period.
> *Interviewer*: Is that only if you're doing poorly or is it also if you're
>   doing good?
> *Student*: Even if I'm doing good.
> *Interviewer*: Does your mom speak English?
> *Student*: Yes.

This parent obviously has some of the skills necessary, such as language, to be able to actively advocate for her child's education. She also demonstrated a confidence in dealing directly with school staff, showing the importance of maintaining connections between home and school even when things are going well for a student at school. Unfortunately, most of the Mexican immigrant parents of the study participants did not have such skills; descriptions of parents giving tangible help and proactively engaging with school staff were espe-cially rare in the data.

One student very bluntly explained why she was not able to access tangible support from her mother when she stated, "My parents don't help with my education. It's not that they're ignorant; they just don't know specifically how to help." A 12-year-old female reiterated this point when explaining why she did not go to her parents for tangible academic help: "Well, they got really bad educations because they were like in Mexico. Both of my parents only went to like the eighth grade, eighth or ninth grade."

Ideally, students with immigrant parents and families with low educational levels and limited knowledge of how to navigate the U.S. educational system would be able to rely on the academic support of teachers and other non-relative adults. Lamentably, the data showed that few students found these individuals to be available as sources of aid.

Academic support from teachers. While the quantitative data showed that academic support provided by teachers and other non-relative adults was not as frequent as support given by parents, the qualitative data revealed insight into how teachers were quite helpful when they did provide assistance. A 17-year-old female described the tangible support she typically seeks out and receives from teachers: "If I miss school, I go to teachers and ask about what I missed. If there's a lesson I don't understand, I go after school so a teacher will explain it to me." In this case teacher assistance seems to be the result of the student's initiative to seek out help. An instance of an exemplary teacher providing concrete academic support is described in the following quote from a 17-year-old female:

> *Student*: So this teacher I had for freshman, sophomore and junior year. So last year he told me, he knows I like math and that I'm good at it. So he told me to take [calculus] as an elective. And he's like, I'm sure you're going to do well. It's complicated at the beginning because you're not used to it, but as time goes you're going to get it. It's going to get easier for you. And AP Psychology is the same teacher.
> *Interviewer*: The math teacher and the psychology teacher?
> *Student*: Yeah, he is very smart. And, um, he told me, I'm also going to teach psychology, so if you want to participate.

This collaborative planning of coursework that demonstrated an empathic understanding of this student's abilities and needs is not only an example of concrete support provided in a caring manner, but is also emblematic of how social capital can generate access to opportunities previously unavailable. This same student went on to describe how this same teacher would be a ready source of help to students by providing regular after-school and weekend study sessions:

He takes his time to teach us. Like if we're behind, he's like we could stay after school, or you can come on Saturday and we can make it up or we could practice a little bit more.

Again, it is apparent that this particular teacher was willing to go above and beyond the limits of a school day to ensure the success of his students. His extra effort appeared to have made quite an impact on this student. Given the potential influence of highly motivated and engaging teachers on students from immigrant families, it is an unfortunate missed opportunity given that these descriptions of receiving concrete support from non-relative adults were rare in the qualitative data. At the same time, given the scarce resources that many urban schools have to work with, the inexperience of the urban teaching corps, and the pressure to focus on a standardized curriculum rather than relationship-building, it is not that surprising that more teachers do not provide this type of extra support (Noguera, 2003).

Very few students had any other place to turn to receive this critical tangible academic assistance. One 13-year-old male student touched on the lack of academic support that he received from peers in this exchange:

> *Student*: When I get homeworks [sic] I don't understand I try hard to see that I'm correct, that I know what I did.
> *Interviewer*: If you don't know it, you ask somebody? Who do you usually ask for help?
> *Student*: Sometimes I call my friends.

Academic support from peers. While students did not describe peers offering much in the form of tangible support, they did occasionally describe friends as encouraging academics. For example, a 16-year-old female described a message she received from friends: "They always telling me to just do my homework and the days will pass by quick." Not only is this advice vague, but it also implies that schoolwork is something to be endured rather than a vehicle for learning.

My following exchange with a 14-year-old female student shows the basic nature of academic support that peers provided:

> *Interviewer*: Are there people in your life that influence you to be a certain type of student?
> *Student*: Just friends.
> *Interviewer*: Anyone else?
> *Student*: No.

Interviewer: What kind of things do your friends say that influence you to be a certain type of student?
Student: To start going to school and to like pay attention in class, so I could like have a good future and everything.

This peer support, while well-intentioned, did not provide much information beyond the most rudimentary skills for school success. This is problematic given the fact that this student described feeling that peers were the only ones to whom she could turn for academic support. Another female student described encouragement provided by peers:

Interviewer: Are there other people that influence you?
Student: My friends.
Interviewer: And how do they influence you?
Student: Like they give me advice to not get in trouble in school. Like they used to get mad and be like stop it. Like, "think of your mom."
Interviewer: So, what would they tell you to think about your mom?
Student: Like to think how she's working her ass off and I'm doing my . . . (trails off).
Interviewer: So, they would say to think of the fact that your mom was sacrificing and working hard. And did you think of that?
Student: Well at first I didn't.
Interviewer: You didn't really care.
Student: And then in a way I started seeing life quite different.

The peers, whom this student later described as also being of immigrant background, appealed to parental authority and their sacrifice as motivation to do well; this focus on motivation and encouragement ultimately frames the issue of doing well in school as one of personal effort and responsibility rather than being about access to information and resources. It is thus not surprising that many students saw the key to academic success as resting squarely on their own shoulders.

Developing Self-Reliance

Another interesting theme that emerged was an extreme self-reliance related to academics. The following exchange I had with a 15-year-old female is indicative of students not receiving influential messages or support from others.

Interviewer: Are there people that influence you to be a certain
    type of student?
Student: No. It's just me, myself, and I.

A 16-year-old female student stated, "I think to myself, 'It's me and
nobody else that will get me into college.' I have to think about myself
because nobody else will." These sentiments are not entirely surprising given that specific and tangible academic support was infrequent or
nonexistent for many students.

DISCUSSION OF THE FINDINGS

This chapter examined the size and composition of the social networks
of Mexican immigrant youth in New York City as well as the types of
academic and emotional support that the members of their networks
provided. Family members dominated the social network composition
of nearly all participants. Students rarely considered non-relative adults
as important members of their social networks, although peers were
a sizeable presence in the social networks of most youth. Given that
the youth in this sample were in the stage of adolescence, a time when
young people move away from the family for support and rely more on
same-age peers, one would have expected them to comprise an even
greater proportion of the participants' social networks (Berndt & Keefe,
1995; Steinberg, 2001). The reliance on family by these youth may be
a unique characteristic of the Mexican immigrant population with its
strong cultural value of familism (see Chapters 10 and 11). Because this
ethnic group is relatively recent to New York, they may have not fully
integrated into the social fabric of their school peers.

Another issue that was possibly related to the immigrant background
of this sample was the homogeneity of their social networks in terms of
educational, linguistic, and ethnic characteristics. The Mexican-descent
students in this sample had social networks with generally low levels
of education and low levels of English dominance and that were predominantly composed of co-ethnic Mexicans or Latinos. Given that
New York is a highly diverse context with other large immigrant group
populations, it is important to note that these youth are separated along
these dimensions and consequently report few significant relationships
that demonstrate higher levels of education, English-language ability,
and cultural diversity. This lack of access to a diverse group of social
network members may limit opportunities to expand the socioeconomic and adaptive opportunities of these ethnic minority youth. Indeed,

looking at the data around the types of support provided by different network members of different backgrounds suggested this was the case.

Only a small minority reported having academically supportive school adults in their social networks. This occurred even though this sample was comprised of mostly second-generation youth, who generally do not have the same degree of cultural and linguistic limitations as first-generation adolescents. Heavy reliance on family and peers for support belies their educational, linguistic, and cultural limitations. This is of particular concern when the language and cultural background of Mexican individuals are generally not those that are valued by American educational institutions and do not lead to upward mobility.

The qualitative findings provided further insight into the nature of the support offered by different network members. Overall, general encouragement characterized the academic support that network members provided, rather than tangible information and resources. There was an emphasis on hard work, seen in other research with Mexican-descent youth (López, 2001), as well as a focus on how not to be in terms of academics, which has also been shown to be particular to the support that Mexican immigrant parents provide to their children (Azmitia, Cooper, Garcia, & Dunbar, 1996; Sanchez, Reyes, & Singh, 2005; Yowell, 2000). Concrete support and specific examples of how to enact productive educational behaviors were least prominent among family and peers despite the fact that these two groups dominated participants' social networks. This was likely the result of their own limited knowledge of the cultural, linguistic, and academic skills necessary to do well in school. In contrast, a study by Useem (1992) showed that parents with high levels of education and concrete and specific knowledge about math placement were able to more effectively advocate for the educational needs of their children. Such social and cultural capital is thus critical in student success.

Non-relative adults, and teachers in particular, gave the most specific and usable academic resources for the students in the sample; while this support was the most useful, it also occurred with the least frequency. As such, a number of students voiced a strong belief in self-reliance when it came to being academically successful. With no one else to turn to as a reliable source of assistance, students accepted full responsibility for their academic achievement, which was unfortunate given their restricted academic resources due to their youth and immigrant status. The solace that came from seeking out peers was offset by their similar lack of resources and reliable academic information, in essence creating negative social capital (Wacquant, 1998) and limiting opportunities because of the peer group's endogenous nature.

CONCLUSION

There are some key educational responses that can be taken from these findings. First, educators should build on the existing asset of strong familial and co-ethnic relationships in the lives of Mexican youth in New York City. Using culturally sensitive approaches, parents could be recruited and taught to draw on their existing resources to support the education of their children more effectively. A study of Mexican American families and students in the Southwest revealed that culturally sensitive connections between family and school can have a positive impact on student learning (Moll, Amanti, Neff, & González, 1992). In that action-research study immigrant parents were brought into the classrooms as teachers and consultants interweaving Mexican cultural practices and knowledge with the traditional curriculum. This raised great interest in students while involving parents more actively in the school, in essence creating the bridging social capital that is often absent among this group. This could also serve to teach parents more about how American schools function and the skills that their children need to be successful in that context.

A second educational response involves developing formal and informal mentoring relationships with school and community members to help bridge the gap between home and school for immigrant students (Roffman, Suárez-Orozco, & Rhodes, 2002). Mentors, defined broadly as caring and supportive adults, might serve as cultural brokers who could bridge the home and school worlds. They could describe the cultural "rules of engagement in the new society" (p. 2). By doing so, mentors might serve as role models for both parents and students about how one must interact with the school system and staff to achieve academic success.

Because Mexican parents already have the cultural concept of support through close family-like relationships, a culturally sensitive, caring, and respectful teacher or mentor might prove to be an invaluable resource for the education of their children. In an ethnographic study of a Southwestern high school with a large Mexican student population, findings demonstrated that genuine caring and respect on the part of adults were related to better academic outcomes and a higher motivation to engage with school (Valenzuela, 1999). Experiencing such caring can have the effect of validating one's upbringing and background and, ultimately, the development of a coherent sense of self, a central task of adolescence (Erikson, 1968).

By implementing such thoughtful, intentional, and culturally sensitive approaches in educational settings we can help determine the future for this large and growing group of Mexican youth coming of age in the nation's premier metropolis, New York City. Securing their success will ultimately determine the outlook of the city and the nation as the numbers of this group increase.

REFERENCES

Azmitia, M., Cooper, C., Garcia, E. E., & Dunbar, N. (1996). The ecology of family guidance in low-income Mexican-American and European-American families. *Social Development, 5*, 1–23.

Berndt, T. J., & Keefe, K. (1995). Friends' influence on adolescents' adjustment to school. *Child Development, 66*, 1312–1329.

Bernstein, N. (2007, June 4). A Mexican baby boom in New York shows the strength of a new immigrant group. *The New York Times*. Retrieved June 4, 2007, from http://nytimes.com

Bourdieu, P. (1986). Forms of capital. In J. G. Richardson (Ed.), *Handbook of theory and research for the sociology of education* (pp. 241–258). New York: Greenwood Publishing Group.

Bronfenbrenner, U. (1977). Toward an experimental ecology of human development. *American Psychologist, 32*, 513–531.

Coleman, J. S. (1988). Social capital in the creation of human capital. *American Journal of Sociology, 94*, S95–S120.

Cortina, R., & Gendreau, M. (2003). *Immigrants and schooling: Mexicans in New York*. New York: Center for Migration Studies.

Croninger, R. G., & Lee, V. E. (2001). Social capital and dropping out of high school: Benefits to at-risk students of teachers' support and guidance. *Teachers College Record, 103*, 548–581.

Erikson, E. H. (1968). *Identity: Youth and crisis*. New York: Norton.

Fry, R. (2004). *Latino youth finishing college: The role of selective pathways*. Washington, DC: Pew Hispanic Center.

Granovetter, M. (1973). The strength of weak ties. *American Journal of Sociology, 78*, 1360–1380.

López, G. R. (2001). The value of hard work: Lessons on parent involvement from an (im)migrant household. *Harvard Educational Review, 71*, 416–437.

Maxwell, J. (1996). *Qualitative research design: An interactive approach*. Thousand Oaks, CA: Sage.

Moll, L. C., Amanti, C., Neff, D., & González, N. (1992). Funds of knowledge for teaching: Using a qualitative approach to connect homes and classrooms. *Theory into Practice, 31*, 132–141.

New York City Department of City Planning. (2004). *The newest New Yorkers 2000*. New York: Author.

Noguera, P. A. (2003). "Welcome to New York, now go home!" Multiple forces within the urban environment and their impact upon recent Mexican immigrants in New York City. In R. Cortina & M. Gendreau (Eds.), *Immigrants and schooling* (pp. 79–89). New York: Center for Migration Studies.

Noguera, P. A. (2004). Social capital and the education of immigrant students: Categories and generalizations. *Sociology of Education, 77,* 180–183.

Portes, A., & Zhou, M. (1993). The new second generation: Segmented assimilation and its variants. *Annals of the American Academy of Political and Social Science, 530,* 74–93.

Putnam, R. (2000). *Bowling alone: The collapse and revival of American community.* New York: Simon & Schuster.

Rivera-Batiz, F. L. (2004). The state of NewYorktitlan: The socioeconomic status of Mexican New Yorkers. *Regional Labor Review, 6,* 33–45.

Roffman, J. G., Suárez-Orozco, C., & Rhodes, J. E. (2002). Facilitating positive development in immigrant youth: The role of mentors and community organizations. In F. A. Villaruel, D. F. Perkins, L. M. Borden, & J. G. Keith (Eds.), *Community youth development: Practice, policy and research* (pp. 90–117). Thousand Oaks, CA: Sage Press.

Sanchez, B., Reyes, O., & Singh, J. (2005). Making it in college: The value of significant individuals in the lives of Mexican American adolescents. *Journal of Higher Education, 5,* 48–67.

Smith, R. C. (2005). *Mexican New York: The transnational lives of new immigrants.* Berkeley: University of California Press.

Stanton-Salazar, R. D. (2001). *Manufacturing hope and despair: The school and kin support networks of U.S.-Mexican youth.* New York: Teachers College Press.

Steinberg, L. (2001). We know some things: Adolescent-parent relationships in retrospect and prospect. *Journal of Research on Adolescence, 11,* 1–20.

Suárez-Orozco, C., Suárez-Orozco, M., & Todorova, I. (2008). *Learning a new land: Immigrant students in American society.* Cambridge, MA: Harvard University Press.

Tashakkori, A., & Teddlie, C. (1998). *Mixed methodology: Combining qualitative and quantitative approaches.* Thousand Oaks, CA: Sage.

U.S. Census Bureau. (2007). *American Community Survey.* Table S0201. Selected Population Profile in the United States, New York City, New York (Mexican). Washington, DC: Author.

Useem, E. (1992). Middle schools and math groups: Parents' involvement in children's placement. *Sociology of Education, 65,* 263–279.

Valenzuela, A. (1999). *Subtractive schooling: U.S.-Mexican youth and the politics of caring.* Albany, NY: SUNY Press.

Wacquant, L. J. D. (1998). Negative social capital: State breakdown and social destitution in America's urban core. *The Netherlands Journal of the Built Environment, 13,* 25–40.

Woolcock, M., & Narayan, D. (2000). Social capital: Implications for development theory, research, and policy. *The World Bank Research Observer, 15,* 225–249.

Yowell, C. M. (2000). Dreams of the future: The pursuit of education and career possible selves among ninth grade Latino youth. *Applied Developmental Science, 6,* 62–72.

Part V

BI-NATIONAL POSSIBILITIES

A series of arguments have been made in this book that rethinking Mexican American schooling requires a more thorough assessment of educational well-being on both sides of the border. It requires deeper engagement among policymakers, educators, and education scholars between the United States and Mexico. In this section authors address historical efforts by federal bodies to establish bi-national collaborations, and offer conceptual shifts needed to meet the educational needs of Mexican-origin children. Mary Martinez-Wenzl in Chapter 13 reviews bi-national education initiatives to date, their merit, and ways to consider expansion to improve schooling opportunities for Mexican American students. And finally, in Chapter 14, Bryant Jensen discusses ways by which a closer, more thoughtful application of learning theory to learning environments for Mexican-origin children in both countries can improve opportunities while advancing theory, especially in regard to the roles of culture and socioemotional development in academic learning.

CHAPTER 13

Bi-National Education Initiatives:
A Brief History

Mary Martinez-Wenzl

As a nation, Mexico defines itself as a cultural entity not restricted by geographic borders. This pluralistic and dynamic construction of Mexico posits unity with the more than 30 million persons of Mexican origin living in the United States today (Alba, 2010). Thus, the Mexican government develops and implements policies and programs to continuously foster its relationship with Mexicans abroad, among which educational programs are prominent. For the most part, these programs have very limited visibility in the United States, in spite of their presence throughout most of the United States and the national emphasis on closing the achievement gap between Mexican students and their peers. At present, the collective impact of these educational programs is unclear, as there have been very few evaluations by researchers or the Mexican or U.S. government.

This chapter aims to foster greater understanding of the Mexican educational presence in the United States and an analysis of how these efforts could be strengthened and expanded. The focus is specifically on the initiatives advanced by the Mexican government; there are numerous partnerships between Mexican universities and local educational agencies that are beyond the scope of this chapter. I begin with a brief history of the evolution of Mexico's educational initiatives in the United States, focusing on the period from 1970 to present. Next, the Mexican-sponsored educational programs that this evolution has made possible are described. I summarize what is known about the levels of usage and impact of these programs to date and offer recommendations as to additional resources needed to sustain and expand Mexico's current efforts to meet the educational needs of Mexicans in the United States.

MEXICO'S RELATIONSHIP WITH ITS NATIONALS
IN THE UNITED STATES

Mexico has strategically cultivated its relationships with co-nationals in the United States over the past 40 years, shifting from a long-standing policy of non-intervention in foreign affairs to a multipronged approach that seeks to foster connections with the Mexican diaspora abroad. Motivations for maintaining ties to co-nationals in the United States are both economic and political.

This diaspora of Mexican nationals represents not only a significant portion of the overall Mexican population, but also a significant source of foreign revenue. Annual remittances to Mexico are second only to oil as a source of revenue to the Mexican economy (Alba, 2010). In 2007, remittances from Mexican workers in the United States to Mexico reached a record high of $26.1 billion (Bank of Mexico, cited by Alba, 2010). While remittances declined with the economic recession, they have begun increasing once again in 2011, and are still Mexico's second-largest source of foreign exchange.

The strong national political focus on Mexicans abroad is indicative of a more institutionalized form of diaspora membership (Smith, 2003). "Rather than simply being transcended, the Mexican state actively created a diasporic public sphere for its own domestic and foreign policy reasons" (p. 749). The potential for political influence via Latino voters and the economic importance of remittances to Mexico are key motivating factors for the Mexican government to foster ties with Mexicans in the United States. Mexico has looked to Israel and the relationship it has developed with the Jewish diaspora as a model; the Anti-Discrimination Group Mexico formed in 2007 shares many similarities with the Anti-Defamation League (Laglagaron, 2010). Fitzgerald (2008) suggests that the Mexican Catholic church's migrant solidarity and efforts to maintain symbolic and material ties to its flock on both sides of the border have provided the Mexican government with a non-coercive model to emulate.

In the United States, there is tacit and overt fostering of political mobilization along ethnic lines, which provides additional motivation for Mexico to nurture its relationship with Mexican nationals in the United States (Smith, 2003). González Gutiérrez (1997) notes that Mexican consulates in the United States interact with large numbers of Mexicans, and that consulates consider first-generation Mexican immigrants a captive audience. De la Garza (1997) states that Mexican officials deny they are pursuing an ethnic lobby in the United States when addressing non-Hispanics, but affirm their desire for such a relationship when addressing Mexican Americans. Since all of Mexico's relations with Mexican Americans occur within the context of ethnic-minority/majority relations in the United States, it is important to note that the host state plays an important role in determining the potential for diasporic membership.

1970s and 1980s: Outreach to Mexicans Abroad Increases

In the 1970s the Mexican government began to strategically cultivate and expand its long-term relations with the Mexican diaspora in the United States. President Luis Echeverría sought to establish ties with the leaders of the U.S. Chicano movement. Mexico promoted networks between Chicano leaders and activists, developed scholarships for Mexican Americans to study in Mexico, provided funding to establish cultural centers, and began to distribute textbooks in Spanish to libraries and schools with large Mexican populations (González Gutiérrez, 1993).

Presidents José López Portillo (1976–1982) and Miguel de la Madrid Hurtado (1982-1988) continued to follow an agenda of fostering long-term ties to Mexican nationals abroad. The López Portillo administration created the Comisión Mixta de Enlace (Bi-National Outreach Commission) to manage relations between the Mexican government and several Mexican American organizations (Cano & Delano, 2007). The finalization of Mexico's General Protection Directive, established in 1980, directed increased and better human resources, materials, and finances toward labor protection of Mexicans in the United States. At the same time Mexican cultural clubs in the United States continued to flourish and eventually took on broader economic and political agendas as well. While these initiatives were less comprehensive in scope than later efforts, they nonetheless laid the groundwork for outreach programs established during subsequent administrations.

The passage of the Immigration Reform and Control Act (IRCA) in 1986 permitted 2.3 million undocumented Mexicans in the United States to adjust their legal status, which greatly increased the demand for Mexican consular services. González Gutiérrez (1997) notes that Mexican consulates in the United States became entrusted with carrying out Mexico's foreign policies, as the Mexican governmental presence in the United States was increasingly in consular offices outside of Washington, DC.

In 1988 the election of President Carlos Salinas de Gortari was surrounded by charges of election fraud, embarrassing and angering many Mexicans in the United States. Many Mexicans had supported the candidacy of Cárdenas, the opposition candidate (Dresser, 1993). Mexicans in the United States subsequently mobilized politically and formed many new organizations during this time, and the Mexican government began to recognize the resentment among Mexicans abroad for the perceived lack of attention. From this time Mexicans in the United States became more powerful actors in the Mexican political arena, and were more valued for their potential political influence in both Mexico and the United States. Latino leaders called upon the Mexican government to create a program for Mexican communities abroad, and the eventual development of such programs represented acquiescence to their demands (González Gutiérrez, 1997).

Dresser (1993) notes that "by assuming a leading role in the defense of Mexicans abroad via its consulates, the Mexican government hoped to repair its tarnished image" (p. 104). Mexicans in the United States had long been treated as *pochos* by their home country, a term that is used for Americanized Mexicans and often has a negative connotation of having betrayed their home country by leaving it.

Salinas Policy Shift: The Program for Mexican Communities Abroad

The Salinas administration's (1988–1994) modernization of Mexican economic and political structures spurred a reevaluation of the principles that had historically guided Mexico's policies abroad. Rodolfo de la Garza (1997) asserts that Mexican political identity from the 1930s through the 1990s had been defined in large part by its *opposition* to the United States. The Estrada Doctrine, for example, claimed that foreign governments should not judge the governments of other nations. It was used to justify the exclusion of foreigners from Mexican affairs and to prevent Mexicans from participating in the politics of foreign countries while abroad. Under Salinas this approach to foreign policy began to change.

According to Manuel García y Griego and Mónica Verea Campos (1998), non-intervention in U.S. domestic affairs was interpreted much more loosely under the Salinas administration, allowing the Mexican government to implement more policies to engage with its co-nationals abroad. Decision making was decentralized as the Mexican government recognized the utility of fostering contact with state and local actors via its consular offices. While the administrations of Echeverría and de la Madrid had established the foundations for government programs to foster relationships with Mexicans abroad, the Salinas administration initiated the *Programa para las Comunidades Mexicanas en el Exterior* (PCME, or Program for Mexican Communities Abroad) within the

Ministry of Foreign Affairs. De la Garza (1997) characterizes the PCME as "the first example of a coherent and continuous effort conducted within the United States designed to have American political actors influence US policies to make them compatible with the preference of the Mexican government" (p. 85).

The PCME was created in 1990 through a comprehensive initiative that involved state, federal, and nongovernmental actors with the objective of extending and regulating relations with the Mexican population in the United States. It was implemented via Mexican consulates, cultural centers, and institutes in the United States, which all received a clear mandate to continue protecting fundamental human rights while fostering long-term relations with the diverse Mexican diaspora through education, culture, sports, business, and community programs and also to attract capital, technology, and foreign commerce (González Gutiérrez, 1997).

The PCME called for a change in the role of consulates from one that had primarily focused on processing travel documents and protecting Mexican nationals to being charged with promoting the interests of the Mexican government. This shift required Mexican consulates to expand their diplomatic role and take on the primary responsibility for coordinating Mexico's relationship with its Mexican diaspora across the United States (González Gutiérrez, 1997).

As it was initiated, the PCME enjoyed extensive resources, autonomy, and political power. New personnel were hired, including more specialized and better-trained administrators. In the most important consular offices press offices were created and representatives of the Mexican Attorney General and Social Security Office were stationed.

Notes from a 2002 meeting of the Bi-National Migrant Education Program (PROBEM) suggest that the objectives of the PCME were four-fold:

To recognize the needs, interests, and aspirations of Mexican
   communities
To develop programs and activities in education, health, culture,
   and sports
To facilitate the establishment of hometown associations
To support mechanisms that facilitate the flow of remittances,
   investments, goods, and services

Meeting notes from the same document continue to describe Mexico's relationship in economic terms, defining the PCME mission as "to strengthen the abilities of Mexicans abroad so that they may live better, to help them maintain solid bonds with Mexico and its population . . .

to support federal and municipal entities so that they can make the most of the opportunities globalization offers for development" (Secretaría de Educación Pública [SEP], 2002, p. 76). The PCME vision is defined as "migrants capable of exercising their rights abroad and solidly linked to their communities of origin and federal and municipal entities" (SEP, 2002, p. 77).

The PCME was structured in eight parts: community organization, education, culture, sports, health, business contacts, information, and fundraising. Among these program areas, education was the highest priority. Key problem areas for Mexicans in the United States were identified as the following:

- The loss of Spanish
- The loss of Mexican identity
- High dropout and/or expulsion rates after 9th grade
- The lack of an understanding of Mexican culture and the Mexican educational system among U.S. teachers
- The achievement gap (as a consequence of not knowing English) with White students

Zedillo and Fox Continue to Reach Out to the Diaspora

President Ernesto Zedillo (1994–2000) continued and strengthened the Mexican government's policies and programs for Mexicans abroad. His administration renewed foreign policies to deepen connections with Mexican communities abroad, paying special attention to the challenges, successes, culture, and feeling of belonging of Mexicans in the United States. Mexico's 1995–2000 National Development Plan defined the Mexican community in the United States as an integral part of the "global Mexican nation" (Secretaría de Programación y Presupuesto, 1995). During this period there was a marked interest in fostering feelings of identity, cultural belonging, and ethnicity among Mexicans abroad. The National Plan stated that it would "give priority to the initiative titled 'Mexican Nation,' which integrated a set of programs to strengthen cultural linkages and connections between communities of Mexicans and persons of Mexican origin abroad" (Diaz de Cossío, Orozco, & González, 1997).

President Vicente Fox (2000–2006) reached out to Mexicans abroad as well, characterizing them as heroes in recognition of the success many had attained, as well as their significant contributions to the Mexican economy through remittances. Some consider Fox's declaration of Mexicans in the United States as "heroes" as the culmination of the political evolution that began decades earlier with the efforts of Mexican presidents who reached out to Chicanos in the 1970s (Garcia-Acevedo, 2003). But it was the Fox administration that finally broke with the Estrada Doctrine in its foreign policy, promoting a new foreign policy of openness and increased national involvement in foreign affairs.

Like Zedillo, Fox viewed Mexicans in the United States as part of the global Mexican nation. His campaign for the presidency had emphasized the interests of the more than 30 million Mexicans in the United States, and he made frequent references to "all Mexicans," making reference to the Mexican nationals in the United States (Sheridan & Stewart, 2000). A presidential decree on April 16, 2003, created the *Instituto para los Mexicanos en el Exterior* (IME, or Institute for Mexicans Abroad), which united with the Program for Mexican Communities Abroad. The IME operates according to directives set forth by the National Board for Mexican Communities Abroad, which is composed of 10 ministers and coordinated by the head of that IME. Laglagaron (2010) suggests that "IME's work represents one of the most significant, if overlooked, factors in U.S. immigrant integration policy" (pp. 28–29).

Calderón Administration

Felipe Calderón became Mexico's president in 2006, and has focused his administration on national security, restoring the rule of law, and fighting drug trafficking and organized crime. Alba (2010) notes that the Calderón government has adopted a more subdued approach to migration matters, likely in reaction to the lack of immigration reform legislation in the United States. Nonetheless, Calderón and the IME have taken a strong stance against anti-immigrant laws in the United States such as Arizona's SB1070. Extensive resources have been directed to the military-led crackdown against drug cartels, reducing the resources available for programs for Mexicans abroad. And in May 2011 Mexico passed a new federal immigration law, mostly in response to concerns about the safety and welfare of Central American immigrants. Thus, while the Mexican government continues to attempt to cultivate an ethnic lobby in the United States, these efforts have been mostly overshadowed by difficult domestic concerns.

BI-NATIONAL EDUCATION PROGRAMS FOR MEXICANS IN THE UNITED STATES

The Mexican government is keenly aware of the gaps in educational achievement and attainment between its nationals abroad and the rest of the U.S. student population. Reducing the inequalities between Mexicans and other U.S. ethnic groups is considered an economic imperative for the complete incorporation of Mexicans into the social and economic fabric of American society (SRE, 2004). In addition to being concerned with how such educational discrepancies impact Mexicans in the United States (e.g., less educated persons find fewer opportunities in the labor market), the government of Mexico worries that its nationals in the United States will lose their culture and language. Educational programs the Mexican government promotes in the United States tend to have strong cultural and language components to teach Mexicans in the United States about their cultural and historical heritage along with academic content.

This educational agenda is advanced through IME, which partners with North American institutions on formal and informal education programs for Mexicans in the United States. Collaboration has occurred at the federal, state, and local levels. U.S. partners include state, county, and city governments, school districts, migrant health centers, corrections facilities, and nonprofit organizations.

Mexico has declared four action areas for its educational programs: migrant education, bilingual education, adult education, and higher education. Efforts on the part of the Mexican government have been made to link these areas with U.S. educational programming (Miller, 1995). Since the 1980s Mexico's Ministry of Foreign Affairs has collaborated with the U.S. Office of Bilingual and Minority Language Affairs (now the Office of English Language Acquisition [OELA]) to increase the number of qualified bilingual teachers, as well as to assist other teachers in increasing their understanding of the history and culture of students of Mexican origin.

The Mexican government recognizes that second-language acquisition requires literacy in one's first language. Mexican consulates in the United States often offer classes in Spanish literacy and basic adult education. Consular educational programs also support organizations promoting bilingual education, and work with such groups on campaigns for the education of immigrant students. In 1997 the Mexican government received an award from the National Association for Bilingual Education in recognition of its advances in bilingual education.

On August 17, 1990, Mexico's Secretariat of Public Education and the U.S. Department of Education entered into a Memorandum of Understanding (MOU) on Education. The Memorandum resulted from the efforts of the Bi-National U.S.-Mexico Commission (see http://www.state.gov/p/wha/ci/mx/c10787.htm) and was signed by U.S. Secretary of Education Lauro Cavazos and his Mexican counterpart, Manuel Bartlett-Diaz (Varisco de García & Garcia, 1996). The document was and remains the most comprehensive agreement the U.S. Department of Education has with any foreign nation and establishes links between Mexico and the United States to cooperate to improve the quality of education. Since 1991, the MOU on Education has been renewed with annexes every 2 years. The most recent renewal was scheduled for 2006 was delayed due to the presidential election, but the 2004 memorandum remains in effect.

Mexico has also entered into educational partnerships at the state level. Such partnerships typically are oriented to meeting bi-national goals, such as closing the achievement gap between Mexican-origin children and their peers. There are currently official educational partnerships between the IME and the state departments of education in California, North Carolina, and Oregon. One of the most important outcomes of the relationships Mexico has developed at the state level in the United States has been curriculum alignment. Many of Mexico's textbooks are aligned with Oregon's K–12 curriculum. Several *Colegio de Bachilleres* courses–Mexico's college-prep high school curriculum–are aligned with state standards in Texas, California, Washington, and Oregon. Given the extent to which educational policy, curricula, and administration is a decentralized state- and district-level operation in the United States, these types of partnerships seem to offer the potential to have more than just a symbolic impact. Much more research is needed to conceptualize and evaluate the impact of these programs to date, as little is actually known about their scope and operation.

Teacher Exchange

Teachers in the United States tend to know very little about the schooling experiences of their Mexican-origin students in Mexico, and the same can be said for Mexican teachers whose students have returned to Mexico after a period of time in the United States. Two types of teacher exchange programs between countries aim to bridge these disconnects. The larger of the two brings qualified teachers from Mexico to teach in the United States for 4 to 6 weeks, typically through the summer Migrant Education programs. The Migrant Education Program is federally funded under Title I of the Elementary and Secondary Education Act. The program operates in 48 states in the United States. There were 557,424 students eligible for the Migrant Education Program in the 2006–2007 academic year, and about 63% of these students enrolled in Migrant Education courses that year (Terrazas & Fix, 2009).

At present, 22 U.S. states participate in the Bi-National Migrant Education Teacher Exchange Program. Mexican teachers' participation in the program initially grew steadily, rising from 50 teachers in

1996 and peaking at 272 in 2003. Since 2003 the number of teachers participating annually has declined. In 2009 it was down to 159, which was attributed to budget cuts resulting from the economic downturn (Terrazas & Fix, 2009).

Mexican teachers apply and are selected through a competitive process each year, often coming from migrant-sending regions of Mexico. The Mexican government provides an annual training seminar to exchange teachers each year and issues a clear mandate for teachers to design lessons on Mexican culture to support identity formation among students. Gándara (2007) notes a program emphasis on cultural diffusion. The extent to which teachers interacted with the school system is generally limited, as there is little contact with regular classroom teachers via the summer Migrant Ed programs. Generally, the focus of these exchanges is on students. Nonetheless, Mexican teachers on exchange in United States are able to improve their English and learn about U.S. schooling systems.

Teacher exchanges between the United States and Mexico also occur through the Fulbright-Hays program. In contrast to the student focus of the Migrant Education teacher exchanges, the Fulbright-Hays exchanges emphasize teacher development and educational and cultural exchanges (Terrazas & Fix, 2009). Fulbright exchanges provide U.S. teachers with the opportunity to live and work in Mexico for a year- or a semester-long direct exchange with a colleague who teaches the same subject and level. These exchanges can result in sustained school and community partnerships across borders.

Gándara (2007) suggests that U.S.-Mexico teacher exchanges could be improved through various means, recommending exchanges of teacher trainers and lengthening their duration.

Transfer Document

Students who come to the United States from Mexico run the risk of being enrolled in courses that they have already taken, or that are at the incorrect level. Much of this results from a lack of understanding of students' prior educational experiences. The *Documento de Transferencia del Estudiante Migrante* is a student school history record provided through the state offices of the Binational Migrant Education Program (PROBEM) that includes information about grade level, subject matter, and grades. It is intended to facilitate smoother transitions for students going between U.S. and Mexican schools. Gándara's (2007) evaluation found that U.S. schools were largely unaware of the documents, and that in 2002–2003, only 1,099 students had them. IME offices at the

Mexican consulates have borne much of the responsibility for processing transfer documents. IME reports that only a quarter of Mexican students returning to Mexico from the United States each year have a transfer document.

The University of Texas at Austin LUCHA (Language Learners at the University of Texas at Austin Center for Hispanic Achievement) program, which has been in operation since 2006, has developed a transcript request and analysis program. This program is similar to the transfer document effort in that the goal is to assist counselors in placing newcomer immigrant youth in the correct grades and courses. However, instead of relying on the transfer document, the LUCHA program requests transcripts directly from Mexico, which are then carefully analyzed by LUCHA staff for alignment with Texas graduation requirements. Gutiérrez-González (2009) suggests that one of the greatest outcomes of this effort has been that it provides U.S. teachers and counselors with irrefutable evidence that "the students coming from Mexico are intelligent and have knowledge and skills and that the fact that they do not presently speak English cannot negate this reality" (p. 98).

Free Textbook Donation

In many regions of the United States, bilingual textbooks are difficult to come by, which presents a challenge to schools and teachers implementing bilingual educational programs. Many of the IME offices distribute Mexican educational materials upon request, depending on the availability and at the discretion of the consulate. This distribution of free textbooks is called the *Consejo Nacional de Libros de Texto Gratis* (CoNaLiTeG). Resources for students include textbooks and workbooks from the Mexican elementary school curriculum for grades K through 6. All textbooks distributed to students are given to them (not loaned), as is required by the CoNaLiTeG policy of free textbook distribution.

Teachers in the United States can also access pedagogical information on classroom settings, reference materials, supplemental instruction, differentiated instruction, and dual and bilingual instruction. Didactic support aims to assist teachers in preserving Mexican roots and identity among students. In total, the program distributes 50 collections of Spanish-language textbooks for teachers and students in history, mathematics, Spanish, and geography. Mexican textbooks for primary grades emphasize Mexican history and the development of national pride, identity, and respect.

Current data on the size and scope of the textbook distribution program are not readily available. A 2007–2008 IME report stated that 9,750 textbooks had been distributed in 2000 (as cited by Laglagaron, 2010). The extent to which students and teachers can access these free textbooks is limited in important ways. First of all, given the limited supply, IME offices do not advertise their availability, so many teachers who might use them are unaware of their existence. People tend to find out about the free textbooks via word of mouth. Second, Mexico requires that the books be given to the students—they cannot be retained by the school from one year to the next. This requirement further limits the supply of textbooks, which are purportedly of very good quality. As noted previously, given the costs associated with printing and shipping textbooks, there has been a shift toward offering electronic versions of curricula.

Telesecundaria

Part of Mexico's electronic educational resources made available to nationals in the United States are a virtual middle and high school curriculum, *la telesecundaria*: a video curriculum beamed via satellite from studios in Mexico City to all rural areas in Mexico (see Chapter 7, this volume). In the United States, *telesecundaria* programs are broadcast on twelve educational channels such as the History Channel, Discovery Kids, CNN, and Bravo. The video curriculum has accompanying teacher guides, student texts, and workbooks.

The *telesecundaria* curriculum is aligned with Oregon state curriculum standards. In Oregon, *telesecundaria* is intended to be taught in a classroom setting with direct instruction from a Spanish-speaking teacher. Data on the extent to which it is actually being used in U.S. secondary schools are not readily available, suggesting that its impact has not been realized to date.

Adult Education

Many of the Mexican immigrants in the United States have low levels of education. In 2003, the average number of years of schooling completed by Mexican immigrants ages 15 and older was 7.3, and over half of adults report having never gone to school or failing to complete basic education (Santibañez, Vernez, & Razquin, 2005). Thus, while many of Mexico's educational efforts in the United States target students in the K–12 system, Mexico also recognizes the educational needs among adult immigrants. Mexico's *Instituto Nacional para la Educación de los Adultos* (INEA, or National Institute for Adult Education) is the primary government agency dedicated to adult education.

It is designed for students ages 14 and older to provide literacy and primary and secondary education as well as life skills and parenting classes. INEA courses are intended for independent study supported by a Spanish-speaking instructor, and as such have been promoted for use by Mexicans in the United States. The materials available through INEA include textbooks, online courses and books, online consultation with INEA consultants, academic credits, academic testing, and certification of program completion.

In the United States, INEA resources have been used to supplement GED instructional materials for Spanish speakers, and also to provide basic adult education as part of workforce development programs. It has also been used in corrections institutions among Mexican inmates, where it reportedly has been very well received. The Corrections Corporation of America (2011) reports that more than 2,000 Mexican educational certificates have been issued in the last decade.

Open and Online High School Programs

In keeping with the trend toward offering educational resources online at a comparatively lower cost, Mexico's *Colegio de Bachilleres* is an online distance-learning program that allows students to finish their high school studies and prepare for college or university study. It is not a part of Mexico's basic education and is not obligatory in Mexico; it is considered "upper middle education." The materials available through the *Colegio de Bachilleres* include student textbooks, online courses, teleconferencing between Mexican teachers and U.S. teachers and students, and an online video component. Study is primarily independent, with support from both Mexican professors and Spanish-speaking instructors in the United States. Mexico's Universidad Nacional de Mexico (UNAM) and Tecnológico de Monterey also provide online distance-learning programs similar to the *Colegio de Bachilleres* that are beyond the scope of this chapter.

The University of California, Los Angeles has been conducting a pilot study using the *Colegio de Bachilleres* math and science courses in four Southern California high schools. The courses are aligned with California content standards and meet the "A-G requirements"–the prerequisite course sequence for admission to the University of California and California State University systems–and thus afford Spanish-dominant students the opportunity to work toward their A-G requirements as they are acquiring English. Now in its 4th year, this project has provided hundreds of newcomer immigrant high school students with access to math and science courses they otherwise would not have been able to take. However, with the exception of this grant-funded project, there are no other examples of systematic use of the *Colegio de Bachilleres* curriculum embedded in high school courses. At present, students who wish to access the *Colegio de Bachilleres* curriculum must do so independently and at their own expense.

Scholarships

Mexico provides scholarship funding for students to access its courses in the form of IME *Becas.* These scholarships can be used for course and exam fees. In recent years, the scholarships have been extended for use in higher education as well. The scholarships are administered through the University of California Office of the President and are granted in amounts of up to $15,000 per year. Between 2005 and 2007, IME provided 210 scholarships (Laglagaron, 2010).

Plazas Comunitarias

All of the electronic educational resources described thus far can be accessed at one of the 262 *Plazas Comunitarias* in existence throughout the United States. INEA estimated that 16,758 students visited one of these *Plazas* in 2007 (Laglagaron, 2010). *Plazas Comunitarias* are learning centers, typically computer labs already established at a host school or organization, that are designed to support individuals over the age of 15 to complete their basic education through online independent study. *Plazas* are sites at which students can access all of Mexico's online educational resources, from INEA adult basic education courses to the *Colegio de Bachilleres* college preparatory curriculum.

In the United States, *Plazas Comunitarias* are typically located in community centers, schools, workplaces, community colleges, and correctional institutions with computer labs already in place. They require a host with a minimum of 10 computers, Internet access, Spanish-speaking instructors, classrooms, a TV/VCR, a satellite dish and receiver, and direct instruction.

As of 2010, there were 261 *Plazas Comunitarias* in the United States in 27 different states. Almost a third of them are located in California (78 in all). A complete listing of the number of plazas by state is provided in Table 13.1.

Table 13.1. States with *Plazas Comunitarias*

State	Number of Plazas	State	Number of Plazas
California	78	Nevada	5
Texas	28	Pennsylvania	5
Washington State	25	South Carolina	4
Illinois	20	Colorado	4
Oregon	15	Utah	4
Georgia	13	Nebraska	2
North Carolina	11	Tennessee	2
New York	9	Washington, DC	2
Indiana	7	Arkansas	1
Missouri	6	Michigan	1
Arizona	5	New Mexico	1
Florida	5	Ohio	1
Idaho	5	Rhode Island	1
		Wisconsin	1

CONCLUSION

There is surprisingly little research on the educational programs Mexico has sponsored in the United States. The number of individuals using the programs and services is unknown, but anecdotal evidence suggests that is it likely quite small in comparison to the population that could potentially use and benefit from the programs. A handful of university researchers in the United States focused on meeting the needs of Latino and English learner students have taken an interest in the potential of Mexico's educational resources to meet the needs of these students. Researchers at the University of California, Los Angeles, and University of Texas, Austin, have launched pilot projects to study the use of Mexico-based resources among Spanish-speaking high school students in the United States. With the exception of these two projects, however, there has been little attention given to understanding the impact and potential of these programs.

Terrazas and Fix (2009) point to a lack of systemic evaluation of the teacher exchange programs, which has hindered an understanding of their impacts to date. In 2004–2005, Gándara (2007) conducted a preliminary evaluation of Mexican-sponsored programs. This evaluation included interviews with more than 25 informants. Participants included program directors and staff, consular staff in Sacramento, representatives from several Mexican states, Mexican academics, and the director of PROBEM. Evaluation of the teacher exchange program concluded that the program's small size, short duration, and segregation from regular schools limited its impact.

Limited evaluations are likely closely linked to insufficient funding for these programs. *Plazas Comunitarias* have in many places opened only to close soon after, lacking a consistent revenue stream. In some cases Mexico has been able to partner with U.S. agencies and organizations to provide funding, but revenue in the form of temporary or short-term funds has hindered program stability, as evidenced by the frequency with which *Plazas Comunitarias* seem to become inactive. While the U.S. Department of Education and a handful of state-level departments of education have signed Memoranda of Understandings with Mexico establishing a commitment to collaborate bi-nationally to work toward closing the achievement gap, these agreements have not included any commitments in the form of tangible resources and/or funding streams. An agreement to work together without the necessary substance to carry out said work has little more than symbolic value.

Mexico has offered many resources free of charge, but seems reluctant to widely advertise or promote the resources because the supply is limited. In general, Mexico seems to be promoting use of the resources it has made available online, as these are less expensive because they do not require printing and shipping. However, accessing resources online is not always practical for classroom teachers, particularly since the schools in which Mexican immigrant students are concentrated tend to have fewer technological resources.

In addition, while many resources are available online, the web platform is dated in comparison to many other educational resources, and the end-user support available is minimal to nonexistent. Finally, the current infrastructure presents another limitation, with only a handful of North American host servers. If all of the potential users of Mexico's educational resources became aware of them and began accessing them, the servers on which they are hosted would likely not be able to accommodate the increased demand.

Inadequate resource and reluctant advertising, thus, mean that some Mexican-origin children and families in the United States discover these bi-national programs via word of mouth, while most probably have no idea they exist. And even fewer use the programs in a meaningful way.

These resources and the potential for partnering with Mexico are a tremendous opportunity. However, to fully work toward the stated goal of maximizing use of Mexican educational resources to close the achievement gap among language-minority students, greater political and administrative will are needed to direct more resources to the partnership. As long as the primary form of support offered by partners in the United States is endorsing the programs without actively seeing that they are implemented as fully as possible, the partnership's value is largely symbolic in nature.

POLICY RECOMMENDATIONS

The United States and Mexico should commit to collaborating more meaningfully to meet the needs of the students they share. The educational outcomes of Mexican immigrants in the United States will have long-term impacts on the economies of the two countries, and the matter is made all the more urgent by the continued low levels of educational achievement and attainment among Mexicans in the United States. In light of the importance of this issue, I offer the following recommendations:

1. *Increase Research on Program Impact.* At present it is difficult to draw any conclusions about the effect of Mexico's educational initiatives, as there is almost no research in this area. With the exception of a few doctoral dissertations employing a case study approach to examine programs in California and Texas (Guerrero, 2009; Gutierrez-Gonzalez, 2009) and a few white papers (Gándara, 2007; Laglagaron, 2010), Mexico's educational initiatives in the United States have received little attention from researchers.

2. *Make Records of Program Usage Available.* Conducting research on these programs is complicated by the fact that there is little information readily available on even the most basic program indicators; the Mexican government should make present and historical records of program participation and completion publicly available. Without knowing how many people have accessed the available programs and resources, it is impossible to gauge their demand and impact. Records of how many people have successfully completed programs of study will help to identify areas where these

programs have been most successful, which will allow for defining best practices and strategic scale-up.

3. *Align Mexican Curriculum with U.S. Common Core Standards.* As 46 states and the District of Columbia move toward adoption of the Common Core Standards, it will become critical for Mexico to align the curriculum it offers both in Mexico and the United States with these new standards.

4. *Launch Additional Pilot Demonstration Projects.* UCLA's Project Secondary Online Learning (SOL) and UT Austin's LUCHA program have demonstrated the potential for expanding the scope and use of Mexico's educational resources with support from institutions of higher education. Additional and sustained piloting of initiatives such as LUCHA and SOL are needed to increase understanding of how such programs might be improved and expanded.

5. *Expand the Bilateral Agenda.* At present counternarcotics, border, and trade issues dominate the U.S.-Mexico bilateral agenda. The U.S. Congress has appropriated $1.3 billion in assistance to Mexico through the Mérida Initiative. One of the Mérida Initiative's four pillars is to build strong and resilient communities; education for Mexicans both in Mexico and abroad should be incorporated into this framework.

6. *Renew Commitment to Bi-National Educational Collaboration.* The fact that the U.S.-Mexico Memorandum of Understanding on Education has not been officially renewed since 2004 is problematic and suggests a lack of commitment at the federal level to fostering bi-national initiatives. The U.S. and Mexico should not only renew their memorandum of understanding on education, but also attach funding provisions so that it moves from a symbolic document to a substantive policy intervention.

REFERENCES

Alba, F. (2010). *Mexico: A crucial crossroads.* Washington, DC: Migration Information Source, Migration Policy Institute. Retrieved from http://www.migrationinformation.org/Profiles/display.cfm?ID=772

Cano, G., & Delano, A. (2007). The Mexican government and organised Mexican immigrants in the United States: A historical analysis of political transnationalism (1848-2005). *Journal of Ethnic and Migration Studies, 33*(5), p. 695.

Corrections Corporation of America. (2011). *CCA strengthens partnership with Mexico's National Institute for Adult Education.* http://www.insidecca. com/cca-source/cca-strengthens-partnership-mexicos-national-insti/

de la Garza, R. O. (1997). Foreign policy comes home: The domestic consequences of the program for Mexican communities living in foreign countries. In R. O. de la Garza & J. Velasco (Eds.), *Bridging the border: Transforming Mexico-U.S. relations* (pp. 69–88). Lanham, MD: Rowman & Littlefield Publishers.

Diaz de Cossío, R. D., Orozco, G., & González, E. (1997). *Los mexicanos en Estados Unidos.* México: Sistemas Técnicos de Edición.

Dresser, D. (September, 1992). Exporting conflict: Transboundary consequences of Mexican politics. Unpublished paper presented at the XVII International Congress of the Latin American Studies Association. Los Angeles, California. Retrieved from http://lasa.international.pitt.edu/members/congress-papers/lasa1992/files/DresserDenise.pdf

Fitzgerald, D. (2008). *A nation of emigrants: How Mexico manages its migration.* Berkeley, CA: University of California Press.

Gándara, P. (2007). A preliminary evaluation of Mexican-sponsored educational programs in the United States: Strengths, weaknesses, and potential. *Resource Book, Second Binational Symposium.* Tempe, AZ: Arizona State University. Retrieved from http://sts-rd.asu.edu/sites/default/files/gandara_PDF.pdf

García y Griego, M., & Campos, M. V. (1998). Colaboración sin concordancia: La Migración en la nueva agenda bilateral México-Estados Unidos. In M. Verea, R. Fernández de Castro, & S. Weintraub (Eds.). *Nueva agenda bilateral in la relación México-Estados Unidos* (pp. 107–134). México: Fondo de Cultura Económica.

Garcia-Acevedo, M. R. (2003). Politics across borders: Mexico's policies toward Mexicans in the United States. *Journal of the Southwest, 45*(4), 533–556.

Guerrero, L. (2009). Project SOL: Shining light on teaching secondary level, Spanish-dominant English Learners using Colegio de Bachilleres content. (Doctoral dissertation). Retrieved from Proquest (No. 3394889).

González Gutiérrez, C. (1993). The Mexican diaspora in California: The limits and possibilities for the Mexican government. In R. O. de la Garza & J. Velasco (Eds.), *The California-Mexico connection* (pp. 221–235). Stanford, CA: Stanford University Press.

González Gutiérrez, C. (1997). Decentralized diplomacy: The role of consular offices in Mexico's relations with its diaspora. In R. O. de la Garza & J. Velasco (Eds.), *Bridging the border: Transforming Mexico-U.S. relations,* (pp. 49–57). Lanham, MD: Rowman & Littlefield Publishers.

Gutierrez-Gonzalez, B. I. (2009). Binational cooperation for high school ELL immigrant students: The LUCHA program at The University of Texas at Austin. (Doctoral dissertation.) Retrieved from Proquest (No. 3389908).

Laglagaron, L. (2010). *Protection through integration: The Mexican Government's efforts to aid migrants in the United States*. Washington, DC: Migration Policy Institute.

Miller, R. (1995). Mexico's role in U.S. education: A well-kept secret. *Phi Delta Kappan, 76*(6), 470–474.

Santibañez, L., Vernez, G., & Razquin, P. (2005). *Education in Mexico: Challenges and opportunities*. Santa Monica, CA: Rand Corporation.

Secretaría de Programación y Presupuesto. (1995). *Plan nacional de desarrollo 1995-2000*. México: Secretaría de Programación y Presupuesto.

Sheridan, M. B., & Stewart, J. (2000, May 9). Mexican candidates' visits highlight California clout. *Los Angeles Times*, p. A3.

Smith, R. C. (2003). Diasporic memberships in historical perspective: Comparative insights from the Mexican, Italian and Polish cases. *International Migration Review, 37*(3), 724–759.

Terrazas, A., & Fix, M. (2009). *The binational option: Meeting the instructional needs of limited English proficient students*. Washington, DC: Migration Policy Institute.

Varisco de García, N., & García, E. E. (1996). Teachers for Mexican migrant and immigrant students: Meeting an urgent need. In J. L. Flores (Ed.), *Children of la frontera: Binational efforts to serve Mexican migrant and immigrant students*. Washington, DC: ERIC Clearinghouse.

CHAPTER 14

Finding Synergy to Improve Learning Opportunities for Mexican-Origin Children and Youth

Bryant Jensen

In large part, this chapter ends the volume where it began: envisioning possibilities. Authors from diverse disciplines with varied interests have addressed the Mexican American educational dilemma. Essentially, they articulated two views of the Mexican-origin student. One conveys a long list of school-related challenges, from poverty to poor academic performance, from school segregation to school dropouts. The other identifies key assets related to schooling and human development more broadly: from familism to cultural and linguistic adaptability. Certainly much more exploration and rigorous study are needed to discover over-lapping space between these perspectives. To some extent this has been a goal of this book.

In this chapter I explore this "overlapping space" as it relates to student learning. I grapple with the latest advances in learning theory to imagine what learning research (and associated practice) concerning Mexican-origin students in both countries *could* look like in the 21st century. My thesis is that a closer application of learning theory to schools and classrooms for Mexican-origin children can improve opportunities while advancing theory. Said accomplishments would reap benefits for other students as well who share key attributes with Mexican-origin children:

a. socioemotional assets (Crosnoe, 2006; Fuller & García Coll, 2010) associated with agrarian cultures (LeVine & White, 1986),

b.   persistent academic underperformance, and

c.   inadequately understood cultural clashes between school and home settings.

Of course, arguing for school learning improvements by applying learning theory to school and classroom settings is nothing new. Schiefelbein and McGinn (2008), for example, recently suggested that greater applications in learning theory to primary and secondary schools throughout Latin America countries (LAC) would reap benefits for children and families, teachers and school leaders, and economic and civil society. They concluded that policymakers throughout LAC should enact measures that

a.   emphasize learning how to learn,

b.   convert teachers from producers to managers of learning,

c.   infuse learning principles to teacher training, and

d.   shift emphasis for change from the central to the local level.

Though suggestions like these are relevant and timely, they tend to neglect a few important points with regard to learning theory. First, in reality there is no unitary theory of learning, but many theories, each with disparate foci, including skills (e.g., learning to type, read, write, compute), understanding (i.e., development of cognitive schema), social interactions in different settings (e.g., laboratory, classrooms), and time scales (from milliseconds to several years) (Bransford et al., 2006). We might use the singular "theory" to reference an era of research or an underlying paradigm that encompasses a series of learning principles–like "behaviorism" (Martinez, 2010, p. 6)–but it should be understood that any singular use implies a multitude of fine-grain theories.

Second, theory is always contested and, therefore, fluid. Our assertions about what constitutes "learning" and its associated principles change with new research technologies, units of analysis, and interdisciplinary frameworks (Bransford et al., 2006). For example, brain-imaging technologies since the 1990s allowing live study of the brain have confirmed the presence of "mirror neurons" in the frontal lobes, activated equally when an individual either *performs* or simply *observes* an action (Meltzoff & Decety, 2003). Interestingly, mirror neurons are found in primates as well, but they do not activate when observing another's action. Thus, imitation as a uniquely human attribute is now understood in neurological terms. This gives new importance to the study of incidental learning (e.g., children learning from adult models, or children learning by observing peer behavior) to design school improvements. In addition, mirror neurons could very well constitute the biological explanation for the preservation of cultural practices (Meltzoff, 2005) as well as individual variation in empathic ability (Jackson, Meltzoff, & Decety, 2005).

Third, there is a difference between the breadth of human competencies on the one hand, and those valued explicitly in schools (e.g., curricular standards) on the other. For good reason, schools have long valued *individual* competencies such as reading, writing, computation, and information processing. There is evidence to suggest that in the coming years these competencies will be demanded at increasingly complex levels (e.g., Carnegie Council on Advancing Adolescent Literacy, 2010). At the same time, employers from emergent and promising industries increasingly demand *interpersonal* competencies such as collaboration, adaptability, and oral communication (Wagner, 2008) in order to innovate through purposeful group work. These, too, should be valued and more systematically nurtured in schools.

In what follows I discuss possibilities for applied research to improve school learning opportunities for Mexican-origin children and youth in the coming years. This means more consistently applying concepts already understood from learning theory (e.g., building on students' preexisting knowledge), as well as addressing unsettled issues like the role of social and emotional competence in academic learning (e.g., Galindo & Fuller, 2010). I describe metaphors for dominant learning theories past and present, and suggest a new metaphor for moving forward. Whereas this new metaphor is particularly important to learning improvements for Mexican-origin students, it is also appropriate in general for children and youth living in high-tech societies. I address challenges ahead, and offer some recommendations for finding "synergy" (Bransford et al., 2006) between research and theory traditions. This synergy, I argue, is imperative to nurture a cultural hybridity for Mexican American students that can optimize their learning of and interest in school-related content.

AN EVOLVING SCIENCE OF LEARNING

Learning scientists over more than the past half-century have embodied different epistemological traditions (Greeno, Collins, & Resnick, 1996), addressing various learning phenomena. Bransford and colleagues (2006) categorize these phenomena within three "research strands" (p. 210): (a) implicit learning and the brain, (b) informal learning, and (c) designs for formal learning. Each strand uses its own set of technologies, methodologies, and theoretical assumptions. Studies of implicit learning address how information is acquired effortlessly by individuals, and sometimes without conscious recollection. They show that many early cognitive and language skills are learned relatively effortlessly, in responses to stimuli in children's environments (Kuhl, 2004).

With new technologies, brain research has accelerated rapidly in recent years (Meltzoff, Kuhl, Movellan, & Sejnowski, 2009). Neuro-imaging studies reveal that neural transformations precede behavioral changes, and that similarly appearing learning behaviors can have very different underlying neural networks between any two persons (Brans-ford et al., 2006). From this we can infer that the synaptic causes and consequences of the same learned behavior can be very different across individuals.

Studies of informal learning rely primarily on anthropological and observational techniques to understand how certain knowledge and skills are acquired outside of formal settings like classrooms. This includes designed settings (e.g., museums, zoos, libraries; Bell, Lewenstein, Shouse, & Feder, 2009) as well as emergent ones (e.g., homes, playgrounds, market) where children learn through everyday activity and experience (Scribner, 1997). These studies offer various units of analysis (e.g., setting elements, activity types, forms of participation, dimensions of social interaction) for fine-tuned research, demonstrating how real learning happens outside of the school through interpersonal competencies like listening, observing, and participation (e.g., Paradise & Rogoff, 2009).

A majority of learning research, however, has focused on the intentional acquisition of knowledge and skills in formal settings, especially in schools and classrooms. This includes articulating what students should know and do, how to best assess that knowledge (Pellegrino, Chudowski, & Glaser, 2001), and how learning processes (e.g., instruction, curriculum) can be optimized to achieve learning goals. Several research syntheses published by the National Research Council (NRC) of the National Academies and the Institute for Education Sciences (IES) of the U.S. Department of Education summarize findings across hundreds of studies. These syntheses address an array of topics, such as reading difficulties among young children (Snow, Burns, & Griffin, 1998), reading comprehension (Shanahan et al., 2010), teacher preparation (Darling-Hammond & Bransford, 2005; NRC, 2010), adolescent literacy (Carnegie Council, 2010; Kamil et al., 2008), interventions for struggling math students (Gersten et al., 2009), and much more.

Whereas the criteria used to establish "evidence" across these syntheses differ, they coalesce around the idea that an individual's organization of knowledge (within academic disciplines) matters for subsequent learning (Bransford, Brown, & Cocking, 2000). Experts in mathematics, history, or physics not only have attained a great deal of content knowledge related to their respective discipline, but they also possess a sophisticated organization of this knowledge that allows them to detect meaningful patterns, quickly retrieve relevant information, and identify important applications across varied contexts and conditions.

I mention these research strands both to highlight the ground covered in learning research and to foreground current limitations, especially in relation to improving the academic performance of Mexican-origin children and youth. Bransford et al. (2006) and others argue for a new science of learning by which the three strands mentioned better inform one another to understand how, when, where, and why children and youth from diverse backgrounds learn (p. 227). The point is not to devise some "grand learning theory" but to share research methodologies across traditions, better understand the social nature of learning, and generate consequential products to improve learning opportunities for diverse groups in diverse settings.

Research across these strands points to three principles, which I consider components of a useful working definition of "learning." First, learning constitutes a change in performance across formal and informal settings. Cognitivists refer to this as *transfer* (Bransford & Schwartz, 1999). Understanding or skill acquisition must be demonstrated across various settings in order for learning to occur. Second, learning is accumulative. Understanding builds on preexisting knowledge and experience. Children come to classrooms with varied experiences. If their initial understanding is not engaged in the classroom, they may not comprehend new concepts and information being taught (Dochy, Segers, & Buehl, 1999). Finally, learning is inextricably social. It occurs in close, regular contact with others in day-to-day settings (Meltzoff et al., 2009).

As important as it is to school improvements for Mexican-origin children, however, learning research is unsettled with regard to at least three issues. First, we need to know how incidental learning–i.e., the unintended acquisition of knowledge and skills through repeated observation and social interaction–can be assessed and incorporated into formal settings (like classrooms) to enhance performance. Some studies show, for example, that Mexican-origin children from agrarian cultures are particularly adept at learning through observation and imitation (López, Correa-Chávez, Rogoff, & Gutiérrez, 2010), but it is not clear how these competencies can or should be integrated into classroom settings to improve student interest and performance. Second, it is important to know how emotions (like joy, hope, pride, anxiety, hopelessness, shame, and anger) moderate academic learning (Denham, 2006;

Pekrun, 2006; Zins et al., 2004). In other words, how do students' emotions in classroom activities inhibit or facilitate the acquisition of academic knowledge and skills? This includes studying how task demands (Wolters, 2003), social interactions (Jensen, Rueda, Reese, & Garcia, Under Review), previous successes and failures (Stöber, 2000), and learning motivations (Guthrie & Wigfield, 1999) are associated with students' feelings in the classroom. And third, we need to know much more about how cultural dimensions are associated with the previous two limitations. Cognitive anthropologists have provided useful units of analysis to do this, including cultural settings (Weisner, 2002), cultural models (Gallimore & Goldenberg, 2001), and sociocultural interactions (Jensen, Rueda, Reese, & Garcia, Under Review).

Learning Metaphors Past

Again, my thesis is that a closer application of learning theory—as just described—to schools and classrooms not only can improve learning opportunities for Mexican-origin students (in both countries) but also advance theory by addressing the research limitations identified. Mexican-origin students present an interesting case to study current limitations because, on the whole, they demonstrate (a) poor academic performance (see Chapters 4 and 5, this volume), (b) relatively strong socioemotional competencies (see Chapter 11, this volume), and (c) broad yet inadequately understood home-school cultural disparities (see Chapters 10 and 11). Improvements of this sort, however, require a new dominant metaphor for learning.

The pigeon. For more than the first half of the 20th century most learning studies drew on conceptual and methodological tools from behaviorism (e.g., Skinner, 1953), which posited that all processes that mattered to learning were directly observable. Thinking and learning could be understood simply by observing individual responses to tasks in controlled settings, altering aspects of the reinforcement schedule, creating new associations between learning stimuli, and so on. Much of this work was developed with animals, so a useful metaphor for the research genre is the pigeon.

Some contributions from the pigeon era continue with us today. Behaviorism was particularly useful in understanding human learning that can be automatized relatively easily (e.g., letter-naming). Gambling behavior, for example, was explained relatively well as a series of responses to an immediate reinforcement schedule. In schools, the management of student behavior in the classroom continues to draw on the pigeon metaphor (e.g., Kern & Clemens, 2007). We know that reinforcing desired student behavior (e.g., attentiveness, task orientation) through genuine reinforcement like praise is more effective than addressing undesirable behavior through punishments. Moreover, the frequency, intensity, and rate of reinforcements can matter to behavioral improvement.

But the pigeon paradigm met its match when it tried explaining complex learning processes like language (Skinner, 1957). The theory dismissed "imagined internal causes" associated with learning, including cognitive abilities like memory or pattern recognition, which made it impossible to explain how higher-order thinking develops in absence of concrete reinforcements. Behaviorism simply did not possess the conceptual or methodological tools to account for cognitive processing, abilities, or schema.

The computer. Thus emerged information-processing theories in the mid-20th century. This approach to human learning developed gradually, closely following the development of hardware and operating systems in computers (Kendler, 1987), which serves as an appropriate metaphor for this genre. Computer studies specify cognitive processes involved in human learning through cognitive tasks and sophisticated statistical modeling (Siegler, 1996). Step-by-step models are developed to articulate the sequence of processing abilities used to solve problems inherent in cognitive tasks, analogous to designing program language for computers. In addition to observation, information-processing researchers use computer programming and simulation to understand moment-to-moment learning episodes (some using analysis units as brief as milliseconds) in perception, sensation, memory, and attention (Siegler, 1996).

Several important teaching strategies for classroom learning emerged out of the computer metaphor. Especially useful has been our understanding of both short- and long-term memory—appreciating the limitations of the former while purposefully expanding the ability of the latter. That is, all learning passes through the gateway of short-term memory, our ability to retain and process information for up to a minute or two. Educators should be mindful of limits of students' working memory (e.g., Miller, 1956) by not giving too much information at once, by chunking information into meaningful and manageable pieces, identifying big or important ideas, seeking automaticity of underlying skills (like calculation in math), dividing study time into multiple sessions, and reiterating the most important ideas at the beginning and end of learning sessions. Research on long-term memory underscores the value of relating school content to students through multiple modalities (e.g., language, mental imagery, personal experience), and to connect new information with students' preexisting knowledge to optimize understanding.

Toward A New Metaphor

The *How People Learn* report by the National Research Council (Bransford, Brown, & Cocking, 2000) is probably the most comprehensive and authoritative source summarizing learning research into a set of digestible principles for teachers and other practitioners. Drawing mostly from research based on the computer metaphor, it highlights what has been learned about learning from multiple disciplines and theoretical perspectives, with a focus on practice improvement. The report concludes that for school learning environments to have the greatest effect, they should be (a) learner-centered, (b) knowledge-centered, (c) assessment-centered, and (d) community-centered (pp. 131–154). Whereas these components are useful to summarize extant research and to draw associated implications for practice, they also provide a useful schematic to consider the current limitations of learning research to improve opportunities for groups like Mexican-origin students—to rethink our metaphor for learning improvement.

Learner-centered environments. Creating a learner-centered environment in schools means that teachers pay close attention to the knowledge, skills, attitudes, and beliefs of individual students in order to increase their interest in and understanding of school content. It means that teachers make a concerted effort to learn about students' cultural and language practices outside of school (e.g., Heath, 1983) to better connect student knowledge and experience with curricular goals. From the research, we know that classroom learning tasks that provide teachers with diagnostic information (e.g., asking students to make predictions and explain reasoning) can clarify student misconceptions to improve their understanding (Bransford et al., 2000, p. 134). But extant studies do not clarify how teachers should or can increase their awareness of student out-of-school beliefs and practices in ways that are consequential to school learning. We assume that connecting classroom with cultural practices (e.g., Ladson-Billings, 1995; Moll et al., 1992; Villegas & Lucas, 2002) will increase student understanding through more positive learning emotions (Pekrun, 2006), but this process remains largely ambiguous and understudied (Roorda, Koomen, Spilt, & Oort, 2011).

Knowledge-centered environments. In a knowledge-centered classroom environment, the organization of content understanding permeates all lesson plans and activities. Academic gestalts, if you will, should inform curricular content and objectives. Teachers who encourage knowledge-centered classrooms develop curricular goals (in history, math, science, etc.) that are integrated across lessons rather than presenting academic content in isolation (Donovan & Bransford, 2005). We know that classrooms generating students' disciplinary thinking and metacognition (Brown, 1987) are more likely to build the cognitive schema they need to detect important patterns, retrieve relevant information, and make content applications across settings. But research is not clear on (a) how to do this for students with widely different exposure to and experiences with academic content outside of school, (b) what kinds of knowledge are acquired tacitly, and (c) how incidental learning (through observation and imitation) can be exploited to improve students' knowledge structures.

Assessment-centered environments. An array of methods are used in assessment-centered learning environments to make student thinking "visible" as a way to shape instructional decisions in real time (i.e., formative assessment), much more than testing students to categorize their content knowledge and skill acquisition to assign a grade and/ or compare performance (i.e., summative assessment). Effective classroom teachers are purposeful about planning assessment and using it frequently and extemporaneously, through discussions, portfolios, close monitoring, writing activities, and so on (Shepard et al., 2005). They are concerned more with assessing students' content understanding than the acquisition of facts, procedure, or rote skills. They model self-monitoring skills and follow assessments with useful feedback to clarify misconceptions and induce critical thinking through hints, assistance, back-and-forth exchanges, and affirmations.

Unfortunately, rich formative assessment practices in schools tend to be infrequent. More summative assessment practices (e.g., unit exams) are reported than formative practices (Bransford et al., 2000, pp. 140–141). This means that more assessments tend to be used for the purpose of grading and comparing students rather than to improve learning opportunities through useful reflection and revision. Some research shows that students working collaboratively in small groups with peers can improve the frequency and quality of feedback (Barron, 2003), but it is not clear why some students are better at cooperative work than others (Slavin, 2011). Given the social prowess of Mexican-origin students (Fuller & García Coll, 2010) and the sense of social cohesion inherent in Mexican ethnic identity (see Chapter 10), it would be particularly helpful to understand how assessment and feedback through small-group activity can improve academic learning for these students.

Community-centered environments. Finally, Bransford et al., (2000, pp. 144–149) suggest that learning environments should be "community-centered." This includes developing norms and expectations for conduct and social interactions in the classroom that are consistent with the learning principles mentioned, and that the school community "feel connected to the larger community of homes, businesses, states, the nation, and even the world" (p. 145). This can be a tall order when norms vary within schools, not to mention the cultural-historical differences that are likely to exist between the norms of school personnel and those of Mexican-origin parents. For example, some studies show White, non-Hispanic students in the United States to be more competitive and less cooperative than Mexican American students (Knight, Cota, & Bernal, 1993; Tharp, Estrada, Dalton, & Yamauchi, 2000, p. 110) in peer settings, and that U.S. classrooms tend to favor competition and student comparison (Deyhle & Margonis, 1995). Thus, emphasizing comparison and "being right" in the classroom might align poorly with the out-of-school norms and expectations of many Mexican-origin students, setting them at an even further disadvantage.

Of course, we should not think of cultural norms and expectations like these as static or unchangeable, as Leslie Reese reminds us in Chapter 10 of this book. At the same time, we should be aware of ways the classroom community compares with the values, beliefs, and practices of the larger community. Further conceptualization, measurement, and design considerations are needed to provide a body of evidence on how this can be accomplished to improve learning opportunities in classrooms for Mexican-origin students. We especially need to understand how aligning norms and expectations within the school and between the school and broader community affects the achievement motivations and emotions of Mexican-origin (and other culturally diverse) students (Rueda, in press).

Prefrontal Cortex

I argue that it is impossible for past metaphors in and of themselves to address the research limitations and make the needed improvements to educational practice for Mexican-origin students—to understand how academic learning is shaped by imitation and incidental learning, emotional mediation, and cultural differences. They simply do not possess the needed conceptual or methodological tools. We need a new metaphor. As technical or unimaginative as it may sound, I suggest the *prefrontal cortex* of the human brain for this metaphor. Let me explain.

Located at the very front of the brain, just beneath the forehead, the prefrontal cortex is the brain's central command system. In it all human senses are integrated to plan, reason, identify patterns, and balance conflicting thoughts. It is where meaning is made from social cues to identify appropriate responses, regulate emotions, and process moral dilemmas. Most important, all these functions are quickly assimilated in real time to make goal-oriented decisions that take shape in our actions, verbal responses, and social behaviors. This is referred to as the brain's executive functions (Goldberg, 2009).

No other part of our anatomy is so uniquely human. Some have described the study of the prefrontal cortex as the "last frontier" in learning research (Goldberg, 2009, p. 6). I draw on this metaphor to improve learning environments like classrooms for Mexican-origin and other underperforming students not because brain research can somehow magically solve our educational woes (Bruer, 1997), but because the prefrontal cortex clearly illustrates deep relationships among complex thought, socialization, emotional mediation, and cultural difference. For example, in a recent set of experiments, Havas, Glenberg, and Rinck (2007) found reading comprehension of elementary school students to improve when the emotions evoked by sentences or phrases in the text were aligned with the emotional state of the reader. The authors concluded that "emotions literally change affordances" for learning, in this case language-related competencies (p. 440).

SCHOOLS AND LEARNING FOR MEXICAN-ORIGIN STUDENTS

But how would a shift toward the prefrontal cortex metaphor for learning actually matter in schools? How could it enhance the academic success of Mexican-origin students? Chapters 4 and 5 in this volume demonstrate the pervasive academic underachievement of Mexican-origin students in both countries. Mexican American students perform better academically across immigrant generations, but substantive gaps persist between non-Hispanic White students and the third-plus Mexican-origin generation, over and above socioeconomic differences. More students from preschool through college have access to public schooling in Mexico than ever before, but there is evidence to suggest that this rapid expansion has created greater inequalities in learning opportunities (Chapter 6). Rural and indigenous students in Mexico are particularly disadvantaged (Chapter 5).

Authors in this volume also address relative assets among Mexican-origin children and families (Chapters 10 and 11). These include bilingualism, biculturalism, familism, adaptability, group loyalty, good manners, respect (Reese, Balzano, Gallimore, & Goldenberg, 1995), and associated social and emotional competencies (Crosnoe, 2006). So why would a conceptual shift—a new "metaphor"—necessarily improve learning opportunities for Mexican-origin students? How can a greater research emphasis on incidental learning, socioemotional mediation, and cultural difference benefit Mexican-origin students in the 21st century? Two general answers come to mind. First, the prefrontal cortex metaphor can lead to classroom settings that induce a greater sense of *belonging* for Mexican-origin students. Collins and Halverson (2009) recently lamented:

> One of the fundamental problems of school is that children are always comparing themselves to other students, and it is only the best students who feel they are successful. Because school is so competitive, a sense of failure overwhelms many students. Most cope by turning their energies to other activities [. . .]. The majority of students come to regard learning as something to do as little as possible. The goal becomes to get grades that are good enough not to hurt one's future, with a minimum effort. This pervasive attitude is inimical to learning and is a direct product of the competitive nature of school, where only a few students look smart. (p. 110)

Competitiveness is only one of many cultural dimensions likely to undercut academic learning opportunities for Mexican American students (Tharp et al., 2000). With the prefrontal cortex as our learning metaphor, teachers can come to appreciate and understand how students with cultural histories different from their own approach learning academic content. This includes the cultural values—e.g., collaboration, respect for authority, group solidarity—inherent in the traditional Mexican concept of *educación* (Reese, Balzano, Gallimore, & Goldenberg, 1995). Curricular standards can more purposefully integrate social and emotional competencies (Zins et al., 2004), and professional development programs can provide mechanisms for school personnel to understand, appreciate, and apply the out-of-school beliefs, experiences, and practices of their students to learning activities in the classroom.

Second, learning opportunities drawing from the prefrontal cortex metaphor can help to decrease the growing difference between a narrow set of competencies valued in schools, on the one hand, and the widening spectrum of those demanded in civil society and the workforce, on the other. Obviously the traditional knowledge and skill sets associated with reading, writing, computation, and information processing will continue to be essential in society. Evidence suggests that they will be demanded at increasingly complex levels (e.g., Carnegie Council, 2010) in the 21st century, especially the reasoning and problem-solving skills needed to interpret varied forms of digital information (Wagner, 2008): websites, social network platforms, alternative online media like blogs, etc. (Collins & Halverson, 2009).

But the acquisition of complex cognitive and technological competence in students also requires greater interpersonal or socioemotional capabilities (Heckman, 2008). Innovative production, for example, demands intimate teamwork and the interpersonal savvy to negotiate, listen intently, communicate, and share responsibility (Trilling & Fadel, 2009, pp. 54–59). For consequential school learning and success in life alike, children need to know how to think and troubleshoot in groups. They need skills in initiation and to know how to take on varied roles and responsibilities, work with ambiguity, balance diverse perspectives, and communicate effectively across cultural differences (Trilling & Fadel, 2009). In a recent interview, Mark Zuckerberg (2012), chief executive and co-creator of Facebook, commented:

> We're trying to build products for everyone in the world [. . .]. You don't want to get isolated to do that. [. . .] We have a very open culture in the company where we foster a lot of interaction between not just me and people, but between everyone else. [. . .] I think that more flow of information and the ability to stay connected to more people makes people more effective as people. [. . .] I also think in terms of doing work and in terms of learning and evolving as a person, you just grow more when you get more people's perspectives and when you're more connected and have more of a flow from people.

Thus, the social nature of new knowledge and skill acquisition (Brown, Collins, & Duguid, 1989) and the demands of employers and civil society (Winograd & Hais, 2011) require a new metaphor for school learning. I suggest the prefrontal cortex as a viable candidate because of the complex neural interactions that occur there among critical thinking, language, social stimuli, and emotional regulation (Goldberg,

2009). Mexican-origin students are positioned particularly well to benefit from this transformation given their poor academic yet relatively strong developmental profile.

PREFRONTAL CORTEX IN THE CLASSROOM

I say "transformation" because there is yet much to glean from past metaphors to improve learning opportunities for Mexican-origin students in the present. Just as moving from the pigeon to the computer metaphor played out (and continues to play out) gradually and incrementally in research and education practice, Mexican-origin children and other culturally and linguistically diverse students have much to gain from extensive applications of already-established learning principles in classrooms and other settings. This includes developing lesson and curricular planning that orient around big disciplinary ideas; assessing students' understanding much more frequently through discussions, writing activities, and close monitoring; and developing norms and expectations within schools that are consistent with these principles.

With these learning principles applied broadly and consistently across classrooms and schools for Mexican-origin students in both countries, however, my guess is that along with significant improvements we would continue to witness Mexican underachievement. For more far-reaching advancements, we must find "synergy" (Bransford et al., 2006) among research strands and methods, disciplines, and epistemological traditions to expand the learning metaphor–to better address the incidental, social, emotional, and cultural dimensions of academic learning (particularly in classrooms). We need a new science of learning that is mindful of educational practice for culturally and linguistically diverse students. Learning research should be more purposeful about nurturing a cultural hybridity for Mexican-origin students that optimizes their interpersonal and individual competencies in ways consistent with the agrarian values associated with *educación* (Reese et al., 1995).

Beyond Traditional Dichotomies

School classrooms are ideal laboratories to forge this "new frontier." They are socially complex, emotionally fluid cultural settings where subtle, rapid-fire decisions bear on students' interest in, appreciation for, and understanding of academic content (Brophy, 1999; Jensen et al., Under Review). However, for researchers and practitioners to incorporate a "prefrontal cortex" framework, a series of long-standing dichotomies in traditional classrooms must be revolutionized. Many if not all of these dichotomies were born in the industrial age, when the factory model for school replaced the single-room schoolhouse—when teaching became an institutionalized profession.

Teacher versus learner. In the factory model, teacher and learner roles are separate and rigid. Classrooms are didactic rather than social. Student autonomy and initiative are restrained rather than fostered. The teacher is the source of knowledge, and the student (or learner) the receptacle. Of course, few classrooms today completely fit this stereotype, but in many there is little flexibility between the social roles of teachers and learners. The prefrontal cortex paradigm has teacher learning and role flexibility at its core. We need to know how teacher understanding of students' experiences, knowledge, beliefs, and practices, for example, can be linked with curricular goals to improve student interest in, involvement with, and understanding of academic content. Students' understanding and experiences with digital technologies outside school is a prime example of this (Collins & Halverson, 2009)—a fantastic resource for teachers to build on.

School versus home. Experiences outside school are essentially irrelevant in the factory model. Students are treated as blank slates upon school entry. All school learning is formal. From a prefrontal cortex perspective, however, the content and social means of learning inside and outside school are very relevant. Informal learning occurs in school and non-school settings. Indeed, much incidental learning occurs in classrooms, and researchers drawing on the new metaphor are deeply interested in how this occurs (through observation, participation, and imitation) in order to build interest in and understanding of academic content. They are also interested in how continuities and connections between school and non-school content and experiences are associated with the academic learning emotions and motivations of students (Rueda, in press).

Individual versus interpersonal. In the factory model, interpersonal competence is only addressed in the face of pathology. That is, asocial manifestations like withdrawal or aggressive behavior are targeted through some intervention separate from the general curriculum, which focuses mostly on the traditional individual competencies—e.g., reading fluency, writing composition, math calculation. From a prefrontal cortex perspective, interpersonal competencies are systematically nurtured, particularly in classroom activities designed to expand students' higher-order thinking skills such as pattern recognition, comparison, inference, and other analytic skills. We are interested in understanding how prosocial competencies (e.g., empathy, cooperation, and responsibility) can facilitate academic learning (Malecki & Elliot, 2002).

Research versus practice. Developing evidence for any practice or program intended to improve student learning involves a cyclical process of development, implementation, analysis, and revision—what Bryk and colleagues (2009) refer to as "plan-do-study-act cycles." In the factory model, teachers and other practitioners implement and researchers do the rest. Researchers and practitioners work separately. There is little cross-pollination of expertise. In a prefrontal cortex perspective, researchers and practitioners merge their respective expertise (e.g., Goldenberg & Gallimore, 1991) through intimate collaborations to develop, test, and refine practices and programs (Reinking, 2010). Because classroom learning constitutes a complex integration of social, emotional, and academic competencies, close research-practitioner collaborations are vital to developing evidence-based improvements.

Inference versus description. Understanding how emotions and motivations interact with academic learning in socially complex classrooms for students from different cultural heritages requires multiple data sources. Goal-oriented collaborations between researchers and practitioners require gathering information on implementation (e.g., amount of time), classroom climate (e.g., clarity of learning objectives, discussion opportunities), and the learning and dispositions of individual students (Collins, Joseph, & Bielaczyc, 2004). This includes both inferential (e.g., standardized scores of academic performance) and descriptive (e.g., field notes, student work samples) data. Under the factory model, inferential and descriptive information are rarely woven in the same analysis to improve learning opportunities. Classroom studies embodied *either* interpretivist *or* positivist perspectives, while more pragmatic approaches were largely neglected. In order to understand and leverage the complexities of incidental and socioemotional dimensions of academic learning to improve opportunities for Mexican-origin students, we need thoughtful, purposeful integrations of various data sources.

Synergy in Practice

In this chapter, I have proposed that academic learning improvements for Mexican-origin children in both countries require rethinking our learning metaphor in ways that (a) combine frameworks and methodologies from various strands of learning theory and research and (b) more adequately address the incidental, social, emotional, and cultural dimensions of learning. Teachers and other school practitioners need to know much more about how to connect the out-of-school knowledge and experiences of Mexican-origin (and other linguistically and culturally diverse) students to curricular activities in the classroom. No other ethnic group in U.S. schools is as large, rapidly growing, and severely underperforming as Mexican American children, and our current metaphors for school learning are inadequate to address the improvement challenge in ways that build on their developmental assets.

I suggest the prefrontal cortex as a viable metaphor to address learning challenges for Mexican-origin students precisely because this part of the human brain integrates complex thought, language, social stimuli, and emotions in order to produce culturally appropriate actions and responses within diverse settings. I have made some suggestions for research collaborations to better represent this metaphor in order to establish a larger body of evidence. These suggestions are particularly relevant given the growing emphasis on interpersonal competence in civic society and the labor market alike, including skills like empathy, cooperation, responsibility, and communication (Trilling & Fadel, 2009).

But teachers and other school practitioners do not have the luxury of waiting for research advances to improve their practice–to address social, emotional, incidental, and cultural dimensions of academic learning in the classroom. They need synergy now. How can the prefrontal cortex metaphor for learning inform current practices in classrooms and other school settings while the empirical knowledge base catches up to speed? Below I end with four broad suggestions. Each underscores the idea that effective teachers are first and foremost eager learners. Indeed, relating academic content to speak effectually to Mexican-origin students' lives and capabilities requires the ongoing acquisition of practitioner knowledge and skills.

Draw on the best practices from metaphors past. The computer metaphor clearly demonstrates that understanding in any given domain of academic knowledge is a direct function of time and exposure. Chapters 5 and 6 in this volume demonstrate that the least advantaged children in Mexico not only attend subpar schools, but that they attend for fewer hours. This means that instructional time is limited. A very initial step toward learning improvements in these settings–as with schools in other developing countries–is to increase overall instructional time in the classroom by improving teacher and student attendance, lengthening the school day where feasible, limiting transition time between academic activities, and increasing student task orientation in class (EQUIP2, 2010).

As discussed, extant research based largely on the computer metaphor also points to the importance of developing learner-, knowledge-, assessment-, and community-centered learning environments. Per the suggestions of Bransford and colleagues (2000, pp. 19–21), teachers can do this by (a) drawing out and working with students' pre-existing understandings; (b) teaching big ideas in depth by providing a firm foundation of factual knowledge and multiple examples; and (c) teaching students metacognitive skills (e.g., self-monitoring, reflection, revision) across academic content, so that students become independent thinkers.

Again, we should think of the prefrontal cortex metaphor as a way of adding value to the current knowledge base of practice improvement, rather than somehow being detached from what strong evidence already suggests. Thus, my following three suggestions should be understood in terms of building on (rather than dismissing or overlooking) the suggestions of Bransford and colleagues (2000), as well as the best of learning metaphors past.

Be sensitive to the motivational and emotional dimensions of classroom learning. In a recent research synthesis, Roorda and colleagues (2011) found that the amount of positive affect in teacher-student relationships was associated with greater academic engagement and achievement of students, more so for secondary than elementary school students. In addition, children from families among lower socioeconomic strata (SES) benefited even more (in terms of engagement and achievement), on average, from positive affect than those from higher-SES groups.

Often the motivational and emotional dimensions in classroom learning are either taken for granted or practically invisible. This includes things such as positive communication, enthusiasm, smiling, respectful language, and student comfort (Zins et al., 2004). It is important for teachers to be mindful of these attributes, especially how the emotions (e.g., joy, hope, pride, anxiety, shame) and motivations (e.g., intrinsic vs. extrinsic) of Mexican-origin students differ during any given classroom activity. Thus, in addition to addressing content understanding, teachers and other practitioners should explore ways of connecting content with students' interests and life experiences (Brophy, 2008). In this way not only is student understanding of the academic material improved, but also their appreciation for and identification with the material (Brophy, 1999; Jensen, Rueda, Reese, & Garcia, Under Review).

Connect objectives and activities in the classroom with students' out-of-school interests, knowledge, and experiences. There have been several proposals in the literature, though minimal inferential evidence (Goldenberg, 2008), regarding this suggestion. These proposals draw on three related units of cultural analysis: cultural models, cultural settings, and sociocultural interactions. Cultural models simply refer to the mental schema shared among members of a cultural group, including the mutable beliefs and values that underpin how individuals think, perceive, and store information. Gonzalez and colleagues (2005) suggest that teachers make regular home visits to better understand the cultural models and the knowledge resources (e.g., mechanics, carpentry, masonry, botany, animals) of students' families. Classroom materials and learning goals can then draw on these resources.

Cultural settings refer to the day-to-day activities (e.g., meals, exercise, chores, sports) of children and youth (Weisner, 2002). As Reese discussed in Chapter 10 of this volume, knowing the daily routines of students is important for teachers to understand their students' goals, responsibilities, and values. Teachers can be creative in doing this, through interviews, surveys, class discussions, and teacher-parent conferences. Again, with this information teachers are able to connect academic content and classroom activity with students' out-of-school knowledge and experiences.

Sociocultural interactions refer to the behaviors or actions that occur between two or more persons in response to one another (Jensen et al., Under Review). The idea is that children from different cultural groups tend to interact differently, based on associated beliefs and values. Invisible cultural rules underlie how/whether children cooperate, use language, and negotiate roles, for example, between siblings, peers, and parents in different settings. Teachers can find ways to observe these interactions (during peer play, for example, or conversations with parents or siblings) in order to (a) interpret the meaning of student behavior during social interactions in the classroom and (b) find ways to make classroom interactions more familiar to increase student interest and learning.

Design classroom activities that exercise and integrate students' social competencies. Teachers and other practitioners in schools should come closer to terms with the social nature of learning in academic settings. Social competencies like empathy, cooperation, responsibility, and communication are especially important to small-group projects and peer assistance in the classroom. Teachers should be mindful of students' relative social strengths, and systematically integrate opportunities to practice and develop social skills in their lesson plans, classroom activities, and learning objectives. For example, a teacher might allow a student to lead a book chapter discussion to develop leadership skills, let students design a science experiment of choice to develop autonomy skills, or have students defend a peer's perspective of some controversy within a historical event to develop empathy skills.

CONCLUSION

Finding synergy between research traditions to account for a broader array of human capabilities (social, emotional, cognitive) presents an awesome opportunity to advance the academic well-being of Mexican-origin students at a crucial point in history. Now is a prime time to take advantage of this opportunity. Schools in the United States, Mexico, and other countries are at the dawn of a new era. Though schools by and large operate much the same way they did 50 years ago, pressures are mounting to deliver meaningful innovations that enhance learning for diverse, historically underserved students. New digital technologies are creating personalized learning opportunities (Collins & Halverson, 2009). Fast-growing industries are demanding socially savvy workers (Trilling & Fadel, 2009). And the impatience with the pervasive underperformance of Mexican American students in the United States (Gándara & Contreras, 2009), and rural and indigenous students in Mexico (Andere, 2006), has reached a breaking point.

Meeting the Mexican-origin student learning challenge through ongoing research and practice improvements will require embracing two essential values. First is *intense pragmatism*—as mentioned, pursuing the prefrontal cortex as a new metaphor for learning does not in any way dismiss the research and practice contributions of metaphors past. Indeed, new research and practice improvements addressing socioemotional and cultural dimensions of school learning should build on rather than dismiss the contributions of past research. This pragmatism also means that researchers and practitioners collaborate much more intensively with one another to identify and address problems of practice (Bryk, Gomez, & Grunow, 2010). Close collaborations will also be needed among disparate social science traditions (e.g., anthropology and psychology, computer science and linguistics).

Second is *authentic relationships*—teachers need to know much more about the out-of-school lives of their Mexican-origin students in order to enhance student interest in and understanding of academic content. Teachers need to be more genuine with regard to their relationship with the academic content as well, which involves conveying more enthusiasm for the material, as well as curiosity, and admitting ignorance when appropriate. From an incidental learning perspective, students–especially Mexican-origin children who demonstrate strong observation and imitation skills (López, Correa-Chávez, Rogoff, & Gutiérrez, 2010)–are much more likely to reflect on their own relationship with the curricula when this is genuinely modeled for them. Deeper, interpersonal connections between teachers and learners with divergent cultural histories and more intimate personal relationships with the academic content will allow Mexican-origin students to see how the things they already know and do well are not only relevant to academic activities, but actually contribute to their understanding.

REFERENCES

Andere, E. (2006). *México sigue en riesgo: El monumental reto de la educación.* México: Editorial Planeta Mexicana.

Barron, B. (2003). When smart groups fail. *Journal of the Learning Sciences, 12*(3), 307–359.

Bell, P., Lewenstein, B., Shouse, A. W., & Feder, M. A. (2009). *Learning science in informal environments.* Washington, DC: National Research Council.

Bransford, J. D., et al. (2006). Learning theories and education: Toward a decade of synergy. In P. Alexander & P. Winne (Eds.), *Handbook of Educational Psychology* (2nd ed.) (pp. 209–244). Mahwah, NJ: Lawrence Erlbaum Associates.

Bransford, J. D., Brown, A. L., & Cocking, R. R. (Eds.). (2000). *How people learn: Brain, mind, experience, and school.* Washington, DC: National Academies Press.

Bransford, J. D., & Schwartz, D. L. (1999). Rethinking transfer: A simple proposal with multiple implications. *Review of Research in Education, 24,* 61–101.

Brophy, J. (2008). Developing students' appreciation for what is taught in school. *Educational Psychologist, 43*(3), 132–141.

Brophy, J. (1999). Toward a model of the value aspects of motivation in education: Developing appreciation for particular learning domains and activities. *Educational Psychologist, 34*(2), 75–85.

Brown, A. (1987). Metacognition, executive control, self-regulation, and other more mysterious mechanisms. In F. Reiner & R. Kluwe (Eds.), *Metacognition, motivation, and understanding* (pp. 65–116). Mahwah, NJ: Lawrence Erlbaum Associates.

Brown, J. S., Collins, A., & Duguid, P. (1989). Situated cognition and the culture of learning. *Educational Researcher, 18*(1), 32–42.

Bruer, J. (1997). Education and the brain: A bridge too far. *Educational Researcher,* *26*(8), 4–16.

Bryk, A. S., Gomez, L. M., & Grunow A. (2010). *Getting ideas into action: Building networked improvement communities in education.* Stanford, CA: Carnegie Foundation for the Advancement of Teaching.

Carnegie Council on Advancing Adolescent Literacy. (2010). *Time to act: An agenda for advancing adolescent literacy for college and career success.* New York: Carnegie Corporation of New York.

Collins, A., & Halverson, R. (2009). *Rethinking education in the age of technology: The digital revolution and schooling in American.* New York: Teachers College Press.

Collins, A., Joseph, D., & Bielaczyc, K. (2004). Design research: Theoretical and methodological issues. *The Journal of the Learning Sciences, 13*(1), 15–42.

Crosnoe, R. (2006). *Mexican roots, American schools: Helping Mexican immigrant children succeed.* Palo Alto, CA: Stanford University Press.

Darling-Hammond, L., & Bransford, J. (Eds.) (2005). *Preparing teachers for a changing world: What teachers should learn and be able to do.* Washington, DC: National Academy of Education.

Denham, S. (2006). Social-emotional competence as support for school readiness: What is it and how do we assess it? *Early Education and Development, 17*(1), 57–89.

Deyhle, D., & Margonis, F. (1995). Navajo mothers and daughters: Schools, jobs, and the family. *Anthropology & Education Quarterly, 26*, 135–167.

Dochy, F., Segers, M., & Buehl, M. M. (1999). The relation between assessment practices and outcomes of studies: The case of prior knowledge. *Review of Educational Research, 69*(2), 145–186.

Donovan, M. S., & Bransford, J. D. (Eds.). (2005). *How students learn: History, mathematics, and science in the classroom.* Washington, DC: The National Academies Press.

EQUIP2. (2010). *Using opportunity to learn and early grade reading fluency to measure school effectiveness in Ethiopia, Guatemala, Honduras, and Nepal.* Washington, DC: USAID.

Fuller, B., & García Coll, C. (2010). Learning from Latinos: Contexts, families, and child development in motion. *Developmental Psychology, 46*(3), 559–565.

Galindo, C., & Fuller, B. (2010). The social competence of Latino kindergartners and growth in mathematical understanding. *Developmental Psychology, 46*(3), 579–592.

Gallimore, R., & Goldenberg, C. (2001). Analyzing cultural models and settings to connect minority achievement and school improvement research. *Educational Psychologist, 36*(1), 45–56.

Gándara, P., & Contreras, F. (2009). *The Latino education crisis: The consequences of failed social policies*. Cambridge, MA: Harvard University Press.

Gersten, R., Beckmann, S., Clarke, B., Foegen, A., Marsh, L., Star, J. R., & Witzel, B. (2009). *Assisting students struggling with mathematics: Response to Intervention (RtI) for elementary and middle schools* (NCEE 2009-4060). Washington, DC: U.S. Department of Education.

Goldberg, E. (2009). *The new executive brain: Frontal lobes in a complex world*. New York: Oxford University Press.

Goldenberg, C. (2008). Teaching English language learners: What the research does–and does not–say. *American Educator, 32*(2), 8–44.

Goldenberg, C., & Gallimore, R. (1991). Local knowledge, research knowledge, and educational change: A case study of early Spanish reading improvement. *Educational Researcher, 20*(8), 2–14.

Gonzalez, N., Moll, L., & Amanti, C. (Eds.). (2005). *Funds of knowledge: Theorizing practices in households and classrooms*. Mahwah, NJ: Lawrence Erlbaum Associates.

Greeno, J., Collins, A., & Resnick, L. (1996). Cognition and learning. In R. Calfee & D. Berliner (Eds.), *Handbook of educational psychology* (pp. 15–46). New York: Macmillan.

Guthrie, J. T., & Wigfield, A. (1999). How motivation fits into a science of reading. *Scientific Studies of Reading, 3*(3), 199–205.

Havas, D. A., Glenberg, A. M., & Rinck, M. (2007). Emotion simulation during language comprehension. *Psychological Bulletin & Review, 14*(3), 436–441.

Heath, S. B. (1983). *Ways with words: Language, life, and work in communities and classrooms*. New York: Cambridge University Press.

Heckman, J. (2008). Schools, skills, and synapses. *Economic Inquiry, 46*(3), 289–324.

Jackson, P. L., Meltzoff, A. N., & Decety, J. (2005). How do we perceive the pain of others? A window into the neural processes involved in empathy. *NeuroImage, 24*, 771–779.

Jensen, B., Rueda, R., Reese, L. & Garcia, E. (Under Review). Designing sociocultural interactions to improve relevant learning opportunities for underperforming minority students. *Educational Psychologist*.

Kamil, M. L., Borman, G. D., Dole, J., Kral, C. C., Salinger, T., & Torgesen, J. (2008). *Improving adolescent literacy: Effective classroom and intervention practices* (NCEE 2008-4027). Washington, DC: National Center for Education Evaluation and Regional Assistance, Institute of Education Sciences, U.S. Department of Education.

Kendler, H. H. (1987). *Historical foundations of modern psychology*. Chicago: Dorsey Press.

Kern, L., & Clemens, N. H. (2007). Antecedent strategies to promote appropriate classroom behavior. *Psychology in the Schools, 44*(1), 65–75.

Knight, G. P., Cota, M. K., & Bernal, M. E. (1993). The socialization of cooperative, competitive, and individualistic preferences: The mediating role of ethnic identity. *Hispanic Journal of Behavioral Sciences, 15*(3), 291–309.

Kuhl, P. K. (2004). Early language acquisition: Cracking the speech code. *Nature Reviews Neuroscience, 5*, 831–843.

Ladson-Billings, G. (1995). Toward a theory of culturally relevant pedagogy. *American Journal of Educational Research, 32*(3), 465–491.

LeVine, R. A., & White, M. I. (1986). *Human conditions: The cultural basis of educational development.* New York: Routledge & Kegan Paul.

López, A., Correa-Chávez, M., Rogoff, B., & Gutiérrez, K. (2010). Attention to instruction directed to another by U.S. Mexican-heritage children of varying cultural backgrounds. *Developmental Psychology, 46*(3), 593–601.

Malecki, C. K., & Elliott, S. N. (2002). Children's social behaviors as predictors of academic achievement: A longitudinal analysis. *School Psychology Quarterly, 17*(1), 1–23.

Martinez, M. (2010). *Learning and cognition: The design of the mind.* Upper Saddle River, NJ: Pearson.

Meltzoff, A. N. (2005). Imitation and other minds: The "like me" hypothesis. In S. Hurley & N. Chater (Eds.), *Perspectives on imitation: From neuroscience to social science* (Vol. 2, pp. 55–77). Cambridge, MA: MIT Press.

Meltzoff, A. N., & Decety, J. (2003). What imitation tells us about social cognition: A rapprochement between developmental psychology and cognitive neuroscience. *Philosophical Transactions of the Royal Society of London: Biological Sciences, 358*, 491–500.

Meltzoff, A. N., Kuhl, P. K., Movellan, J., & Sejnowski, T. J. (2009). Foundations for a new science of learning. *Science, 325*, 284–288.

Miller, G. A. (1956). The magical number seven, plus or minus two. *Psychological Review, 63*, 81–97.

National Research Council. (2010). *Preparing teachers: Building evidence for sound policy.* Washington, DC: The National Academies Press.

Paradise, R., & Rogoff, B. (2009). Side by side: Learning by observing and pitching it. *Ethos, 37*(1), 102–138.

Pekrun, R. (2006). The control-value theory of achievement emotions: Assumptions, corollaries, and implications for educational research and practice. *Educational Psychology Review, 18*(4), 315–341.

Pelligrino, J. W., Chudowski, N., & Glaser, R. (2001). *Knowing what students know: The science and design of educational assessment.* Washington, DC: National Academy Press.

Reese, L., Balzano, S., Gallimore, R., & Goldenberg, C. (1995). The concept of *educación*: Latino family values and American schooling. *International Journal of Educational Research, 23*(1), 57–81.

Reinking, D. (2010). *Beyond the laboratory and lens: New metaphors for literacy research.* Address given at the meeting for the Literacy Research Association in Fort Worth, TX.

Roorda, D. L., Koomen, H. M. Y., Spilt, J. L., & Oort, F. J. (2011). The influence of affective teacher-student relationships on students' school engagement and achievement: A meta-analytic approach. *Review of Educational Research, 81*(4), 493–529.

Rueda, R. (In Press). Twenty first century skills: Cultural, linguistic, and motivational perspectives. In D. Alverman & N. Unrau (Eds.), *Theoretical Models & Processes of Reading.* Newark, DE: International Reading Association.

Schiefelbein, E., & McGinn, N. F. (2008). *Learning to educate: Proposals for the reconstruction of education in Latin America.* Paris, France: UNESCO.

Scribner, S. (1997). Knowledge at work. In E. Tobach, R. J. Falmagne, M. B. Parlee, L. M. W. Martin, & A. S. Kapelman (Eds.), *Mind & social practice: Selected writings of Sylvia Scribner* (pp. 308–318). Cambridge, UK: Cambridge University Press.

Shanahan, T., Callison, K., Carriere, C., Duke, N. K., Pearson, P. D., Schatschneider, C., & Torgesen, J. (2010). *Improving reading comprehension in Kindergarten through 3rd grade* (NCEE 2010-4038). Washington, DC: National Center for Education Evaluation and Regional Assistance, Institute of Education Sciences, U.S. Department of Education.

Shepard, L., Hammerness, K., Darling-Hammond, L., Rust, F., Baratz Snowden, J., Gordon, E., Gutierrez, C., & Pacheco, A. (2005). Assessment. In L. Darling-Hammond & J. Bransford (Eds.), *Preparing teachers for a changing world: What teachers should learn and be able to do* (pp. 275–326). San Francisco, CA: Jossey-Boss.

Siegler, R. S. (1996). Emerging minds: The process of change in children's thinking. New York: Oxford University Press.

Skinner, B. F. (1953). *Science and human behavior.* New York: Macmillan.

Skinner, B. F. (1957). *Verbal behavior.* New York: Appleton Century Crofts.

Slavin, R. E. (2011). Instruction based on cooperative learning. In R. Mayer (Ed.), *Handbook of research on learning and instruction* (pp. 344–360). London, UK: Taylor & Francis.

Snow, C., Burns, M. S., & Griffin, P. (1998). *Preventing reading difficulties in young children.* Washington, DC: National Academies Press.

Stöber, J. (2000). Prospective cognitions in anxiety and depression: Replication and methodological extension. *Cognition and Emotion, 14,* 725–729.

Tharp, R., Estrada, P., Dalton, S., & Yamauchi, L. A. (2000). *Teaching transformed: Achieving excellence, fairness, inclusion, and harmony.* Boulder, CO: Westview Press.

Trilling, B., & Fadel, C. (2009). *21st century skills: Learning for life in our times.* San Francisco: Jossey-Bass.

Villegas, A. M., & Lucas, T. (2002). Preparing culturally responsive teachers: Rethinking the curriculum. *Journal of Teacher Education, 53*(1), 20–32.

Wagner, T. (2008). *The global achievement gap.* New York: Basic Books.

Weisner, T. S. (2002). Ecocultural understanding of children's developmental pathways. *Human Development, 45,* 275–281.

Winograd, M., & Hais, M. D. (2011). *Millennial momentum: How a new generation is remaking America.* Piscataway, NJ: Rutgers University Press.

Wolters, C. A. (2003). Regulation of motivation: Evaluating an underemphasized aspect of self-regulated learning. *Educational Psychologist, 38,* 189–205.

Zins, J. E., Weissberg, R. P., Wang, M. C., & Walberg, H. J. (2004). *Building academic success on social and emotional learning: What does the research say?* New York: Teachers College Press.

Zuckerberg, M. (2012). With the highly anticipated Facebook IPO announcement, we look back at Charlie's exclusive interview with Mark Zuckerberg and Sheryl Sandberg. Accessed on February 9, 2012, at http://www.charlierose.com/view/clip/12125

About the Editors and the Contributors

Bryant Jensen is assistant professor of Teacher Education at Brigham Young University. He earned a Ph.D. in educational psychology at Arizona State University. Bryant is a former Fulbright scholar in Mexico and Institute of Education Sciences (IES) post-doctoral fellow at the University of Oregon. He is interested in improving academic learning opportunities for culturally and linguistically diverse children from low-income households by applying principles of sociocultural theory and design-based research in classrooms and other settings.

Adam Sawyer is assistant professor of Education in the Bard College Master of Arts in Teaching Program. He is devoted to improving schooling opportunities for students impacted by migration in both the United States and Latin America. His research seeks to inform teaching and policy through exploration of the interplay of schooling with student social context, family life, culture, and language. Adam has worked as a bilingual teacher in East Palo Alto, San Francisco, and Los Angeles, and as a consultant to the Mexican Secretariat of Education. He holds a doctorate in International Education from the Harvard Graduate School of Education.

James D. Bachmeier is a post-doctoral research associate in the Population Research Institute at Pennsylvania State University. His research focuses on Mexican immigration to the United States and intergenerational patterns of educational attainment among the U.S. Mexican-origin population

Frank D. Bean is Chancellor's Professor of Sociology and Director of the Center for Research on Immigration, Population and Public Policy at the University of California, Irvine. His latest book, *The Diversity Paradox: Immigration and the Color Line in Twenty-First Century America*, received the 2011 American Sociological Association's Population Section's Otis Dudley Duncan Award for Distinguished Scholarship in Social Demography.

Susan K. Brown is associate professor of sociology at the University of California, Irvine. She is the author of *Beyond the Immigrant Enclave: Network Change and Assimilation* (2004). Her research focuses on the incorporation of immigrants to the United States, residential segregation, and inequality of access to higher education.

Benilde García Cabrero is professor of Educational Psychology at the Universidad Nacional Autónoma de México. She also serves in consultant capacities for several national and international institutions, including the Consejo Nacional de Fomento Educativo, the Instituto Nacional para la Evaluación de la Educación, and the Secretaría de Educación Pública in Mexico; UNICEF and UNESCO at the United Nations; as well as private companies that design educational programs, curriculum, and materials.

Cynthia García Coll is the Charles Pitts Robinson and John Palmer Barstow Professor of Education, Psychology and Pediatrics at Brown University and Assistant Dean of Research at the University of Puerto Rico. She has published extensively on the sociocultural influences in child development, with particular emphasis on at-risk and minority populations. She has been on the editorial boards of several research journals and co-edited several books, most recently *The Immigrant Paradox in Children and Adolescents*.

Regina Cortina is associate professor of Education and coordinator of the International and Comparative Education Program at Teachers College, Columbia University. Her areas of expertise include the education and employment of teachers, international and comparative education, gender and education, public policy and education in Mexico, educational attainment among the poor in Latin America, and the schooling of Latin American-born students in the United States.

Ivania de la Cruz is a doctoral candidate in International Educational Development at Teachers College, Columbia University. Her research interests are in educational reforms in Latin America and educational development of indigenous youth in Mexico. Ivania is currently writing her doctoral dissertation on indigenous students' access and completion of high school in Oaxaca, Mexico.

Guadalupe Ruiz Cuéllar is a professor at the Universidad Autónoma de Aguascalientes in Mexico. She coordinates the Masters Program in

Educational Research, and teaches undergraduate and graduate courses in research methods and academic writing. Her research interests focus on evaluating primary school quality, teacher training, and school administration in Mexico.

Claudia Galindo is an assistant professor at the University of Maryland, Baltimore County. She was a post-doctoral fellow at the Center for Social Organization of Schools at Johns Hopkins University, studying longitudinal effects of district support on the quality of school partnership programs. She focuses on issues of educational inequality, minority students' educational experiences, and Latino students and families. Her work integrates sociology of education, educational policy, immigration, and psychology.

Francisco X. Gaytan is an assistant professor of social work at Northeastern Illinois University in Chicago. His research focuses on community organizing, education, and youth development in Latino and immigrant communities in urban areas. He received his M.S.W. from the University of California at Berkeley, his Ed.M. from Harvard University, and his Ph.D. in Applied Psychology from New York University.

Edmund "Ted" Hamann is an associate professor in the Department of Teaching, Learning, and Teacher Education at the University of Nebraska-Lincoln. An anthropologist of education, he studies the local formations of education policy in response to student mobility, particularly the movement of students between the United States and Mexico. He is co-editor of Information Age Press's *Education Policy in Practice: Critical Cultural Studies* book series.

Nadia Huq is a doctoral student in Clinical Psychology at the University of North Carolina, Greensboro. Her current research interests include acculturative stress and depressive symptoms in Latino youth, with an emphasis on ethnic identity as a protective factor.

Mark A. Leach is assistant professor of Rural Sociology and Demography at Pennsylvania State University. His recent research focuses on implications of parental unauthorized status for educational attainment of immigrant children, effects of state and local restrictions directed at unauthorized immigrants, and living arrangements of Mexican immigrant families.

Carmina Makar is a doctoral candidate in International Educational Development at Teachers College, Columbia University. She has served as lecturer for the department of Communication and Urban Planning and program coordinator for Distance Education at a university in Guadalajara, Mexico. Her research interests include language, literacy, and transnational approaches to education, as well as emerging methodological issues in education research.

María Guadalupe Pérez Martínez is a research associate and teaches courses in research methods at the Universidad Autónoma de Aguascalientes in Mexico. Her scholarship has focused on preschool evaluation, teacher assessment practices, and professional development in Mexico. She is interested in education policy, teacher learning, and the conditions that influence teacher practice.

Mary Martinez-Wenzl is a doctoral student at the University of California, Los Angeles. She conducts research for the UCLA Civil Rights Project/Proyecto Derechos Civiles and the RAND Corporation. Her research interests include college preparation and access among newcomer immigrant students, community colleges, and binational educational partnerships. She received a B.A. in Public Policy/International Studies and an M.P.A. from the University of Oregon.

Vilma Ortíz is professor of Sociology at the University of California, Los Angeles. Her research addresses broad theoretical issues on racial/ethnic stratification and social inequality. For more than 20 years, she has studied the socioeconomic experiences of Latinos in the United States, focusing both on specific Latino groups as well as comparative studies with other racial/ethnic groups. She and Edward Telles are co-authors of the award-winning *Generations of Exclusion: Mexican Americans, Assimilation, and Race*.

Leslie Reese is the Executive Director of the Center for Language Minority Education and Research at California State University, Long Beach. A former bilingual teacher, Leslie has worked in Perú, Mexico, and Guatemala on research, community development, and professional learning projects. Her research interests include education of Latino children in the United States, early literacy development among dual language children, and home-school connections.

Gabriela Livas Stein graduated from Columbia University and received her Ph.D. in clinical psychology from the University of North

Carolina-Chapel Hill. She was awarded the APA/APAGS Award for Distinguished Graduate Student in Professional Psychology in 2007. She is an assistant professor in Psychology at the University of North Carolina-Greensboro. Her research focuses on the interplay between culture and risk factors in predicting psychopathology in ethnic minority youth.

Rosaura Tafoya-Estrada is assistant professor of sociology at Boise State University. She received her Ph.D. in sociology from the University of California, Irvine. Her scholarly areas of interest are immigrant adaptation and incorporation, gendered selective acculturation processes, and the intersection of race/ethnicity, gender, education, and employment dynamics.

Edward Telles is professor of sociology at Princeton University. With Vilma Ortiz, he published *Generations of Exclusion: Mexican Americans, Assimilation, and Race* in 2008, and he published *Race in Another America: The Significance of Skin Color in Brazil* in 2008 as well. He currently directs the Project on Ethnicity and Race in Latin America (PERLA) and is Vice President of the American Sociological Association.

Ernesto Treviño is the executive director of the Centro de Políticas Comparadas de Educación at the Universidad Diego Portales in Santiago, Chile. Ernesto has worked on policy and learning assessment in Latin America and the Caribbean, collaborating with UNESCO, the Organization of American States, Programa de Promoción de la Reforma Educativa en América Latina (PREAL), and UNICEF. Currently he evaluates "Un Buen Comienzo," a professional development program in preschool that enhances educational opportunities for poor children in Chile. He is also senior advisor to UNESCO's Laboratorio Latinoamericano de Evaluación de la Calidad.

Victor Zúñiga is Dean of Research and Extension at the Universidad de Monterrey and holds his Ph.D. in sociology from the Université de Paris VIII-Vincennes. He specializes in international migrant communities, cultural border issues, and the schooling of migrant students, both in Mexico and the United States. He is a tier-3 (highest level) member of Mexico's Sistema Nacional de Investigadores.

Index